D1575423

The Little Big
COOKIES BOOK

The Little Big Cookies Book
was created and produced by McRae Books Srl
Borgo Santa Croce, 8 – Florence (Italy)
info@mcraebooks.com
www.mcraebooks.com
Publishers: Anne McRae and Marco Nardi

Text: Pamela Egan, Brenda Moore, Ting Morris
Photography: Lorenzo Borri, Keeho Casati, Mauro Corsi, Walter Mericchi, Leonardo Pasquinelli, Gianni Petronio, Studio Marco Lanza
Food Styling: Arianna Cappellini, Francesco Piccardi
Pastry Chef for Photography: Masha Caputo Innocente
Editing: Helen Farrell
Indexing: Ellie Smith
Art Director: Marco Nardi
Layout: Adina Stefania Dragomir, Sara Mathews, Filippo Delle Monache
Repro: Litocolor, Florence - Fotolito Toscana, Florence

The Publishers would like to thank:

Bellini Più, Montespertoli (Florence); Ceramiche il Pozzo, Montespertoli (Florence); Ceramiche Virginia, Montespertoli (Florence); CIVE Vetreria in Toscana. Co s.coop.r.l., Empoli (Florence); Il Nodo Ceramiche, Montelupo Fiorentino (Florence); Ceramiche Toscane, Montelupo Fiorentino (Florence); Vetreria Lux, Montelupo Fiorentino (Florence); Ceramiche Nicola Fasano, Grottaglie; Decortex Tessuti, Calenzano (Prato); Ceramiche D'Arte, Milano.

ISBN 88-89272-51-1

Printed and bound in China by C&C Offset Printing Co., Ltd.

The Little Big
COOKIES
BOOK

M^cRAE BOOKS

CONTENTS

CHOCOLATE
COOKIES

CHOCOLATE RASPBERRY BARS

Preheat the oven to 325°F/170°C/gas 3. • Line a 13 x 9-inch (33 x 23-cm) baking pan with aluminum foil, letting the edges overhang. • Base: Sift the flour, cocoa, and salt into a medium bowl. • Beat the butter, sugar, and vanilla in a large bowl with an electric mixer at high speed until creamy. • Mix in the dry ingredients. • Firmly press the mixture into the prepared pan to form a smooth, even layer. Prick all over with a fork. • Bake for 15–20 minutes, or until firm to the touch. • Increase the oven temperature to 375°F/190°C/gas 5. • Filling: Mix the preserves and liqueur in a small bowl and spread it evenly over the base. Sprinkle with the chocolate chips. • Process the finely ground almonds, egg whites, sugar, and almond extract in a food processor or blender until well blended. • Pour the mixture over the preserves and sprinkle with the flaked almonds. • Bake for 20–25 minutes, or until lightly browned. • Using the foil as handles, lift onto a rack and let cool completely. • Remove the foil and cut into bars.

Makes: 30 bars

Preparation: 25'

Cooking: 35–45'

Level of difficulty: 1

BASE
- 1 cup/150 g all-purpose/plain flour
- 2 tbsp unsweetened cocoa powder
- 1/4 tsp salt
- 1/2 cup/125 g butter, softened
- 1/2 cup/100 g granulated sugar
- 1/2 tsp vanilla extract/essence

FILLING
- 1/2 cup/160 g raspberry preserves
- 1 tbsp raspberry liqueur
- 1 cup/180 g semisweet/dark chocolate chips
- 1 1/2 cups/150 g finely ground almonds
- 4 large egg whites
- 1 cup/200 g granulated sugar
- 1/2 tsp almond extract/essence
- 2 tbsp flaked almonds

PIQUANT MOCHA COOKIES

Preheat the oven to 350°F/180°C/gas 4. •
Butter two cookie sheets. • Sift the flour,
baking powder, pepper, and salt into a small bowl.
• Heat the raisins with the coffee liqueur in a small
saucepan over low heat. • Melt the chocolate with
the butter in a double boiler over barely simmering
water. Set aside to cool. • Beat the eggs and
sugar in a large bowl until creamy. • Beat in the
melted chocolate and vanilla. • Beat in the dry
ingredients, followed by the raisin mixture and the
chocolate chips. • Drop tablespoons of the dough
2 inches (5 cm) apart onto the prepared cookie
sheets. • Bake for 10–12 minutes, or until set but
still slightly soft. • Cool until the cookies firm
slightly. • Transfer to racks to finish cooling.

Makes: 25–30
  cookies

Preparation: 20'

Cooking: 10–12'

Level of difficulty: 1

- 2 cups/300 g all-
  purpose/plain flour
- ½ tsp baking
  powder
- ½ tsp freshly
  ground black
  pepper
- ¼ tsp salt
- ½ cup/90 g raisins
- 2 tbsp coffee
  liqueur
- 8 oz/250 g
  bittersweet/plain
  chocolate,
  coarsely chopped
- 4 tbsp butter
- 2 large eggs
- ¾ cup/150 g
  granulated sugar
- 2 tsp vanilla
  extract/essence
- 1 cup/180 g
  semisweet/dark
  chocolate chips

CHOCOLATE CHIP AND CANDIED CHERRY COOKIES

Makes: 18–20
cooking: 15–20'

Preparation: 20'

Cooking: 15–20'

Level of difficulty: 1

- ¾ cup/125 g all-purpose/plain flour
- ½ tsp baking powder
- ⅛ tsp salt
- ½ cup/125 g butter, softened
- ¼ cup/50 g granulated sugar
- ½ tsp vanilla extract/essence
- ½ cup/50 g coarsely chopped candied cherries
- 2 oz/60 g semisweet/dark chocolate, coarsely chopped

Preheat the oven to 375°F/190°C/gas 5. •
Butter two cookie sheets. • Sift the flour, baking powder, and salt into a large bowl. • Beat the butter, sugar, and vanilla in a large bowl with an electric mixer at high speed until creamy. • Mix in the dry ingredients, cherries, and chocolate.
• Drop rounded teaspoons of the dough 1 inch (2.5 cm) apart onto the prepared cookie sheets.
• Bake for 15–20 minutes, or until just golden. •
Cool on the sheets until the cookies firm slightly. •
Transfer to racks to finish cooling.

CHOCOLATE AND HAZELNUT COOKIES

Preheat the oven to 325°F/170°C/gas 3. • Set out three cookie sheets. • Spread the hazelnuts on a baking sheet. Toast for 7 minutes, or until lightly golden. • Let cool completely. Transfer to a food processor, add $^1/_2$ cup (100 g) of the granulated sugar and process until the nuts are coarsely chopped. • Sift the flour, baking powder, and salt into a medium bowl. • Beat the butter and remaining granulated sugar and brown sugar in a large bowl with an electric mixer at high speed until creamy. • Add the eggs, beating until just blended. Add the vanilla. • Mix in the dry ingredients and enough orange juice to make a smooth dough. • Stir in the chocolate and hazelnuts. • Drop teaspoons of the dough 1 inch (2.5 cm) apart onto the cookie sheets. • Bake, one sheet at a time, for 10–12 minutes, or until golden brown. • Cool the cookies for 3 minutes on each cookie sheet. • Transfer to racks to finish cooling.

12

Makes: 45 cookies

Preparation: 40'

Cooking: 10–12'

Level of difficulty: 1

- **$^3/_4$ cup/90 g hazelnuts**
- **1 cup/200 g granulated sugar**
- **2 cups/300 g all-purpose/plain flour**
- **1 tsp baking powder**
- **$^1/_8$ tsp salt**
- **1 cup/250 g butter, softened**
- **$^1/_2$ cup/100 g firmly packed light brown sugar**
- **2 large eggs**
- **1 tsp vanilla extract/essence**
- **1–2 tbsp fresh orange juice**
- **7 oz/200 g semisweet/dark chocolate, coarsely chopped**

COCOA CORN FLAKE COOKIES

P reheat the oven to 350°F/180°C/gas 4. •
Butter two cookie sheets. • Beat the butter and
sugar in a large bowl with an electric mixer at high
speed until creamy. • Sift in the flour and cocoa.
Stir in the corn flakes until well mixed. • Drop
teaspoons of the dough 1 inch (2.5 cm) apart onto
the prepared cookie sheets. • Bake for 10–15
minutes, or until firm to the touch. • Transfer to
racks to cool. • Frosting: Mix the confectioners'
sugar, butter, water, cocoa, and vanilla in a small
bowl until well blended. • Spread the frosting over
the tops of the cooled cookies. Decorate with the
walnut halves.

Makes: 30 cookies

Preparation: 15'

Cooking: 10–15'

Level of difficulty: 1

- ¾ cup/180 g
  butter, softened
- ½ cup/100 g
  granulated sugar
- 2 cups/300 g all-
  purpose/plain flour
- 2 tbsp unsweetened
  cocoa powder
- ¼ cup/50 g corn
  flakes, lightly
  crushed

FROSTING
- 1 cup/150 g
  confectioners'/
  icing sugar
- 2 tbsp butter,
  softened
- 1 tbsp boiling water
- 1 tbsp unsweetened
  cocoa powder
- 1 tsp vanilla
  extract/essence
- 30 walnut halves, to
  decorate

CHOCOLATE CHIP HALLOWEEN COOKIES

Makes: 20–25 cookies

Preparation: 20'

Cooking: 8–10'

Level of difficulty: 1

- 1 cup/150 g all-purpose/plain flour
- ½ tsp baking powder
- ½ tsp baking soda
- ½ tsp ground cinnamon
- ⅛ tsp salt
- 4 tbsp butter, softened
- ½ cup/100 g granulated sugar
- ½ cup/125 ml canned pumpkin purée
- ½ tbsp finely grated orange zest
- ½ cup/90 g semisweet/dark chocolate chips

Preheat the oven to 375°F/190°C/gas 5. • Set out two cookie sheets. • Sift the flour, baking powder, baking soda, cinnamon, and salt into a large bowl. • Use a pastry blender to cut in the butter until the mixture resembles fine crumbs.
• Stir in the sugar, pumpkin, and orange zest.
• Stir in the chocolate chips. • Drop teaspoons of the dough 2 inches (5 cm) apart onto the cookie sheets. • Bake for 8–10 minutes, or until golden.
• Transfer to racks to cool.

MINTY CHOCOLATE SANDWICHES

Makes: 24 cookies

Preparation: 40' + 90' to chill

Cooking: 6–8'

Level of difficulty: 2

- 1 cup/150 g all-purpose/plain flour
- 2 tbsp unsweetened cocoa powder
- 1/8 tsp salt
- 1/2 cup/125 g butter, softened
- 1/4 cup/50 g granulated sugar
- 1 tsp mint extract/essence
- 1 large egg

FILLING
- 1/2 cup/125 ml heavy/double cream
- 7 oz/200 g white chocolate, coarsely chopped
- 1 tsp mint extract/essence

GLAZE
- 5 oz/150 g bittersweet/plain chocolate, coarsely chopped
- 6 tbsp butter

Sift the flour, cocoa, and salt into a medium bowl. • Beat the butter and sugar in a large bowl with an electric mixer at high speed until creamy. • Add the mint extract and egg, beating until just blended. • Mix in the dry ingredients. • Press the dough into a disk, wrap in plastic wrap, and refrigerate for 30 minutes. •

For best results, make sure that the dough is well chilled before rolling it out.

Preheat the oven to 350°F/180°C/gas 4. • Butter two cookie sheets. • Roll out the dough on a lightly floured surface to a thickness of 1/8 inch (3 mm). • Use a 2-inch (5-cm) cookie cutter to cut out the cookies. Gather the dough scraps, re-roll, and continue cutting out cookies until all the dough is used. • Use a spatula to transfer the cookies to the prepared cookie sheets, placing them 1 inch (2.5 cm) apart. • Bake for 6–8 minutes, or until just golden at the edges. • Transfer to racks and let cool completely. • Filling: Bring the cream to a boil in a small saucepan over low heat.

• Remove from the heat and stir in the white chocolate. Add the mint extract and transfer to a medium bowl. • Cool for 30 minutes, or until firm but not set. • Stick the cookies together in pairs with filling. • Glaze: Melt the chocolate and butter in a double boiler over barely simmering water.

• Spread on top of the cookies and refrigerate for 30 minutes.

PEANUT BUTTER SLICES

Sift the all-purpose and rice flours, baking powder, and salt into a large bowl. • Beat the butter, brown sugar, and peanut butter in a medium bowl until creamy. • Mix in the dry ingredients and milk until firm. • Melt the chocolate in a double boiler over barely simmering water. Mix the chocolate into the dough. • Form the dough into two 8-inch (20-cm) logs. Refrigerate for 2 hours. Slice the dough $1/4$ inch (5 mm) thick and place 2 inches (5 cm) apart on the prepared cookie sheets. • Preheat the oven to 350°F/180°C/gas 4. • Line two cookie sheets with parchment paper. • Bake for 8–10 minutes, until golden brown and firm around the edges. • Transfer to racks to cool. Spread the frosting over the cookies.

18

Makes: 64 cookies

Preparation: 60' + 2 h to chill

Cooking: 8–10'

Level of difficulty: 2

- 2 cups/300 g all-purpose/plain flour
- $2/3$ cup/100 g rice flour
- $1\frac{1}{2}$ tsp baking powder
- $1/8$ tsp salt
- $3/4$ cup/180 g butter, softened
- 1 cup/200 g firmly packed light brown sugar
- 6 tbsp crunchy peanut butter
- 1 oz/30 g semisweet/dark chocolate, coarsely chopped
- 2 tbsp milk
- 2 cups/500 ml Chocolate Frosting (see page 952)

CHOCOLATE SANDWICHES

Makes: 15 cookies
Preparation: 45'
Cooking: 10–12'
Level of difficulty: 1

- 1 cup/150 g all-purpose/plain flour
- 1/3 cup/50 g custard powder
- 2 tbsp unsweetened cocoa powder
- 1/8 tsp salt
- 1/2 cup/125 g butter, softened
- 1 cup/200 g granulated sugar
- 1 large egg
- superfine sugar, to sprinkle

- 1/3 cup/50 g Italian Buttercream flavored with cocoa (see page 954)

Sift the flour, custard powder, cocoa, and salt into a medium bowl. • Beat the butter and granulated sugar in a large bowl with an electric mixer at high speed until creamy. • Add the egg, beating until just blended. • Mix in the dry ingredients. Press the dough into a disk, wrap in plastic wrap, and refrigerate for 30 minutes. • Preheat the oven to 350°F/180°C/ gas 4. • Butter two cookie sheets. • Roll out to a thickness of 1/4 inch (5 mm). Cut into rectangles. • Arrange the cookies 1 inch (2.5 cm) apart on the sheets. Prick all over and sprinkle with the superfine sugar. • Bake for 10–12 minutes, or until lightly browned. • Cool completely on the sheets. • Stick the cookies together in pairs with the buttercream.

CUTE CHOCOLATE COOKIES

Preheat the oven to 375°F/190°C/gas 5. • Butter two cookie sheets. • Sift the flour and cocoa into a medium bowl. • Beat the butter and sugar in a large bowl with an electric mixer at medium speed until creamy. • Add the egg yolk, beating until just blended. • Mix in the dry ingredients. • Form the dough into three equal-size disks, wrap in plastic wrap, and refrigerate for 30 minutes. • Roll out the dough on a lightly floured surface to a thickness of $^1/_4$ inch (5 mm). • Use a 2-inch (5-cm) cutter to cut out twenty circles and use a $1^1/_2$-inch (4-cm) cutter to cut out another twenty circles, re-rolling the dough as necessary. • Place one of the larger circles on a cookie sheet. Place a piece of chocolate in the center. Cover with one of the smaller circles. • Working carefully, mold the smaller circle over the chocolate and turn the edges of the larger circle upward. Press around the edges with a fork to seal the chocolate completely. • Repeat with the rest of the circles, spacing 2 inches (5 cm) apart. • Bake for 8–10 minutes, or until the cookies have spread slightly. • Cool on the sheet for 5 minutes. • Transfer to racks to cool.

Makes: 20 cookies

Preparation: 20' + 30' to chill

Cooking: 8–10'

Level of difficulty: 2

- 1$^2/_3$ **cups/250 g self-rising flour**
- **2 tbsp unsweetened cocoa powder**
- $^2/_3$ **cup/150 g butter, softened**
- $^3/_4$ **cup/150 g granulated sugar**
- **1 large egg yolk**
- **20 chocolate drops (buttons) or small squares of semisweet chocolate**

APRICOT AND CHOCOLATE PRETZELS

Makes: 35–40 cookies

Preparation: 45'

Cooking: 12–15' per batch

Level of difficulty: 2

- 1 cup/100 g finely chopped dried apricots
- 6 tbsp orange juice
- 5 tbsp butter
- 1⅓ cups/180 g all-purpose/plain flour
- 1 tsp baking powder
- ¼ tsp salt
- ¼ cup/50 g granulated sugar
- 2 large egg yolks, lightly beaten
- 2 oz/60 g semisweet/dark chocolate, finely grated

Preheat the oven to 350°F/180°C/gas 4. • Line three cookie sheets with parchment paper. • Mix the apricots, orange juice, and 1 tablespoon butter in a small saucepan. Cook over low heat for 5 minutes, or until the apricots have softened. • Let cool completely. • Sift the flour, baking powder, and salt into a large bowl. Stir in the sugar. • Use a pastry blender to cut in the remaining butter until the mixture resembles fine crumbs. • Add the egg yolks, chocolate, and apricot mixture to make a stiff dough. • Form tablespoons of the dough into 6-inch (15-cm) ropes. • Make each rope into a pretzel shape by twisting the two ends around each other, then bringing both back near to the center of the strip, about 1 inch apart. • Use a spatula to transfer the cookies to the cookie sheet, spacing 1 inch (2.5 cm) apart. • Bake, one sheet at a time, for 12–15 minutes, or until just golden. • Transfer to racks to cool.

CHOCOLATE-FROSTED OAT BARS

Makes: 22–33 bars

Preparation: 25'

Cooking: 15–20'

Level of difficulty: 1

- ¾ cup/125 g all-purpose/plain flour
- ⅛ tsp salt
- 1 cup/250 g butter, softened
- 1 cup/200 g firmly packed light brown sugar
- 2 large egg yolks
- ¾ cup/125 g old-fashioned rolled oats

FROSTING
- 6 oz/180 g semisweet/dark chocolate, coarsely chopped
- 2 tbsp butter

Preheat the oven to 375°F/190°C/gas 5. • Butter an 11 x 7-inch (28 x 18-cm) baking pan. • Sift the flour and salt into a medium bowl. • Beat the butter and brown sugar in a large bowl with an electric mixer at high speed until creamy. • Add the egg yolks, beating until just blended. • Mix in the dry ingredients and oats. • Firmly press the mixture into the prepared pan to form a smooth, even layer. • Bake for 15–20 minutes, or until firm to the touch. • Cool completely in the pan. • Frosting: Melt the chocolate and butter in a double boiler over barely simmering water. • Spread the chocolate mixture over and let stand for 30 minutes until set. • Cut into bars.

BANANA BROWNIES

Preheat the oven to 325°F/170°C/gas 3. •
Butter an 11 x 7-inch (28 x 18-cm) baking pan.
• Sift the flour, cocoa, baking powder, and salt
into a medium bowl. • Melt the chocolate with the
butter and brown sugar in a double boiler over
barely simmering water. • Remove from the heat
and stir in the pecans, eggs, and bananas. • Mix
in the dry ingredients. • Spoon the mixture evenly
into the prepared pan. • Bake for 25–35 minutes,
or until dry on top and almost firm to the touch.
Do not overbake. • Cool completely before cutting
into bars.

Makes: 22–33 bars

Preparation: 20'

Cooking: 25–35'

Level of difficulty: 1

- ¾ cup/225 g all-purpose/plain flour
- 2 tbsp unsweetened cocoa powder
- 1 tsp baking powder
- ⅛ tsp salt
- 6 oz/180 g semisweet/dark chocolate, coarsely chopped
- ¾ cup/180 g butter, cut up
- 1¼ cups/250 g firmly packed dark brown sugar
- 1 cup/100 g coarsely chopped pecans
- 3 large eggs, lightly beaten
- 2 firm-ripe bananas, mashed

CHOCOLATE MUNCHIES

Sift the flour, cocoa, baking powder, baking soda, and salt into a medium bowl. • Beat the butter and sugar in a large bowl until creamy. • Add the egg, beating until just blended. • Beat in 4 oz (125 g) of the chocolate and vanilla. • Mix in the dry ingredients. • Divide the dough in half. Form into two long logs each 2 inches (5 cm) in diameter, wrap in waxed paper, and freeze for at least 4 hours. • Preheat the oven to 350°F/ 180°C/gas 4. • Line two cookie sheets with foil. • Slice the dough $1/4$ inch (5 mm) thick and place 1 inch (2.5 cm) apart on the sheets. • Bake for 10–12 minutes, or until lightly browned. • Transfer the cookies to racks to cool. • Drizzle the remaining semisweet and white chocolate over the cookies.

Makes: 30 cookies

Preparation: 40' + 4 h to freeze

Cooking: 10–12'

Level of difficulty: 1

- **2¼ cups/330 g all-purpose/plain flour**
- **⅓ cup/50 g unsweetened cocoa powder**
- **½ tsp baking powder**
- **½ tsp baking soda**
- **⅛ tsp salt**
- **7 oz/200 g semisweet/dark chocolate, melted**
- **¾ cup/180 g butter, softened**
- **1 cup/200 g granulated sugar**
- **1 large egg**
- **1 tsp vanilla extract/essence**
- **3 oz/90 g white chocolate, melted**

CHOCOLATE ALMOND BITES

Makes: 20 cookies

Preparation: 40'

Cooking: 20–30'

Level of difficulty: 1

- ¾ cup/125 g almonds
- 2 large egg whites
- ½ cup/100 g superfine/caster sugar
- 2 tbsp vanilla sugar
- ⅛ tsp cream of tartar
- ⅛ tsp salt
- 2 oz/60 g bittersweet/plain chocolate, grated

Preheat the oven to 325°F/170°C/gas 3. • Line two cookie sheets with rice paper. • Sprinkle half the almonds on a large baking sheet. Toast for 7 minutes, or until lightly golden. Lower the oven temperature to 300°F/150°C/gas 2. • Place the almonds on a clean kitchen towel and rub off the skins. • Coarsely chop half the peeled almonds. • Process the remaining almonds in a food processor until finely chopped. Set aside. • Beat the egg whites in a medium bowl until frothy. • Beat in the superfine sugar, vanilla sugar, cream of tartar, and salt. • Fold in all the almonds and chocolate. • Form domes the size of apricots. • Place 2 inches (5 cm) apart on the prepared baking sheets. • Bake for 20–30 minutes, or until golden. • Cool on the cookie sheets.

Makes: 16–20 squares	
Preparation: 40' + 90' to chill	
Cooking: 30–35'	
Level of difficulty: 2	

COCOA AND MARMALADE SQUARES

BASE
- 1 cup/150 g all-purpose/plain flour
- 2 tbsp unsweetened cocoa powder
- ¼ tsp salt
- 1 cup/250 g butter
- ⅓ cup/70 g granulated sugar
- ⅓ cup/50 g confectioners'/icing sugar

FILLING
- Zest of 1 orange
- ½ cup/125 ml orange juice
- ½ cup/125 ml water
- ⅓ cup/50 g cornstarch
- 1 tsp lemon juice
- 1 tbsp butter
- ½ cup/160 g orange marmalade

GLAZE
- 3 tbsp heavy/double cream
- 1½ tsp corn syrup/golden syrup
- 3 oz/90 g semisweet/dark chocolate, chopped

Preheat the oven to 325°F/170°C/gas 3. • Line an 8-inch (20-cm) square baking pan with aluminum foil, letting the edges overhang. • Chocolate Base: Sift the flour, cocoa, and salt into a medium bowl. • Beat the butter, granulated sugar, and confectioners' sugar in a large bowl with an electric mixer at high speed until creamy. • Mix in the dry ingredients. • Firmly press the mixture into the prepared pan to form a smooth, even layer. • Prick all over with a fork. • Bake for 25–30 minutes, or until firm to the touch. • Let cool for 10 minutes. • Filling: Mix the orange zest and juice, water, cornstarch, and lemon juice in a small saucepan over medium heat. • Bring to a boil and boil, stirring constantly, for 1 minute, or until thickened. • Remove from the heat and mix in the butter and marmalade until well blended. • Pour the filling evenly over the cookie base. • Bake for 5 minutes. • Cool completely in the pan. • Refrigerate for 1 hour, or until set. • Glaze: Bring the cream to a boil with the corn syrup in a small saucepan. • Remove from the heat and stir in the chocolate until melted and smooth. • Spoon the glaze into a small freezer bag and cut off a tiny corner. • Pipe over the filling in a decorative manner and refrigerate for 30 minutes. • Using the foil as handles, transfer to a cutting board. • Cut into squares.

CHOCOLATE MINT SQUARES

Preheat the oven to 350°F/180°C/gas 4. • Butter a 11 x 7-inch (28 x 18-cm) baking pan. • Base: Sift the flour, cocoa, baking powder, and salt into a large bowl. Stir in the sugar. • Cut in the butter until the mixture resembles fine crumbs. • Mix in the egg mixture. • Firmly press the mixture into the prepared pan to form a smooth layer. • Bake for 15–20 minutes, or until firm to the touch. • Filling: Mix the confectioners' sugar and mint liqueur until well blended. • Stir in enough milk to achieve a spreadable consistency. • Spread the peppermint mixture over the base. • Frosting: Melt the chocolate and butter over barely simmering water. • Pour the frosting over the peppermint layer. Make a swirling pattern with a fork. • Let stand for 30 minutes until set. • Cut into squares.

Makes: 36–45 squares

Preparation: 40' + 30' to set

Cooking: 15–20'

Level of difficulty: 1

BASE
- ²/₃ cup/100 g all-purpose/plain flour
- 2 tbsp unsweetened cocoa powder
- 1 tsp baking powder
- ¼ tsp salt
- ⅓ cup/70 g granulated sugar
- 2 tbsp butter
- 1 large egg, lightly beaten with 6 tbsp water

FILLING
- 2¼ cups/330 g confectioners'/icing sugar
- 1 tbsp mint liqueur
- 1–2 tbsp milk

FROSTING
- 4 oz/125 g semisweet/dark chocolate, coarsely chopped
- 6 tbsp butter

- **4 large egg whites**
- **1¼ cups/250 g granulated sugar**
- **3 cups/300 g finely ground almonds**
- **2 oz/60 g bittersweet/plain chocolate, finely grated**
- **1 tsp vanilla extract/essence**
- **2 cups/500 ml Chocolate Frosting (see page 952) (optional)**

CHOCOLATE SQUARES

Preheat the oven to 350°F/180°C/gas 4. • Butter a 13 x 9-inch (33 x 23-cm) baking pan. • Beat 3 of the egg whites in a large bowl with an electric mixer at medium speed until soft peaks form. • With mixer at high speed, gradually beat in 1 cup (200 g) of the sugar, beating until stiff, glossy peaks form. • Use a large rubber spatula to fold in the almonds, chocolate, and vanilla. • Spread the mixture evenly in the prepared pan. • Beat the remaining egg white and remaining sugar until frothy. Brush over the top. • Bake for 20–25 minutes, or until lightly browned. • Cool completely in the pan. If desired, spread with the frosting. Make a swirled pattern with a fork.

• Cut into squares.

33

RICH CHOCOLATE BROWNIES

Preheat the oven to 325°F/170°C/gas 3. •
Butter and flour a 13 x 9-inch (33 x 23-cm)
baking pan. • Sift the flour, baking powder, and salt
into a large bowl. • Melt the chocolate and butter in
a double boiler over barely simmering water.
Remove from the heat and let cool. • Beat the
eggs, brown sugar, and vanilla in a large bowl with
an electric mixer at high speed until pale and thick.
• Use a large rubber spatula to fold in the
chocolate mixture, followed by the dry ingredients.
• Pour the batter into the prepared pan. • Bake for
35–40 minutes, or until dry on top and almost firm
to the touch. Do not overbake. • Cool completely
before cutting into squares.

*Makes: 16–25
  squares*

Preparation: 35'

Cooking: 35–40'

Level of difficulty: 1

- ½ cup/75 g all-
  purpose/plain flour
- ½ tsp baking
  powder
- ⅛ tsp salt
- 6 oz/180 g
  bittersweet/plain
  chocolate,
  coarsely chopped
- 1½ cups/375 g
  butter, cut up
- 5 large eggs
- 2¼ cups/440 g
  firmly packed light
  brown sugar
- 1 tsp vanilla
  extract/essence

MILK CHOCOLATE FROSTED BARS

Makes: 22–33 bars

Preparation: 40' + 30' to set

Cooking: 35–45'

Level of difficulty: 1

- 1½ cups/225 g all-purpose/plain flour
- 1 tbsp unsweetened cocoa powder
- 2 tsp baking powder
- ⅛ tsp salt
- 1 cup/250 g butter, softened
- 1 cup/200 g granulated sugar
- 4 large eggs, lightly beaten
- 2 tbsp milk
- ½ tsp vanilla extract/essence

FROSTING
- ¾ cup/125 g milk chocolate chips
- 4 tbsp butter
- 2 tbsp milk
- 1 cup/150 g confectioners'/icing sugar

Preheat the oven to 350°F/180°C/gas 4. • Butter an 11 x 7-inch (28 x 18-cm) baking pan. • Sift the flour, cocoa, baking powder, and salt into a medium bowl. • Beat the butter and sugar in a large bowl with an electric mixer at high speed until creamy. • Add the eggs, beating until just blended. • Mix in the dry ingredients, milk, and vanilla until well blended. • Spread the mixture evenly in the prepared pan. • Bake for 35–45 minutes, or until firm to the touch and a toothpick inserted into the center comes out clean. • Cool completely in the pan. • Frosting: Melt the chocolate chips and butter with the milk in a double boiler over barely simmering water until well blended. Remove from the heat and beat in the confectioners' sugar until thick and spreadable. • Spread the frosting over the cookie base. Let stand for 30 minutes, or until set. • Cut into bars.

Makes:	30 squares
Preparation:	45'
Cooking:	60–75'
Level of difficulty:	2

- 1½ cups/225 g self-rising flour
- ½ tsp ground cinnamon
- ½ tsp ground cloves
- ¼ tsp ground cardamom
- ¼ tsp salt
- ½ cup/90 g dark raisins
- ½ cup/90 g golden raisins/sultanas
- ½ cup/125 ml dark rum mixed with 1 tbsp cold water
- ¾ cup/75 g candied cherries, halved
- 1 cup/100 g chopped walnuts
- 1 cup/100 g chopped almonds
- 3 oz/90 g semisweet/dark chocolate, chopped
- ¾ cup/180 g butter
- 1 cup/200 g firmly packed light brown sugar
- zest of 1 orange
- 3 large eggs, lightly beaten
- 3 tbsp orange juice

BOOZY CHOCOLATE SQUARES

Preheat the oven to 325°F/170°C/gas 3. • Butter an 11 x 7-inch (28 x 18-cm) baking pan. Line with parchment paper, letting the edges overhang. • Sift the flour, cinnamon, cloves, cardamom, and salt into a large bowl. • Bring the dark raisins, golden raisins, and rum mixture to a boil in a large saucepan. Remove from the heat and set aside for 15 minutes to allow the raisins to soak up the liquid. • Mix the raisin mixture, cherries, walnuts, and almonds in a large bowl. Use a large rubber spatula to fold in 1 tablespoon of the dry ingredients and stir until well coated. • Melt the chocolate in a double boiler over barely simmering water. • Beat the butter and brown sugar in a large bowl with an electric mixer at high speed until creamy. • Add the orange zest and melted chocolate. • Add the eggs, beating until just blended, adding 1 tablespoon of the dry ingredients. • Use a large rubber spatula to fold in the remaining dry ingredients, followed by the raisin mixture and orange juice. • Spoon the batter into the prepared pan, smoothing the top. • Bake for 60–75 minutes, or until a toothpick inserted into the center comes out clean. • Cool completely before cutting into squares.

CHOCOLATE VANILLA COOKIES

Line an 8^1/$_2$ x 4^1/$_2$-inch (21 x 11-cm) loaf pan with waxed paper. • Sift the flour, baking powder, and salt into a medium bowl. • Beat the butter and sugar in a large bowl until creamy. • Add the vanilla, egg yolk, and dry ingredients. • Divide the dough into three bowls. • Melt the chocolate in a double boiler over barely simmering water. • Add the almond extract to one bowl, the chocolate to the second bowl, and the walnuts to the third bowl. • Spread the almond mixture in the pan, followed by the walnut mixture. Finish with the chocolate mixture. • Refrigerate for 4 hours. • Preheat the oven to 350°F/180°C/gas 4. • Butter four cookie sheets. • Cut the dough into ^{1}/$_4$-inch (5-mm) thick slices. • Place 1 inch (2.5 cm) apart on the sheets. • Bake for 10–12 minutes, or until browned. • Cool on racks.

Makes: 30–35 cookies ·

Preparation: 40' + 4 h to chill

Cooking: 10–12'

Level of difficulty: 2

- 1^1/$_3$ cups/200 g all-purpose/plain flour
- 1 tsp baking powder
- ^{1}/$_8$ tsp salt
- ^{1}/$_2$ cup/125 g butter, softened
- ^{1}/$_2$ cup/100 g granulated sugar
- 1 tsp vanilla extract/essence
- 1 large egg yolk, lightly beaten
- 1 oz/30 g semisweet/dark chocolate, coarsely chopped
- ^{1}/$_2$ tsp almond extract/essence
- ^{2}/$_3$ cup/70 g chopped walnuts

ORANGE CHOCOLATE CHIP COOKIES

Makes: 40 cookies

Preparation: 20'

Cooking: 10–12'

Level of difficulty: 1

- 2 cups/300 g all-purpose/plain flour
- ½ cup/75 g whole-wheat flour
- 1 tsp baking soda
- ½ tsp salt
- 1 cup/200 g granulated sugar
- ½ cup/100 g firmly packed dark brown sugar
- ¾ cup/180 g butter, softened
- 2 tbsp finely grated orange zest
- 2 large eggs
- 1 cup/100 g chopped walnuts
- 1 cup/180 g semisweet/dark chocolate chips

Preheat the oven to 350°F/180°C/gas 4. • Butter two cookie sheets. • Sift the all-purpose and whole-wheat flours, the baking soda, and salt into a medium bowl. • Beat the granulated and brown sugars, butter, and orange zest in a large bowl with an electric mixer at high speed until creamy. • With mixer at medium speed, add the eggs, beating until just blended. • With mixer at low speed, gradually beat in the dry ingredients, followed by the walnuts and the chocolate chips. • Drop tablespoons of the dough 2 inches (5 cm) apart onto the prepared cookie sheets. • Bake for 10–12 minutes, or until lightly browned. • Cool on the sheets until the cookies firm slightly. • Transfer to racks to finish cooling.

CHOCOLATE NUT BARS

Makes: 16–25 bars

Preparation: 25' + 10'
  to plump the raisins

Cooking: 15–20'

Level of difficulty: 1

- ½ cup/90 g golden raisins/sultanas
- 1¼ cups/180 g whole-wheat flour
- 1 tsp baking powder
- ⅛ tsp salt
- 2 large eggs
- ½ cup/100 g granulated sugar
- ¼ tsp vanilla extract/essence
- Grated zest of ½ lemon
- 2 tbsp milk
- 1 tbsp dark rum
- ¾ cup/75 g finely chopped hazelnuts
- ½ cup/50 g chopped walnuts
- 3 oz/90 g bittersweet/plain chocolate, finely grated

- 1 cup/250 g Chocolate Frosting (see page 952)

Preheat the oven to 400°F/200°C/gas 6. • Butter a 9-inch (23-cm) square baking pan. • Plump the raisins in hot water to cover in a small bowl for 10 minutes. • Drain well and pat dry with paper towels. • Sift the flour, baking powder, and salt into a medium bowl. • Beat the eggs and sugar in a large bowl with an electric mixer at high speed until pale and thick. • Add the vanilla and lemon zest. • Mix in the dry ingredients, followed by the milk, rum, raisins, hazelnuts, walnuts, and chocolate. • Pour the mixture into the prepared pan. • Bake for 15–20 minutes, or until a toothpick inserted into the center comes out clean. • Cool completely in the pan. • Chocolate Frosting: Mix the confectioners' sugar, cocoa, vanilla, and enough water to make a smooth frosting. • Spread with the frosting and cut into bars.

MARZIPAN-FILLED COOKIES

Sift the flour, ginger, baking soda, and salt into a medium bowl. • Heat the honey and sugar in a small saucepan over low heat until the sugar has dissolved completely. • Let cool for 5 minutes. • Use a wooden spoon to work in the dry ingredients, almonds, and candied peel to form a smooth dough. • Cover with a clean kitchen towel and let rest for 2 days. • Preheat the oven to 375°F/190°C/gas 3. • Line four cookie sheets with parchment paper. • Marzipan Filling: Knead the marzipan and preserves in a medium bowl until smooth. Work in the almonds and candied lemon peel. Form the dough into two 6-inch (15-cm) logs. • Roll out each log on a lightly floured surface to a thickness of 1/4 inch (5 mm). • Cut into two 12 x 6-inch (30 x 15-cm) rectangles. • Cover the dough strips with the marzipan and sprinkle with currants. • Roll the dough strips up tightly to form logs about 2 inches (5 cm) in diameter. Slice 1/2 inch (1 cm) thick. Use a spatula to transfer the slices to the prepared cookie sheets, placing them 1 inch (2.5 cm) apart, cut-side up. • Bake, one sheet at a time, for 15–20 minutes, or until just golden. • Let cool completely. • Drizzle the frosting over the cookies, letting it run down the sides. • Decorate with pistachios and candied fruit.

Makes: 30–35 cookies

Preparation: 60' + 2 days to rest

Cooking: 15–20' per batch

Level of difficulty: 2

- 2 1/3 cups/350 g all-purpose/plain flour
- 1 tbsp ginger
- 2 tsp baking soda
- 1/8 tsp salt
- 1 cup/250 g honey
- 2/3 cup/140 g sugar
- 2 cups/200 g finely ground almonds
- 3/4 cup/75 g chopped candied peel

MARZIPAN FILLING
- 7 oz/200 g marzipan, softened
- 3/4 cup/240 g white currant preserves
- 1 cup/100 g chopped almonds
- 1/2 cup/50 g chopped lemon peel
- 1/2 cup/90 g dried currants
- 1 cup/250 ml Chocolate Frosting (see page 952)
- 3–4 tbsp chopped pistachios
- 2 tbsp finely chopped candied fruit

CHOCOLATE CHIP WEDGES

Preheat the oven to 375°F/190°C/gas 5. • Set out a 14-inch (35-cm) pizza pan. • Sift the flour, baking soda, and salt into a medium bowl. • Beat the butter and granulated and brown sugars in a large bowl with an electric mixer at high speed until creamy. • Add the vanilla and eggs, beating until just blended. • Mix in the dry ingredients and chocolate chips. • Spread the mixture in the pan. • Bake for 20–25 minutes, or until lightly browned. • Cool completely in the pan. • Cut into wedges.

Bake this fun cookie pie for Halloween or for children's birthday parties.

Makes: 16 wedges
Preparation: 20'
Cooking: 20–25'
Level of difficulty: 1

- 2¼ cups/330 g all-purpose/plain flour
- 1 tsp baking soda
- ½ tsp salt
- 1 cup/250 g butter, softened
- ¾ cup/150 g granulated sugar
- ¾ cup/150 g firmly packed light brown sugar
- ½ tsp vanilla extract/essence
- 2 large eggs
- 1 cup/180 g semisweet/dark chocolate chips

44

GLAZED CHOCOLATE COFFEE COOKIES

Makes: 20–25 cookies

Preparation: 45' + 2 h to chill

Cooking: 12–15'

Level of difficulty: 2

- 3 oz/90 g semisweet/dark chocolate, coarsely chopped
- 1 cup/150 g all-purpose/plain flour
- 2 tbsp unsweetened cocoa powder
- 1 tsp espresso coffee powder
- 1 tsp baking soda
- 1/4 tsp salt
- 2/3 cup/150 g butter, softened
- 1/2 cup/100 g firmly packed light brown sugar
- 1 large egg, lightly beaten
- 1 tsp vanilla extract/essence

FROSTING

- 1 1/3 cups/200 g confectioners'/icing sugar
- 1 tsp espresso coffee powder
- 1–2 tbsp warm water

Melt the chocolate in a bowl set over simmering water. • Sift the flour, cocoa, espresso powder, baking soda, and salt into a medium bowl. • Beat the butter and brown sugar in a large bowl with an electric mixer at high speed until creamy. • Add the egg and vanilla and beat for 1 minute. • Stir in the melted chocolate. • Mix in the dry ingredients. • Divide the dough in half. Form the dough into two 9 x 2-inch (23 x 5-cm) logs, wrap in plastic wrap, and refrigerate for at least 2 hours. • Preheat the oven to 350°F/180°C/gas 4. • Butter two cookie sheets. • Slice the dough 2/3 inch (1.5 cm) thick and place 1 inch (2.5 cm) apart on the prepared cookie sheets. • Bake for 12–15 minutes, or until the edges are firm and the bottoms are lightly browned. • Cool on the sheets until the cookies firm slightly. • Transfer to racks to cool. • Frosting: Mix the sugar and espresso powder in a small bowl. Stir in enough warm water to make a drizzling consistency. • Drizzle over the cookies and let set.

OVER THE TOP CHOCOLATE SQUARES

Preheat the oven to 350°F/180°C/gas 4. •
Butter a 9-inch (23-cm) baking pan. • Cream
Cheese Mixture: Beat the cream cheese and sugar
in a large bowl until creamy. • Beat in the orange
zest and juice and cornstarch. Add the egg. •
Chocolate Mixture: Melt the chocolate and butter in
a double boiler over barely simmering water. Set
aside to cool. • Stir in the sugar and vanilla. • Add
the beaten egg mixture, followed by the flour. •
Pour the chocolate mixture into the prepared pan.
• Drop tablespoons of the cream cheese mixture
over the chocolate base. • Swirl the mixtures
together to create a marbled effect. • Bake for
25–30 minutes, or until slightly risen around the
edges and set in the center. • Cool before cutting
into squares.

Makes: 16–25 squares

Preparation: 35'

Cooking: 25–30'

Level of difficulty: 2

CREAM CHEESE MIXTURE
- 1 cup/250 ml cream cheese, softened
- ¼ cup/50 g granulated sugar
- 2 tbsp finely grated orange zest
- 3 tbsp orange juice
- 1 tsp cornstarch/cornflour

CHOCOLATE MIXTURE
- 7 oz/200 g semisweet/dark chocolate, coarsely chopped
- 4 tbsp butter
- ¾ cup/150 g granulated sugar
- 2 tsp vanilla extract/essence
- 2 large eggs, lightly beaten with 2 tbsp cold water
- ½ cup/75 g all-purpose/plain flour

GREENTOP COOKIES

Makes: 15 bars

Preparation: 25'

Cooking: 25–30'

Level of difficulty: 1

BASE

- 1 cup/150 g all-purpose/plain flour
- 1 cup/125 g shredded/desiccated coconut
- ¼ cup/50 g granulated sugar
- 1 tbsp unsweetened cocoa powder
- ½ tsp baking powder
- ⅛ tsp salt
- ½ cup/125 g butter, cut up

MINT TOPPING

- 1⅔ cups/250 g confectioners'/icing sugar
- ½ tsp mint extract/essence
- ½ tsp green food coloring
- 4 tbsp warm water (105°–115°F), or more as needed

Base: Preheat the oven to 350°F/180°C/ gas 4. • Set out a 10½ x 15½-inch (26 x 36-cm) jelly-roll pan. • Stir together the flour, coconut, sugar, cocoa, baking powder, and salt in a large bowl. • Use a pastry blender to cut in the butter until the mixture resembles fine crumbs. • Press the mixture evenly into the pan. • Bake for 25–30 minutes, or until lightly browned. • Cool completely in the pan on a rack. • Mint Topping: Mix the confectioners' sugar, mint extract, and green food coloring in a small bowl. Add enough water to make a spreadable paste. • Spread the topping over the crispy base. • Cut into bars.

BANANA CARAMEL COOKIES

Sift the flour, baking powder, baking soda, and salt into a medium bowl. • Beat the butter and the brown sugars in a large bowl with an electric mixer at high speed until creamy. • Add the eggs, beating until just blended. • Mix in the dry ingredients, chocolates, banana chips, and milk. • Divide the dough in half. Form the dough into two 8-inch (20-cm) logs, wrap in plastic wrap, and refrigerate for at least 2 hours. • Preheat the oven to 350°F/180°C/gas 4. • Line two cookie sheets with parchment paper. • Slice the dough $^{1}/_{2}$ inch (1 cm) thick and place 1 inch (2.5 cm) apart on the prepared cookie sheets. • Bake for 15–18 minutes, or until the edges are firm and the centers are still slightly soft. • Cool on the sheets until the cookies firm slightly. • Transfer to racks to cool.

Makes: 30–40 cookies

Preparation: 60' + 2 h to chill

Cooking: 15–18'

Level of difficulty: 2

- 2²/₃ cups/400 g all-purpose/plain flour
- 1 tsp baking powder
- ¹/₄ tsp baking soda
- ¹/₄ tsp salt
- ³/₄ cup/180 g butter, softened
- ³/₄ cup/150 g firmly packed light brown sugar
- 2 tbsp firmly packed dark brown sugar
- 2 large eggs, lightly beaten
- 7 oz/200 g caramel-filled chocolates, such as Rolos, cut into small chunks
- 3 oz/90 g dried banana chips, coarsely chopped
- 2 tbsp milk

DRIZZLED CHOCOLATE FINGERS

Makes: 18–20 cookies

Preparation: 30' + 30' to set

Cooking: 12–15'

Level of difficulty: 1

- 1 cup/150 g all-purpose/plain flour
- ½ cup/75 g cornstarch/cornflour
- ⅛ tsp salt
- ¾ cup/180 g butter, softened
- ⅓ cup/50 g confectioners'/icing sugar
- ½ tsp vanilla extract/essence
- 2 oz/60 g semisweet/dark chocolate, coarsely chopped
- 2 oz/60 g white chocolate, coarsely chopped

Preheat the oven to 350°F/180°C/gas 4. • Line two cookie sheets with parchment paper. • Sift the flour, cornstarch, and salt into a medium bowl. • Beat the butter, confectioners' sugar, and vanilla in a large bowl with an electric mixer at high speed until creamy. • Mix in the dry ingredients. • Fit the pastry bag with a ¹/₂-inch (1-cm) tip. Fill the pastry bag, twist opening tightly closed, and squeeze out 3-inch (8-cm) lines, spacing 2 inches (5 cm) apart on the prepared cookie sheets. • Bake for 12–15 minutes, or until just golden at the edges and firm to the touch. • Transfer to racks to cool. • Melt the semisweet and white chocolate separately in double boilers over barely simmering water. • Spoon the chocolates into separate small freezer bags and cut off tiny corners. • Drizzle over the cookies in a decorative manner. • Let stand for 30 minutes until set.

COCONUT AND CHOCOLATE SPRITZERS

Makes: 60 cookies

Preparation: 40' + 30' to set

Cooking: 10–15' per batch

Level of difficulty: 2

- 3⅓ cups/500 g all-purpose/plain flour
- ⅛ tsp salt
- 1 cup/250 g butter, softened
- 1¼ cups/250 g granulated sugar
- 1 large egg
- ½ tsp vanilla extract/essence
- grated zest of 1 lemon
- 7 oz/200 g semisweet/dark chocolate, coarsely chopped
- ¾ cup/90 g shredded/desiccated coconut

Preheat the oven to 325°F/170°C/gas 3. • Butter four cookie sheets. • Sift the flour and salt into a medium bowl. • Beat the butter and sugar in a large bowl with an electric mixer at high speed until creamy. • Add the egg and vanilla, beating until just blended. • Mix in the dry ingredients and lemon zest to form a stiff dough. • Insert the chosen design plate into a cookie press by sliding it into the head and locking in place. Press out the cookies, spacing about 1 inch (2.5 cm) apart on the prepared cookie sheets. • Bake, one sheet at a time, for 10–15 minutes, or until golden brown. • Transfer to racks to cool. • Melt the chocolate in a double boiler over barely simmering water. • Spread the melted chocolate over the tops of the cookies and sprinkle with the coconut. Let stand for 30 minutes until set.

Use a pastry bag with a wide tip if you don't have a cookie press on hand.

ANGELICA-TOPPED COOKIES

Preheat the oven to 350°F/180°C/gas 4. • Butter four cookie sheets. • Sift the flour and salt into a medium bowl. • Melt the chocolate in a double boiler over barely simmering water. • Beat the butter and sugar in a large bowl with an electric mixer at high speed until creamy. • Add the vanilla, milk, and egg, beating until just blended. • Mix in the dry ingredients and chocolate. • Insert the chosen design plate into the press by sliding it into the head and locking in place. Press out the cookies, spacing about $1^1/_2$ inches (4 cm) apart on the prepared cookie sheets. • Place a piece of angelica into the center of each cookie. • Bake, one sheet at a time, for 8–10 minutes, or until just colored and crisp. • Transfer to racks to cool.

Makes: 40–48 cookies

Preparation: 50'

Cooking: 8–10'

Level of difficulty: 2

- **2 cups/300 g all-purpose/plain flour**
- **$1/_4$ tsp salt**
- **2 oz/60 g semisweet/dark chocolate, coarsely chopped**
- **$1/_2$ cup/125 g butter, softened**
- **1 cup/200 g granulated sugar**
- **1 tsp vanilla extract/essence**
- **2 tbsp milk**
- **1 large egg, lightly beaten**
- **2 tbsp chopped angelica**

CITRUS CHOCOLATE TWISTS

Preheat the oven to 350°F/180°C/gas 4. • Line four cookie sheets with parchment paper. • Sift the flour, baking powder, and salt into a medium bowl. • Beat the butter and sugar in a large bowl with an electric mixer at high speed until creamy. • Add the egg, beating until just blended. • Finely grate 2 oz (60 g) of the chocolate and beat into the mixture. • Beat in the orange zest. • Mix in the dry ingredients to form a soft dough. • Turn the dough out onto a lightly floured surface and knead until smooth. • Form tablespoons of the dough into 8-inch (20-cm) ropes. • Fold in half and twist, pressing the ends of the rope together. • Transfer to the prepared cookie sheets, placing them 2 inches (5 cm) apart. • Bake, one batch at a time, for 10–12 minutes, or until just firm. • Transfer to racks to cool. • Melt the remaining chocolate in a double boiler over barely simmering water. • Dip in the tops of cookies and let set for 30 minutes.

Makes: 40–45 cookies

Preparation: 40' + 30' to set

Cooking: 10–12'

Level of difficulty: 2

- 3 cups/450 g all-purpose/plain flour
- 2 tsp baking powder
- ¼ tsp salt
- ¾ cup/180 g butter, softened
- ½ cup/100 g granulated sugar
- 1 large egg
- 5 oz/150 g semisweet/dark chocolate
- 1 tbsp finely shredded orange zest

PECAN AND CHOCOLATE CHIP WEDGES

Preheat the oven to 350°F/180°C/gas 4. • Set out a 12-inch (30-cm) pizza pan. • Sift the flour, baking soda, and salt into a medium bowl. • Beat the butter and granulated and brown sugars in a large bowl with an electric mixer at high speed until creamy. • Add the vanilla and egg, beating until just blended. • Mix in the dry ingredients, chocolate chips, pecans, and M&Ms. • Spread the mixture in the pan. • Bake for 12–15 minutes, or until lightly browned. • Cool completely in the pan. • Cut into wedges.

Makes: 16 wedges

Preparation: 20'

Cooking: 12–15'

Level of difficulty: 1

- **2 cups/300 g all-purpose/plain flour**
- **1 tsp baking soda**
- **½ tsp salt**
- **½ cup/125 g butter, softened**
- **⅓ cup/70 g granulated sugar**
- **½ cup/100 g firmly packed light brown sugar**
- **½ tsp vanilla extract/essence**
- **1 large egg**
- **¾ cup/125 g semisweet/dark chocolate chips**
- **½ cup/50 g finely chopped pecans**
- **½ cup/50 g M&Ms**

CHOCOLATE ARCHES

Makes: 20–25 cookies

Preparation: 30' + 30' to set

Cooking: 10–15'

Level of difficulty: 2

- ¾ cup/125 g all-purpose/plain flour
- ¾ cup/125 g finely ground yellow cornmeal
- ⅛ tsp salt
- ⅓ cup/70 g granulated sugar
- ½ tsp vanilla extract/essence
- 2 large eggs
- ⅔ cup/150 g butter, softened
- 7 oz/200 g semisweet/dark chocolate, coarsely chopped

Sift the flour, cornmeal, and salt into a large bowl. • Stir in the sugar and vanilla. • Add the eggs, beating until just blended. • Stir in the butter to form a stiff dough. • Cover with a clean kitchen towel and let stand for 30 minutes. • Preheat the oven to 400°F/200°C/gas 6. • Line two cookie sheets with parchment paper. • Fit a pastry bag with a ½-inch (1-cm) star tip. Fill the pastry bag, twist the opening tightly closed, and squeeze out 4-inch (10-cm) tall arches (horseshoes) spacing them 2 inches (5 cm) apart on the prepared cookie sheets. • Bake for 10–15 minutes, or until just golden. • Cool the cookies completely on the cookie sheets. • Melt the chocolate in a double boiler over barely simmering water. • Dip the cookies halfway into the chocolate and let stand until set, about 30 minutes.

CRUNCHY HAZELNUT ROUNDS

Makes: 16–20
  cookies

Preparation: 30'

Cooking: 10–15'

Level of difficulty: 1

- ½ cup/125 g
  butter, softened
- ⅔ cup/140 g
  firmly packed dark
  brown sugar
- 1 large egg, lightly
  beaten
- ⅔ cup/100 g all-
  purpose/plain flour
- ⅓ cup/50 g old-
  fashioned rolled
  oats
- 1½ tbsp
  unsweetened
  cocoa powder
- ½ tsp baking
  powder
- ⅛ tsp salt
- 3 oz/90 g white
  chocolate,
  coarsely chopped
- 3 oz/90 g milk
  chocolate,
  coarsely chopped
- 1 cup/100 g
  coarsely chopped
  hazelnuts

Preheat the oven to 350°F/180°C/gas 4. •
Butter a cookie sheet. • Beat the butter and
brown sugar in a large bowl with an electric mixer
at high speed until creamy. • Add the egg, beating
until just blended. • Mix in the flour, oats, cocoa,
baking powder, and salt. • Stir in the white and
milk chocolates and hazelnuts. • Drop teaspoons
of the mixture ½ inch (1 cm) apart on the
prepared baking sheet. • Bake for 10–15 minutes,
or until risen and craggy. • Cool on the sheet until
the cookies firm slightly. Transfer to racks and let
cool completely.

CHOCOLATE SPICE COOKIES

Makes: 25–30 cookies

Preparation: 20'

Cooking: 12–15'

Level of difficulty: 1

- 1 cup/150 g all-purpose/plain flour
- 4 tbsp unsweetened cocoa powder
- 1 tsp baking powder
- 1/8 tsp freshly grated nutmeg
- 1/8 tsp salt
- 1/2 cup/125 g butter, softened
- 1/2 cup/100 g granulated sugar
- 1 large egg yolk

Preheat the oven to 350°F/180°C/gas 4. • Butter two cookie sheets. • Sift the flour, cocoa, baking powder, nutmeg, and salt into a medium bowl. • Beat the butter and sugar in a large bowl with an electric mixer at high speed until creamy. • Add the egg yolk, beating until just blended. • Mix in the dry ingredients. • Drop teaspoons of the dough 1 inch (2.5 cm) apart onto the prepared cookie sheets. • Bake for 12–15 minutes, or until firm around the edges. • Transfer to racks to cool.

WHITE CHOCOLATE CHIP REFRIGERATOR COOKIES

Sift the flour, baking powder, and salt into a medium bowl. • Beat the butter, oil, and brown sugar in a large bowl with an electric mixer at high speed until creamy. • Add the egg and vanilla, beating until just blended. • Mix in the dry ingredients, chocolate chips, and walnuts. • Form the dough into a 7-inch (18-cm) log, wrap in plastic wrap, and refrigerate for at least 30 minutes. • Preheat the oven to 375°F/190°C/gas 5. • Butter two cookie sheets. • Slice the dough ¼ inch (5-mm) thick and place 2 inches (5 cm) apart on the prepared cookie sheets. • Bake for 8–10 minutes, or until just golden at the edges.
• Transfer to racks to cool.

Makes: 28 cookies

Preparation: 40' + 30' to chill

Cooking: 8–10'

Level of difficulty: 1

- 1²⁄₃ cups/250 g all-purpose/plain flour
- 1½ tsp baking powder
- ¼ tsp salt
- ½ cup/125 g butter, softened
- 4 tbsp sunflower or peanut oil
- ¾ cup/150 g firmly packed light brown sugar
- 1 large egg, lightly beaten
- ½ tsp vanilla extract/essence
- 1 cup/180 g white chocolate chips
- 1 cup/100 g chopped walnuts

CHOCOLATE AND BUTTER WHEEL COOKIES

Makes: 36 cookies

Preparation: 45'+ 80' to chill

Cooking: 12–15'

Level of difficulty: 2

- 1²/₃ cups/250 g all-purpose/plain flour
- 1 tsp baking powder
- ⅛ tsp salt
- ²/₃ cup/150 g butter
- ¾ cup/150 g firmly packed light brown sugar
- 1 large egg, lightly beaten
- 2 tsp rum extract/essence
- 1 tsp vanilla extract/essence
- 2 oz/60 g semisweet/dark chocolate, coarsely chopped
- 2 tbsp vanilla sugar
- 2 tbsp unsweetened cocoa powder
- 1 tbsp milk

Sift the flour, baking powder, and salt into a large bowl. • Cut in the butter until it resembles fine crumbs. • Mix in the brown sugar, egg, and rum and vanilla extracts. Divide the dough in half. Refrigerate for 30 minutes. • Melt the chocolate in a double boiler over simmering water. Mix in the vanilla sugar, cocoa, and milk. • Take one half of the dough and knead in the chocolate mixture. • Form the chocolate dough into a 9-inch (23-cm) log. Refrigerate for 30 minutes. • Roll out the plain dough on a surface to fit around the chocolate roll. Wrap the plain dough around the chilled chocolate dough to form a larger roll. • Refrigerate for 20 minutes. • Preheat the oven to 350°F/180°C/gas 4. • Line two cookie sheets with parchment paper. • Slice ¼ inch (5 mm) thick and place 1 inch (2.5 cm) apart on the sheets. • Bake for 12–15 minutes, or until lightly browned. • Transfer to racks to cool.

CHOCOLATE-FLECKED COOKIES

Preheat the oven to 350°F/180°C/gas 4. • Butter two cookie sheets. • Sift the flour, baking powder, and salt into a large bowl. • Beat the butter and sugar in a large bowl with an electric mixer at high speed until creamy. • Add the egg, beating until just blended. • Mix in the dry ingredients and chocolate. • Drop teaspoons of the mixture 1 inch (2.5 cm) apart onto the prepared cookie sheets. • Bake for 15–20 minutes, or until golden brown. • Cool on the sheets for 15 minutes. • Transfer to racks to cool.

Makes: 30 cookies

Preparation: 15'

Cooking: 15–20'

Level of difficulty: 1

- 1 cup/150 g all-purpose/plain flour
- 1½ tsp baking powder
- ½ tsp salt
- ½ cup/125 g butter, softened
- ¼ cup/50 g granulated sugar
- 1 large egg, lightly beaten
- 6 oz/180 g semisweet/dark chocolate, coarsely chopped

DUSKY CHOCOLATE COOKIES

Makes: 25–30 cookies

Preparation: 40' + 30' to chill

Cooking: 12–15'

Level of difficulty: 1

- $^2/_3$ cup/100 g all-purpose/plain flour
- $^1/_2$ cup/75 g semolina flour
- 2 tbsp unsweetened cocoa powder
- $^1/_8$ tsp salt
- 6 tbsp butter, softened
- $^1/_2$ cup/100 g granulated sugar
- 1 large egg, lightly beaten

Sift the flour, semolina, cocoa, and salt into a medium bowl. • Beat the butter and sugar in a large bowl until creamy. • Add the egg, beating until just blended. • Mix in the dry ingredients. • Press the dough into a disk, wrap in plastic wrap, and refrigerate for 30 minutes. • Preheat the oven to 375°F/190°C/gas 5. • Set out two cookie sheets. • Roll out the dough on a lightly floured surface to a thickness of $^1/_4$ inch (5 mm). • Use a 2-inch (5-cm) cookie cutter to cut out the cookies. Gather the dough scraps, re-roll, and continue cutting out cookies until all the dough is used. Use a spatula to transfer the cookies to the cookie sheets. • Bake for 12–15 minutes, or until lightly browned. • Transfer to racks to cool.

ALMOND CHOCOLATE CHIP COOKIES

Preheat the oven to 325°F/170°C/gas 3. • Butter two cookie sheets. • Sift the flour and confectioners' sugar into a large bowl. • With an electric mixer at high speed, beat in the butter and egg yolk until well blended. • Mix in the almond extract, almonds, and chocolate chips. • Form the dough into balls the size of walnuts and place 1 inch (2.5 cm) apart on the prepared cookie sheets. • Bake for 20–25 minutes, or until just golden. • Cool on the sheets until the cookies firm slightly. • Transfer to racks to finish cooling.

Makes: 30 cookies

Preparation: 25'

Cooking: 20–25'

Level of difficulty: 1

- 1²⁄₃ cups/250 g all-purpose/plain flour
- ¾ cup/125 g confectioners'/icing sugar
- 1 cup/250 g butter, softened
- 1 large egg yolk, lightly beaten
- 1 tsp almond extract/essence
- 1 cup/100 g finely chopped almonds
- ½ cup/90 g semisweet/dark chocolate chips

PEANUT BUTTER CHOCOLATE CHIP COOKIES

Makes: 16 cookies

Preparation: 20'

Cooking: 10–12'

Level of difficulty: 1

- 1¼ cups/180 g all-purpose/plain flour
- ½ tsp baking soda
- ¼ tsp salt
- ½ cup/125 g butter, softened
- ½ cup/100 g raw sugar (Demerara or Barbados)
- ½ cup/125 g smooth peanut butter
- 1 tsp vanilla extract
- 1 large egg
- 4 oz/125 g semisweet/dark chocolate, coarsely chopped

Preheat the oven to 375°F/190°C/gas 5. • Butter a cookie sheet. • Sift the flour, baking soda, and salt into a large bowl. • Beat the butter and sugar in a large bowl with an electric mixer at high speed until creamy. • Beat in the peanut butter. • Add the vanilla and egg, beating until just blended. • Mix in the dry ingredients, followed by the chocolate. • Drop tablespoons of the dough 2 inches (5 cm) apart onto the prepared cookie sheet. • Bake for 10–12 minutes, or until just golden at the edges. • Transfer to racks and let cool completely.

Use crunchy or smooth peanut butter to change the texture of these cookies.

LUNCHBOX SQUARES

Butter an 8-inch (20-cm) square baking pan. •
Melt the butter in a small saucepan over low
heat. Stir in the cocoa, brown sugar, and corn
syrup. Bring to a boil and let boil for 1 minute. •
Remove from the heat and stir in the crumbs. •
Spoon the mixture into the prepared pan, pressing
down lightly . • Melt the chocolate in a double
boiler over barely simmering water. Pour the
melted chocolate over the cookie base. Use a knife
to decorate the chocolate in a decorative manner.
• Refrigerate for 1 hour. • Cut into squares.

Makes: 16–25 squares

Preparation: 15' + 1 h to chill

Level of difficulty: 1

- **1 cup/250 g butter, cut up**
- **4 tbsp unsweetened cocoa powder**
- **1 tbsp firmly packed light brown sugar**
- **2 tbsp light corn syrup/golden syrup**
- **2 cups/250 g graham cracker crumbs/crushed digestive biscuits**
- **4 oz/125 g semisweet/dark chocolate, coarsely chopped**

CHOCOLATE-TOPPED DROPS

Makes: 36 cookies

Preparation: 25'

Cooking: 8–10' per batch

Level of difficulty: 1

- 1⅓ cups/200 g all-purpose/plain flour
- ½ tsp baking soda
- ⅛ tsp salt
- 2 oz/60 g semisweet/dark chocolate, coarsely chopped
- ½ cup/125 g butter, softened
- 1 cup/200 g granulated sugar
- 1 tsp vanilla extract/essence
- 1 large egg, lightly beaten
- 2 tbsp milk

- 1 cup/250 ml Chocolate Frosting (see page 952)
- ½ cup/50 g pecans, halved

Preheat the oven to 400°F/200°C/gas 6. • Butter three cookie sheets. • Sift the flour, baking soda, and salt into a large bowl. • Melt the chocolate in a double boiler over barely simmering water. • Beat the butter, sugar, and melted chocolate in a large bowl with an electric mixer at high speed until creamy. • Add the vanilla and egg, beating until just blended. • Mix in the dry ingredients and milk until well blended. • Drop teaspoons of the dough 1 inch (2.5 cm) apart onto the prepared cookie sheets. • Bake, one sheet at a time, for 8–10 minutes, or until slightly risen. • Cool on the sheets until the cookies firm slightly. Transfer to racks to finish cooling. • Spread the frosting over the tops of the cookies and decorate with the pecans.

AFRICAN CHOCOLATE CHIP COOKIES

Butter and flour two 12-cup muffin pans, or line with foil or paper baking cups. • Sift the flour and salt into a medium bowl. • Beat the butter and both sugars in a large bowl with an electric mixer at high speed until creamy. • Add the vanilla and egg and egg yolk, beating until just blended. • Mix in the baking soda mixture, followed by the dry ingredients. • Stir in the chocolate chips. • Spoon the cookie dough evenly into the prepared cups and refrigerate for 30 minutes. • Preheat the oven to 350°F/180°C/gas 4. • Bake for 15–18 minutes, or until set. • Cool completely in the pans.

Makes: 20–24 cookies

Preparation: 20' + 30' to chill

Cooking: 15–18'

Level of difficulty: 2

- 2 cups/300 g all-purpose/plain flour
- ¼ tsp salt
- 1 cup/250 g butter, softened
- 1½ cups/300 g firmly packed dark brown sugar
- ¼ cup/50 g granulated sugar
- 1 tsp vanilla extract/essence
- 1 large egg + 1 large egg yolk
- 1 tsp baking soda dissolved in 1 tbsp hot water
- 1¼ cups/230 g semisweet/dark chocolate chips

CHOCOLATE PRETZELS WITH WHITE CHOCOLATE

Makes: 20–25 cookies

Preparation: 40' + 1 h to chill and set

Cooking: 10–12'

Level of difficulty: 2

- 2 cups/300 g all-purpose/plain flour
- 2 tbsp unsweetened cocoa powder
- 1 tsp baking powder
- ½ tsp salt
- ¾ cup/180 g butter, softened
- 1 cup/200 g granulated sugar
- 1 large egg
- ½ tsp almond extract/essence
- ½ cup/50 g finely ground almonds
- 8 oz/250 g white chocolate, coarsely chopped

Sift the flour, cocoa, baking powder, and salt into a medium bowl. • Beat the butter and sugar in a large bowl until creamy. • Add the egg and almond extract, beating until just blended. • Mix in the dry ingredients and almonds. • Divide the dough in half. Press into disks, wrap each in plastic wrap, and refrigerate for 30 minutes. • Preheat the oven to 350°F/180°C/gas 4. • Butter two cookie sheets. • Form the dough into 1½-inch (4-cm) balls and roll each into a 12-inch (30-cm) rope. • Make each rope into a pretzel shape by twisting the two ends around each other, then bringing both back near to the center of the strip, about 1 inch (2.5 cm) apart. • Bake for 10–12 minutes, or until golden. • Transfer to racks to cool. • Melt the white chocolate in a double boiler over barely simmering water. • Dip the cookies halfway into the chocolate and let stand for 30 minutes until set.

CHERRY AND WHITE CHOCOLATE COOKIES

Makes: 18–20 cookies

Preparation: 20'

Cooking: 15–20'

Level of difficulty: 1

- 1 cup/150 g all-purpose/plain flour
- ½ tsp baking powder
- ⅛ tsp salt
- ½ cup/125 g butter, softened
- ¼ cup/50 g granulated sugar
- ½ tsp vanilla extract/essence
- ⅓ cup/40 g finely chopped candied cherries
- 1 oz/30 g white chocolate, finely chopped

Preheat the oven to 375°F/190°C/gas 5. • Butter two cookie sheets. • Sift the flour, baking powder, and salt into a large bowl. • Beat the butter, sugar, and vanilla in a large bowl with an electric mixer at high speed until creamy. • Mix in the dry ingredients, cherries, and white chocolate. • Drop rounded teaspoons of the dough 1 inch (2.5 cm) apart onto the prepared cookie sheets. • Bake for 15–20 minutes, or until just golden. • Cool on the sheets until the cookies firm slightly. Transfer to racks to finish cooling.

HOT CHOCOLATE COOKIES

Preheat the oven to 350°F/180°C/gas 4. •
Butter two cookie sheets. • Sift the flour, red
pepper, baking powder, and salt into a medium
bowl. • Beat the butter and granulated and brown
sugars in a large bowl with an electric mixer at high
speed until creamy. • Add the egg and vanilla,
beating until just blended. • Mix in the dry
ingredients and chopped chocolate. • Drop
teaspoons of the dough 1 inch (2.5 cm) apart onto
the prepared cookie sheets. • Bake for 12–15
minutes, or until firm to the touch. • Transfer to
racks to cool.

*Makes: 20–25
cookies*

Preparation: 20'

Cooking: 12–15'

Level of difficulty: 1

- ¾ cup/125 g all-
  purpose/plain flour
- 1 tsp ground red
  pepper
- ½ tsp baking
  powder
- ⅛ tsp salt
- ½ cup/125 g
  butter, softened
- 2 tbsp granulated
  sugar
- ¼ cup/50 g firmly
  packed dark brown
  sugar
- 1 large egg
- ½ tsp vanilla
  extract/essence
- 3 oz/90 g
  semisweet/dark
  chocolate, finely
  chopped

Makes: 16 cookies
Preparation: 25'
Cooking: 20–25'
Level of difficulty: 1

- 1½ cups/225 g all-purpose/plain flour
- 2 tbsp unsweetened cocoa powder
- ½ tsp baking powder
- ⅛ tsp salt
- ½ cup/125 g butter, softened
- ½ cup/125 g lard or vegetable shortening, softened
- ½ cup/100 g granulated sugar
- 1 cup/150 g old-fashioned rolled oats
- 4 tbsp light corn syrup/golden syrup dissolved in 1 tbsp hot water

FILLING

- 4 tbsp butter, softened
- 2 tbsp confectioners'/icing sugar
- 2 tbsp unsweetened cocoa powder
- ½ tsp vanilla extract/essence

CHOCOLATE CREAM KISSES

Preheat the oven to 350°F/180°C/gas 4. • Butter two cookie sheets. • Sift the flour, cocoa, baking powder, and salt into a medium bowl. • Beat the butter, lard, and sugar in a large bowl with an electric mixer at high speed until creamy. • Mix in the dry ingredients, followed by the oats and corn syrup mixture to form a smooth dough. • Form the dough into balls the size of walnuts, and place 1 inch (2.5 cm) apart on the prepared cookie sheets, flattening them slightly. • Bake for 20–25 minutes, or until firm to the touch. • Transfer to racks to cool. • Filling: Beat the butter and confectioners' sugar in a small bowl until creamy. • Mix in the cocoa and vanilla. • Stick the cookies together in pairs with the chocolate filling.

DARK CHOCOLATE CARAMEL DELIGHT

Preheat the oven to 325°F/170°C/gas 3. • Line a 12 x 9-inch (30 x 23-cm) jelly-roll pan with aluminum foil. • Cookie Base: Sift the flour, baking powder, and salt into a large bowl. • Beat the butter and sugar in a large bowl with an electric mixer at high speed until creamy. • Mix in the dry ingredients. • Spread the mixture evenly in the prepared pan. • Bake for 10–15 minutes, or until golden brown. • Topping: Melt the butter with the sugar, corn syrup, and condensed milk in a medium saucepan over low heat, stirring constantly. Bring to a boil and let boil for 5 minutes. Remove from the heat and let cool slightly. • Spread the caramel topping evenly over the cookie base. • Melt the chocolate in a double boiler over barely simmering water. Pour the chocolate over the caramel topping and let stand for 30 minutes until set. • Cut into squares.

Makes: 20–24 squares

Preparation: 20' + 30' to set

Cooking: 10'

Level of difficulty: 2

BASE
- 1 cup/150 g all-purpose/plain flour
- 1 tsp baking powder
- 1/8 tsp salt
- 1/2 cup/125 g butter, softened
- 1/4 cup/50 g granulated sugar

TOPPING
- 1/2 cup/125 g butter, cut up
- 1/2 cup/100 g granulated sugar
- 2 tbsp light corn syrup/golden syrup
- 1 can (14 oz/400 g) sweetened condensed milk
- 8 oz/250 g semisweet/dark chocolate, coarsely chopped

CLASSIC REFRIGERATOR COOKIES

Makes: 20 cookies

Preparation: 50' + 90' to chill

Cooking: 10–15'

Level of difficulty: 2

- 1⅓ cups/200 g all-purpose/plain flour
- ½ tsp baking powder
- ⅛ tsp salt
- ⅔ cup/150 g butter, softened
- ⅓ cup/70 g vanilla sugar
- 2 tbsp unsweetened cocoa powder
- 1 large egg white, lightly beaten

Sift the flour, baking powder, and salt into a medium bowl. • Beat the butter and vanilla sugar in a large bowl with an electric mixer at high speed until creamy. • Mix in the dry ingredients to form a stiff dough. • Lightly dust a surface with confectioners' sugar and divide the dough in half. • Knead the cocoa powder into one half of the dough until well blended. Wrap each dough portion in plastic wrap and refrigerate for at least 30 minutes. • Cut each chilled portion in thirds and form into long logs 1 inch (2.5 cm) in diameter. Press the edges of the logs to make them into even-sided oblongs. • Arrange the three chocolate logs and the three plain logs on top of each other in a checkerboard pattern. To do so, place one light log next to one dark log, then set a dark log on top of the light log to make a roll with alternating chocolate and plain sections. • Seal the sections together by brushing them with a little egg white. The dough will now be rectangular in shape. • Wrap in plastic wrap and refrigerate for at least 1 hour. • Preheat the oven to 375°F/190°C/gas 5. • Butter two large cookie sheets. • Slice the dough ¼ inch (5 mm) thick and place 1½ inches (4 cm) apart on the prepared cookie sheets. • Bake for 10–15 minutes, or until lightly browned and the edges are firm. • Transfer to racks to cool.

BANANA CHIP COOKIES

Preheat the oven to 375°F/190°C/gas 5. • Butter three cookie sheets. • Sift the flour, baking soda, and salt into a medium bowl. • Beat the butter and both sugars in a large bowl with an electric mixer at high speed until creamy. • Add the vanilla and eggs, beating until just blended. • Mix in the banana and dry ingredients, followed by the chocolate and banana chips. • Drop teaspoons of the dough 1 inch (2.5 cm) apart onto the prepared cookie sheets. • Bake, one sheet at a time, for 15–20 minutes, or until just golden. • Cool on the sheets until the cookies firm slightly. • Transfer to racks to finish cooling.

Makes: 36 cookies

Preparation: 20'

Cooking: 15–20' per batch

Level of difficulty: 1

- 2⅓ cups/350 g all-purpose/plain flour
- 1 tsp baking soda
- ⅛ tsp salt
- 1 cup/250 g butter, softened
- ¾ cup/150 g firmly packed dark brown sugar
- ½ cup/100 g granulated sugar
- 1 tsp vanilla extract/essence
- 2 large eggs
- 1 large banana, peeled and lightly mashed
- ½ cup/125 g semisweet/dark chocolate chips
- ½ cup/50 g coarsely chopped dried banana chips

HONEY WALNUT BROWNIES

Makes: 36–45 bars

Preparation: 20'

Cooking: 30–35'

Level of difficulty: 1

- 1 cup/150 g all-purpose/plain flour
- ½ tsp baking powder
- ⅛ tsp salt
- 6 oz/180 g semisweet/dark chocolate, coarsely chopped
- ½ cup/125 g butter, cut up
- ½ cup/100 g granulated sugar
- ½ cup/125 ml honey
- 2 large eggs
- 1 cup/100 g finely chopped walnuts

Preheat the oven to 350°F/180°C/gas 4. • Butter a 13 x 9-inch (33 x 23-cm) baking pan. • Sift the flour, baking powder, and salt into a medium bowl. • Melt the chocolate with the butter in a double boiler over barely simmering water. Transfer the chocolate mixture to a large bowl and let cool for 5 minutes. • Beat in the sugar and honey. • Add the eggs, beating until just blended. • Mix in the dry ingredients and walnuts. • Spoon the mixture evenly into the prepared pan. • Bake for 30–35 minutes, or until dry on top and almost firm to the touch. Do not overbake. • Cool completely before cutting into bars.

FANCY COOKIES

Butter Cookies: Preheat the oven to 375°F/180°C/gas 4. • Set out two cookie sheets. • Sift the flour and salt into a medium bowl. • Beat the butter and sugar in a large bowl with an electric mixer at high speed until creamy. • Add the egg yolk, beating until just blended. • Beat in the sour cream and almond extract. • Mix in the dry ingredients to form a smooth dough. • Insert a Christmas tree design plate into a cookie press by sliding it into the head and locking in place. Press out the cookies, spacing about $^1/_2$ inch (1 cm) apart on the cookie sheets. • Bake for 12–15 minutes, or until lightly browned. • Cool on the sheets until the cookies firm slightly. Transfer to racks to finish cooling. • Chocolate Glaze: Cook the sugar, water, butter, and corn syrup in a small saucepan over low heat until the sugar has dissolved. • Remove from the heat and stir in the chocolate chips. • Return the saucepan to the heat and stir until the glaze is smooth. • Dip the cookies halfway into the glaze and decorate with the sprinkles. • Let stand until the glaze has dried, about 30 minutes.

Serve these bright and cheerful cookies at a children's Christmas party.

94

Makes: 20–24 cookies

Preparation: 45' + 30' to set

Cooking: 12–15'

Level of difficulty: 2

BUTTER COOKIES
- 1 cup/150 g all-purpose/plain flour
- $^1/_8$ tsp salt
- 6 tbsp butter, softened
- $^1/_4$ cup/50 g granulated sugar
- 1 large egg yolk, lightly beaten
- 2 tbsp sour cream
- $^1/_4$ tsp almond extract/essence

CHOCOLATE GLAZE
- $^1/_2$ cup/100 g granulated sugar
- 2 tbsp water
- 1 tbsp butter
- 2 tsp dark corn syrup/golden syrup
- $^1/_4$ cup/50 g semisweet/dark chocolate chips
- colored sprinkles or sugar crystals, to decorate

TWO-TONE CRUNCHIES

Sift the flour, baking powder, and salt into a large bowl. • Cut in the butter until it resembles fine crumbs. • Mix in the sugar, egg, and vanilla. • Divide the dough in half. • Mix the cocoa and milk in a small bowl. • Knead the cocoa mixture into one half of the dough. • Form the plain dough into a 12-inch (30-cm) log. Brush with cold water. • Roll out the cocoa dough on a surface into a 12 x 6-inch (30 x 15-cm) rectangle. • Place the plain dough log in the center of the cocoa rectangle and wrap the cocoa dough around it. • Wrap in plastic wrap and refrigerate for 30 minutes. • Preheat the oven to 375°F/180°C/gas 4. • Butter three cookie sheets. • Slice the dough ¹/₄ inch (5 mm) thick and place 2 inches (5 cm) apart on the sheets. • Bake, one sheet at a time, for 8–10 minutes, or until lightly browned. • Let cool completely.

Makes: 48 cookies

Preparation: 40' + 30' to chill

Cooking: 8–10' per batch

Level of difficulty: 2

- 1²/₃ cups/250 g all-purpose/plain flour
- 1 tsp baking powder
- ¹/₈ tsp salt
- ¹/₂ cup/125 g butter, cut up
- ³/₄ cup/150 g granulated sugar
- 1 large egg, lightly beaten
- 1 tsp vanilla extract/essence
- 4 tbsp unsweetened cocoa powder
- 1 tbsp milk

CHOCOLATE FRUIT CHEWIES

Makes: 16 squares

Preparation: 40' + 2 h 20' to chill and set

Level of difficulty: 1

- ½ cup/125 g butter, cut up
- ½ cup/100 g granulated sugar
- 1¾ cups/175 g finely chopped pitted dates
- ⅔ cup/70 g finely chopped candied cherries
- ⅓ cup/45 g golden raisins/sultanas
- 2 cups/200 g rice krispies
- 8 oz/250 g semisweet/dark chocolate, coarsely chopped

Set out a 10½ x 15½-inch (26 x 36-cm) jelly-roll pan. • Melt the butter and sugar in a large saucepan over medium heat. • Remove from the heat and stir in the dates, cherries, raisins, and rice krispies until well coated. • Spoon the mixture evenly into the pan, pressing down firmly. • Refrigerate for 2 hours, or until set. • Melt the chocolate in a double boiler over barely simmering water. Pour the chocolate over and let stand for 20 minutes until set. • Use a sharp knife to cut into squares.

CHOCOLATE NUT BISCOTTI

Preheat the oven to 325°F/170°C/gas 3. •
Spread the hazelnuts on a large baking sheet. •
Toast for 7 minutes, or until lightly golden. Transfer
the nuts to a clean kitchen towel. Fold the kitchen
towel over and gently rub the nuts to remove the
skins. Pick out the nuts. • Increase the oven
temperature to 350°F/180°C/gas 4. • Butter two
cookie sheets. • Sift the flour, cocoa, baking
powder, cinnamon, cloves, and salt. Stir in the
sugar. • Beat the eggs, egg white, and vanilla in a
large bowl with an electric mixer at high speed until
frothy. • Mix in the dry ingredients, coffee,
hazelnuts, almonds, and chocolate chips to form a
stiff dough. • Divide the dough in four. • Form into
four logs about 1 inch (2.5 cm) in diameter and
place 4 inches (10 cm) apart on the prepared
cookie sheets, flattening them slightly. • Glaze:
Beat the yolk and milk in a small bowl and brush it
over the logs. • Bake for 25–30 minutes, or until
firm to the touch. Transfer to a cutting board to
cool for 15 minutes. • Reduce the oven
temperature to 300°F/150°C/gas 2. • Cut on the
diagonal into 1-inch (2.5 cm) slices. • Arrange the
slices cut-side up on the cookie sheets and bake
for about 10 minutes more. • Transfer to racks
to cool.

Makes: 30–35 biscotti

Preparation: 40'

Cooking: 35–40'

Level of difficulty: 2

- 1/3 cup/50 g shelled hazelnuts
- 2 cups/300 g all-purpose/plain flour
- 2 tbsp unsweetened cocoa powder
- 1 tsp baking powder
- 1/2 tsp ground cinnamon
- 1/4 tsp ground cloves
- 1/8 tsp salt
- 3/4 cup/150 g granulated sugar
- 3 large eggs + 1 large egg white
- 1 tsp vanilla extract/essence
- 2 tsp freeze-dried coffee granules dissolved in 1 tbsp hot water
- 1–2 tbsp slivered almonds
- 2 tbsp semisweet chocolate chips

GLAZE
- 1 large egg yolk
- 1–2 tbsp milk

DOUBLE CHOCOLATE NUT BISCOTTI

Preheat the oven to 325°F/170°C/gas 3. • Line a cookie sheet with parchment paper. • Sift the flour, cocoa, baking powder, and salt into a medium bowl. • Beat the butter and sugar in a large bowl with an electric mixer at high speed until creamy. • Add the vanilla and eggs, beating until just blended. • Mix in the dry ingredients, walnuts, and chocolate to form a stiff dough. • Divide the dough in half. • Form the dough into two 12-inch (30-cm) logs and place 3 inches (8 cm) apart on the prepared cookie sheet, flattening the tops. • Bake for 25–35 minutes, or until firm to the touch. • Transfer to a cutting board to cool for 15 minutes. • Cut on the diagonal into 1-inch (2.5-cm) slices. • Arrange the slices cut-side up on two cookie sheets and bake for 10–15 minutes more. • Cool on racks.

Makes: 48 cookies

Preparation: 40'

Cooking: 35–50'

Level of difficulty: 2

- 2½ cups/375 g all-purpose/plain flour
- ¾ cup/125 g unsweetened cocoa powder
- 2 tsp baking powder
- ¼ tsp salt
- ½ cup/125 g butter, softened
- 1⅓ cups/240 g granulated sugar
- ½ tsp vanilla extract/essence
- 3 large eggs
- 1 cup/100 g coarsely chopped walnuts
- 4 oz/125 g semisweet/dark chocolate, coarsely chopped

MARBLED BROWNIES

Makes: 36–40 brownies

Preparation: 30'

Cooking: 40–45'

Level of difficulty: 1

BASE
- 1 cup/250 g butter, cut up
- 5 oz/150 g semisweet/dark chocolate, coarsely chopped
- 2½ cups/500 g granulated sugar
- 3 large eggs, lightly beaten
- 1 cup/150 g all-purpose/plain flour
- 1¼ cups/125 g coarsely chopped walnuts
- 1 tsp vanilla extract/essence
- ½ tsp salt

TOPPING
- 1 package (8 oz/ 250 g) cream cheese, softened
- ⅔ cup/140 g granulated sugar
- 1 large egg, lightly beaten
- 1 tsp vanilla extract/essence

Preheat the oven to 350°F/180°C/gas 4. • Butter a 13 x 9-inch (33 x 23-cm) baking pan. • Chocolate-Walnut Base: Melt the butter and chocolate in a double boiler over barely simmering water. • Remove from the heat and add the sugar and eggs, beating until just blended. • Mix in the flour, walnuts, vanilla, and salt. • Spoon the mixture into the prepared pan. • Topping: Beat the cream cheese, sugar, egg, and vanilla in a large bowl with an electric mixer at high speed until smooth. • Spoon the mixture over the chocolate base. • Use a knife to draw decorative lines across the topping. • Bake for 40–45 minutes, or until almost firm to the touch. • Cool completely before cutting into bars.

HAZELNUT FLORENTINES WITH WHITE CHOCOLATE

Preheat the oven to 325°F/170°C/gas 3. •
Spread the hazelnuts on a large baking sheet.
Toast for 7 minutes, or until lightly golden. •
Transfer to a food processor or blender with
$1/4$ cup (50 g) of sugar and process until very finely
chopped. • Increase the oven temperature to
375°F/170°C/gas 3. • Set out three cookie
sheets. • Melt the butter with the honey, cream,
and the remaining sugar in a small saucepan over
low heat until the sugar has dissolved completely.
• Bring to a boil and boil for 2 minutes. • Remove
from the heat and stir in the nut mixture and salt.
• Drop teaspoons of the mixture 3 inches (8 cm)
apart onto the cookie sheets. • Bake, one sheet at
a time, for 8–10 minutes, or until golden brown.
• Cool on the sheets until the cookies firm slightly.
• Transfer to racks to cool. • Melt the chocolate in
a double boiler over barely simmering water. Dip
the bottoms of the cookies into the chocolate and
let stand for 30 minutes until set.

Makes: 30–40 cookies

Preparation: 40' + 30' to set

Cooking: 8–10'

Level of difficulty: 3

- 1 lb/500 g hazelnuts
- 1 cup/200 g granulated sugar
- 1 cup/250 g butter, softened
- $1/2$ cup/125 g honey
- $1/2$ cup/125 ml heavy/double cream
- $1/8$ tsp salt
- 6 oz/180 g white chocolate, coarsely chopped
- 6 oz/180 g semisweet/dark chocolate, coarsely chopped

WHITE FLORENTINES

Makes: 18–20
cookies

Preparation: 45'

Cooking: 10–12'

Level of difficulty: 3

- ½ cup/125 ml heavy/double cream
- ¼ vanilla pod
- 2 tbsp butter
- ½ cup/100 g granulated sugar
- ½ cup/50 g coarsely chopped almonds
- ¼ cup/30 g coarsely chopped hazelnuts
- 1 cup/100 g finely chopped mixed candied peel
- ¼ cup/25 g finely sliced red candied cherries
- 1 tbsp finely chopped candied angelica
- 2 tbsp all-purpose/plain flour
- 7 oz/200 g white chocolate, coarsely chopped

Preheat the oven to 325°F/170°C/gas 3. • Line four cookie sheets with parchment paper. • Heat the cream with the vanilla pod, butter, and sugar in a medium saucepan over medium heat, stirring constantly, until the sugar has dissolved. Bring to a boil and remove from the heat immediately. Discard the vanilla pod and let cool. • Mix the almonds, hazelnuts, candied peel, cherries, angelica, and flour in a large bowl. • Stir in the cooled cream mixture and mix well. • Drop heaping teaspoons of the mixture 4 inches (10 cm) apart onto the prepared cookie sheets, flattening them to make 2-inch (5 cm) circles. Do not place more than five cookies on one sheet. • Bake, one sheet at a time, for 10–12 minutes, or until golden around the edges. • Cool on the sheets until the cookies firm slightly. Transfer to racks and let cool completely. • Melt the white chocolate in a double boiler over barely simmering water. • Lay the cold florentines flat-side upwards on a sheet of waxed paper, and spread the chocolate over them with a pastry brush. For a thick coating, paint the cookies several times. • When they are nearly set, make swirly patterns with a fork on the white chocolate base.

EXOTIC WAFERS

Preheat the oven to 350°F/180°C/gas 4. • Line four cookie sheets with parchment paper. • Sift the flour and salt into a medium bowl. • Melt the butter with the sugar and honey in a medium saucepan over low heat, stirring often, until the sugar has dissolved completely. • Increase the heat and bring the mixture almost to a boil. • Remove from the heat and mix in the almonds and dried fruit. • Add the dry ingredients all at once and stir until well blended. • Drop teaspoons of the dough 3 inches (8 cm) apart onto the prepared cookie sheets, flattening them slightly. • Bake, one sheet at a time, for 8–10 minutes, or until golden brown on top and slightly darker brown at the edges. • Cool on the sheets until the cookies firm slightly. Transfer to racks to finish cooling. • Melt the chocolate in a double boiler over barely simmering water. Arrange the cookies flat-side up on a sheet of waxed paper. • Brush with the melted chocolate and let stand for 30 minutes until set.

Makes: 45 cookies

Preparation: 25' + 30' to stand

Cooking: 8–10'

Level of difficulty: 1

- ¾ cup/125 g all-purpose/plain flour
- ⅛ tsp salt
- ½ cup/125 g butter, cut up
- ¾ cup/140 g granulated sugar
- 2 tsp honey
- ½ cup/50 g flaked almonds, toasted
- ⅔ cup/70 g finely chopped dried cranberries
- ⅔ cup/70 g finely chopped dried pineapple
- ⅔ cup/70 g finely chopped dried apricots
- 4 oz/125 g semisweet/dark chocolate, coarsely chopped

MARSHMALLOW ROUNDS

Set out an 8-inch (20-cm) square of plastic wrap. • Melt the butter with the brown sugar, cacoa powder, and corn syrup in a small saucepan over low heat until the sugar has dissolved completely. • Melt the chocolate in a double boiler over barely simmering water. Stir the chocolate into the butter mixture. Mix in the marshmallows and raisins. • Spoon the mixture onto the center of the plastic wrap. Roll the mixture to form a cylinder. • Refrigerate for 4 hours, or until firm. • Cut into rounds.

Makes: 16–25 rounds

Preparation: 25' + 4 h to chill

Level of difficulty: 1

- ½ cup/125 g butter, cut up
- 1 tbsp dark brown sugar
- ⅓ cup/50 g unsweetened cocoa powder
- 2 tbsp light corn syrup
- 8 oz/250 g semisweet/dark chocolate, coarsely chopped
- 2 cups/250 g snipped marshmallows, mixed colors
- 1 cup/180 g raisins

CAROB BROWNIES

Makes: 16–25
  brownies

Preparation: 20' + 2 h
  to chill

Level of difficulty: 1

- 1 cup/250 ml honey
- ¾ cup/125 g old-fashioned rolled oats
- ½ cup/75 g carob powder
- 2 tbsp sesame seeds
- 2 tbsp sunflower seeds
- 1 cup/100 g finely chopped walnuts

Line an 8-inch (20-cm) baking pan with aluminum foil. • Warm the honey in a small saucepan over low heat until liquid. • Mix the oats, carob powder, sesame seeds, sunflower seeds, honey, and walnuts in a large bowl. • Firmly press the mixture into the prepared pan to form a smooth, even layer. • Refrigerate for 2 hours, or until set. • Cut into squares.

PECAN BROWNIES

Preheat the oven to 350°F/180°C/gas 4. • Line a 13 x 9-inch (33 x 23-cm) baking pan with aluminum foil, letting the edges overhang. • Sift the flour, baking powder, and salt into a medium bowl. • Melt the butter and chocolate in a double boiler over barely simmering water. • Remove from the heat and stir in the sugar. • Add the eggs, beating until just blended. • Mix in the dry ingredients, vanilla, and pecans. • Pour the batter into the prepared pan. • Bake for 25–30 minutes, or until dry on top and almost firm to the touch. Do not overbake. • Cool completely in the pan. • Using the foil as handles, lift onto a cutting board. Peel off the foil. Cut into squares.

Makes: 36–40 brownies

Preparation: 20'

Cooking: 25–30'

Level of difficulty: 1

- 3 cups/450 g all-purpose/plain flour
- 2 tsp baking powder
- 1/4 tsp salt
- 1/2 cup/125 g butter, cut up
- 4 oz/125 g semisweet/dark chocolate, coarsely chopped
- 2 cups/400 g granulated sugar
- 4 large eggs, lightly beaten
- 1 tsp vanilla extract/essence
- 3/4 cup/125 g coarsely chopped pecans

CHOCOLATE VANILLA DROP COOKIES

Preheat the oven to 375°F/190°C/gas 5. •
Butter two cookie sheets. • Sift the flour,
cocoa, baking powder, and salt into a medium
bowl. • Beat the butter and sugar in a large bowl
with an electric mixer at high speed until creamy.
• Mix in the vanilla and dry ingredients. • Drop
tablespoons of the dough 2 inches (5 cm) apart
onto the prepared cookie sheets. • Bake for
15–18 minutes, or until firm to the touch.
• Cool on the sheets until the cookies firm slightly.
• Transfer to racks to finish cooling.

Makes: 15–20
cookies

Preparation: 20'

Cooking: 15–18'

Level of difficulty: 1

- 1 cup/150 g all-
  purpose/plain flour
- 2 tbsp unsweetened
  cocoa powder
- 1 tsp baking
  powder
- ⅛ tsp salt
- ⅔ cup/175 g
  butter, softened
- ½ cup/100 g
  granulated sugar
- ½ tsp vanilla
  extract/essence

SIMPLE CHOCOLATE BROWNIES

Makes: 16–25 bars

Preparation: 20'

Cooking: 35–40'

Level of difficulty: 1

- 1½ cups/225 g all-purpose/plain flour
- ⅛ tsp salt
- 7 oz/200 g semisweet/dark chocolate, coarsely chopped
- ½ cup/125 g butter, cut up
- 1 cup/180 g white chocolate chips
- 1 cup/180 g milk chocolate chips
- 1 cup/100 g coarsely chopped pecans
- 2 large eggs

Preheat the oven to 350°F/180°C/gas 4. • Butter an 8-inch (20-cm) square baking pan. • Sift the flour and salt into a medium bowl. • Melt the semisweet chocolate with the butter in a double boiler over barely simmering water. • Transfer the chocolate mixture to a medium bowl and let cool for 5 minutes. • Mix in the white and milk chocolate chips and the pecans. • Add the eggs, beating until just blended. • Mix in the dry ingredients. • Spoon the batter evenly into the prepared pan. • Bake for 35–40 minutes, or until dry on top and almost firm to the touch. Do not overbake. • Cool completely before cutting into bars.

AMARETTI CHOCOLATE CRUNCH

L ine an 8-inch (20-cm) square baking pan with parchment paper. • Melt the white chocolate with the butter and cream in a double boiler over barely simmering water. • Mix in the amaretti cookies, coconut, cherries, and almonds until well coated. • Spoon into the prepared pan, spreading it evenly. • Refrigerate for 4 hours, or until set. • Use a knife dipped in hot water to cut into bars.

Makes: 20 bars

Preparation: 30' + 4 h to chill

Level of difficulty: 1

- **10 oz/300 g white chocolate, coarsely chopped**
- **²/₃ cup/150 g butter, cut up**
- **4 tbsp heavy/ double cream**
- **3 oz/90 g amaretti cookies, crushed**
- **2 tbsp shredded coconut**
- **1 cup/100 g coarsely chopped candied cherries**
- **½ cup/50 g flaked almonds, toasted**

CHOCOLATE ALMOND MICE

Makes: 12 cookies

Preparation: 20' + 3 h
   to chill

Level of difficulty: 1

- 5 oz/150 g
  semisweet/dark
  chocolate,
  coarsely chopped
- 6 tbsp heavy/
  double cream
- 1 cup/125 g
  chocolate wafer
  crumbs
- 1/3 cup/50 g
  confectioners'/
  icing sugar
- 24 silver balls, to
  decorate
- 24 flaked almonds,
  to decorate
- Red licorice whips,
  to decorate

Melt the chocolate with the cream in a double boiler over barely simmering water. • Mix in the chocolate wafer crumbs until well blended. • Cover with plastic wrap and refrigerate for 1 hour, or until firm. • Form the dough into balls the size of tangerines, tapering one end to resemble the nose. • Roll half the balls in the confectioners' sugar until well coated. • Decorate all with the silver balls to resemble the eyes, almonds for ears, and a small length of licorice for the tail. • Refrigerate for 2 hours.

EASY CHOCOLATE CARAMEL SQUARES

Makes: 16 squares

Preparation: 25'

Level of difficulty: 1

- ¾ cup/180 ml sweetened condensed milk
- 12 oz/350 g semisweet/dark chocolate, coarsely grated
- 2 tbsp butter, softened
- 2 cups/200 g rice krispies

Grease an 11 x 7-inch (28 x 18-cm) baking pan with sunflower oil. • Heat the condensed milk in a medium saucepan over low heat for 3 minutes, stirring constantly. • Stir in the chocolate and butter and cook until smooth and well blended. • Remove from the heat and stir in the rice krispies until well coated. • Pour the mixture into the pan, smoothing the top. • Let cool for 5 minutes. Use a sharp knife to score the mixture into bars. • When set, cut into squares.

FROSTED BRANDY CRUNCH

Makes: 10 cookies

Preparation: 20' + 4 h to stand

Cooking: 15'

Level of difficulty: 1

- **3 eggs**
- **1²⁄₃ cups/250 g all-purpose/plain flour**
- **½ cup/125 g butter, softened**
- **¼ tsp salt**
- **3 tbsp brandy**
- **2²⁄₃ cups/400 g confectioners'/icing sugar**
- **1 tbsp lemon juice**

Preheat the oven to 350°F/180°C/gas 4. • Separate two of the eggs, place the whites in a large bowl, and set aside for the frosting. • Sift the flour into a large bowl. • Break in the remaining egg and add the yolks, butter, salt, and brandy. • Gradually work these ingredients into the flour, first with a fork, then by hand until the dough is smooth and elastic. • Divide the dough into 4 or 5 portions and roll each into a long cylinder about as thick as a finger. Slice ¹⁄₂ inch (1 cm) thick. • Grease a baking sheet with the remaining butter and bake for 15 minutes, or until they are pale golden brown. • Remove from the oven and set aside to cool. • Frosting: Add the sifted confectioners' sugar and lemon juice to the egg whites and mix until smooth. • Set aside 7 tablespoons of this frosting in a small bowl. • Working fast (so that the frosting doesn't have time to set), add the baked dough pieces to the icing left in the large bowl and stir gently to coat all over. • Divide the mixture into 4–6 portions and heap it up on confectioners' or ice cream wafers, cut into squares or disks. • Spoon some of the extra frosting over each one. • Set aside for several hours before serving.

HAZELNUT AND CHOCOLATE HEARTS

Sift the flour, cocoa, and salt into a medium bowl. • Beat the butter and brown sugar in a large bowl with an electric mixer at high speed until creamy. • Add 1 whole egg and 1 egg yolk, beating until just blended. • Mix in the dry ingredients and ground hazelnuts to form a smooth dough. • Press the dough into a disk, wrap in plastic wrap, and refrigerate for 30 minutes. • Preheat the oven to 350°F/180°C/gas 4. • Line two cookie sheets with parchment paper. • Discard the plastic wrap. Roll out the dough on a lightly floured surface to a thickness of $1/4$ inch (5 mm). • Use a $1^1/2$-inch (4-cm) heart-shaped cookie cutter to cut out the cookies. Gather the dough scraps, re-roll, and continue cutting out cookies until all the dough is used. • Use a spatula to transfer the cookies to the prepared cookie sheets, placing them 1 inch (2.5 cm) apart. • Use a wire whisk to beat the remaining egg white in a small bowl until frothy and brush over the tops of the cookies. Sprinkle with the chopped hazelnuts. • Bake for 10–15 minutes, or until golden brown. • Transfer to racks to cool.

Makes: 25–30 cookies

Preparation: 40' + 30' to chill

Cooking: 10–15'

Level of difficulty: 1

- 1$1/3$ cups/200 g all-purpose/plain flour
- $1/3$ cup/50 g unsweetened cocoa powder
- $1/8$ tsp salt
- $1/2$ cup/125 g butter, softened
- $2/3$ cup/140 g firmly packed light brown sugar
- 2 large eggs, 1 separated
- $1/2$ cup/75 g finely ground hazelnuts
- $1/2$ cup/50 g finely chopped hazelnuts

124

CHOCOLOGS

Sift the flour, cocoa, and salt into a large bowl. •
Use a pastry blender to cut in the butter until
the mixture resembles fine crumbs. • Stir in the
sugar and vanilla. • Add the milk to form a stiff
dough. • Form the dough into a log 1 inch (2.5 cm)
in diameter, wrap in plastic wrap, and refrigerate
for 30 minutes. • Preheat the oven to 400°F/
200°C/gas 6. • Butter a cookie sheet. • Slice the
dough into 2-inch (5-cm) lengths and place 1 inch
(2.5 cm) apart on the prepared cookie sheet. •
Bake for 20–25 minutes, or until lightly browned
and firm to the touch. • Transfer to racks to cool.
• Frosting: Mix the cocoa with the water until
smooth. • Beat the butter in a medium bowl until
creamy. • Beat the confectioners' sugar and the
cocoa mixture until smooth. • Use a thin metal
spatula to spread the tops of the cookies with the
frosting. • Draw the tines of a fork across the
frosting to resemble the bark of a log.

*Makes: 14–16
cookies*

*Preparation: 30' + 30'
to chill*

Cooking: 20–25'

Level of difficulty: 1

- ³/₄ cup/125 g all-
  purpose/plain flour
- ¹/₃ cup/50 g
  unsweetened
  cocoa powder
- ¹/₈ tsp salt
- 6 tbsp butter
- ¹/₄ cup/50 g
  granulated sugar
- ¹/₂ tsp vanilla
  extract/essence
- 2 tbsp milk

FROSTING

- 1 tbsp unsweetened
  cocoa powder
- 2 tsp cold water
- 4 tbsp butter,
  softened
- 1 cup/150 g
  confectioners'/
  icing sugar

OAT SQUARES WITH CHOCOLATE WALNUT TOPPING

Preheat the oven to 375°F/190°C/gas 5. •
Butter a 10 1/2 x 15 1/2-inch (26 x 36-cm) jelly-roll pan. • Beat the butter and brown sugar in a large bowl with an electric mixer at high speed until creamy. • Add the egg yolk, beating until just blended. • Mix in the flour, oats, and salt until well blended. • Firmly press the mixture into the prepared pan to form a smooth, even layer.
• Bake for 15–20 minutes, or until just golden.
• Topping: Melt the chocolate and butter in a double boiler over barely simmering water.
• Spread the melted chocolate mixture over the oat base and sprinkle with the chopped walnuts.
• Cut into squares.

Makes: 24 squares

Preparation: 25'

Cooking: 15–20'

Level of difficulty: 1

- 1/2 cup/125 g butter, softened
- 2/3 cup/140 g firmly packed light brown sugar
- 1 large egg yolk
- 1/3 cup/50 g all-purpose/plain flour
- 2 tbsp old-fashioned rolled oats
- 1/8 tsp salt

TOPPING
- 3 oz/90 g semisweet/dark chocolate
- 1 tbsp butter
- 1/2 cup/50 g finely chopped walnuts

DUSTED COOKIES

Makes: 20–25
cookies

Preparation: 35'

Cooking: 15–20'

Level of difficulty: 1

- 1²⁄₃ cups/250 g all-purpose/plain flour
- 1 tsp baking powder
- ⅛ tsp salt
- 6 tbsp butter, softened
- ¼ cup/50 g granulated sugar
- 2 large eggs
- 1 tbsp milk
- 4 tbsp confectioners'/icing sugar
- 2 tbsp unsweetened cocoa powder

Preheat the oven to 350°F/180°C/gas 4. • Butter two cookie sheets. • Sift the flour, baking powder, and salt into a large bowl and make a well in the center. • Add the butter, sugar, eggs, and milk. • Use your hands to knead the mixture into a smooth dough. • Form the dough into balls the size of walnuts and place 1 inch (2.5 cm) apart on the prepared cookie sheets. • Bake for 15–20 minutes, or until just golden. • Transfer to racks and let cool completely. • Dip half of each cookie in the confectioners' sugar and the remaining half in the cocoa.

PECAN TORTOISES

Makes: 24 cookies

Preparation: 20'

Cooking: 8–10'

Level of difficulty: 1

- ½ cup/75 g all-purpose/plain flour
- 1 tbsp freeze-dried coffee granules
- ½ tsp baking powder
- ⅛ tsp salt
- 14 oz/400 g semisweet/dark chocolate, coarsely chopped
- 4 tbsp butter
- 1½ cups/300 g granulated sugar
- 1 tsp vanilla extract/essence
- 4 large eggs
- 2 cups/200 g finely chopped pecans + 1 cup/100 g pecan halves
- 1 cup/180 g semisweet/dark chocolate chips

Preheat the oven to 350°F/180°C/gas 4. • Line two cookie sheets with parchment paper. • Sift the flour, coffee granules, baking powder, and salt into a large bowl. • Melt the chocolate and butter in a double boiler over barely simmering water. • Stir in the sugar until completely dissolved. • Remove from the heat and mix in the vanilla and eggs. • Mix in the dry ingredients, finely chopped pecans, and chocolate chips. • Drop tablespoons of the dough 3 inches (8 cm) apart onto the prepared cookie sheets. • Press four pecan halves into each corner of the cookies to resemble the legs of a turtle and an additional one to resemble a head. • Bake for 8–10 minutes, or until just set. • Let cool completely.

COCOA WEDDING CAKES

Makes: 40–45
  cookies

Preparation: 20'

Cooking: 35–40'

Level of difficulty: 1

- 1½ cups/225 g all-purpose/plain flour
- ⅔ cup/100 g cornstarch/cornflour
- 2 tbsp unsweetened cocoa powder
- ⅛ tsp salt
- 1 cup/250 g butter, softened
- ¼ cup/50 g granulated sugar
- ⅔ cup/100 g confectioners'/icing sugar, to dust

Preheat the oven to 325°F/170°C/gas 3. • Line three cookie sheets with parchment paper. • Sift the flour, cornstarch, cocoa, and salt into a medium bowl. • Beat the butter and granulated sugar in a large bowl with an electric mixer at high speed until creamy. • Mix in the dry ingredients to make a smooth dough. • Form heaping teaspoons of the dough into balls the size of walnuts and place 2 inches (5 cm) apart on the prepared cookie sheets. • Bake, one sheet at a time, for 35–40 minutes, or until pale gold. • Cool on the sheets until the cookies firm slightly. Transfer to racks to finish cooling. • Put the confectioners' sugar in a small bowl and dip in the cookies until well coated

COCOA AND ORANGE SQUARES

Preheat the oven to 350°F/180°C/gas 4. •
Butter an 11 x 7-inch (28 x 18-cm) baking pan.
• Sift the flour, cocoa, baking powder, and salt into
a medium bowl. • Beat the butter and brown sugar
in a large bowl with an electric mixer at high speed
until creamy. • Add the eggs and orange zest,
beating until just blended. • Mix in the dry
ingredients, orange juice, and dates. • Pour the
mixture into the prepared pan. • Bake for 30–35
minutes, or until a toothpick inserted into the
center comes out clean. • Cool completely in the
pan. • Cut into bars.

Makes: 22–33 bars

Preparation: 20'

Cooking: 30–35'

Level of difficulty: 1

- 1½ cups/225 g all-purpose/plain flour
- 3 tbsp unsweetened cocoa powder
- 2 tsp baking powder
- ¼ tsp salt
- ½ cup/125 g butter, softened
- ¾ cup/150 g firmly packed light brown sugar
- 3 large eggs
- 1 tbsp finely grated orange zest
- ¾ cup/180 ml fresh orange juice
- 1 cup/100 g finely chopped pitted dates

WHITE CHOCOLATE AND PECAN COOKIES

Makes: 20 cookies

Preparation: 20'

Cooking: 10–12'

Level of difficulty: 1

- 1⅓ cups/200 g all-purpose/plain flour
- ½ tsp baking soda
- ⅛ tsp salt
- ½ cup/125 g butter, softened
- ⅔ cup/140 g raw sugar (Demerara or Barbados)
- 1 tsp vanilla extract/essence
- 1 large egg
- 4 oz/125 g white chocolate, coarsely chopped
- ½ cup/50 g finely chopped pecans

Preheat the oven to 350°F/180°C/gas 4. • Butter a cookie sheet. • Sift the flour, baking soda, and salt into a medium bowl. • Beat the butter and raw sugar in a large bowl with an electric mixer at high speed until creamy. • Add the vanilla and egg, beating until just blended. • Mix in the dry ingredients, white chocolate, and pecans. • Form the dough into balls the size of walnuts and place 2 inches (5 cm) apart on the prepared cookie sheet. • Bake for 10–12 minutes, or until just golden. • Cool on the sheet until the cookies firm slightly. • Transfer to racks and let cool completely.

PEANUT BUTTER PIZZA COOKIE

Preheat the oven to 375°F/190°C/gas 5. • Set out two 12-inch (30-cm) pizza pans. • Sift the flour, baking soda, and salt into a medium bowl. • Beat the butter, brown sugar, peanut butter, milk, and vanilla in a large bowl with an electric mixer at high speed until creamy. • Add the egg, beating until just blended. • Mix in the dry ingredients. • Divide the dough in half. • Spread the dough halves in the pans. • Bake for 10–12 minutes, or until lightly browned. • Cool completely in the pans. • Melt the white and semisweet chocolates in separate double boilers over barely simmering water. • Drizzle the chocolate over the cookies and let stand for 30 minutes to set. • Cut into wedges.

Makes: 30 wedges

Preparation: 20' + 30' to stand

Cooking: 10–12'

Level of difficulty: 1

- 1¾ cups/275 g all-purpose/plain flour
- ½ tsp baking soda
- ½ tsp salt
- ½ cup/125 g butter, softened
- 1¼ cups/250 g firmly packed light brown sugar
- ¾ cup/180 ml smooth peanut butter
- 4 tbsp milk
- ½ tsp vanilla extract/essence
- 1 large egg
- 4 oz/125 g white chocolate, coarsely chopped
- 4 oz/125 g semisweet/dark chocolate, coarsely chopped

CHOCOLATE MUNCHIES

Preheat the oven to 350°F/180°C/gas 4. •
Butter two cookie sheets. • Sift the flour,
cocoa, baking powder, cinnamon, and salt into a
medium bowl. • Beat the butter and sugar in a
large bowl with an electric mixer at high speed until
creamy. • Add the egg yolk, beating until just
blended. • Mix in the dry ingredients. • Drop
teaspoons of the dough 1 inch (2.5 cm) apart onto
the prepared cookie sheets. • Bake for 12–15
minutes, or until firm around the edges. • Transfer
to racks to cool. • Melt the chocolate in a double
boiler over barely simmering water. Drizzle the tops
with the melted chocolate.

*Makes: 25–30
cookies*

Preparation: 20'

Cooking: 12–15'

Level of difficulty: 1

- 1 cup/150 g all-
  purpose/plain flour
- 2 tbsp unsweetened
  cocoa powder
- 1 tsp baking
  powder
- 1/8 tsp ground
  cinnamon
- 1/8 tsp salt
- 1/2 cup/125 g
  butter, softened
- 1/2 cup/100 g
  granulated sugar
- 1 large egg yolk
- 2 oz/60 g
  semisweet/dark
  chocolate,
  coarsely chopped

CHOCOLATE ORANGE COOKIES

Makes: 25–30 cookies

Preparation: 45' + 60' to chill and set

Cooking: 10–15'

Level of difficulty: 1

- 1 cup/150 g all-purpose/plain flour
- 1/8 tsp salt
- 6 tbsp butter, cut up
- 1/3 cup/50 g finely ground almonds
- 1/4 cup/50 g granulated sugar
- 1 tbsp finely grated orange zest
- 1 large egg yolk, lightly beaten
- 2 tbsp fresh orange juice
- 4 oz/125 g semisweet/dark chocolate, coarsely chopped

Sift the flour and salt into a large bowl. • Cut in the butter until the mixture resembles fine crumbs. • Mix in the ground almonds, sugar, and orange zest. • Add the egg yolk and orange juice until smooth. • Refrigerate for 30 minutes. • Preheat the oven to 350°F/180°C/gas 4. • Line two cookie sheets with parchment paper. • Roll out the dough to a thickness of 1/4 inch (5 mm). • Use a 2-inch (5-cm) cookie cutter to cut out the cookies. Continue cutting out cookies until all the dough is used. • Transfer the cookies to the prepared cookie sheets, placing them 1 inch (2.5 cm) apart. • Bake for 10–15 minutes, or until golden. • Transfer to racks to cool. • Melt the chocolate in a double boiler over barely simmering water. • Dip the cookies halfway into the chocolate and let stand for 30 minutes until set.

CHOCOLATE WAFERS

Makes: 20–22
  cookies

Preparation: 30'

Cooking: 8–10'

Level of difficulty: 3

- 1 cup/100 g flaked almonds
- 2 tsp all-purpose/plain flour
- 2 tbsp unsweetened cocoa powder
- 1/8 tsp salt
- 1 large egg + 1 large egg white, lightly beaten
- 1/2 cup/100 g granulated sugar
- 2 tbsp butter, softened

Preheat the oven to 325°F/170°C/gas 3. •
Spread the almonds on a large baking sheet.
• Toast for 7 minutes, or until lightly golden.
• Butter four cookie sheets. • Set out two rolling pins. • Sift the flour, cocoa, and salt into a medium bowl. • Use a wooden spoon to mix the egg and egg white and sugar in a large bowl. • Mix in the dry ingredients and butter.
• Drop tablespoons of the mixture 2 inches (5 cm) apart onto the prepared cookie sheets. Do not place more than five cookies on one sheet. Spread the mixture out into thin circles. Sprinkle with the almonds. • Bake, one sheet at a time, for 8–10 minutes, or until firm at the edges. • Working quickly, use a spatula to lift each cookie from the sheet and drape it over a rolling pin.
• Let cool completely.

These deliciously crisp wafers are so good that it is well worth the effort of learning how to make them.

DOUBLE CHOCOLATE CHERRY COOKIES

Preheat the oven to 350°F/180°C/gas 4. • Line three cookie sheets with parchment paper. • Soak the cherries in the kirsch in a medium bowl for 15 minutes. • Drain well. • Sift the flour, baking soda, and salt into a medium bowl. • Beat the butter and granulated and raw sugars in a large bowl with an electric mixer at high speed until creamy. • Add the vanilla and almond extracts and egg, beating until just blended. • Mix in the dry ingredients, followed by the cherries, white and semisweet chocolates, and macadamia nuts. • Drop heaping tablespoons of the dough 2 inches (5 cm) apart onto the prepared cookie sheets. • Bake, one sheet at a time, for 12–15 minutes, or until lightly browned. • Cool the cookies on the sheets for 15 minutes. • Transfer to racks and let cool completely.

These easy rich chocolate and cherry cookies are sure to please family and friends.

Makes: 36 cookies

Preparation: 20' + 15' to soak the cherries

Cooking: 12–15'

Level of difficulty: 1

- 1 can (7 oz/200 g) pitted sour cherries, drained
- 1/2 cup/125 ml kirsch
- 1 1/2 cups/225 g all-purpose/plain flour
- 1/2 tsp baking soda
- 1/4 tsp salt
- 1/2 cup/125 g butter, softened
- 1/2 cup/100 g granulated sugar
- 1/2 cup/100 g raw sugar (Demerara or Barbados)
- 1 1/2 tsp vanilla extract/essence
- 1/4 tsp almond extract/essence
- 1 large egg
- 5 oz/150 g white chocolate, coarsely chopped
- 5 oz/150 g semisweet/dark chocolate, coarsely chopped
- 1/2 cup/50 g finely chopped macadamia nuts

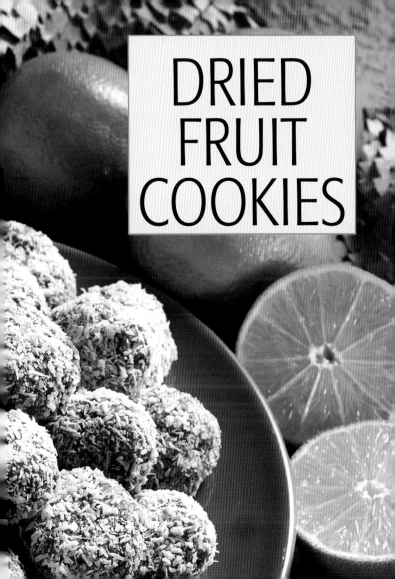

DRIED
FRUIT
COOKIES

COCONUT, ALMOND, AND OAT SQUARES

Preheat the oven to 350°F/180°C/gas 4. •
Butter an 8-inch (20-cm) square baking pan.
• Base: Beat the butter and brown sugar in a large
bowl with an electric mixer at high speed until
creamy. • Mix in the flour, oats, wheat germ,
orange juice, and salt until well blended. • Firmly
press the mixture into the prepared pan to form a
smooth, even layer. • Topping: With mixer at high
speed, beat the eggs and brown sugar in a large
bowl until pale and thick. • Stir in the almonds and
coconut. • Spread the topping evenly over the
base. • Bake for 30–35 minutes, or until just
golden. • Cool completely before cutting
into squares.

148

Makes: 16–20 squares

Preparation: 30'

Cooking: 30–35'

Level of difficulty: 1

BASE

- ½ cup/125 g butter, softened
- ⅔ cup/140 g firmly packed light brown sugar
- ⅔ cup/100 g all-purpose/plain flour
- 2 tbsp old-fashioned rolled oats
- 2 tbsp toasted wheat germ
- 1 tbsp finely grated orange zest
- ⅛ tsp salt

TOPPING

- 2 large eggs, lightly beaten
- ¼ cup/50 g firmly packed light brown sugar
- ¾ cup/125 g blanched almonds, halved
- ½ cup/60 g shredded coconut

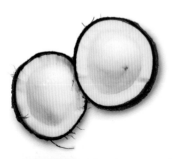

CRUNCHY COCONUT SQUARES

Makes: 35–40 squares

Preparation: 40' + 30' to chill

Cooking 15–20'

Level of difficulty: 1

- 1⅓ cups/200 g all-purpose/plain flour
- 1 tsp baking powder
- ¼ tsp salt
- 3 tbsp granulated sugar
- ½ cup/125 g butter, cut up
- 1 large egg yolk, lightly beaten with 2 tbsp cold water

FROSTING

- 1 large egg white
- 5 tbsp confectioners'/icing sugar, sifted
- 3 tbsp shredded/desiccated coconut
- Colored sprinkles, chopped Brazil nuts, or hazelnuts (optional)

Preheat the oven to 325°F/170°C/gas 3. • Line two cookie sheets with parchment paper. • Sift the flour, baking powder, and salt into a large bowl. • Stir in the sugar. • Use a pastry blender to cut in the butter until the mixture resembles fine crumbs. • Stir the egg yolk mixture into the mixture and knead into a stiff dough, adding more water if needed. • Wrap in plastic wrap and refrigerate for 30 minutes. • Frosting: Beat the egg white with an electric mixer at medium speed until frothy. With mixer at high speed, gradually add the confectioners' sugar, beating until stiff. • Roll out the dough on a lightly floured surface to a thickness of ¼ inch (5 mm). Cut into 3 x 8-inch (8 x 20-cm) strips. • Spread the frosting over and sprinkle with coconut. Sprinkle with sprinkles or nuts, if using. • Cut the strips in half lengthwise and into 1½-inch (4-cm) squares. • Gather the dough scraps, re-roll, and continue cutting out the cookies until all the dough is used. • Use a spatula to transfer the cookies to the prepared cookie sheets, placing them 1 inch (2.5 cm) apart. • Bake for 15–20 minutes, or until lightly golden. • Transfer to racks to cool.

APRICOT, PINEAPPLE, AND CHERRY CRUNCHIES

Preheat the oven to 400°F/200°C/gas 6. • Line two cookie sheets with parchment paper.
• Sift the flour, baking powder, and salt into a large bowl. • Use a pastry blender to cut in the butter until the mixture resembles coarse crumbs.
• Stir in the granulated sugar, apricots, pineapple, and cherries. • Beat the egg and orange juice and zest in a small bowl until pale. • Add the egg mixture to the dry ingredients and mix until well blended. • Drop teaspoons of the mixture 2 inches (5 cm) apart onto the prepared cookie sheets.
• Sprinkle with the brown sugar. • Bake for 15–20 minutes, or until golden brown. • Cool the cookies on the cookie sheets for 5 minutes. • Transfer to racks to cool.

Makes: 15–18 cookies

Preparation: 20'

Cooking: 15–20'

Level of difficulty: 1

- 1⅓ cups/200 g all-purpose/plain flour
- 2 tsp baking powder
- ½ tsp salt
- ½ cup/125 g cold butter, cut up
- ¼ cup/50 g granulated sugar
- 3 tbsp coarsely chopped dried apricots
- 1 tbsp coarsely chopped candied pineapple
- 1 tbsp coarsely chopped candied cherries
- 1 large egg
- 1 tbsp orange juice
- 1 tsp finely grated orange zest
- 2 tbsp firmly packed light brown sugar, to sprinkle

ZESTY COCONUT COOKIES

Makes: 36 cookies

Preparation: 40' + 30' to chill

Cooking: 10–12'

Level of difficulty: 1

- 2¼ cups/330 g all-purpose/plain flour
- ½ tsp salt
- 1 cup/250 g butter, softened
- 1 cup/200 g granulated sugar
- 2 large eggs, lightly beaten
- Grated zest of 1 lime
- 1 tbsp fresh lime juice
- ½ tsp vanilla extract/essence
- ½ tsp almond extract/essence
- 1 cup/125 g shredded/desiccated coconut

Sift the flour and salt into a medium bowl. • Beat the butter and sugar in a large bowl with an electric mixer at high speed until creamy. • Add the eggs, beating until just blended. • Add the lime zest, lime juice, and vanilla and almond extracts. • Mix in the dry ingredients and ¾ cup (90 g) coconut to form a stiff dough. • Divide the dough in half. Form the dough into two logs 2 inches (5 cm) in diameter, wrap each in plastic wrap, and flatten slightly to form oblongs. • Refrigerate for at least 30 minutes. • Preheat the oven to 375°F/190°C/gas 5. • Butter three cookie sheets. • Discard the plastic wrap. • Slice the dough ¼ inch (5 mm) thick and place 1 inch (2.5 cm) apart on the prepared cookie sheets. • Sprinkle with the remaining coconut. • Bake, one sheet at a time, for 10–12 minutes, or until just golden. • Transfer to racks and let cool completely.

BUTTER CURRANT BARS

S ift the flour, confectioners' sugar, and salt into a large bowl. • Use a pastry blender to cut in the butter until the mixture resembles fine crumbs. • Add the whole egg to form a stiff dough. • Divide the dough in half. Press each half into a disk, wrap in plastic wrap, and refrigerate for 30 minutes. • Preheat the oven to 400°F/200°C/gas 6. • Butter four cookie sheets. • Roll out one disk on a lightly floured surface to a thickness of $1/8$ inch (3 mm) and to a 14 x 12-inch (35 x 30-cm) rectangle. Sprinkle with the currants. • Roll out the remaining dough to the same dimensions and place on top of the currants, pressing down lightly. • Cut into 2 x $1^1/_2$-inch (5 x 4-cm) strips. • Use a spatula to transfer the cookies to the prepared cookie sheets, placing them 1 inch (2.5 cm) apart. Brush with the remaining beaten egg yolk. • Bake, one sheet at a time, for 10–12 minutes, or until golden brown. • Transfer to racks to cool.

Makes: 56 bars

Preparation: 40' + 30' to chill

Cooking: 10–12'

Level of difficulty: 1

- 2^1/$_3$ cups/350 g all-purpose/plain flour
- ^{2}/$_3$ cup/100 g confectioners'/icing sugar
- ^{1}/$_8$ tsp salt
- ^{3}/$_4$ cup/180 g butter, cut up
- 1 large egg + 1 large egg yolk, lightly beaten
- ^{1}/$_3$ cup/45 g dried currants

COCONUT SQUARES WITH CANDIED CHERRIES

Makes: 15 squares

Preparation: 15'

Cooking: 15–20'

Level of difficulty: 1

- **10 oz/300 g semisweet/dark chocolate, coarsely chopped**
- **$1/2$ cup/125 g butter, softened**
- **$1 1/4$ cups/250 g granulated sugar**
- **2 large eggs**
- **$2/3$ cup/70 g candied cherries, coarsely chopped**
- **2 cups/250 g shredded/ desiccated coconut**

Preheat the oven to 325°F/170°C/gas 3. • Line a $10^1/2$ x $15^1/2$-inch (26 x 36-cm) jelly-roll pan with aluminum foil. • Melt the chocolate in a double boiler over barely simmering water. Spread the chocolate over the foil and set aside to cool. • Beat the butter and sugar in a large bowl with an electric mixer at high speed until creamy. • Add the eggs, beating until just blended after each addition. • Use a large rubber spatula to fold in the cherries and coconut. • Spread over the cooled chocolate. • Bake for 15–20 minutes, or until a toothpick inserted into the center comes out clean. • Cool completely before cutting into squares.

COCONUT COOKIES

Preheat the oven to 350°F/180°C/gas 4. • Set out two cookie sheets. • Sift the flour, baking soda, and salt into a medium bowl. Stir in the coconut. • Beat the butter, brown sugar, and vanilla in a large bowl with an electric mixer at high speed until creamy. • Add the egg, beating until just blended. • With mixer at low speed, gradually add the dry ingredients. • Form the dough into balls the size of walnuts and place 1 inch (2.5 cm) apart on the sheets. • Use your thumb to make a slight hollow in each center and fill with a small amount of preserves. • Bake for 12–15 minutes, or until golden brown. • Transfer to racks to cool.

Makes: 25–30 cookies

Preparation: 20'

Cooking: 12–15'

Level of difficulty: 1

- 1¼ cups/180 g all-purpose/plain flour
- 2 tsp baking soda
- ¼ tsp salt
- ⅔ cup/40 g shredded/desiccated coconut
- ½ cup/125 g butter, softened
- ½ cup/100 g firmly packed light brown sugar
- 1 tsp vanilla extract/essence
- 1 large egg
- 3 tbsp raspberry or strawberry preserves

CUT OUT RAISIN COOKIES

Sift the flour, baking powder, and salt into a large bowl. • Stir in the sugar. • Rub in the butter until the mixture resembles coarse crumbs. • Mix in the egg, wine, and lemon zest to form a smooth dough. Knead in the raisins. • Press the dough into a disk, wrap in plastic wrap, and refrigerate for 30 minutes. • Preheat the oven to 400°F/200°C/gas 6. • Butter two cookie sheets. • Roll out the dough on a lightly floured surface to a thickness of $^{1}/_{4}$ inch (5 mm). • Use a 2-inch (5-cm) cookie cutter to cut out the cookies. Continue cutting out cookies until all the dough is used. • Transfer the cookies to the prepared cookie sheets, spacing them 1 inch (2.5 cm) apart. • Bake for 12–15 minutes, or until just golden. • Transfer to racks to cool.

Makes: 25 cookies

Preparation: 40' + 30' to chill

Cooking: 12–15'

Level of difficulty: 1

- 1½ cups/225 g all-purpose/plain flour
- 1 tsp baking powder
- ⅛ tsp salt
- ½ cup/100 g granulated sugar
- 6 tbsp butter, cut up
- 1 large egg, lightly beaten
- 3 tbsp dry white wine
- grated zest of 1 lemon
- ½ cup/90 g golden raisins/sultanas

CURRENT OAT SQUARES

Makes: 16–25 squares

Preparation: 20'

Cooking: 25–30'

Level of difficulty: 1

- 1 cup/250 g butter
- ¾ cup/180 g light corn syrup/ golden syrup
- ½ cup/100 g firmly packed light brown sugar
- 1 cup/150 g old-fashioned rolled oats
- ⅔ cup/100 g all-purpose/plain flour
- ⅛ tsp salt
- ½ cup/90 g currants
- 3 oz/90 g white chocolate, coarsely chopped

Preheat the oven to 325°F/170°C/gas 3. • Butter a 9-inch (23-cm) square baking pan. • Melt the butter with the corn syrup and brown sugar in a small saucepan until smooth. • Stir together the oats, flour, salt, and currants in a large bowl. • Stir in the butter mixture until well blended. • Spoon the mixture into the prepared pan, pressing down firmly. • Bake for 25–30 minutes, or until lightly browned. • Cool completely in the pan. • Melt the white chocolate in a double boiler over barely simmering water. Use a thin metal spatula to spread the chocolate over and cut into squares.

COCONUT KISSES WITH CHOCOLATE CREAM

Preheat the oven to 300°F/150°C/gas 2. • Set out two cookie sheets. • Sift the flour, baking powder, and salt into a medium bowl. • Beat the butter, sugar, and vanilla in a large bowl with an electric mixer at medium speed until creamy. • Add the egg, beating until just blended. • Mix in the dry ingredients. • Place the coconut in a small bowl. • Roll teaspoons of the dough in the coconut and place 1 inch (2.5 cm) apart on the cookie sheets. • Bake for 18–20 minutes, or until lightly browned. • Transfer to racks to cool. • Chocolate Filling: Beat the confectioners' sugar and melted butter in a small bowl. • Mix in the cocoa powder. • Stick the cookies together in pairs with the chocolate filling.

Roll the finished cookies in chocolate or sugar sprinkles as a variation.

Makes: 15–20 cookies

Preparation: 25'

Cooking: 18–20'

Level of difficulty: 1

- 1⅓ cups/200 g all-purpose/plain flour
- 1 tsp baking powder
- ⅛ tsp salt
- ¾ cup/180 g butter, softened
- ⅓ cup/70 g granulated sugar
- ½ tsp vanilla extract/essence
- 1 large egg
- 3 tbsp shredded/desiccated coconut

CHOCOLATE FILLING
- 1 cup/150 g confectioners'/icing sugar
- 4 tbsp butter, melted
- 1 tbsp unsweetened cocoa powder

COCONUT CRESCENTS

Blanch the pistachios in boiling water for 1 minute. Drain well and use a clean cloth to rub off the skins. • Let cool, then transfer to a food processor and process until very finely chopped. • Sift the flour onto a surface and make a well in the center. • Cut in the butter, coconut, confectioners' sugar, and the egg and egg yolk to make a smooth dough. • Wrap in plastic wrap and refrigerate for at least 2 hours. • Divide the dough into balls the size of walnuts. Form into crescent shapes, wrap individually in plastic wrap, and refrigerate for 1 hour more. • Preheat the oven to 350°F/180°C/gas 4. • Butter and flour a large baking sheet. • Sprinkle the cookies with the sugar. Dip in the finely chopped pistachios until well coated. • Arrange on the prepared baking sheet. • Bake for 15–20 minutes, or until firm to the touch. • Cool the cookies completely on the baking sheet.

Makes: 15–20 cookies

Preparation: 40' + 3 h to chill

Cooking: 15–20'

Level of difficulty: 2

- 1¼ cups/190 g pistachios, shelled
- 1⅓ cups/200 g all-purpose/plain flour
- 6 tbsp butter, softened
- 2 tbsp freshly grated coconut
- ⅓ cup/50 g confectioners'/icing sugar
- 1 egg + 1 egg yolk
- ½ cup/100 g granulated sugar

CHEWY RAISIN COOKIES

Makes: 36 cookies

Preparation: 15'

Cooking: 10–12'

Level of difficulty: 1

- ½ cup/125 g vegetable shortening
- ⅔ cup/140 g firmly packed brown sugar
- 1 egg
- 1 cup/180 g raisins
- ½ cup/125 ml water
- 2 cups/300 g all-purpose/plain flour
- ½ tsp baking soda
- ¼ tsp salt
- ½ tsp ground cinnamon
- ½ tsp ground nutmeg
- ½ cup/50 g chopped walnuts

Preheat the oven to 350°F/180°C/gas 4. • Stir together the shortening and sugar in a medium bowl until well blended. • Beat in the egg and add the raisins. Gradually stir in the water, salt, cinnamon, nutmeg, and walnuts until well mixed. Mix in the flour and baking soda. • Using a tablespoon, drop spoonfuls onto lightly greased cookie sheets. • Bake for about 10 minutes, or until golden brown. • Let cool completely.

OLD-FASHIONED COCONUT COOKIES

Makes: 25–30 cookies

Preparation: 40' + 30' to chill

Cooking: 25–30'

Level of difficulty: 1

- ¾ cup/125 g all-purpose/plain flour
- ⅛ tsp salt
- ½ cup/125 g vegetable shortening
- 1 cup/125 g shredded/desiccated coconut
- 1 cup/150 g old-fashioned rolled oats
- ½ cup/100 g granulated sugar
- 2 tbsp cold water
- 1 tbsp light molasses
- 1 tsp baking soda

Preheat the oven to 300°F/150°C/gas 2. • Butter two cookie sheets. • Sift the flour and salt into a large bowl. • Use a pastry blender to cut in the shortening until the mixture resembles fine crumbs. • Stir in the coconut, oats, and sugar. • Mix the water, molasses, and baking soda in a small bowl. • Stir the baking soda liquid into the oat mixture to form a stiff dough. Press the dough into a disk, wrap in plastic wrap, and refrigerate for 30 minutes. • Roll out the dough on a lightly floured surface to a thickness of ¼ inch (5 mm). • Use a 3-inch (8-cm) cookie cutter to cut out the cookies. Gather the dough scraps, re-roll, and continue cutting out cookies until all the dough is used. • Use a spatula to transfer the cookies to the prepared cookie sheet, placing them 1 inch (2.5 cm) apart. • Bake for 25–30 minutes, or until just golden at the edges. • Transfer to racks and let cool completely.

COCONUT CITRUS BITES

Preheat the oven to 350°F/180°C/gas 4. • Line two cookie sheets with parchment paper. • Melt the chocolate in a double boiler over barely simmering water. • Beat the butter and sugar in a medium bowl with an electric mixer at high speed until creamy. • Add the coconut extract, cream of coconut, melted chocolate, and the lemon and lime zests. • Mix in $^1/_2$ cup (60 g) of shredded coconut and flour. • Turn the dough onto a lightly floured surface and knead until smooth. • Form the dough into balls the size of walnuts. Roll in the remaining coconut and place 2 inches (5 cm) apart on the prepared cookie sheet, flattening them slightly. • Bake for 15–20 minutes, or until just golden. • Transfer to racks to cool.

Makes: 25–30 cookies

Preparation: 30'

Cooking: 15–20'

Level of difficulty: 1

- 2 oz/60 g semisweet/dark chocolate, coarsely chopped
- 6 tbsp butter, softened
- $^1/_3$ cup/70 g granulated sugar
- 1 tsp coconut extract/essence
- 2 tbsp cream of coconut
- 1 tsp finely shredded lemon zest
- 1 tsp finely shredded lime zest
- $^3/_4$ cup/90 g shredded/desiccated coconut
- $1^3/_4$ cups/275 g all-purpose/plain flour

PRUNE SQUARES

Preheat the oven to 350°F/180°C/gas 4. •
Butter a 9-inch (23-cm) baking pan. • Cookie
Base: Sift the flour, baking powder, and salt into a
large bowl. • Beat the butter and brown sugar in a
large bowl with an electric mixer at high speed until
creamy. • Add the vanilla and egg, beating until just
blended. • Mix in the dry ingredients until well
blended. • Prune Filling: Bring the prunes and
water to a boil in a large saucepan. • Reduce the
heat and simmer for 3 minutes. • Drain well and
transfer the prunes to a food processor or blender.
Add the honey and lemon zest and juice and
process until smooth. • Firmly press one third of
the cookie base into the prepared pan to form a
smooth, even layer. Spoon over half of the prune
filling and spread it evenly. Sprinkle with half the
remaining cookie base and spread with the
remaining prune filling. Sprinkle with the remaining
cookie base to finish. • Bake for 55–65 minutes,
or until lightly browned. • Cool completely before
cutting into squares.

*Makes: 16–25
    squares*

Preparation: 30'

Cooking: 55–65'

Level of difficulty: 1

COOKIE BASE
- 1²/₃ cups/250 g all-
  purpose/plain flour
- 1 tsp baking
  powder
- ½ tsp salt
- ¾ cup/180 g
  butter, softened
- 1½ cups/300 g
  firmly packed light
  brown sugar
- 1 tsp vanilla
  extract/essence
- 1 large egg, lightly
  beaten

PRUNE FILLING
- 1¼ cups/310 g
  pitted prunes
- 2 cups/500 ml
  water
- 4 tbsp honey
- Grated zest and
  juice of ¼ lemon

SPICY APPLESAUCE COOKIES

Makes: 36 cookies

Preparation: 20'

Cooking: 5–7'

Level of difficulty: 1

- **2 cups/300 g all-purpose/plain flour**
- **1 tsp ground cinnamon**
- **1 tsp ground ginger**
- **½ tsp ground cloves**
- **½ tsp baking soda**
- **½ tsp salt**
- **½ cup/125 g butter, softened**
- **½ cup/100 g firmly packed light brown sugar**
- **⅓ cup/70 g granulated sugar**
- **1 tsp vanilla extract/essence**
- **1 large egg**
- **1 cup/250 ml applesauce**
- **1 cup/180 g golden raisins/sultanas**
- **¾ cup/75 g finely chopped walnuts**

Preheat the oven to 350°F/180°C/gas 4. • Butter three cookie sheets. • Sift the flour, cinnamon, ginger, cloves, baking soda, and salt into a medium bowl. • Beat the butter and brown and granulated sugars in a large bowl with an electric mixer at high speed until creamy. • Add the vanilla and egg, beating until just blended. • Stir in the applesauce. • Mix in the dry ingredients, followed by the raisins and walnuts. • Drop tablespoons of the dough 2 inches (5 cm) apart onto the prepared cookie sheets. • Bake, one sheet at a time, for 5–7 minutes, or until just golden. • Transfer to racks and let cool.

SOFT COCONUT COOKIES

Preheat the oven to 400°F/200°C/gas 6. •
Butter two cookie sheets. • Sift the flour,
baking powder, and salt into a medium bowl.
• Beat the butter and sugar in a large bowl with an
electric mixer at high speed until creamy. • Add the
egg, beating until just blended. • Mix in the dry
ingredients and coconut until well blended. • Drop
tablespoons of the dough 2 inches (5 cm) apart
onto the prepared cookie sheets, pressing down
lightly with a fork. • Bake for 10–15 minutes, or
until golden brown. • Cool on the cookie sheets for
15 minutes. • Transfer to racks to cool.

Makes: 15 cookies

Preparation: 20'

Cooking: 10–15'

Level of difficulty: 1

- **1 cup/150 g all-purpose/plain flour**
- **1 tsp baking powder**
- **⅛ tsp salt**
- **½ cup/125 g butter, softened**
- **½ cup/100 g granulated sugar**
- **1 large egg**
- **1 cup/125 g shredded/desiccated coconut**

Makes: 36 cookies

Preparation: 20' + 15' to soak

Cooking: 6–8'

Level of difficulty: 1

- 3 cups/540 g raisins
- 1 cup/250 g dried cranberries
- 1 cup/250 ml hot water
- 2½ cups/375 g all-purpose/plain flour
- 2 tsp ground cinnamon
- 1½ tsp baking soda
- 1 tsp ground ginger
- ½ tsp baking powder
- ½ tsp allspice
- ½ tsp salt
- ¾ cup/180 g butter, softened
- 1½ cups/300 g firmly packed light brown sugar
- 1½ tsp vanilla extract/essence
- 2 large eggs
- 2 cups/300 g old-fashioned rolled oats
- 2 cups/200 g coarsely chopped walnuts
- 1¼ cups/280 g coarsely chopped pitted prunes
- 1¼ cups/280 g coarsely chopped pitted dates

PRUNE, RAISIN, AND OAT COOKIES

Preheat the oven to 400°F/200°C/gas 6. • Butter three cookie sheets. • Soak the raisins and cranberries in the water in a large bowl for 15 minutes. • Drain well, reserving 6 tablespoons liquid, and set aside. • Sift the flour, cinnamon, baking soda, ginger, baking powder, allspice, and salt into a medium bowl. • Beat the butter and brown sugar in a large bowl with an electric mixer at high speed until creamy. • Add the vanilla and eggs, beating until just blended. • Mix in the dry ingredients and reserved liquid. • Stir in the oats, walnuts, prunes, dates, raisins, and cranberries until well blended. • Drop tablespoons of the dough 3 inches (8 cm) apart onto the prepared cookie sheets, flattening them slightly. • Bake, one sheet at a time, for 6–8 minutes, or until just golden at the edges and set. • Transfer to racks and let cool completely.

FRUITY RAISIN MOMENTS

Preheat the oven to 400°F/200°C/gas 6. •
Butter two cookie sheets. • Sift the flour,
baking powder, nutmeg, and salt into a large bowl.
• Use a pastry blender to cut in the butter until the
mixture resembles coarse crumbs. • Stir in the
brown sugar, candied peel, raisins, and egg.
• Drop tablespoons of the dough 2 inches (5 cm)
apart onto the prepared cookie sheets. • Bake for
20–25 minutes, or until golden brown. • Transfer
the cookies to racks to cool.

Makes: 20–25
  cookies

Preparation: 30'

Cooking: 20–25'

Level of difficulty: 1

- **2 cups/300 g all-purpose/plain flour**
- **1 tsp baking powder**
- **¼ tsp freshly grated nutmeg**
- **⅛ tsp salt**
- **½ cup/125 g butter, cut up**
- **½ cup/100 g firmly packed light brown sugar**
- **⅔ cup/70 g finely chopped candied peel**
- **⅓ cup/45 g raisins**
- **1 large egg, lightly beaten**

OAT AND HAZELNUT COOKIES

Makes: 45 cookies

Preparation: 20'

Cooking: 12–15'

Level of difficulty: 1

- **2 large egg whites**
- **½ cup/100 g raw sugar (Demerara or Barbados)**
- **1 tbsp vanilla sugar**
- **½ cup/75 g old-fashioned rolled oats**
- **½ cup/50 g finely ground hazelnuts**
- **1 tbsp very finely chopped dried figs**
- **1 tbsp fresh lemon juice**
- **Grated zest of 1 lemon**
- **2 tbsp sunflower seeds**

Preheat the oven to 350°F/180°C/gas 4. • Line three cookie sheets with parchment paper. • Beat the egg whites and 1 tablespoon raw sugar in a large bowl with an electric mixer at medium speed until soft peaks form. • With mixer at high speed, gradually add the remaining raw sugar, beating until stiff peaks form. • Use a large rubber spatula to fold in the vanilla sugar, oats, hazelnuts, and figs. • Drizzle with the lemon juice and sprinkle with the zest. • Drop teaspoons of the mixture 1 inch (2.5 cm) apart onto the prepared cookie sheets. Sprinkle with the sunflower seeds. • Bake, one sheet at a time, for 12–15 minutes, or until lightly browned. • Cool the cookies on the cookie sheet for 15 minutes. Transfer to racks and let cool completely.

SOFT DATE COOKIES

Preheat the oven to 375°F/190°C/gas 5. •
Butter two cookie sheets. • Beat the butter,
sugar, and vanilla in a large bowl with an electric
mixer at high speed until creamy. • Mix in the flour
and dates. • Drop rounded teaspoons of the dough
1 inch (2.5 cm) apart onto the prepared cookie
sheets. • Bake for 15–20 minutes, or
until just golden. • Cool on the sheets until the
cookies firm slightly. • Transfer to racks to
finish cooling.

Soft and sumptuous, these delicious cookies won't last long in your cookie jar!

182

Makes: 18–20
    cookies

Preparation: 20'

Cooking: 15–20'

Level of difficulty: 1

- ½ cup/125 g
  butter, softened
- ¼ cup/50 g
  granulated sugar
- ½ tsp vanilla
  extract/essence
- ¼ cup/60 g finely
  chopped dates
- ¾ cup/125 g all-
  purpose/plain flour

LEMON, RAISIN AND OAT COOKIES

Makes: 16 cookies

Preparation: 20'

Cooking: 15–20'

Level of difficulty: 1

- 1½ cups/225 g all-purpose/plain flour
- 1 tsp baking powder
- ⅛ tsp salt
- ½ cup/125 g butter, softened
- ½ cup/100 g granulated sugar
- grated zest of 1 lemon
- 1 large egg
- 2 tbsp old-fashioned rolled oats
- 1 cup/180 g raisins

Preheat the oven to 375°F/190°C/gas 5. • Butter a cookie sheet. • Sift the flour, baking powder, and salt into a large bowl. • Beat the butter, sugar, and lemon zest in a large bowl with an electric mixer at high speed until creamy. • Add the egg, beating until just blended. • Mix in the dry ingredients, oats, and raisins. • Drop tablespoons of the dough 3 inches (8 cm) apart onto the prepared cookie sheet. • Bake for 10–15 minutes, or until just golden at the edges. • Transfer to racks to cool.

BUSY BEE BISCOTTI

These chewy, twice-baked Italian cookies are ideal for school lunchboxes as well as for grown-up teas.

Preheat the oven to 325°F/170°C/gas 3. •
Spread the whole almonds on a large baking sheet. Toast for 7 minutes, or until lightly golden.
• Let cool completely and chop coarsely. • Sift the flour, baking powder, cinnamon, cloves, and salt into a medium bowl. • Beat the butter and sugar in a large bowl with an electric mixer at high speed until creamy. • Add 2 eggs, beating until just blended. • Heat the honey in a small saucepan over low heat until liquid. Stir the warm honey, candied lemon and orange peel, and chopped almonds into the mixture. • Mix in the dry ingredients to form a smooth dough. • Press the dough into a disk, wrap in plastic wrap, and refrigerate for 1 hour. • Preheat the oven to 350°F/180°C/gas 4. • Line three cookie sheets with parchment paper. • Roll out the dough on a lightly floured surface to a thickness of $1/4$ inch (5 mm). • Use a $2^1/2$-inch (6-cm) cookie cutter to cut out the cookies. Gather the dough scraps, re-roll, and continue cutting out cookies until all the dough is used. • Use a spatula to transfer the cookies to the prepared cookie sheets, placing them 1 inch (2.5 cm) apart. • Lightly beat the remaining egg and brush over the tops of the cookies. • Decorate with the flaked almonds and candied peel. • Bake, one sheet at a time, for 10–12 minutes, or until just golden and crisp around the edges. • Transfer to racks to cool.

Makes: 50–60 cookies

Preparation: 50' + 1 h to chill

Cooking: 10–12'

Level of difficulty: 2

- 1 cup/150 g whole almonds
- 3⅓ cups/500 g all-purpose/plain flour
- 1½ tsp baking powder
- 2 tsp ground cinnamon
- ½ tsp ground cloves
- ⅛ tsp salt
- ½ cup/125 g butter, softened
- ½ cup/100 g granulated sugar
- 3 large eggs
- ¾ cup/180 ml honey
- 1 cup/50 g chopped candied lemon peel
- 1 cup/100 g chopped candied orange peel
- 2 tbsp flaked almonds
- 1–2 tbsp chopped mixed candied peel

CURRANT SQUARES

Makes: 12–16
squares

Preparation: 40' + 30'
to chill

Cooking: 8–10'

Level of difficulty: 1

- ¾ cup/125 g all-purpose/plain flour
- ½ tsp baking powder
- ⅛ tsp salt
- 1 tbsp granulated sugar
- 6 tbsp vegetable shortening or lard
- ½ cup/90 g dried currants
- 2 tbsp ice water + more as needed

Sift the flour, baking powder, and salt into a medium bowl. Stir in the sugar. • Use a pastry blender to cut in the shortening until the mixture resembles fine crumbs. • Stir in the currants. • Mix in enough water to form a stiff dough. • Press the dough into a disk, wrap in plastic wrap, and refrigerate for 30 minutes. • Preheat the oven to 400°F/200°C/gas 6. • Butter a cookie sheet. • Roll out the dough on a lightly floured surface to a thickness of ¼ inch (5 mm). • Use a sharp knife to cut the dough into 2-inch (5-cm) squares. Gather the dough scraps, re-roll, and continue cutting out cookies until all the dough is used. • Use a spatula to transfer the cookies to the prepared cookie sheet, placing them 1 inch (2.5 cm) apart. • Bake for 8–10 minutes, or until golden. • Transfer to racks to cool.

DIAMOND COOKIES

S tir together the flour, granulated sugar, vanilla sugar, lemon zest, and salt in a medium bowl.
• Add the butter, distributing the pieces evenly over the mixture. Use a pastry blender to cut in the butter until the mixture resembles coarse crumbs.
• Make a well in the center and add the egg, mixing until a dough is formed. • Turn out onto a lightly floured surface, working in the candied cherries, candied peel, and nuts. Knead until smooth. • Return to the bowl, cover with plastic wrap, and refrigerate for 30 minutes. • Preheat the oven to 350°F/180°C/gas 4. • Line two cookie sheets with parchment paper. • Roll out the dough to a thickness of $^1/_2$ inch (1 cm). Use a $2^1/_2$-inch (6-cm) round or diamond-shaped cutter to stamp out shapes. • Use a metal spatula to transfer the cookies to the prepared cookie sheets, spacing 1 inch (2.5 cm) apart. • Mix the egg yolk and water in a small bowl. • Brush the cookies with the egg yolk mixture. • Bake for 12–15 minutes, or until lightly browned. • Cool the cookies on the sheets for 10 minutes. Use a metal spatula to transfer to racks to cool.

Makes: 40 cookies

Preparation: 45' + 30' to chill

Cooking: 12–15'

Level of difficulty: 2

- **2 cups/300 g all-purpose/plain flour**
- **$^1/_2$ cup/100 g granulated sugar**
- **1 tbsp vanilla sugar**
- **grated zest of $^1/_2$ lemon**
- **$^1/_4$ tsp salt**
- **$^3/_4$ cup/180 g cold butter, cut up**
- **1 large egg, lightly beaten**
- **1 tbsp candied cherries, chopped**
- **2 tbsp mixed candied peel, chopped**
- **2 tbsp sugared nuts, crushed**
- **1 large egg yolk, to brush**
- **$^1/_2$ cup/125 ml water**

CURRANT ROUNDS

Makes: 15–20
cookies

Preparation: 40' + 30'
to chill

Cooking: 12–15'

Level of difficulty: 1

- 1²/₃ cups/250 g all-purpose/plain flour
- ¹/₈ tsp salt
- ¹/₂ cup/125 g butter, softened
- ¹/₂ cup/100 g granulated sugar
- 2 large eggs
- ²/₃ cup/120 g currants

Sift the flour and salt into a medium bowl. • Beat the butter and sugar in a large bowl with an electric mixer at high speed until creamy. • Add the eggs, beating until just blended. • Mix in the dry ingredients and currants. • Press the dough into a disk, wrap in plastic wrap, and refrigerate for 30 minutes. • Preheat the oven to 325°F/170°C/ gas 3. • Butter two cookie sheets. • Roll the dough out on a lightly floured surface to a thickness of ³/₄ inch (2 cm). • Use a 2-inch (5-cm) cookie cutter to cut out the cookies. Gather the dough scraps, re-roll, and continue cutting out cookies until all the dough is used. • Use a spatula to transfer the cookies to the prepared cookie sheets, placing them 2 inches (5-cm) apart. • Bake for 12–15 minutes, or until golden. • Transfer to racks to cool.

MELTING RAISIN COOKIES

Plump the raisins in hot water to cover in a small bowl for 10 minutes. • Drain well and pat dry with paper towels. • Sift the flour, baking powder, and salt into a large bowl. • Stir in the sugar. • Use a pastry blender to cut in the butter until the mixture resembles coarse crumbs. • Mix in the egg, wine, and lemon zest to form a smooth dough. Knead in the raisins until well blended. • Press the dough into a disk, wrap in plastic wrap, and refrigerate for 30 minutes. • Preheat the oven to 400°F/200°C/gas 6. • Butter two cookie sheets. • Roll out the dough on a lightly floured surface to a thickness of $^1/_4$ inch (5 mm). • Use a 2-inch (5-cm) cookie cutter to cut out the cookies. Gather the dough scraps, re-roll, and continue cutting out cookies until all the dough is used. • Use a spatula to transfer the cookies to the prepared cookie sheets, spacing them 1 inch (2.5 cm) apart. • Bake for 12–15 minutes, or until just golden. • Transfer to racks to cool.

Makes: 25 cookies

Preparation: 40' + 30' to chill

Cooking: 12–15'

Level of difficulty: 1

- ½ cup/90 g golden raisins/sultanas
- 1½ cups/225 g all-purpose/plain flour
- 1 tsp baking powder
- ⅛ tsp salt
- ½ cup/100 g granulated sugar
- 6 tbsp butter, cut up
- 1 large egg, lightly beaten
- 3 tbsp dry white wine
- grated zest of 1 lemon

CHEWY FRUIT BARS

Makes: 36–45 bars
Preparation: 25'
Cooking: 40–45'
Level of difficulty: 1

- **2 cups/200 g dried apricots, soaked overnight**
- **2 tbsp sunflower oil**
- **1 cup/180 g raisins**
- **⅔ cup/100 g old-fashioned rolled oats**
- **grated zest of 1 lemon**
- **½ tsp ground cardamom**
- **⅛ tsp salt**

Preheat the oven to 400°F/200°C/gas 6. • Butter a 13 x 9-inch (33 x 23-cm) baking pan. • Bring the apricots and their soaking liquid to a boil in a small saucepan over low heat and simmer for 5 minutes, or until softened. • Drain and transfer to a food processor or blender. Process until smooth. • Transfer to a large bowl and add the oil. • Mix in the raisins, oats, lemon zest, cardamom, and salt until well blended. • Spread the mixture evenly in the prepared pan. • Bake for 40–45 minutes, or until firm to the touch. • Cool completely in the pan. • Cut into bars.

GOLDEN WALNUT SQUARES

Preheat the oven to 350°F/180°C/gas 4. •
Place a large baking sheet in the hot oven. ·
Butter an 8-inch (20-cm) baking pan. • Base: Mix
the flour and brown sugar in a large bowl. • Use a
pastry blender to cut in the butter until the mixture
resembles coarse crumbs. • Firmly press the
mixture into the prepared pan to form a smooth,
even layer. • Place the pan on the heated baking
sheet. • Bake for 12–15 minutes, or until lightly
browned. • Cool the base completely in the pan.
• Topping: Mix the orange and lemon juices with
enough water to make ²/₃ cup (150 ml) liquid.
• Simmer the apricots in the liquid in a large
saucepan for 15 minutes, or until they have
softened. • Drain the apricots, reserving the liquid
in a small bowl. • Finely chop the apricots and
return to the saucepan. Add both zests, the brown
sugar, cornstarch, and 4 tablespoons apricot
liquid. • Bring to the boil and boil for 1 minute,
stirring constantly. Let cool, then spread it over the
base. Sprinkle with walnuts. • Bake for 15–20
minutes, or until golden brown. • Cool completely
before cutting into bars.

Makes: 16–25 bars

Preparation: 30'

Cooking: 30–35'

Level of difficulty: 2

BASE
- ³/₄ cup/120 g all-purpose/plain flour
- ²/₃ cup/140 g firmly packed light brown sugar
- 4 tbsp cold butter, cut up

TOPPING
- zest and juice of 1 orange
- zest and juice of ½ lemon
- water
- ³/₄ cup/75 g dried apricots
- ¹/₃ cup/70 g firmly packed light brown sugar
- 2 tsp cornstarch/cornflour
- ½ cup/50 g finely chopped walnuts

GINGER CHERRY SQUARES

Makes: 22–33 bars

Preparation: 10'

Cooking: 40–45'

Level of difficulty: 1

- 1 cup/150 g all-purpose/plain flour
- 1 tsp baking powder
- ⅛ tsp salt
- 1 cup/100 g finely chopped mixed dried fruit
- ½ cup/50 g finely chopped crystallized ginger
- ½ cup/125 g butter, softened
- ¾ cup/150 g granulated sugar
- 1 large egg

Preheat the oven to 300°F/150°C/gas 2. • Butter an 11 x 7-inch (28 x 18-cm) baking pan. • Sift the flour, baking powder, and salt into a medium bowl. • Stir in the dried fruit and ginger. • Beat the butter and sugar in a large bowl with an electric mixer at high speed until creamy. • Add the egg. • Mix in the dry ingredients. • Spoon the mixture into the prepared pan. • Bake for 40–45 minutes, or until golden brown. • Cool completely before cutting into bars.

GLAZED DIAMONDS

Makes: 36–45 bars

Preparation: 25'

Cooking: 20–25'

Level of difficulty: 1

Preheat the oven to 350°F/180°C/gas 4. •
Butter a 13 x 9-inch (33 x 23-cm) baking pan.
• Sift the flour, cinnamon, baking powder, baking
soda, and salt into a large bowl. • Stir in the brown
sugar. • Add the eggs, beating until just blended.
• Beat in the butter and sour cream. • Stir in the
dates and walnuts. • Pour the mixture into the
prepared pan. • Bake for 20–25 minutes, or until
golden brown and a toothpick inserted into the
center comes out clean. • Cool completely in the
pan. • Lemon Glaze: Mix the confectioners' sugar,
butter, and lemon juice in a small bowl. • Add
enough water to create a glazing consistency.
• Spread the glaze over the cooled cake. • Cut
lengthwise into long strips. • Cut the strips into
diamonds by running the knife diagonally from one
side of the pan to the other.

- 1⅔ cups/250 g all-purpose/plain flour
- 1 tsp ground cinnamon
- 1 tsp baking powder
- ½ tsp baking soda
- ½ tsp salt
- 1 cup/200 g firmly packed dark brown sugar
- 2 large eggs, lightly beaten
- 1 cup/250 g butter, melted
- ½ cup/125 ml sour cream
- 1⅓ cups/140 g finely chopped dates
- ¾ cup/75 g finely chopped walnuts or pecans

LEMON GLAZE

- 1⅓ cups/200 g confectioners'/icing sugar
- 3 tbsp butter, melted
- 1 tbsp fresh lemon juice
- 1–2 tbsp water

FRUIT AND NUT COOKIES

Makes: 26 cookies

Preparation: 20'

Cooking: 8–10'

Level of difficulty: 1

- 1 cup/150 g all-purpose/plain flour
- ½ tsp ground cinnamon
- ¼ tsp baking soda
- 2 tbsp water
- ¾ cup/75 g finely chopped dates
- ¾ cup/135 g golden raisins/sultanas
- 6 tbsp butter, softened
- ½ cup/100 g granulated sugar
- 1 large egg
- ½ cup/50 g finely chopped walnuts

Preheat the oven to 400°F/200°C/gas 6. • Butter two cookie sheets. • Sift the flour and cinnamon into a medium bowl. • Mix the baking soda and water in a small bowl. Add the dates and raisins. • Beat the butter and sugar in a large bowl with an electric mixer at high speed until creamy. • Add the egg, beating until just blended. • Stir in the date and raisin mixture. • Mix in the dry ingredients and walnuts. • Drop tablespoons of the dough 1 inch (2.5 cm) apart onto the prepared cookie sheets. • Bake for 8–10 minutes, or until lightly browned. • Cool on the sheets until the cookies firm slightly. • Transfer to racks and let cool completely.

CHEWY ROLLED OAT COOKIES

Preheat the oven to 350°F/180°C/gas 4. • Line an 8-inch (20-cm) baking pan with aluminum foil, letting the edges overhang. • Sift the flour and salt into a medium bowl. • Beat the butter and brown sugar in a large bowl with an electric mixer at high speed until creamy. • Mix in the dry ingredients and oats. • Firmly press two-thirds of the mixture into the prepared pan to form a smooth, even layer. • Mix the cranberry sauce and walnuts in a small bowl and spread over the base. • Spoon the remaining oat mixture over the top, pressing down gently. • Bake for 15–20 minutes, or until lightly browned. • Cool completely in the pan. • Using the foil as handles, lift onto the cutting board. Peel off the foil. Cut into squares.

Cranberries are native to North America and are rich in vitamin C.

206

Makes: 16–25 squares

Preparation: 20'

Cooking: 15–20'

Level of difficulty: 1

- 1 cup/150 g all-purpose/plain flour
- ¼ tsp salt
- ½ cup/125 g butter, softened
- ½ cup/100 g firmly packed dark brown sugar
- 2½ cups/375 g old-fashioned rolled oats
- ½ cup/125 ml store-bought cranberry sauce
- ½ cup/50 g coarsely chopped walnuts

PEANUT BUTTER AND ORANGE COOKIES

Makes: 20–25 cookies

Preparation: 20'

Cooking: 12–15'

Level of difficulty: 1

- 1 cup/150 g all-purpose/plain flour
- 1 tsp baking powder
- 1/8 tsp salt
- 1/2 cup/125 ml smooth peanut butter
- 1/2 cup/100 g granulated sugar
- 1 tbsp finely grated orange zest
- 1 large egg
- 1/2 cup/90 g raisins

Preheat the oven to 325°F/170°C/gas 3. • Butter three cookie sheets. • Sift the flour, baking powder, and salt into a medium bowl. • Beat the peanut butter, sugar, and orange zest in a large bowl with an electric mixer at high speed until creamy. • Add the egg, beating until just blended. • Mix in the raisins. • Mix in the dry ingredients. • Form the dough into balls the size of walnuts and place 2 inches (5 cm) apart on the prepared cookie sheets. • Dip a fork in flour and press lines into the tops. • Bake, one sheet at a time, for 12–15 minutes, or until golden brown. • Transfer to racks to cool.

DRIED FRUIT SQUARES

Preheat the oven to 375°F/190°C/gas 5. • Line an 8-inch (20-cm) baking pan with aluminum foil, letting the edges overhang. • Sift the flour, baking powder, and salt into a medium bowl. • Mix the pears, apricots, honey, and applesauce in a large bowl. • Beat in the oil and eggs until well blended. • Mix in the dry ingredients. • Pour the mixture into the prepared pan. • Sprinkle with the almonds. • Bake for 25–30 minutes, or until just golden and a toothpick inserted into the center comes out clean. • Using the foil as handles, lift onto a rack to cool. • Cut into bars.

Makes: 16–25 bars

Preparation: 20'

Cooking: 20–25'

Level of difficulty: 1

- 1½ cups/225 g whole-wheat flour
- 1½ tsp baking powder
- ¼ tsp salt
- 3 large firm-ripe pears, peeled, cored, and finely chopped
- 1½ cups/150 g finely chopped dried apricots
- 2 tbsp honey
- 1 tbsp applesauce
- 2 tbsp vegetable oil
- 2 large eggs, lightly beaten
- ½ cup/50 g flaked almonds, to decorate

CHEWY BROWN COOKIES

Makes: 25 cookies

Preparation: 20'

Cooking: 25–30'

Level of difficulty: 1

- 1¾ cups/175 g
  finely chopped
  pitted dates
- 1¾ cups/175 g
  finely chopped
  almonds
- 2 large egg whites
- 1 cup/150 g
  confectioners'/
  icing sugar
- 1 tbsp unsweetened
  cocoa powder
- juice of 1 lemon

Preheat the oven to 325°F/170°C/gas 3. •
Butter two cookie sheets. • Chop the dates
very finely and place in a large bowl. Add the
almonds. • Stir in the egg whites, confectioners'
sugar, cocoa, and lemon juice and mix until well
blended. • Drop teaspoons of the dough 1 inch
(2.5 cm) apart onto the prepared cookie sheets.
• Bake for 25–30 minutes, or until just golden at
the edges. • Transfer to racks to cool.

MIDDLE EASTERN SQUARES

Preheat the oven to 350°F/180°C/gas 4. • Line a 13 x 9-inch (33 x 23-cm) baking pan with aluminum foil, letting the edges overhang. • Date Filling: Cook the dates with the brown sugar and water in a saucepan over medium heat until the sugar has dissolved completely. • Remove from the heat and add the vanilla and cinnamon. • Transfer to a food processor or blender and process until pureed. • Return to the bowl and let cool completely. • Oat Crust: Mix the flour, brown sugar, cinnamon, baking soda, and salt in a large bowl. • Use a pastry blender to cut in the butter until the mixture resembles coarse crumbs. Stir in the oats and walnuts. • Firmly press half the mixture into the prepared pan to form a smooth, even layer. • Pour the filling over the oat crust and sprinkle with the remaining oat crust mixture. • Bake for 30–35 minutes, or until lightly browned. • Using the foil as handles, lift onto a rack and let cool completely. • Cut into squares.

Makes: 36–40 squares

Preparation: 40'

Cooking: 30–35'

Level of difficulty: 1

DATE FILLING
- 1 lb/500 g pitted dates
- 1 cup/200 g firmly packed dark brown sugar
- 1 cup/250 ml water
- ½ tsp vanilla extract/essence
- ½ tsp ground cinnamon

OAT CRUST
- 1½ cups/225 g all-purpose/plain flour
- 1 cup/200 g firmly packed dark brown sugar
- 1 tsp ground cinnamon
- ½ tsp baking soda
- ⅛ tsp salt
- 1 cup/250 g butter, cut up
- ⅔ cup/150 g old-fashioned rolled oats
- ½ cup/50 g finely chopped walnuts

CINNAMON AND RAISIN COOKIES

Makes: 24–30 cookies

Preparation: 20' + 30' to chill

Cooking: 8–10'

Level of difficulty: 1

- 2⅓ cups/350 g all-purpose/plain flour
- 2 tsp ground cinnamon
- 1 tsp baking powder
- 1 tsp ground cloves
- ½ tsp freshly grated nutmeg
- ¼ tsp salt
- ½ cup/125 g butter, softened
- ¾ cup/150 g firmly packed dark brown sugar
- 2 large eggs
- ½ cup/90 g raisins
- ½ cup/50 g flaked almonds

Sift the flour, cinnamon, baking powder, cloves, nutmeg, and salt into a medium bowl. • Beat the butter, brown sugar, and eggs in a large bowl with an electric mixer at medium speed until well combined. • Mix in the dry ingredients, followed by the raisins and almonds. • Cover with plastic wrap and refrigerate for 30 minutes. • Preheat the oven to 375°F/190°C/gas 5. • Butter two cookie sheets. • Drop heaped teaspoons of the cookie dough 2 inches (5 cm) apart onto the prepared cookie sheets. • Bake for 8–10 minutes, or until golden brown. • Transfer to racks and let cool.

AMERICAN COOKIES

Preheat the oven to 375°F/190°C/gas 5. • Line two cookie sheets with parchment paper. • Sift the flour, baking soda, and salt into a medium bowl. • Beat the butter, shortening, and granulated and brown sugars in a large bowl with an electric mixer at high speed until creamy. • Add the vanilla and egg, beating until just blended. • Mix in the dry ingredients, cranberries, candied peel, and pecans. • Drop tablespoons of the dough 1^1/$_2$ inches (4 cm) apart onto the prepared cookie sheets. • Bake for 8–10 minutes, or until golden at the edges. • Cool on the sheets until the cookies firm slightly. • Transfer to racks to finish cooling.

Makes: 25–30 cookies

Preparation: 20'

Cooking: 8–10'

Level of difficulty: 1

- 1 cup/150 g all-purpose/plain flour
- ^{1}/$_4$ tsp baking soda
- ^{1}/$_8$ tsp salt
- 2 tbsp butter, softened
- 2 tbsp vegetable shortening
- ^{1}/$_4$ cup/50 g granulated sugar
- ^{1}/$_4$ cup/50 g firmly packed light brown sugar
- ^{1}/$_2$ tsp vanilla extract/essence
- 1 large egg
- ^{1}/$_2$ cup/50 g coarsely chopped dried cranberries
- ^{1}/$_4$ cup/30 g finely chopped mixed candied peel
- ^{1}/$_4$ cup/30 g finely chopped pecans

CHERRY ALMOND BISCOTTI

Makes: 30 cookies

Preparation: 25'

Cooking: 35–45'

Level of difficulty: 2

- ¼ cup/30 g candied cherries
- 1 tbsp cherry brandy
- 1½ cups/225 g all-purpose/plain flour
- ½ tsp baking powder
- ⅛ tsp salt
- 4 tbsp butter, softened
- ½ cup/100 g granulated sugar
- 2 large eggs
- ½ tsp vanilla extract/essence
- ½ cup/50 g coarsely chopped almonds

Soak the cherries in the cherry brandy in a small bowl for 15 minutes. Drain and pat dry with paper towels. • Preheat the oven to 375°F/190°C/gas 5. • Butter a cookie sheet. • Sift the flour, baking powder, and salt into a large bowl. • Beat the butter and sugar in a large bowl with an electric mixer at high speed until creamy. • Add the eggs and vanilla, beating until just blended. • Mix in the dry ingredients, almonds, and cherries to form a stiff dough. • Divide the dough in half. Form the dough into two 12-inch (30-cm) logs and place 2 inches (5-cm) apart on the prepared cookie sheet, flattening them slightly. • Bake for 20–25 minutes, or until firm to the touch. • Transfer to a cutting board to cool for 15 minutes. • Reduce the oven temperature to 325°F/170°C/gas 3. • Cut on the diagonal into 1-inch (2.5-cm) slices. • Arrange the slices cut-side up on two cookie sheets and bake for 10–15 minutes, or until golden and toasted. • Transfer to racks to cool.

PEGGY'S COOKIES

Preheat the oven to 375°F/190°C/gas 5. •
Butter two cookie sheets. • Sift the flour,
baking powder, and salt into a medium bowl. •
Beat the butter and sugar in a large bowl with an
electric mixer at high speed until creamy. • Add the
egg and vanilla, beating until just blended. • Mix in
the dry ingredients, followed by the raisins and
orange zest. • Drop tablespoons of the dough
2 inches (5 cm) apart onto the prepared cookie
sheets. • Bake for 12–15 minutes, or until just
golden. • Cool on the sheets until the cookies firm
slightly. • Transfer to racks to finish cooling.

Makes: 25 cookies

Preparation: 25'

Cooking: 12–15'

Level of difficulty: 1

- 1⅓ cups/200 g all-
  purpose flour
- ½ tsp baking
  powder
- ½ tsp salt
- ½ cup/125 g
  butter, softened
- ⅔ cup/140 g
  granulated sugar
- 1 large egg, lightly
  beaten
- ½ tsp vanilla
  extract/essence
- ⅔ cup/120 g
  raisins
- 1 tbsp finely grated
  orange zest

ALADDIN'S LAMP COOKIES

Makes: 24 cookies

Preparation: 20'

Cooking: 20–25'

Level of difficulty: 1

- 1¼ cups/180 g all-purpose/plain flour
- 1 tsp baking powder
- ⅛ tsp salt
- 6 tbsp butter, softened
- ⅓ cup/70 g firmly packed light brown sugar
- 1 large egg, lightly beaten
- 1 tsp almond extract/essence
- Seeds of 8 cardamom pods, crushed
- ½ cup/50 g finely chopped candied cherries
- ½ cup/50 g finely chopped dried apricots
- ½ cup/50 g finely chopped crystallized ginger

Preheat the oven to 350°F/180°C/gas 4. • Butter two cookie sheets. • Sift the flour, baking powder, and salt into a medium bowl. • Beat the butter and brown sugar in a large bowl with an electric mixer at high speed until creamy. • Add the egg, beating until just blended. • Mix in the dry ingredients, almond extract, and crushed cardamom, followed by the cherries, apricots, and ginger. • Drop rounded teaspoons of the dough 1 inch (2.5 cm) apart onto the prepared cookie sheets. • Bake for 20–25 minutes, or until lightly browned. • Transfer to racks and let cool.

RUSTIC COOKIES

Preheat the oven to 425°F/220°C/gas 7. • Butter a cookie sheet. • Sift the flour and salt into a large bowl. Stir in the coconut, sugar, and lemon zest. • Use a pastry blender to cut in the butter until the mixture resembles coarse crumbs. • Add the lemon juice and eggs, mixing until a smooth dough has formed. • Drop heaping tablespoons of the dough 2 inches (5 cm) apart onto the prepared cookie sheet. • Bake for 8–10 minutes, or until lightly browned. • Transfer to racks to cool.

Makes: 12 cookies
Preparation: 20'
Cooking: 8–10'
Level of difficulty: 1

- ¾ cup/125 g whole-wheat flour
- ⅛ tsp salt
- 1 cup/125 g shredded/desiccated coconut
- ¼ cup/50 g granulated sugar
- grated zest and juice of ½ lemon
- 4 tbsp butter, cut up
- 2 large eggs, lightly beaten

MANHATTAN FORTUNE COOKIES

Makes: 30 cookies

Preparation: 25'

Cooking: 5–7'

Level of difficulty: 3

- **2 large egg whites**
- **⅓ cup/70 g granulated sugar**
- **⅓ cup/50 g all-purpose/plain flour**
- **2 tbsp butter, melted**
- **1 tsp coconut extract/essence**
- **⅛ tsp salt**
- **2 tbsp shredded/desiccated coconut**

Preheat the oven to 350°F/180°C/gas 4. • Butter four cookie sheets. • Beat the egg whites and sugar in a large bowl with an electric mixer at high speed until frothy. • With mixer at low speed, beat in the flour, butter, coconut extract, and salt. • Use a large rubber spatula to fold in the melted butter, flour, and salt. • Drop teaspoons of the batter onto the prepared cookie sheets, spreading it out to 3-inch (8-cm) circles. • Sprinkle with the coconut. • Bake, one sheet at a time, for 5–7 minutes, or until lightly browned. • Use a spatula to remove the cookies, placing a message in the center. Fold the cookies in half, enclosing the message to form a semicircle. Hold the rounded edges of the semicircle between your thumb and index finger. Place your other index finger at the center of the folded edge and push in. • Let cool completely.

DATE AND CHOCOLATE CHEWIES

Set out a 10^1/$_2$ x 15^1/$_2$-inch (26 x 36-cm) jelly-roll pan. • Melt the butter and sugar in a large saucepan over medium heat. • Remove from the heat and stir in the dates, cherries, raisins, and rice krispies until well coated. • Spoon the mixture evenly into the pan, pressing down firmly. • Refrigerate for 2 hours, or until set. • Melt the chocolate in a double boiler over barely simmering water. Pour the chocolate over and let stand for 20 minutes until set. • Use a sharp knife to cut into squares.

Makes: 16 squares

Preparation: 40' + 2 h 20' to chill and set

Level of difficulty: 1

- ^{1}/$_2$ cup/125 g butter, cut up
- ^{1}/$_2$ cup/100 g granulated sugar
- 1^3/$_4$ cups/175 g finely chopped pitted dates
- ^{2}/$_3$ cup/70 g finely chopped candied cherries
- ^{1}/$_3$ cup/60 g golden raisins/sultanas
- 2 cups/200 g rice krispies
- 8 oz/250 g semisweet/dark chocolate, coarsely chopped

DRIED APRICOT AND CHOCOLATE SALAMI

Makes: 20 cookies

Preparation: 20' + 12 h to chill

Level of difficulty: 1

- ⅔ cup/80 g graham cracker crumbs/crushed digestive biscuits
- ½ cup/50 g coarsely chopped toasted almonds
- ½ cup/50 g finely chopped dried apricots
- ½ cup/50 g coarsely chopped candied cherries
- ⅓ cup/70 g white chocolate chips
- 5 oz/150 g semisweet/dark chocolate, coarsely chopped
- 4 tbsp butter, cut up
- 2 oz/60 g white chocolate, coarsely chopped

Stir together the graham cracker crumbs, almonds, apricots, candied cherries, and chocolate chips in a large bowl. • Melt the semisweet chocolate with the butter in a double boiler over barely simmering water. Remove from the heat and let cool for 5 minutes. • Pour the chocolate mixture over the graham cracker mixture and mix well. • Turn the mixture onto a sheet of plastic wrap and form into a 10-inch (25-cm) log. • Wrap in the plastic wrap and refrigerate for 12 hours. • Slice the log ½ inch (1-cm) thick. • Melt the white chocolate in a double boiler over barely simmering water and drizzle over the tops of the cookies.

CARIBBEAN SQUARES

Line a $10^1/2$ x $15^1/2$-inch (26 x 36-cm) jelly-roll pan with aluminum foil. • Beat the butter and confectioners' sugar in a large bowl with an electric mixer at high speed until creamy. • Use a large rubber spatula to fold in the coconut, graham cracker crumbs, and vanilla. • Dust your hands lightly with confectioners' sugar. • Press into a disk, wrap in plastic wrap, and refrigerate for 30 minutes. • Divide into ten equal portions. Form each portion into a square or rectangle. • Melt the chocolate in a double boiler over barely simmering water. Use tongs to dip the bars into the chocolate to cover completely. • Place the bars on the prepared baking sheet and let stand for 30 minutes until set.

Makes: about 10 squares

Preparation: 30' + 60' to chill and set

Level of difficulty: 1

- ¾ cup/180 g butter, softened
- 1 cup/150 g confectioners'/icing sugar
- 1 cup/125 g shredded/desiccated coconut
- 1 cup/125 g graham cracker crumbs/crushed digestive biscuits
- 1 tsp vanilla extract/essence
- 8 oz/250 g semisweet/dark chocolate, coarsely chopped

ALLSPICE COOKIES

Makes 24 cookies

Preparation: 40' + 30' to chill

Cooking: 15–20'

Level of difficulty: 1

- 1¼ cups/180 g all-purpose/plain flour
- 1 tsp baking powder
- ½ tsp ground allspice
- ⅛ tsp salt
- 6 tbsp butter, softened
- ⅓ cup/70 g + 2 tsp granulated sugar
- 1 large egg, separated
- ⅓ cup/45 g currants
- 1 tbsp finely chopped mixed candied peel
- ¼ tsp brandy
- 2 tbsp milk or more as needed

Preheat the oven to 375°F/190°C/gas 5. • Butter two cookie sheets. • Sift the flour, baking powder, allspice, and salt into a medium bowl. • Beat the butter and ⅓ cup (70 g) of sugar in a large bowl with an electric mixer at high speed until creamy. • Add the egg yolk, beating until just blended. • Mix in the dry ingredients, currants, candied peel, and brandy until well blended. • Add enough milk to form a soft, but not sticky, dough. • Cover with plastic wrap and refrigerate for 30 minutes. • Roll out the dough to a thickness of ¼ inch (5 mm). • Use a 2-inch (5-cm) cookie cutter to cut out the cookies. Gather the dough scraps, re-roll, and continue cutting out cookies until all the dough is used. Use a spatula to transfer the cookies to a cookie sheet, placing them 1 inch (2.5 cm) apart. Prick all over with a fork. • Bake, one sheet at a time, for 10 minutes. • Beat the egg white lightly in a small bowl. • Remove the cookie sheet from the oven and brush the cookies with the beaten egg white. Sprinkle with the remaining sugar. • Bake for 5–10 minutes more, or until lightly browned. • Cool on the sheets until the cookies firm slightly. Transfer to racks to finish cooling.

BRITISH COOKIES

Preheat the oven to 375°F/190°C/gas 5. •
Butter three cookie sheets. • Sift the flour,
baking soda, and salt into a medium bowl. • Beat
the butter and granulated and brown sugars in a
large bowl with an electric mixer at high speed until
creamy. • Add the egg, beating until just blended. •
Mix in the dry ingredients,
mincemeat, and brandy. • Drop heaped teaspoons
of the dough 2 inches (5 cm) apart onto the
prepared cookie sheets. • Bake, one sheet at a
time, for 10–12 minutes, or until golden brown.
Transfer to racks to cool

238

*Mincemeat is a British delicacy used to make
Christmas cakes and cookies.*

*Makes: 40–50
  cookies*

Preparation: 40'

Cooking: 10–12'

Level of difficulty: 1

- 1¼ cups/180 g all-
  purpose/plain flour
- ¼ tsp baking soda
- ⅛ tsp salt
- 6 tbsp butter,
  softened
- ¼ cup/50 g
  granulated sugar
- ¼ cup/50 g firmly
  packed light brown
  sugar
- 1 large egg
- ¾ cup/180 ml
  mincemeat
- 2 tsp brandy

PECAN DELIGHT COOKIES

Makes: 25 cookies

Preparation: 20'

Cooking: 25–30'

Level of difficulty: 1

- 1¾ cups/175 g finely chopped pitted dates
- 1¾ cups/175 g finely chopped pecans
- 2 large egg whites
- 1 cup/150 g confectioners'/icing sugar
- 1 tbsp unsweetened cocoa powder
- juice of 1 lemon

Preheat the oven to 325°F/170°C/gas 3. • Butter two cookie sheets. • Chop the dates very finely and place in a large bowl. Add the pecans. • Stir in the egg whites, confectioners' sugar, cocoa, and lemon juice and mix until well blended. • Drop teaspoons of the dough 1 inch (2.5 cm) apart onto the prepared cookie sheets. • Bake for 25–30 minutes, or until just golden at the edges. • Transfer to racks to cool.

ALI BABA BITES

Makes: 25 cookies

Preparation: 20'

Cooking: 25–30'

Level of difficulty: 1

- 1¾ cups/175 g finely chopped pitted dates
- 1¾ cups/175 g finely chopped walnuts
- 2 large egg whites
- 1 cup/150 g confectioners'/icing sugar
- 1 tbsp unsweetened cocoa powder
- Juice of 1 lemon

Preheat the oven to 325°F/170°C/gas 3. • Butter two cookie sheets. • Chop the dates very finely and place in a large bowl. Add the walnuts. • Stir in the egg whites, confectioners' sugar, cocoa, and lemon juice and mix until well blended. • Drop teaspoons of the dough 1 inch (2.5 cm) apart onto the prepared cookie sheets. • Bake for 25–30 minutes, or until just golden at the edges. • Transfer to racks and let cool.

FIJIAN COOKIES

Beat the butter and cream cheese in a large bowl with an electric mixer at medium speed for 1 minute. • Beat in the confectioners' sugar, baking soda, and salt. • Add the egg, beating until just blended. • Beat in the orange zest, juice, and vanilla. • Mix in the flour to form a soft dough. • Turn the dough out on a lightly floured surface and knead until smooth. • Divide the dough in half. Form the dough into two 8-inch (20-cm) logs and roll each in the coconut. Wrap in plastic wrap, and refrigerate for at least 30 minutes. • Preheat the oven to 375°F/190°C/gas 5. • Set out three cookie sheets. • Slice the dough ¹/₄ inch (5 mm) thick and place 1 inch (2.5 cm) apart on the cookie sheets. • Bake, one sheet at a time, for 8–10 minutes, or until just golden. • Cool on the sheet until the cookies firm slightly. • Transfer to racks to finish cooling.

Makes: 64 cookies

Preparation: 40' + 30' to chill

Cooking: 8–10'

Level of difficulty: 2

- ¹/₂ cup/125 g butter, softened
- ¹/₂ cup/125 g cream cheese, softened
- 1¹/₄ cups/180 g confectioners'/icing sugar
- ¹/₄ tsp baking soda
- ¹/₄ tsp salt
- 1 large egg, lightly beaten
- 1 tbsp finely grated orange zest
- 1 tbsp fresh orange juice
- ¹/₂ tsp vanilla extract/essence
- 2¹/₄ cups/330 g all-purpose/plain flour
- ¹/₂ cup/60 g shredded/desiccated coconut

CANDIED FRUIT DELIGHTS

Makes: 35–40 cookies

Preparation: 25'

Cooking: 10–12' per batch

Level of difficulty: 1

- 1½ cups/225 g all-purpose/plain flour
- ⅛ tsp salt
- 3 large eggs, separated
- 1 cup/200 g granulated sugar
- ½ cup/50 g very finely chopped mixed candied peel
- 2 tbsp confectioners'/icing sugar, to sprinkle

Preheat the oven to 350°F/180°C/gas 4. • Line three cookie sheets with parchment paper. • Sift the flour and salt into a medium bowl. • Beat the egg whites in a large bowl with an electric mixer at medium speed until frothy. • With mixer at high speed, gradually add the granulated sugar, beating until stiff, glossy peaks form. • Use a large rubber spatula to fold in the candied peel and dry ingredients. • With mixer at high speed, beat the egg yolks in a small bowl until frothy. • Fold the beaten egg yolks into the batter. • Drop teaspoons of the dough 2 inches (5 cm) apart onto the prepared cookie sheets. • Sprinkle with confectioners' sugar. • Bake, one batch at a time, for 10–12 minutes, or until pale gold. • Cool on the sheets until the cookies firm slightly. • Transfer to racks to finish cooling.

RAW SUGAR RAISIN COOKIES

Preheat the oven to 350°F/180°C/gas 4. • Butter two cookie sheets. • Plump the raisins in hot water to cover in a small bowl for 10 minutes. • Drain well and pat dry with paper towels. • Sift the flour, baking powder, cinnamon, nutmeg, and salt into a medium bowl. • Mix the milk and lemon juice in a small bowl. • Beat the butter and raw and granulated sugars in a large bowl with an electric mixer at high speed until creamy. • Add the eggs, beating until just blended. • Mix in the dry ingredients, milk mixture, and raisins. • Drop teaspoons of the dough 1 inch (2.5 cm) apart onto the prepared cookie sheets. • Bake for 12–15 minutes, or until just golden. • Transfer to racks to cool.

Makes: 32 cookies

Preparation: 25'

Cooking: 12–15'

Level of difficulty: 1

- 1 cup/180 g golden raisins/sultanas
- 2 cups/300 g all-purpose/plain flour
- 1 tsp baking powder
- 1 tsp ground cinnamon
- $1/8$ tsp freshly grated nutmeg
- $1/8$ tsp salt
- 4 tbsp milk
- $1/8$ tsp fresh lemon juice
- $1/2$ cup/125 g butter, softened
- 1 cup/200 g raw sugar (Demerara or Barbados)
- $1/4$ cup/50 g granulated sugar
- 2 large eggs

NUTTY ELEVENSES

Makes: 50 cookies

Preparation: 20'

Cooking: 8–10'

Level of difficulty: 1

- 3¼ cups/480 g all-purpose/plain flour
- ½ tsp ground cinnamon
- ⅛ tsp salt
- 1 cup/250 g butter, softened
- 1½ cups/300 g firmly packed light brown sugar
- 3 large eggs
- 1 tsp baking soda dissolved in 1½ tbsp hot water
- 1 cup/100 g coarsely chopped walnuts
- 1 cup/180 g raisins

Preheat the oven to 350°F/180°C/gas 4. • Butter four cookie sheets. • Sift the flour, cinnamon, and salt into a large bowl. • Beat the butter and brown sugar in a large bowl with an electric mixer at high speed until creamy. • Add the eggs, beating until just blended. • Stir in the baking soda mixture. • Mix in the dry ingredients, walnuts, and raisins. • Drop tablespoons of the dough 3 inches (8 cm) apart onto the prepared cookie sheets. • Bake, one sheet at a time, for 8–10 minutes, or until just golden at the edges. • Transfer to racks and let cool.

SUSANNA SPECIALS

Sift the flour, cornstarch, and salt into a medium bowl. • Beat the butter and sugar in a large bowl with an electric mixer at high speed until creamy. • Add the lemon zest. • With mixer at high speed, beat the egg whites in a large bowl until soft peaks form. • Fold them into the butter mixture. • Mix in the dry ingredients, dates, lemon juice, and rum extract. Refrigerate for 30 minutes. • Preheat the oven to 375°F/190°C/gas 5. • Butter two cookie sheets. • Drop teaspoons of the mixture 1¹/₂ inches (4 cm) apart onto the prepared cookie sheets. • Bake for 8–10 minutes, or until golden brown. • Transfer to racks to cool.

Makes: 30 cookies

Preparation: 20' + 30' to chill

Cooking: 10'

Level of difficulty: 2

- ¹/₂ cup/75 g all-purpose/plain flour
- 2 tbsp cornstarch/cornflour
- ¹/₄ tsp salt
- 6 tbsp butter, softened
- ¹/₂ cup/100 g granulated sugar
- 1 tbsp finely grated lemon zest
- 3 large egg whites
- ¹/₂ cup/50 g finely chopped pitted dates
- 1 tbsp fresh lemon juice
- 1 tsp rum extract/essence

POLISH BREAKFAST COOKIES

Makes: 30–35
  cookies

Preparation: 30' + 30'
  to chill

Cooking: 15–18'

Level of difficulty: 1

- 1 cup/150 g all-
  purpose/plain flour
- 1/8 tsp salt
- 1/2 cup/125 g
  butter, softened
- 1/3 cup/70 g + 1
  tbsp granulated
  sugar
- 1/2 cup/125 ml
  heavy/double
  cream
- 1 large egg, lightly
  beaten
- 3 tbsp sweet white
  wine, such as
  Sauternes
- 1 tsp finely
  chopped mixed
  candied peel
- 1/3 cup/40 g finely
  chopped almonds

Preheat the oven to 400°F/200°C/gas 6. •
Butter a cookie sheet. • Sift the flour and salt
into a large bowl. • Use a pastry blender to cut in
the butter until the mixture resembles fine crumbs.
• Stir in 1/3 cup (70 g) of sugar and make a well in
the center. • Mix in the cream, egg, 2 tablespoons
of the wine, and the candied peel to form a smooth
dough. • Press the dough into a disk, wrap in
plastic wrap, and refrigerate for 30 minutes. • Roll
out the dough on a lightly floured surface to a large
rectangle with a thickness of 1/4 inch (5 mm). •
Use a rolling pin to transfer the dough to the
prepared cookie sheet. • Brush the remaining
1 tablespoon of wine over the dough. Sprinkle with
the remaining sugar and almonds. • Bake for
12–15 minutes, or until just golden. • Cut into
2-inch (5-cm) triangles. • Bake for 3–5 minutes
more, or until firm to the touch and golden brown.
• Cool completely on the cookie sheet.

PECAN BALLS

Preheat the oven to 350°F/180°C/gas 4. • Butter three cookie sheets. • Process the pecans, apricots, and brown sugar in a food processor to a finely ground paste. • Add the eggs and process until blended. • Transfer to a large bowl and mix in 1 1/2 cups (185 g) coconut to form a stiff dough. • Place the remaining coconut in a small bowl. • Form the dough into balls the size of walnuts and roll in the coconut. • Place 1 inch (2.5 cm) apart on the prepared cookie sheets. • Bake, one sheet at a time, for 10–12 minutes, or until golden brown. • Transfer to racks to cool.

Makes: 30–40 cookies

Preparation: 20'

Cooking: 10–12'

Level of difficulty: 1

- 2 cups/200 g coarsely chopped pecans
- 1 cup/100 g coarsely chopped dried apricots
- 1 cup/200 g firmly packed light brown sugar
- 1 large egg, lightly beaten
- 2 1/4 cups/280 g shredded/desiccated coconut

Makes: 22–33 bars	
Preparation: 15'	
Cooking: 40–45'	
Level of difficulty: 1	

FARMER SQUARES

- ¾ cup/125 g all-purpose/plain flour
- ½ tsp baking powder
- ¼ tsp salt
- ½ cup/60 g shredded/desiccated coconut
- ½ cup/50 g finely chopped walnuts
- 2 tbsp finely ground almonds
- ⅓ cup/50 g old-fashioned rolled oats
- ¾ cup/150 g granulated sugar
- ½ cup/125 g butter, cut up
- 1 tbsp light corn syrup/golden syrup
- 1 tbsp milk
- 1 large egg

Preheat the oven to 350°F/180°C/gas 4. • Butter an 11 x 7-inch (28 x 18-cm) baking pan. • Sift the flour, baking powder, and salt into a large bowl. • Stir in the coconut, walnuts, almonds, oats, and sugar. • Use a pastry blender to cut in the butter until the mixture resembles fine crumbs. • Dissolve the corn syrup in the milk in a small saucepan over low heat. Add the egg, beating until just blended. • Pour the egg mixture into the dry ingredients and mix well. • Spread the mixture evenly in the baking pan. • Bake for 40–45 minutes, or until golden brown. • Cool completely before cutting into bars.

WHOLE-WHEAT CINNAMON BARS

Preheat the oven to 350°F/180°C/gas 4. •
Butter an 8-inch (20-cm) square baking pan.
• Heat the milk in a small saucepan over low heat.
• Pour the milk into a large bowl, add the dates,
and let soak for 15 minutes. • Sift the flour, baking
powder, cinnamon, and salt into a medium bowl.
• Beat the egg, butter, and orange zest into the
date mixture. • Mix in the dry ingredients, followed
by the orange flesh until well blended. • Spoon the
batter into the prepared pan. • Bake for 35–40
minutes, or until a toothpick inserted into the
center comes out clean. • Cool completely before
cutting into bars.

Makes: 16–25 bars

Preparation: 20' + 15'
to soak the dates

Cooking: 35–40'

Level of difficulty: 1

- ²⁄₃ cup/150 ml milk
- ¹⁄₂ cup/100 g finely
  chopped dates
- ³⁄₄ cup/125 g
  whole-wheat flour
- ¹⁄₂ tsp baking
  powder
- ¹⁄₂ tsp ground
  cinnamon
- ¹⁄₈ tsp salt
- 1 large egg, lightly
  beaten
- 4 tbsp butter,
  melted
- grated zest and
  chopped flesh of 1
  orange

ROBBIE'S BEST COOKIES

Makes: 20–25 cookies

Preparation: 20'

Cooking: 15–20'

Level of difficulty: 1

- 1 cup/150 g all-purpose/plain flour
- ⅔ cup/100 g whole-wheat flour
- 1 tsp baking powder
- ⅛ tsp salt
- 1 cup/200 g finely chopped pitted dates
- ¾ cup/180 g butter, softened
- ¾ cup/150 g granulated sugar
- 1 large egg

Preheat the oven to 400°F/200°C/gas 6. • Butter two cookie sheets. • Sift the all-purpose and whole-wheat flours, baking powder, and salt into a large bowl. • Beat the butter and granulated sugar in a large bowl with an electric mixer at high speed until creamy. • Add the egg, beating until just blended. • Mix in the dry ingredients and dates to make a stiff dough. • Form the dough into balls the size of walnuts and place 2 inches (5 cm) apart on the prepared cookie sheets, flattening them slightly. • Bake for 15–20 minutes, or until lightly browned. • Transfer to racks and let cool.

CHEWY COCONUT MOMENTS

Preheat the oven to 325°F/170°C/gas 3. • Line three cookie sheets with parchment paper. • Mix the sugar, coconut, egg whites, lemon zest, and vanilla in a large shallow saucepan. • Cook over low heat, stirring constantly, for about 5 minutes, or until creamy. Do not bring to a boil. Remove from the heat and let cool for 15 minutes, or until thickened for piping. • Fit a pastry bag with a $1/4$-inch (5-mm) star tip. Fill the pastry bag, twist the opening tightly closed, and pipe out hazelnut-sized rounds, spacing 1 inch (2.5-cm) apart on the prepared cookie sheets. • Bake, one batch at a time, for 8–10 minutes, or until firm to the touch and golden brown. • Cool the cookies on the cookie sheets for 5 minutes. • Transfer to racks to cool.

Makes: 50 cookies

Preparation: 40'

Cooking: 8–10'

Level of difficulty: 2

- 2 cups/400 g granulated sugar
- 1½ cups/185 g shredded/ desiccated coconut
- 5 large egg whites
- grated zest of ½ lemon
- ¼ tsp vanilla extract/essence

DARWIN'S COOKIES

Makes: 26 cookies

Preparation: 20'

Cooking: 8–10'

Level of difficulty: 1

- 1 cup/150 g all-purpose/plain flour
- ½ tsp ground cinnamon
- ¼ tsp baking soda
- 2 tbsp water
- ¾ cup/75 g finely chopped dates
- ¾ cup/150 g currants
- 6 tbsp butter, softened
- ½ cup/100 g granulated sugar
- 1 large egg
- ½ cup/50 g finely chopped pecans

Preheat the oven to 400°F/200°C/gas 6. • Butter two cookie sheets. • Sift the flour and cinnamon into a medium bowl. • Mix the baking soda and water in a small bowl. Add the dates and currants. • Beat the butter and sugar in a large bowl with an electric mixer at high speed until creamy. • Add the egg, beating until just blended. • Stir in the date and currant mixture. • Mix in the dry ingredients and pecans. • Drop tablespoons of the dough 1 inch (2.5 cm) apart onto the prepared cookie sheets. • Bake for 8–10 minutes, or until lightly browned. • Cool on the sheets until the cookies firm slightly. • Transfer to racks and let cool completely.

COFFEE
& CREAM
COOKIES

BRAZILIAN SPIRALS

Refrigerate four cookie sheets. • Sift the flour, baking powder, and salt into a medium bowl. • Beat the butter and granulated and vanilla sugars in a large bowl with an electric mixer at high speed until creamy. Add the brandy and vanilla. • Add the eggs, beating until just blended. • Mix in the dry ingredients to form a soft dough. • Mix the chocolate hazelnut spread and coffee liqueur in a small bowl. • Roll the dough out into a large rectangle about $1/2$ inch (1 cm) thick. • Spread evenly with the chocolate spread mixture and tightly roll up the dough from the long side. • Wrap in plastic wrap and refrigerate for at least 30 minutes. • Preheat the oven to 375°F/190°C/gas 5. • Cut the dough into $1/2$-inch (1-cm) thick slices. • Place 1 inch (2.5 cm) apart on the prepared cookie sheets. • Bake, one sheet at a time, for 8–10 minutes, or until lightly browned and firm to the touch. • Cool the cookies on the cookie sheets for 5 minutes. • Transfer to racks to cool.

Prepare the dough in the evening and leave in the refrigerator overnight. Bake fresh for breakfast.

Makes: 60–65 cookies

Preparation: 60' + 30' to chill

Cooking: 8–10'

Level of difficulty: 2

- **3$1/3$ cups/500 g all-purpose/plain flour**
- **$1/4$ tsp baking powder**
- **$1/8$ tsp salt**
- **1 cup/250 g butter, softened**
- **$3/4$ cup/150 g granulated sugar**
- **3 tbsp vanilla sugar**
- **1 tbsp brandy**
- **$1/2$ tsp vanilla extract/essence**
- **2 large eggs**
- **4 tbsp chocolate hazelnut spread (Nutella)**
- **1 tbsp coffee liqueur**

VALENTINO COOKIES

Preheat the oven to 375°F/190°C/gas 5. •
Butter two cookie sheets. • Sift the flour,
cornstarch, cocoa, baking powder, and salt into a
large bowl. • Use a pastry blender to cut in the
butter until the mixture resembles coarse crumbs.
• Stir in the sugar. • Add the coffee extract and
enough milk to form a stiff dough. • Turn the dough
out onto a lightly floured surface and knead until
smooth. • Roll out the dough to a thickness of
$1/4$ inch (5 mm). • Use a heart-shaped cookie
cutter to cut out the cookies. Gather the dough
scraps, re-roll, and continue cutting out cookies
until all the dough is used. • Use a spatula to
transfer the cookies onto the prepared cookie
sheets, placing them 1 inch (2.5 cm) apart.
• Bake for 10–15 minutes, or until lightly browned.
• Cool on the sheets until the cookies firm slightly.
Transfer to racks to finish cooling. • Spread with
the frosting. Draw the tines of a fork through the
frosting to make decorative patterns.

Makes: 25 cookies

Preparation: 40'

Cooking: 10–15'

Level of difficulty: 1

- **$2/3$ cup/100 g all-purpose/plain flour**
- **2 tbsp cornstarch/cornflour**
- **1 tbsp unsweetened cocoa powder**
- **$1/2$ tsp baking powder**
- **$1/8$ tsp salt**
- **4 tbsp butter**
- **$1/4$ cup/50 g granulated sugar**
- **1 tsp coffee extract/essence**
- **1 tbsp milk or more as needed**
- **$1/2$ cup/125 ml Chocolate Frosting (see page 952)**

MOCHA NUT COOKIES

Makes: 20 cookies

Preparation: 20'

Cooking: 20–25'

Level of difficulty: 1

- ⅔ cup/100 g all-purpose/plain flour
- ½ tsp baking powder
- ⅛ tsp salt
- 12 oz/350 g bittersweet/plain chocolate, coarsely chopped
- ½ cup/125 g butter, cut up
- 3 large eggs
- 1 cup/200 g granulated sugar
- 1 tbsp freeze-dried coffee granules
- 1 tsp vanilla extract/essence
- 1½ cups/150 g coarsely chopped pecans
- 1½ cups/150 g coarsely chopped hazelnuts
- 1 cup/180 g semisweet/dark chocolate chips

Preheat the oven to 325°F/170°C/gas 4. • Set out two cookie sheets. • Sift the flour, baking powder, and salt into a large bowl. • Melt the chocolate and butter in a double boiler over barely simmering water. • Beat the eggs and sugar in a large bowl with an electric mixer at high speed until pale and thick. • Beat in the chocolate mixture, coffee granules, and vanilla. • Mix in the dry ingredients, pecans, hazelnuts, and chocolate chips. • Drop tablespoons of the dough 3 inches (8 cm) apart onto the cookie sheets. • Bake for 20–25 minutes, or until lightly cracked on top. • Transfer to racks to cool.

MOCHA PINWHEELS

Sift the flour, baking powder, and salt into a medium bowl. • Beat 4 tablespoons of butter and 2 tablespoons sugar in a medium bowl with an electric mixer at high speed until creamy. • Mix in $^3/_4$ cup (125 g) of the dry ingredients. • Stir the coffee granules into the remaining flour. • Beat the remaining butter and sugar until creamy. • Mix in the coffee mixture. • Roll out both doughs on a lightly floured surface into rectangles $^1/_4$ inch (5 mm) thick. • Brush the plain dough with the milk. • Top with the coffee dough and roll up tightly from a long side. Wrap in plastic wrap and refrigerate for at least 30 minutes. • Preheat the oven to 350°F/ 180°C/gas 4. • Butter a cookie sheet. • Slice the dough $^1/_4$ inch (5 mm) thick and place 1 inch (2.5 cm) apart on the prepared cookie sheet.
• Bake for 12–15 minutes, or until just golden.
• Transfer to racks to cool.

Makes: 30 cookies

Preparation: 60' + 30' to chill

Cooking: 12–15'

Level of difficulty: 1

- 1 $^2/_3$ cups/250 g all-purpose/plain flour
- 1 tsp baking powder
- $^1/_8$ tsp salt
- $^1/_2$ cup/125 g butter, softened
- $^1/_3$ cup/70 g granulated sugar
- 2 tsp freeze-dried coffee granules
- 1 tsp milk

MELTING MOMENTS

Stir together the flour, custard powder, sugar, rice flour, baking powder, and salt in a large bowl. • Use a pastry blender to cut in the butter until the mixture resembles coarse crumbs. Pour in the milk to form a firm dough. • Press the dough into a disk, wrap in plastic wrap, and refrigerate for 30 minutes. • Preheat the oven to 350°F/180°C/ gas 4. · Set out two cookie sheets. • Transfer the dough to a lightly floured surface and roll out to a thickness of $1/4$ inch (5 mm). • Use a $1^1/_2$-inch (4-cm) cookie cutter to cut out the cookies. • Gather the dough scraps, re-roll, and continue cutting out the cookies until all the dough is used. • Transfer the cookies to the cookie sheets, placing them 1 inch (2.5 cm) apart. • Bake for 12–15 minutes, or until lightly browned. • Transfer to racks to cool. • Stick pairs of cookies together with the buttercream.

| Makes: 15 cookies |
| Preparation: 45' |
| Cooking: 12–15' |
| Level of difficulty: 1 |

- 1²⁄₃ cups/250 g all-purpose/plain flour
- 1¼ cups/180 g custard powder
- 1 cup/200 g granulated sugar
- ½ cup/75 g rice flour
- 1 tsp baking powder
- ⅛ tsp salt
- ¾ cup/180 g butter, cut up
- 4 tbsp milk
- 1 cup/250 ml Italian Buttercream (see page 954)

BARBADOS CREAMS

Makes: 25 cookies

Preparation: 45' + 30' to chill

Cooking: 6–8'

Level of difficulty: 2

- **2 cups/300 g all-purpose/plain flour**
- **2 tsp baking powder**
- **¼ tsp salt**
- **6 tbsp butter, softened**
- **1 cup/200 g raw sugar (Demerara or Barbados)**
- **1 large egg**
- **1 tbsp fresh orange juice**
- **1 tsp vanilla extract/essence**

FILLING

- **2 tbsp pistachios**
- **¾ cup/150 g firmly packed light brown sugar**
- **6 tbsp butter, softened**
- **2 tbsp fresh orange juice**

Sift the flour, baking powder, and salt into a medium bowl. • Beat the butter and raw sugar in a large bowl until creamy. • Add the egg, beating until just blended. • Beat in the orange juice, vanilla, and the dry ingredients. • Form into two logs about 2 inches (5 cm) in diameter, wrap in plastic wrap, and refrigerate for 30 minutes. • Preheat the oven to 375°F/190°C/gas 5. • Butter four cookie sheets. • Slice the dough ⅛ inch (3 mm) thick. • Place the cookies on the prepared cookie sheets. • Bake, one batch at a time, for 6–8 minutes, or until golden brown. • Cool on the sheets for 2 minutes. Transfer to racks and let cool completely. • Filling: Process the pistachios and brown sugar in a food processor until very finely chopped. • Add the butter and process until smooth. Continue processing, adding enough orange juice to make a thick cream. • Stick the cookies together in pairs with the filling.

COFFEE SANDWICHES

Makes: 12–15
  cookies

Preparation: 20'

Cooking: 10–15'

Level of difficulty: 1

- ¾ cup/125 g all-purpose/plain flour
- 1 tbsp unsweetened cocoa powder
- ½ tsp baking powder
- ⅛ tsp salt
- ½ cup/125 g butter, softened
- ¼ cup/50 g granulated sugar
- ½ tsp vanilla extract/essence
- 1 cup/250 ml Coffee Buttercream (see page 955)

Preheat the oven to 375°F/190°C/gas 5. • Butter two cookie sheets. • Sift the flour, cocoa, baking powder, and salt into a medium bowl. • Beat the butter, sugar, and vanilla in a large bowl with an electric mixer at high speed until creamy. • Mix in the dry ingredients to form a stiff dough. • Form the dough into balls the size of walnuts and place 1 inch (2.5 cm) apart on the prepared cookie sheets. Use a fork to flatten them slightly. • Bake for 10–15 minutes, or until firm to the touch. • Cool on the sheets until the cookies firm slightly. • Transfer to racks to finish cooling. • Stick the cookies together in pairs with the buttercream.

MOCHA HAZELNUT COOKIES

Preheat the oven to 325°F/170°C/gas 3. •
Butter two cookie sheets. • Sift the flour,
baking powder, and salt into a large bowl. • Beat
the butter and sugar in a large bowl with an electric
mixer at high speed until creamy. • Add the coffee
extract and vanilla. • Mix in the dry ingredients to
form a smooth dough. • Roll into balls the size of
walnuts and place 1 1/2 inches (4 cm) apart on the
prepared baking sheet, pressing down lightly.
• Press three hazelnuts into the tops. • Bake for
15–20 minutes, or until firm to the touch.
• Transfer to racks to cool.

Makes: about 30
cookies

Preparation: 15'

Cooking: 15–20'

Level of difficulty: 1

- **1 1/4 cups/180 g all-purpose/plain flour**
- **1 tsp baking powder**
- **1/8 tsp salt**
- **1/2 cup/125 g butter, softened**
- **2/3 cup/140 g granulated sugar**
- **2 tsp coffee extract or 2 tsp freeze-dried coffee granules dissolved in 1 tbsp boiling water**
- **1 tsp vanilla extract/essence**
- **1/2 cup/75 g toasted hazelnuts**

HAZELNUT SLABS
WITH COFFEE GLAZE

Makes: 30–35 cookies

Preparation: 40' + 30' to chill

Cooking: 12–15'

Level of difficulty: 1

- 1²/₃ cups/250 g all-purpose/plain flour
- ¹/₈ tsp salt
- ³/₄ cup/180 g butter, softened
- ³/₄ cup/125 g confectioners'/icing sugar
- 1¹/₄ cups/125 g finely chopped hazelnuts

COFFEE GLAZE

- 1 large egg white, lightly beaten
- 1 tbsp freeze-dried coffee granules dissolved in 2 tsp hot water

S ift the flour and salt into a large bowl. • Beat the butter and confectioners' sugar in a large bowl with an electric mixer at high speed until creamy. • Mix in the dry ingredients, followed by the hazelnuts to form a dough. • Press the dough into a disk, wrap in plastic wrap, and refrigerate for 30 minutes. • Preheat the oven to 375°F/190°C/gas 5. • Butter two cookie sheets. • Roll out the dough on a lightly floured surface to a thickness of ¹/₄ inch (5 mm). • Coffee Glaze: Beat the egg white and coffee in a small bowl. Brush all over the dough. • Cut into 3 x 1¹/₂-inch (8 x 4-cm) bars and use a spatula to transfer to the prepared cookie sheets, placing them 1 inch (2.5 cm) apart. • Bake for 12–15 minutes, or until firm to the touch. • Transfer to racks and let cool completely.

GLIMMERING COOKIES

Sift the flour, baking powder, and salt into a large bowl. • Use a pastry blender to cut in the butter until the mixture resembles fine crumbs. • Stir together the sugar, sour cream, and 1 egg. Stir into the dry ingredients to form a smooth dough. • Press the dough into a disk, wrap in plastic wrap, and refrigerate for 30 minutes. • Preheat the oven to 425°F/220°C/gas 7. • Line two cookie sheets with parchment paper. • Roll out the dough on a lightly floured surface to a thickness of $1/4$ inch (5 mm). Use a 2-inch (5-cm) cookie cutter to cut out the cookies. Gather the dough scraps, re-roll, and continue cutting out until all the dough is used. • Use a spatula to transfer the cookies to the cookie sheets, spacing them 2 inches (5 cm) apart. Prick all over with a fork. • Beat the remaining egg and brush over the tops of the cookies. • Bake for 10–15 minutes, or until golden brown. • Transfer to racks to cool.

Makes: 16–20 cookies

Preparation: 40' + 30' to chill

Cooking: 10–15'

Level of difficulty: 1

- 1 cup/150 g all-purpose/plain flour
- $1/2$ tsp baking powder
- $1/8$ tsp salt
- 2 tbsp butter, cut up
- 3 tbsp granulated sugar
- 5 tbsp sour cream
- 2 large eggs

BREAKFAST BROWNIES

Makes: 16–25 bars

Preparation: 15'

Cooking: 30–35'

Level of difficulty: 1

- 1 cup/150 g all-purpose/plain flour
- 1 tsp baking powder
- ¼ tsp salt
- ½ cup/125 g butter, cut up
- 1⅓ cups/270 g firmly packed light or dark brown sugar
- 1 tbsp freeze-dried coffee granules dissolved in 1 tbsp hot water
- 1 tsp vanilla extract/essence
- 2 large eggs, lightly beaten
- 5 oz/150 g semisweet/dark chocolate, coarsely chopped
- 2 tbsp coarsely chopped walnuts

Preheat the oven to 350°F/180°C/gas 4. • Butter a 9-inch (23-cm) square baking pan. • Sift the flour, baking powder, and salt into a large bowl. • Melt the butter with the brown sugar in a medium saucepan over low heat, stirring constantly. • Stir in the coffee mixture. • Remove from the heat and let cool for 5 minutes. • Add the vanilla and eggs, beating until just blended. • Mix in the dry ingredients, chocolate, and walnuts until well blended. • Pour the mixture into the prepared pan. • Bake for 30–35 minutes, or until dry on the top and almost firm to the touch. Do not overbake. • Cool completely before cutting into bars.

COFFEE DROPS

Preheat the oven to 325°F/170°C/gas 3. • Butter three cookie sheets. • Sift the flour, cocoa, and salt into a medium bowl. • Beat the butter, sugar, and vanilla in a large bowl with an electric mixer at high speed until creamy. • Mix in the dry ingredients, coffee granules, pecans, and cherries until well blended. • Form the dough into balls the size of walnuts and place 1 inch (2.5 cm) apart on the prepared cookie sheets. • Bake, one sheet at a time, for 15–18 minutes, or until firm to the touch. • Transfer to racks and let cool completely. • Dust with the confectioners' sugar.

Makes: 36 cookies

Preparation: 20'

Cooking: 15–18'

Level of difficulty: 1

- 1 cup/150 g all-purpose/plain flour
- 1 tbsp unsweetened cocoa powder
- ¼ tsp salt
- ½ cup/125 g butter, softened
- ¼ cup/50 g granulated sugar
- 1 tsp vanilla extract/essence
- 2 tsp freeze-dried coffee granules
- ½ cup/50 g finely chopped pecans
- 2 tbsp finely chopped candied cherries
- ⅓ cup/50 g confectioners'/icing sugar

COFFEE CRUNCH COOKIES

Makes: 25–30 cookies

Preparation: 20'

Cooking: 15–20'

Level of difficulty: 1

- ¾ cup/125 g all-purpose/plain flour
- ½ tsp baking powder
- ⅛ tsp salt
- ½ cup/125 g butter, softened
- ¼ cup/50 g granulated sugar
- ⅔ cup/70 g finely chopped walnuts
- 2 tsp freeze-dried coffee granules

Preheat the oven to 375°F/190°C/gas 5. • Butter two cookie sheets. • Sift the flour, baking powder, and salt into a large bowl. • Beat the butter and sugar in a large bowl with an electric mixer at high speed until creamy. • Mix in the dry ingredients, walnuts, and coffee granules until well blended. • Drop tablespoons of the dough 1 inch (2.5 cm) apart onto the prepared cookie sheets. • Bake for 15–20 minutes, or until just golden. • Cool on the sheets until the cookies firm slightly. • Transfer to racks to finish cooling.

CREAMY CAFÉ SLICE

Preheat the oven to 350°F/180°C/gas 4. • Butter an 11 1/2 x 9 1/2-inch (27 x 24-cm) baking pan. • Sift the flour, cocoa, baking powder, and salt into a medium bowl. • Beat the butter and sugar in a large bowl with an electric mixer at high speed until creamy. • Beat in the eggs until just blended. • Mix in the dry ingredients and coffee until well blended. • Pour the batter into the prepared pan. • Bake for 25–35 minutes, or until dry on top and almost firm to the touch. • Cool completely in the pan. • Spread the frosting over and cut into bars.

Indulge family and friends with this moorish slice at coffee mornings or afternoon teas.

Makes: 22–33 bars

Preparation: 30'

Cooking: 25–35'

Level of difficulty: 1

- 1 1/2 cups/225 g all-purpose/plain flour
- 2 tbsp unsweetened cocoa powder
- 1 tsp baking powder
- 1/8 tsp salt
- 2 tbsp very strong hot coffee
- 1 cup/250 g butter, softened
- 1 cup/200 g granulated sugar
- 4 large eggs
- 2 cups/500 ml Coffee Buttercream (see page 955)

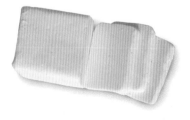

ESPRESSO COOKIES

Preheat the oven to 375°F/190°C/gas 5. •
Butter two cookie sheets. • Sift the flour,
baking powder, and salt into a medium bowl.
• Beat the butter and sugar in a large bowl with an
electric mixer at high speed until creamy. • Mix in
the dry ingredients, pecans, and coffee until well
blended. • Drop tablespoons of the dough 1 inch
(2.5 cm) apart onto the prepared cookie sheets.
• Bake for 15–20 minutes, or until just golden.
• Cool on the sheets until the cookies firm slightly.
• Transfer to racks to finish cooling.

*Makes: 25–30
cookies*

Preparation: 20'

Cooking: 15–20'

Level of difficulty: 1

- **1 cup/150 g all-
  purpose/plain flour**
- **½ tsp baking
  powder**
- **⅛ tsp salt**
- **½ cup/125 g
  butter, softened**
- **¼ cup/50 g
  granulated sugar**
- **⅔ cup/60 g finely
  chopped pecans**
- **2 tbsp strong
  espresso coffee**

VANILLA CRISPS

Makes: 35 cookies

Preparation: 40' + 30' to chill

Cooking: 10–15'

Level of difficulty: 1

- 3 cups/450 g all-purpose/plain flour
- ²⁄₃ cup/100 g cornstarch/cornflour
- 2 tsp baking powder
- ¹⁄₈ tsp salt
- 1 cup/200 g granulated sugar
- ³⁄₄ cup/180 g butter, melted
- 1 large egg
- 6 tbsp light/single cream
- ¹⁄₂ tsp vanilla extract/essence

Preheat the oven to 350°F/180°C/gas 4. • Butter three cookie sheets. • Sift the flour, cornstarch, baking powder, and salt into a large bowl. • Use a wooden spoon to mix in the sugar, butter, egg, cream, and vanilla to form a smooth dough. • Press the dough into a disk, wrap in plastic wrap, and refrigerate for 30 minutes. • Roll out the dough on a lightly floured surface to a thickness of ¹⁄₄ inch (5 mm). • Use a 2¹⁄₂-inch (6-cm) fluted cookie cutter to cut out the cookies. Gather the dough scraps, re-roll, and continue cutting out cookies until all the dough is used. • Use a spatula to transfer the cookies to the prepared cookie sheets, placing them 1 inch (2.5 cm) apart. • Bake, one sheet at a time, for 10–15 minutes, or until just golden at the edges. • Transfer to racks and let cool.

293

NUTTY COFFEE SQUARES

Makes: 16–25
  squares

Preparation: 40'

Cooking: 35–40'

Level of difficulty: 2

- 1⅓ cups/200 g
  whole almonds
- 2 tbsp water
- ¾ cup/150 g
  granulated sugar
- 2 tsp freeze-dried
  coffee granules
- 2 large egg whites
- ⅛ tsp salt
- 1 tbsp
  confectioners'/
  icing sugar

Preheat the oven to 350°F/180°C/gas 4. •
Butter an 8-inch (20-cm) baking pan. • Place
the almonds in a large bowl and pour over enough
hot water to cover them completely. • Let stand
for 5 minutes. • Use a slotted spoon to scoop the
nuts out of the water and place on a kitchen towel.
• Fold over the kitchen towel and gently rub the
nuts to remove the skins. Pick out the skins and
discard them. • Finely chop the almonds. • Bring
2 tablespoons water, the granulated sugar, and the
coffee granules to a boil in a small saucepan until
the sugar and coffee have dissolved completely.
• Stir in the almonds. • Remove from the heat and
set aside. • Beat the egg whites and salt in a large
bowl with an electric mixer at high speed until stiff
peaks form. • Use a large rubber spatula to fold in
the almond mixture. • Pour the batter into the
prepared pan. • Bake for 35–40 minutes, or until a
toothpick inserted into the center comes out clean.
• Cool completely before cutting into squares.
• Dust with the confectioners' sugar.

CAVOUR COFFEE BISCOTTI

Preheat the oven to 350°F/180°C/gas 4. • Line three cookie sheets with parchment paper. • Spread the almonds and pistachios on separate large baking sheets. Toast each for 7 minutes, or until lightly golden. • Transfer the almonds to a food processor and process until finely chopped. • Coarsely grind 2 tablespoons of the beans with a pestle and mortar or in a food processor. • Grind the remaining beans in a coffee grinder until very fine. • Sift the flour, baking powder, and salt into a large bowl. • Use a pastry blender to cut in the butter until the mixture resembles coarse crumbs. • Mix in the almonds, pistachios, coarsely and finely ground espresso beans, sugar, eggs, and coffee to form a stiff dough. • Divide the dough in three. Form into three logs about 2 inches (5 cm) in diameter and place 2 inches (5 cm) apart on the prepared cookie sheets, flattening them slightly. • Dust each log with cocoa powder and cinnamon. • Bake, one sheet at a time, for 25–30 minutes, or until firm to the touch. • Transfer to a cutting board to cool for 15 minutes. • Lower the oven temperature to 300°F/150°C/gas 2. • Cut on the diagonal into 1-inch (2.5-cm) slices. • Arrange the slices cut-side up on the cookie sheets and bake for 15–20 minutes, or golden and toasted. • Transfer to racks to cool.

These twice-baked Italian cookies are great to have in your cookie jar for unexpected guests.

Makes: 40 cookies

Preparation: 40'

Cooking: 40–50'

Level of difficulty: 2

- 1 cup/150 g almonds
- ½ cup/50 g coarsely chopped pistachios
- 5 tbsp espresso coffee beans
- 2⅓ cups/500 g all-purpose/plain flour
- 2 tsp baking powder
- ½ tsp salt
- ½ cup/125 g butter, cut up
- 1 cup/200 g granulated sugar
- 3 large eggs, lightly beaten
- ½ cup/125 ml strong coffee
- 1 tbsp unsweetened cocoa powder
- ⅛ tsp ground cinnamon

RISORGIMENTO COOKIES

Makes: 56 cookies

Preparation: 40' + 1 h
to chill

Cooking: 8–10'

Level of difficulty: 1

- 1 cup/150 g all-
  purpose/plain flour
- $^1/_2$ tsp baking
  powder
- $^1/_2$ tsp ground
  cinnamon
- $^1/_8$ tsp salt
- $^1/_2$ cup/125 g
  butter, softened
- 2 tbsp vegetable
  shortening
- $^1/_2$ cup/100 g + 2
  tbsp granulated
  sugar
- $^1/_4$ cup/50 g firmly
  packed light brown
  sugar
- 1 tbsp + 1 tsp
  freeze-dried coffee
  granules
- 1 large egg
- 2 tsp hot water
- coffee beans, to
  decorate

Sift the flour, baking powder, cinnamon, and salt into a medium bowl. • Beat the butter, vegetable shortening, $^1/_2$ cup (100 g) of granulated sugar, and brown sugar in a large bowl with an electric mixer at high speed until creamy. • Dissolve 1 tablespoon of the coffee granules in the hot water. • Add the coffee mixture and egg, beating until just blended. • Mix in the dry ingredients to form a stiff dough. • Divide the dough in half. Form into two 7-inch (18-cm) logs, wrap in plastic wrap, and refrigerate for 1 hour. • Preheat the oven to 375°F/190°C/gas 5. • Butter four cookie sheets. • Slice the dough $^1/_4$ inch (5 mm) thick and place 1 inch (2.5 cm) apart on the prepared cookie sheets. • Mix the remaining granulated sugar and 1 teaspoon coffee granules in a small bowl. Sprinkle over the tops of the cookies and decorate with the coffee beans. • Bake, one sheet at a time, for 8–10 minutes, or until pale gold. • Cool on the sheets until the cookies firm slightly. • Transfer to racks to finish cooling.

NUT
& SPICE
COOKIES

WEDDING RINGS

Preheat the oven to 350°F/180°C/gas 4. •
Butter two cookie sheets. • Sift the flour,
baking powder, cinnamon, and salt into a medium
bowl. • Stir in the sugar. • Use a wooden spoon to
beat the eggs in a large bowl until pale and thick.
• Beat in the butter and lemon zest until well
blended. • Mix in the dry ingredients and enough
milk to make a stiff dough. • Break off balls of
dough the size of walnuts and form into 4-inch
(10-cm) ropes. Form the ropes into rings and
sprinkle with the pine nuts. • Use a spatula to
transfer the cookies to the prepared cookie sheets,
placing 1 inch (2.5 cm) apart. • Bake for 15–20
minutes, or until just golden. • Transfer to racks
to cool.

Makes: 25–30
  cookies

Preparation: 20'

Cooking: 15–20'

Level of difficulty: 2

- 2²/₃ cups/400 g all-
  purpose/plain flour
- 2 tsp baking
  powder
- ¹/₈ tsp ground
  cinnamon
- ¹/₈ tsp salt
- ³/₄ cup/150 g
  granulated sugar
- 3 large eggs
- 6 tbsp butter,
  softened
- grated zest of ¹/₂
  lemon
- 2–4 tbsp milk
- 2 tbsp pine nuts

BLOOMFIELD COOKIES

Preheat the oven to 350°F/180°C/gas 4. •
Butter two cookie sheets. • Beat the butter and
brown sugar in a large bowl with an electric mixer
at high speed until creamy. • Add the egg yolk,
beating until just blended. • Mix in the flour, lemon
zest and juice, apricots, and pecans. • Press the
dough into a disk, wrap in plastic wrap, and
refrigerate for 30 minutes. • Roll out the dough on
a lightly floured surface to a thickness of $^1/_4$ inch
(5 mm). • Use a 2-inch (5-cm) cookie cutter to cut
out the cookies. Gather the dough scraps, re-roll,
and continue cutting out cookies until all the dough
is used. • Use a spatula to transfer the cookies to
the prepared cookie sheets. • Bake for 15–20
minutes, or until lightly browned. • Transfer to
racks and let cool.

Makes: 16 cookies

Preparation: 40' + 30'
to chill

Cooking: 15–20'

Level of difficulty: 1

- **7 tbsp butter,
  softened**
- **$^1/_3$ cup/70 g firmly
  packed light brown
  sugar**
- **1 large egg yolk**
- **$1^1/_3$ cups/200 g
  whole-wheat flour**
- **grated zest and
  juice of $^1/_2$ lemon**
- **$^1/_2$ cup/50 g finely
  chopped dried
  apricots**
- **$^1/_2$ cup/50 g
  coarsely chopped
  pecans**

CHEWY FROSTED BLISS

Makes: 25 squares

Preparation: 25' + 30'
   to set

Cooking: 25–30'

Level of difficulty: 1

- 1 cup/150 g all-purpose/plain flour
- 1 tsp baking powder
- ¼ tsp salt
- ½ cup/125 g butter, softened
- ¾ cup/150 g granulated sugar
- 1 large egg
- 2½ cups/250 g finely chopped pitted dates
- 1⅓ cups/130 g finely chopped walnuts
- 8 oz/250 g semisweet/dark chocolate, coarsely chopped

Preheat the oven to 350°F/180°C/gas 4. • Butter a 10½ x 15½-inch (26 x 36-cm) jelly-roll pan. • Sift the flour, baking powder, and salt into a medium bowl. • Beat the butter and sugar in a large bowl with an electric mixer at high speed until creamy. • Add the egg, beating until just blended. • Mix in the dry ingredients, dates, and walnuts until well blended. • Spoon the mixture into the prepared pan. • Bake for 25–30 minutes, or until firm to the touch. • Cool completely in the pan. • Melt the chocolate in a double boiler over barely simmering water. • Use a thin metal spatula to spread the chocolate evenly over the top. • Set aside for 30 minutes before cutting into squares.

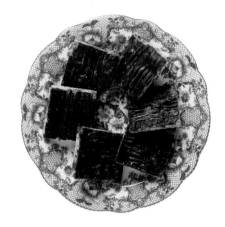

GINGERBREAD PEOPLE

Sift the flour, baking powder, and salt into a medium bowl. • Beat the butter and granulated sugar in a large bowl with an electric mixer at high speed until creamy. • Add the milk, ginger, and egg. • Mix in the dry ingredients. • Press the dough into a disk, wrap in plastic wrap, and refrigerate for 30 minutes. • Preheat the oven to 350°F/180°C/gas 4. • Butter two cookie sheets. • Roll out the dough on a lightly floured surface to a thickness of $^1/_4$ inch (5 mm). • Use large gingerbread people cookie cutters to ut out the figures. • Gather the dough scraps, re-roll, and continue cutting out cookies until all the dough is used. • Use a spatula to transfer them to the prepared cookie sheets, placing them $^1/_2$ inch (1 cm) apart. • Bake for 10–12 minutes, or until just golden at the edges. • Transfer to racks to cool. • Use the candy writers to decorate the cookies.

Makes: 8 cookies

Preparation: 40' + 30' to chill

Cooking: 10–12'

Level of difficulty: 2

- 2 cups/300 g all-purpose/plain flour
- 1 tsp baking powder
- ¼ tsp salt
- ½ cup/125 g butter, softened
- ½ cup/100 g granulated sugar
- 1 tbsp milk
- 1 tbsp ground ginger
- 1 large egg
- colored candy writers, to decorate

TOFFEE PEANUT SQUARES

Preheat the oven to 350°F/180°C/gas 4. • Line a baking sheet with parchment paper. • Beat ²/₃ cup (150 g) of butter, the egg, ¹/₃ cup (70 g) brown sugar, and the baking powder in a large bowl until creamy. • Beat in the flour. • Pour the mixture onto the prepared baking sheet, spreading it out. • Bake for 20–25 minutes, or until a toothpick inserted into the center comes out clean. • Lower the oven temperature to 300°F/150°C/gas 2. • Cook the remaining butter, remaining sugar, condensed milk, and salt in a small saucepan over low heat, stirring constantly, until well blended. • Remove from heat and stir in the peanuts. • Pour the peanut mixture over the baked cake. • Bake for 15 minutes more. • Turn off the oven and let the brownies cool in the oven with the door slightly ajar. • Cut into squares.

Makes: 24 squares
Preparation: 25'
Cooking: 35–40'
Level of difficulty: 1

- ³/₄ cup/180 g butter
- 1 large egg
- ²/₃ cup/140 g firmly packed light brown sugar
- ¹/₂ tsp baking powder
- 1¹/₃ cups/200 g all-purpose/plain flour
- 1³/₄ cups/430 ml sweetened condensed milk
- ¹/₈ tsp salt
- 1 cup/100 g finely chopped peanuts

BALKAN COOKIES

Makes: 20 cookies	
Preparation: 45'	
Cooking: 15–20'	
Level of difficulty: 2	

SYRUP
- 1 cup/200 g sugar
- 1 tbsp water
- 1 vanilla bean
- 3 cloves

COOKIES
- ¾ cup/180 g butter
- 1 cup/200 g sugar
- 2 large egg yolks
- 1¼ cups/180 g all-purpose/plain flour
- ¼ tsp baking soda

Syrup: Bring the sugar, water, vanilla bean, and cloves to a boil. Boil for 15 minutes. • Wash down the pan sides with a pastry brush dipped in cold water to prevent sugar crystals from forming. Cook, without stirring, until the mixture reaches 238°F (114°C) or the soft-ball stage. • Cookies: Preheat the oven to 325°F/170°C/gas 3. • Beat the butter and sugar in a large bowl with an electric mixer at high speed until creamy. • Add the egg yolks, one at a time, until just blended after each addition. • With mixer at low speed, gradually beat in the the flour and baking soda. • Roll to ¼-inch (5-mm) thick on parchment paper. Refrigerate for 15 minutes. • Use a pastry cutter to cut out 1-inch (2.5-cm) disks. Lay them on a cookie sheet covered with waxed paper. • Bake for 15–20 minutes, or until golden brown. • Cool the cookies on the sheet. • Serve in the lukewarm syrup.

309

FRUIT AND NUT TURNOVERS

Preheat the oven to 400°F/200°C/gas 6. •
Butter a large baking sheet. • Sift the flour into
a large bowl. • Use your fingertips to rub in the
butter and cream cheese. Shape into a ball.
• Cover with a clean cloth and refrigerate
overnight. • Divide the dough into 3 pieces. Roll
out to $1/4$-inch (5-mm) thick. • Cut the dough into
2–3-inch (5–8-cm) squares. • Mix the jam, walnuts,
and egg in a small bowl until well blended.
• Spoon a teaspoonful of the filling in the center
of each piece of dough. Fold the dough over the
filling to form small triangles. • Bake for 12–15
minutes, or until lightly browned. • Dust with the
confectioners' sugar.

Makes: 12 cookies
Preparation: 10'
Cooking: 12–15'
Level of difficulty: 1

- **2 cups/300 g all-purpose/plain flour**
- **$2/3$ cup/150 g butter**
- **1 cup/250 g cream cheese, softened**

FILLING
- **1 cup/300 g apple or pineapple jam**
- **1 cup/100 g finely ground walnuts**
- **1 large egg, lightly beaten**
- **$1/2$ cup/75 g confectioners'/icing sugar, to dust**

JUST COOKIES

Makes: 25 cookies

Preparation: 20'

Cooking: 5–7'

Level of difficulty: 1

- 1¼ cups/125 g coarsely chopped hazelnuts
- ⅔ cup/140 g granulated sugar
- 3 tbsp all-purpose/plain flour
- 1 tbsp cornstarch/cornflour
- ⅛ tsp salt
- 3 tbsp butter, melted
- 1 tsp vanilla extract/essence
- 1 tsp ground cinnamon
- 3 large egg whites, lightly beaten

Stir together the hazelnuts, sugar, flour, cornstarch, and salt in a large bowl. • Add the butter, vanilla, and cinnamon. • Stir in the egg whites. • Refrigerate for 30 minutes. • Preheat the oven to 400°F/200°C/gas 6. • Line two cookie sheets with aluminum foil. • Drop ½ tablespoons of the dough 2 inches (5 cm) apart onto the prepared cookie sheets. • Bake for 5–7 minutes, or until golden brown. • Transfer to racks to cool.

PIEDMONT TRUFFLES

Preheat the oven to 350°F/180°C/gas 4. •
Butter two cookie sheets. • Sift the flour and
salt into a large bowl. • Beat the butter and sugar
in a large bowl with an electric mixer at high speed
until creamy. • Add the vanilla. • Stir the ground
hazelnuts and the dry ingredients into the mixture.
• Form the dough into balls the size of marbles and
place 1 inch (2.5 cm) apart on the prepared cookie
sheets. • Bake for 12–15 minutes, or until firm.
• Transfer to racks to cool. • Roll in the cocoa until
well coated.

Makes: 24 cookies

Preparation: 20'

Cooking: 12–15'

Level of difficulty: 1

- ²⁄₃ cup/100 g all-purpose/plain flour
- ⅛ tsp salt
- ½ cup/125 g butter, softened
- 2 tbsp granulated sugar
- 1 tsp vanilla extract/essence
- 1 cup/150 g finely ground hazelnuts
- ⅓ cup/50 g unsweetened cocoa powder

HAZELNUT COOKIES

Makes: 26 cookies

Preparation: 25'

Cooking: 15–20'

Level of difficulty: 1

- 2½ cups/250 g finely chopped hazelnuts
- 1 large egg, lightly beaten
- ¾ cup/150 g granulated sugar
- ½ tsp orange liqueur
- ½ tsp fresh lemon juice
- ½ tsp vanilla extract/essence
- ⅛ tsp salt
- 13 candied cherries, cut in half
- 26 chocolate-coated coffee beans

Preheat the oven to 350°F/180°C/gas 4. • Line two cookie sheets with parchment paper. • Use a wooden spoon to mix the hazelnuts, egg, sugar, orange liqueur, lemon juice, vanilla, and salt until a stiff dough has formed. • Form the dough into balls the size of walnuts and place 1 inch (2.5 cm) apart on the prepared cookie sheets. • Decorate with cherry halves. • Bake, one sheet at a time, for 15–20 minutes, or until just golden at the edges. • Transfer to racks and let cool completely. • Decorate the cookies with the coffee beans.

Replace the hazelnuts with the same quantity of finely chopped almonds for a delicious variation.

TWEEDLEDEE COOKIES

Preheat the oven to 375°F/190°C/gas 5. •
Butter two cookie sheets. • Sift the flour,
baking powder, cinnamon, ginger, and salt into a
large bowl. • Beat the butter, shortening, and
brown sugar in a large bowl with an electric mixer
at high speed until creamy. • Add the eggs,
beating until just blended. • Mix in the dry
ingredients, raisins, and walnuts. • Drop teaspoons
of the dough 1 inch (2.5 cm) apart onto the
prepared cookie sheets. • Bake for 8–10 minutes,
or until just lightly browned at the edges. • Transfer
the cookies to racks to cool. • Milk Frosting: Mix
the confectioners' sugar and enough milk in a small
bowl to make a drizzling consistency. Drizzle the
frosting over the cookies.

Makes:	40 cookies
Preparation:	25'
Cooking:	8–10'
Level of difficulty:	1

- 2½ cups/375 g all-purpose/plain flour
- 1½ tsp baking powder
- ½ tsp ground cinnamon
- ¼ tsp ground ginger
- ¼ tsp salt
- ½ cup/125 g butter, softened
- ½ cup/125 g vegetable shortening
- 2 large eggs
- 1 cup/200 g firmly packed dark brown sugar
- ½ cup/90 g raisins
- ½ cup/50 g coarsely chopped walnuts

MILK FROSTING
- 1½ cups/225 g confectioners'/icing sugar
- ½ cup/125 ml milk or more as needed

Makes: 32 cookies

Preparation: 40' + 30'
to chill

Cooking: 8–10'

Level of difficulty: 2

- 1⅓ cups/200 g all-purpose/plain flour
- 1 tsp baking powder
- ⅛ tsp salt
- ½ cup/125 g butter, softened
- ½ cup/100 g granulated sugar
- 1 tsp ground aniseeds
- 1 tsp finely grated lemon zest
- 1 large egg + 1 large egg yolk + 1 large egg white
- 2 tbsp + 1 tsp milk
- 4 tbsp sesame seeds

ORTHODOX COOKIES

Sift the flour, baking powder, and salt into a medium bowl. • Beat the butter and sugar in a large bowl with an electric mixer at high speed until creamy. • Add the aniseeds and lemon zest. • With mixer at high speed, beat the whole egg and egg yolk and 2 tablespoons milk until frothy in a large bowl. • Beat the egg mixture into the batter. • Mix in the dry ingredients to form a smooth dough. • Divide the dough in half. • Form into 8-inch (20-cm) logs, wrap in plastic wrap, and refrigerate for at least 30 minutes. • Preheat the oven to 375°F/ 190°C/gas 5. • Line two cookie sheets with parchment paper. • Discard the plastic wrap. • Slice the dough ½ inch (1 cm) thick. • Roll each slice into a 6-inch (15-cm) log and form into an S-shape, flattening it slightly. • Place the cookies 1 inch (2.5 cm) apart on the prepared cookie sheets. • Mix the egg white and remaining milk in a small bowl. • Brush over the cookies and sprinkle with sesame seeds. • Bake for 8–10 minutes, or until just golden at the edges. • Transfer to racks and let cool.

BARMAN'S COOKIES

Preheat the oven to 375°F/190°C/gas 5. • Line two cookie sheets with parchment paper. • Sift the flour and baking powder into a large bowl. • Beat the butter, shortening, and brown sugar in a large bowl with an electric mixer at high speed until creamy. • Add the vanilla and egg, beating until just blended. • Mix in the dry ingredients and peanuts. • Drop teaspoons of the dough 2 inches (5 cm) apart onto the prepared cookie sheets. • Bake for 8–10 minutes, or until firm to the touch. • Transfer to racks to cool.

Makes: 20–25 cookies

Preparation: 20'

Cooking: 8–10'

Level of difficulty: 1

- 1 cup/150 g all-purpose/plain flour
- 2 tsp baking powder
- 1/2 cup/125 g butter, softened
- 4 tbsp vegetable shortening
- 1/3 cup/70 g firmly packed light brown sugar
- 1/2 tsp vanilla extract/essence
- 1 large egg
- 1/2 cup/75 g salted peanuts

BROWN PEANUT BITES

Makes: 20–25
   cookies

Preparation: 20'

Cooking: 20–25'

Level of difficulty: 1

- 1 cup/150 g all-purpose/plain flour
- 2 tbsp cocoa powder
- 1 tsp baking powder
- 1/8 tsp salt
- 1/2 cup/125 g butter, softened
- 1/2 cup/100 g granulated sugar
- 1 large egg
- 1 cup/100 g coarsely chopped salted peanuts

Preheat the oven to 325°F/170°C/gas 3. • Butter two cookie sheets. • Sift the flour, cocoa, baking powder, and salt into a large bowl. • Beat the butter and sugar in a large bowl with an electric mixer at high speed until creamy. • Add the egg, beating until just blended. • Mix in the dry ingredients, followed by the peanuts. • Drop teaspoons of the dough 1 inch (2.5 cm) apart onto the prepared cookie sheet. • Bake for 20–25 minutes, or until crisp and golden brown. • Cool on the sheets until the cookies firm slightly. • Transfer to racks to cool.

WALNUT GINGER COOKIES

Preheat the oven to 375°F/190°C/gas 5. • Butter three cookie sheets. • Sift the flour, baking soda, ginger, and salt into a medium bowl. • Beat the brown sugar, corn syrup, water, and egg in a large bowl with an electric mixer at high speed until well blended. • Stir in the dry ingredients, cherries, and walnuts. • Drop teaspoons of the dough 2 inches (5 cm) apart onto the prepared cookie sheets. • Bake, one sheet at a time, for 10–12 minutes, or until just golden at the edges. • Transfer to racks to cool.

Makes: 30 cookies

Preparation: 20'

Cooking: 10–12'

Level of difficulty: 1

- **2 cups/300 g all-purpose/plain flour**
- **1 tbsp baking soda**
- **1 tbsp ground ginger**
- **¼ tsp salt**
- **1 cup/200 g firmly packed light brown sugar**
- **3 tbsp light corn syrup/golden syrup**
- **3 tbsp water**
- **1 large egg**
- **½ cup/50 g finely chopped candied cherries**
- **½ cup/50 g finely chopped walnuts**

GLENFIELD SQUARES

Makes: 30 squares

Preparation: 45' + 4 h to set

Level of difficulty: 1

- 2 cups/400 g granulated sugar
- 2/3 cup/150 ml milk
- 2/3 cup/150 g butter, cut up
- 3 oz/90 g semisweet/dark chocolate, coarsely chopped
- 2 tbsp honey
- 1/3 cup/50 g pistachios, crushed
- 1 cup/150 g old-fashioned rolled oats

Butter a 9-inch (23-cm) square baking pan. • Stir the sugar, milk, butter, chocolate, and honey in a large saucepan over low heat until the ingredients have blended. • Wash down the sides of the pan with a pastry brush dipped in cold water to prevent sugar crystals from forming. Cook, without stirring, until the mixture reaches 238°F (114°C), or the soft-ball stage. • Remove from the heat and let cool for 5 minutes. • Stir in the pistachios and oats until creamy. • Pour the mixture into the prepared pan. • Use a sharp knife to score into 30 squares. • Let stand for at least 4 hours, or until firm.

LIVINGSTON'S DOUBLE CHOCOLATE COOKIES

Makes: 20 cookies

Preparation: 20'

Cooking: 20–25'

Level of difficulty: 1

- ⅔ cup/100 g all-purpose/plain flour
- ½ tsp baking powder
- ⅛ tsp salt
- 6 oz/180 g semisweet/dark chocolate, coarsely chopped
- 6 oz/180 g white chocolate, coarsely chopped
- ½ cup/125 g butter, cut up
- 3 large eggs
- 1 cup/200 g granulated sugar
- 1 tbsp freeze-dried coffee granules
- 1 tsp almond extract/essence
- 3 cups/300 g coarsely chopped almonds
- 1 cup/180 g white chocolate chips

Preheat the oven to 325°F/170°C/gas 3. • Set out two cookie sheets. • Sift the flour, baking powder, and salt into a large bowl. • Melt the semisweet and white chocolates and butter in a double boiler over barely simmering water. • Beat the eggs and sugar in a large bowl with an electric mixer at high speed until pale and thick. • Beat in the chocolate mixture, coffee granules, and almond extract. • Mix in the dry ingredients, almonds, and white chocolate chips. • Drop tablespoons of the dough 3 inches (8 cm) apart onto the cookie sheets. • Bake for 20–25 minutes, or until lightly cracked on top. • Transfer to racks and let cool.

BRANDY SPICE COOKIES

Preheat the oven to 350°F/180°C/gas 4. • Butter two cookie sheets. • Plump the raisins in the brandy in a small bowl for 15 minutes, or until almost all the liquid has been absorbed. • Sift the flour, cinnamon, nutmeg, baking soda, and salt into a medium bowl. • Beat the butter and granulated and brown sugars in a large bowl with an electric mixer at high speed until creamy. • Mix in the milk, raisin mixture, dry ingredients, and orange zest. • Drop teaspoons of the dough 1 inch (2.5 cm) apart onto the prepared cookie sheets. • Bake for 10–15 minutes, or until just golden. • Cool on the sheets until the cookies firm slightly. • Transfer to racks to finish cooling.

Makes: 24–30 cookies

Preparation: 20' + 15' to plump the raisins

Cooking: 10–15'

Level of difficulty: 1

- ⅓ cup/60 g raisins
- 2 tbsp brandy
- 1½ cups/225 g all-purpose/plain flour
- 1 tsp ground cinnamon
- 1 tsp freshly grated nutmeg
- ½ tsp baking soda
- ⅛ tsp salt
- ¾ cup/180 g butter, softened
- ⅔ cup/140 g granulated sugar
- ¼ cup/50 g firmly packed dark brown sugar
- 4 tbsp milk
- grated zest of 1 orange

PECAN CINNAMON COOKIES

Makes: 20–25
  cookies

Preparation: 20'

Cooking: 10–15'

Level of difficulty: 1

- 1¼ cups/180 g all-purpose/plain flour
- 1 tsp baking powder
- ⅛ tsp salt
- ½ cup/125 g butter, softened
- ⅔ cup/140 g granulated sugar
- 1 large egg
- ¾ cup/75 g finely chopped pecans
- 2 tsp ground cinnamon

Preheat the oven to 375°F/190°C/gas 5. • Butter two cookie sheets. • Sift the flour, baking powder, and salt into a medium bowl. • Beat the butter and sugar in a large bowl with an electric mixer at high speed until creamy. • Add the egg, beating until just blended. • Mix in the dry ingredients to form a smooth dough. • Mix the pecans and cinnamon in a small bowl. • Form the dough into balls the size of walnuts and roll them in the nut mixture until well coated. • Place the cookies 2 inches (5 cm) apart on the prepared cookie sheets. • Bake for 10–15 minutes, or until golden. • Transfer to racks to cool.

SPICE AND HONEY GINGER ROUNDS

Preheat the oven to 325°F/170°C/gas 3. • Line two cookie sheets with parchment paper. • Sift the flour, baking powder, baking soda, ground ginger, cinnamon, and salt into a large bowl. Stir in the brown sugar. • Heat the butter, corn syrup, and molasses over low heat until the butter has melted. • Remove from the heat and add the egg, beating until just blended. • Stir in the crystallized ginger. • Beat the butter mixture into the dry ingredients with an electric mixer at low speed until well blended. • Drop teaspoons of the dough $1^1/_2$ inches (4 cm) apart onto the prepared cookie sheets. Use a fork to flatten them slightly. • Bake for 15–20 minutes, or until golden brown. • Cool the cookies on the cookie sheets for 5 minutes. Use a metal spatula to transfer to racks and let cool completely. • Ginger Frosting: Mix the confectioners' sugar, ginger, cocoa, water, and coconut oil to make a smooth paste. Spread the frosting over the cookies.

The irresistible taste of ginger shines through in these scrumptious cookies.

Makes: 35 cookies
Preparation: 30'
Cooking: 15–20'
Level of difficulty: 2

- 1½ cups/225 g all-purpose/plain flour
- 1 tsp baking powder
- 1 tsp baking soda
- 1 tsp ground ginger
- ¼ tsp ground cinnamon
- ⅛ tsp salt
- ½ cup/100 g firmly packed dark brown sugar
- 6 tbsp butter
- 3 tbsp dark corn syrup/golden syrup
- 3 tbsp dark molasses/treacle
- 1 large egg, lightly beaten
- ½ cup/50 g finely chopped crystallized ginger

GINGER FROSTING

- ½ cup/75 g confectioners'/icing sugar
- ⅛ tsp ground ginger
- ¼ tsp unsweetened cocoa powder
- 1 tbsp hot water
- 1 tsp coconut oil or coconut extract

HILTON SQUARES

Preheat the oven to 325°F/170°C/gas 3. • Butter a 13 x 9-inch (33 x 23-cm) baking pan. • Sift the flour, ginger, cream of tartar, baking soda, and salt into a large bowl. • Use a pastry blender to cut in the butter until the mixture resembles coarse crumbs. • Stir in the oats and brown sugar. • Firmly press the mixture into the prepared pan to form a smooth, even layer, pressing down with a floured fork. • Bake for 20–30 minutes, or until lightly browned. • Cool completely before cutting into bars.

Makes: 36–45 bars

Preparation: 20'

Cooking: 20–30'

Level of difficulty: 1

- 2 cups/300 g whole-wheat flour
- 1 tbsp ground ginger
- 1½ tsp cream of tartar
- ¾ tsp baking soda
- ⅛ tsp salt
- 1¼ cups/310 g butter, cut up
- ⅓ cup/50 g old-fashioned rolled oats
- 1½ cups/300 g firmly packed light brown sugar

LOMBARDY COOKIES

Makes: 36 cookies

Preparation: 25'

Cooking: 15–20'

Level of difficulty: 1

- **1 tbsp baking soda**
- **½ cup/125 ml milk**
- **3⅓ cups/500 g all-purpose/plain flour**
- **6 tbsp extra-virgin olive oil**
- **¾ cup/150 g granulated sugar**
- **½ cup/50 g coarsely chopped toasted hazelnuts**
- **4 tbsp grape juice or vincotto**

Preheat the oven to 350°F/180°C/gas 4. • Butter three cookie sheets. • Mix the baking soda and milk in a small bowl. • Use a wooden spoon to mix the flour, olive oil, sugar, hazelnuts, grape juice, and baking soda mixture to make a soft dough. • Form the dough into balls the size of walnuts and place 1 inch (2.5 cm) apart on the prepared cookie sheets, flattening them slightly. • Bake, one sheet at a time, for 15–20 minutes, or until just golden. • Transfer to racks and let cool completely.

INDIAN LADY COOKIES

Butter two cookie sheets. • Sift the flour, cornstarch, cardamom, and salt into a large bowl. • Beat the eggs, sugar, and vanilla in a large bowl with an electric mixer at high speed until pale and thick. • Mix in the dry ingredients. • Drop teaspoons of the dough 2 inches (5 cm) apart onto the prepared cookie sheets.

Cardamom is available in ethnic food stores or well-stocked supermarkets.

334

• Cover with a clean kitchen towel and let rest for 12 hours. • Preheat the oven to 300°F/150°C/gas 2. • Bake for 25–35 minutes, or until golden brown. • Transfer to racks and let cool.

Makes: 25–30 cookies

Preparation: 20' + 12 h

Cooking: 25–35'

Level of difficulty: 1

- ¾ cup/125 g all-purpose/plain flour
- ¾ cup/125 g cornstarch/cornflour
- 1 tbsp ground cardamom
- ⅛ tsp salt
- 3 large eggs
- 1 cup/200 g granulated sugar
- ½ tsp vanilla extract/essence

RUSSIAN HONEY COOKIES

Makes: 24–30
cookies

Preparation: 40' + 60'
to chill

Cooking: 15–20'

Level of difficulty: 1

- 3 cups/450 g all-purpose/plain flour
- 1 tsp baking soda
- 1/2 tsp ground cinnamon
- 1/2 tsp ground cardamom
- 1/4 tsp ground nutmeg
- 1/8 tsp salt
- 2 large eggs
- 1 cup/200 g granulated sugar
- 1 cup/250 ml honey
- 1/2 tsp vanilla extract/essence
- 2 tbsp confectioners'/icing sugar, to dust

Sift the flour, baking soda, cinnamon, cardamom, nutmeg, and salt into a medium bowl. • Beat the eggs and sugar in a large bowl with an electric mixer at high speed until pale and thick. • Heat the honey in a small saucepan over low heat until liquid. • Stir the honey and vanilla into the beaten egg mixture. • Mix in the dry ingredients to form a stiff dough. • Cover with plastic wrap and refrigerate for 1 hour. • Preheat the oven to 375°F/190°C/gas 5. • Butter two cookie sheets. • Roll out the dough on a lightly floured surface to a thickness of 1/2 inch (1 cm). • Use a 2-inch (5-cm) cookie cutter to cut out the cookies. • Gather the dough scraps, re-roll, and continue cutting out cookies until all the dough is used. • Use a spatula to transfer the cookies to the prepared cookie sheets, placing them 2 inches (5 cm) apart. • Bake for 15–20 minutes, or until just golden. • Cool on the sheets until the cookies firm slightly. • Transfer to racks to finish cooling. • Dust with the confectioners' sugar.

LEMON SNACKING COOKIES

Preheat the oven to 350°F/180°C/gas 4. •
Butter two cookie sheets. • Beat the butter and
brown sugar in a large bowl with an electric mixer
at high speed until creamy. • Add the egg yolk,
beating until just blended. • Mix in the flour, lemon
zest and juice, apricots, and pecans. • Press the
dough into a disk, wrap in plastic wrap, and
refrigerate for 30 minutes. • Roll out the dough on
a lightly floured surface to a thickness of $1/4$ inch
(5 mm). • Use a 2-inch (5-cm) cookie cutter to cut
out the cookies. Gather the dough scraps, re-roll,
and continue cutting out cookies until all the dough
is used. • Use a spatula to transfer the cookies to
the prepared cookie sheets. • Bake for 15–20
minutes, or until lightly browned. • Transfer to
racks and let cool completely.

Makes: 16 cookies

Preparation: 40' + 30' to chill

Cooking: 15–20'

Level of difficulty: 1

- **6 tbsp butter, softened**
- **$1/3$ cup/70 g firmly packed light brown sugar**
- **1 large egg yolk**
- **$1\frac{1}{4}$ cups/180 g whole-wheat flour**
- **grated zest and juice of $1/2$ lemon**
- **$1/2$ cup/50 g finely chopped dried apricots**
- **$1/2$ cup/50 g coarsely chopped pecans**

FAREWELL COOKIES

Preheat the oven to 375°F/190°C/gas 5. • Line two cookie sheets with parchment paper.
• Sift the flour, baking powder, cinnamon, nutmeg, cloves, and salt into a large bowl. • Beat the oil, honey, and peanut butter in a large bowl with an electric mixer at high speed until well blended.
• Mix in the dry ingredients, oats, and raisins.
• Drop tablespoons of the dough 1 inch (2.5 cm) apart onto the prepared cookie sheets. • Bake for 8–10 minutes, or until golden brown. • Cool on the sheets until the cookies firm slightly. • Transfer to racks to finish cooling.

Makes: 30 cookies

Preparation: 20'

Cooking: 8–10'

Level of difficulty: 1

- 1²⁄₃ cups/250 g all-purpose/plain flour
- 1 tsp baking powder
- ½ tsp ground cinnamon
- ½ tsp ground nutmeg
- ¼ tsp ground cloves
- ½ tsp salt
- 6 tbsp sunflower or canola oil
- 6 tbsp honey
- 1 cup/250 ml smooth peanut butter
- ½ cup/75 g old-fashioned rolled oats
- ½ cup/90 g raisins

FALL CRESCENTS

Makes: 12 cookies

Preparation: 30' + 30' to chill

Cooking: 15–20'

Level of difficulty: 2

PASTRY
- 1½ cups/225 g all-purpose/plain flour
- ⅛ tsp salt
- 1 tsp sugar
- ½ tsp ground fennel seeds
- ½ cup/125 g cold butter, cut up
- 2 tbsp ice water or more as needed

FILLING
- 2 tsp superfine/caster sugar
- ½ tsp cardamom seeds, lightly crushed
- ¼ tsp ground cinnamon
- ¼ tsp allspice
- 2 cups/200 g chopped walnuts
- 2 tbsp honey
- finely grated zest of 1 lemon
- 1 large egg
- 2 tbsp confectioners'/icing sugar, to dust

Pastry: Sift the flour and salt into a large bowl. Stir in the sugar and fennel seeds. • Use a pastry blender to cut in the butter until the mixture resembles fine crumbs. • Add enough water to form a soft, but not sticky, dough. • Turn the dough out onto a lightly floured surface and knead once or twice. Shape into a ball, wrap in plastic wrap, and refrigerate for 30 minutes. • Filling: Mix the superfine sugar, cardamom seeds, cinnamon, allspice, walnuts, honey, and lemon zest in a medium bowl. • Preheat the oven to 375°F/190°C/gas 5. • Set out a cookie sheet. • Roll out the dough on a lightly floured surface to a thickness of ¼ inch (5 mm). Use a round cutter to stamp out 4-inch (10-cm) circles. • Fill each dough circle with 2 teaspoonfuls of the filling. Fold over to make a half moon, sealing the edges with a fork. • Brush with the beaten egg. • Place on the cookie sheet, spacing 1 inch (2.5 cm) apart. • Bake for 15–20 minutes, or until pale golden. Transfer to racks to cool. • Dust with the confectioners' sugar.

GINGER CRUNCHIES

Preheat the oven to 350°F/180°C/gas 4. •
Butter two cookie sheets. • Sift the flour,
ginger, baking powder, baking soda, and salt into a
large bowl. • Stir in the brown sugar. • Melt the
butter with the corn syrup in a small saucepan over
low heat. • Remove from the heat and let cool.
• Stir the butter mixture into the dry ingredients.
• Add the egg and mix to make a stiff dough.
• Form the dough into twenty balls the size of
walnuts and place 2 inches (5 cm) apart on the
prepared cookie sheets. • Bake for 12–15
minutes, or until just golden and firm to the touch.
• Cool the cookies on the sheets for 5 minutes.
• Transfer to racks and let cool completely.

Makes: 20 cookies

Preparation: 20'

Cooking: 12–15'

Level of difficulty: 1

- 1¼ cups/180 g all-purpose/plain flour
- 2 tsp ground ginger
- 1 tsp baking powder
- ½ tsp baking soda
- ⅛ tsp salt
- ⅓ cup/70 g firmly packed light brown sugar
- 4 tbsp butter, softened
- 3 tbsp light corn syrup/golden syrup
- 1 large egg

ORANGE-GLAZED NUT COOKIES

Makes: 35–40 cookies

Preparation: 45' + 60' to chill and set

Cooking: 12–15'

Level of difficulty: 2

- 1 large egg white
- $^1/_8$ tsp salt
- $^1/_2$ cup/100 g superfine/caster sugar
- 1 cup/150 g finely ground hazelnuts + more as needed
- 1 cup/150 g finely ground almonds+ more as needed
- $^1/_2$ cup/50 g coarsely chopped pistachios
- 2 tsp finely chopped candied peel

ORANGE GLAZE
- $^2/_3$ cup/100 ml confectioners'/ icing sugar
- 1 tbsp orange juice
- grated zest of $^1/_2$ orange

Beat the egg white and salt in a large bowl with an electric mixer at medium speed until frothy. • With mixer at high speed, gradually add the superfine sugar, beating until stiff, glossy peaks form. • Use a large rubber spatula to fold in the hazelnuts, almonds, pistachios, and candied peel to form a stiff dough. Add more ground nuts if the dough is very sticky. • Press the dough into a disk, wrap in plastic wrap, and refrigerate for 30 minutes. • Preheat the oven to 300°F/150°C/ gas 2. • Line three cookie sheets with parchment paper. • Roll out the dough between sheets of waxed paper dusted with confectioners' sugar to a thickness of $^1/_4$ inch (5 mm). • Cut into 2 x $^3/_4$-inch (5 x 4-cm) strips. • Gather the dough scraps, re-roll, and continue cutting out cookies until all the dough is used. • Use a spatula to transfer the cookies to the prepared cookie sheets, placing them 1 inch (2.5 cm) apart. • Bake, one sheet at a time, for 12–15 minutes, or until golden brown. • Transfer to racks to cool. • Orange Glaze: Mix the confectioners' sugar, orange juice, and orange zest in a small bowl. • Dip the cookies halfway into the glaze and let stand for 30 minutes until set.

BEST-EVER GINGER COOKIES

Sift the flour, ginger, baking soda, and salt into a large bowl. • Stir in the sugar, candied peel, and lemon zest. • Heat the butter and molasses in a small saucepan over low heat until liquid. • Mix the molasses mixture into the dry ingredients to form a stiff dough. • Press the dough into a disk, wrap in plastic wrap, and refrigerate for 30 minutes. • Preheat the oven to 350°F/180°C/gas 4. • Butter two cookie sheets. • Roll out the dough on a lightly floured surface to a thickness of $^1/_8$ inch (3 mm). • Use a 2-inch (5-cm) cookie cutter to cut out the cookies. Gather the dough scraps, re-roll, and continue cutting out cookies until all the dough is used. • Use a spatula to transfer the cookies to the prepared cookie sheets, placing them 2 inches (5 cm) apart. • Bake for 8–10 minutes, or until just golden. • Cool on the sheets until the cookies firm slightly. • Transfer to racks to cool.

Makes: 24–30 cookies

Preparation: 40' + 30' to chill

Cooking: 8–10'

Level of difficulty: 1

- 1$^2/_3$ cups/250 g all-purpose/plain flour
- 2 tsp ground ginger
- $^1/_4$ tsp baking soda
- $^1/_8$ tsp salt
- $^2/_3$ cup/140 g granulated sugar
- 1 cup/100 g finely chopped mixed candied peel
- $^1/_2$ tsp grated lemon zest
- $^1/_2$ cup/125 g butter, cut up
- 4 tbsp light molasses/treacle

FAR EAST COOKIES

Sift the flour, baking powder, ginger, and salt into a large bowl. • Use a pastry blender to cut in the butter until the mixture resembles fine crumbs. • Add the egg, beating until just blended. • Stir in the sugar to form a soft dough. • Turn the dough out onto a lightly floured surface and knead until smooth. • Form the dough into a long log 2 inches (5 cm) in diameter, wrap in plastic wrap, and refrigerate for at least 30 minutes. • Preheat the oven to 375°F/190°C/gas 5. • Butter three cookie sheets. • Slice the dough 1/2 inch (1 cm) thick and place 1 inch (2.5 cm) apart on the prepared cookie sheets. • Bake, one sheet at a time, for 8–10 minutes, or until just golden. • Cool on the sheets until the cookies firm slightly. • Transfer to racks to finish cooling.

Makes: 35 cookies

Preparation: 40' + 30' to chill

Cooking: 8–10'

Level of difficulty: 1

- 1²/₃ cups/250 g all-purpose/plain flour
- 1 tsp baking powder
- 2 tsp ground ginger
- ⅛ tsp salt
- ½ cup/125 g butter, cut up
- 1 large egg, lightly beaten
- ¾ cup/150 g granulated sugar

VISITORS' MAPLE COOKIES

Makes: 30 cookies

Preparation: 40' + 30' to chill

Cooking: 8–10'

Level of difficulty: 1

- ½ cup/125 g butter, softened
- ½ cup/100 g granulated sugar
- 2 tsp light brown sugar
- 2 tsp pure maple syrup
- 1⅓ cups/200 g all-purpose/plain flour
- 1 tsp freeze-dried coffee granules
- ⅔ cup/60 g finely chopped walnuts
- ⅛ tsp salt

Beat the butter, granulated and brown sugars, and maple syrup in a large bowl with an electric mixer at high speed until creamy. • Mix in the flour, coffee, walnuts, and salt to form a soft dough. • Turn the dough out onto a lightly floured surface and knead until smooth. • Press the dough into a disk, wrap in plastic wrap, and refrigerate for 30 minutes. • Preheat the oven to 375°F/190°C/gas 5. • Butter and flour two cookie sheets. • Roll out the dough to a thickness of ⅛ inch (3 mm). • Use a 3-inch (8-cm) cookie cutter to cut out the cookies. • Gather the dough scraps, re-roll, and continue cutting out cookies until all the dough is used. • Use a spatula to transfer the cookies to the prepared cookie sheets, placing them 1 inch (2.5 cm) apart. • Bake for 8–10 minutes, or until barely colored. • Transfer to racks to cool.

FILLED HAZELNUT CRUNCHIES

Makes: 30 cookies

Preparation: 40' + 60' to chill

Cooking: 12–15'

Level of difficulty: 2

- 3 cups/450 g all-purpose/plain flour
- 1/8 tsp salt
- 1 cup/200 g superfine/caster sugar
- 1 1/3 cups/130 g finely ground hazelnuts
- 1 cup/250 g cold butter, cut up
- 2 large eggs, lightly beaten
- 1/2 cup/160 g strawberry or raspberry preserves
- 1/4 cup/50 g vanilla sugar

Refrigerate three cookie sheets. • Sift the flour and salt into a large bowl. Stir in the superfine sugar and hazelnuts. • Dot the butter evenly over the mixture. • Use a pastry blender to cut in the butter until the mixture resembles coarse crumbs. • Add the eggs, beating until just blended. • Turn out onto a lightly floured surface and work into a smooth dough. Knead gently once or twice (too much kneading causes cracks when cutting out shapes). • Shape into a ball, wrap in plastic wrap, and refrigerate for at least 1 hour. • Roll out small portions of dough to a thickness of 1/4 inch (5 mm). • Use a cutter to stamp into 1-inch (2.5-cm) circles. Gather the dough scraps, re-roll, and continue cutting out cookies until all the dough is used. • Use a metal spatula to transfer the cookies onto one of the chilled baking sheets, placing them 1 1/2 inches (4 cm) apart. • Preheat the oven to 375°F/190°C/gas 5. • Bake, one batch at a time, for 12–15 minutes, or until just golden. • Cool the cookies on the cookie sheets for 5 minutes. • Spread each cookie with a little preserves and sandwich them together. • Dust with the vanilla sugar.

ALMOND JUMBLES

Beat the butter and sugar in a large bowl with an electric mixer at high speed until creamy. • Mix in the flour, almonds, and salt. • Add the lemon juice to form a stiff dough. • Press the dough into a disk, wrap in plastic wrap, and refrigerate for 30 minutes. • Preheat the oven to 375°F/190°C/gas 5. • Butter a cookie sheet. • Roll out the dough on a lightly floured surface to a thickness of ¹/₄ inch (5 mm). • Use a 2-inch (5-cm) cookie cutter to cut out the cookies. Gather the dough scraps, re-roll, and continue cutting out cookies until all the dough is used. • Use a spatula to transfer the cookies to the prepared cookie sheet, placing them 2 inches (5 cm) apart. • Bake for 12–15 minutes, or until pale golden. • Cool on the sheet until the cookies firm slightly. • Transfer to racks to cool.

Makes: 12–16 cookies

Preparation: 40' + 30' to chill

Cooking: 12–15'

Level of difficulty: 1

- ½ cup/125 g butter, softened
- ¾ cup/150 g granulated sugar
- 1½ cups/225 g all-purpose/plain flour
- ²/₃ cup/100 g finely ground almonds
- ⅛ tsp salt
- juice of 1 lemon

CINNAMON HEARTIES

Makes: 32 cookies

Preparation: 40' + 60' to chill

Cooking: 12–15'

Level of difficulty: 1

- 1 2/3 cups/250 g all-purpose/plain flour
- 1/8 tsp salt
- 3/4 cup/180 g butter, softened
- 1/3 cup/70 g granulated sugar
- 1 tsp almond extract/essence

TOPPING

- 1/3 cup/70 g superfine/caster sugar
- 1/2 tsp ground cinnamon
- 2/3 cup/100 g coarsely chopped blanched almonds, toasted
- 1 large egg white, lightly beaten

Preheat the oven to 375°F/190°C/gas 5. • Butter three cookie sheets. • Sift the flour and salt into a medium bowl. • Beat the butter and sugar in a large bowl with an electric mixer at high speed until creamy. • Mix in the dry ingredients and almond extract. The mixture should be slightly crumbly. • Refrigerate for at least 1 hour, or until the dough can be formed into a firm, smooth dough. • Roll out the dough on a lightly floured surface to a 12 x 8-inch (30 x 20-cm) rectangle. • Cut into 3 x 1-inch (8 x 2.5-cm) bars. • Transfer the cookies to the prepared cookie sheets, placing them 1/2 inch (1 cm) apart. • Almond Cinnamon Topping: Mix the superfine sugar, cinnamon, and almonds in a small bowl. • Brush the cookies with the beaten egg white and sprinkle with the topping. • Bake, one sheet at a time, for 12–15 minutes, or until just golden. • Cool on the sheet until the cookies firm slightly. Transfer to racks to cool.

FRENCH ALMOND PARCELS

358

Sift the flour, cornstarch, baking powder, and salt into a large bowl. • Stir in the granulated and vanilla sugars and the orange zest. • Use a pastry blender to cut in the butter until the mixture resembles coarse crumbs. • Use a fork to mix in the egg to form a smooth dough. • Press the dough into a disk, wrap in plastic wrap, and refrigerate for 30 minutes. • Set out two cookie sheets. • Roll out the dough on a lightly floured surface to a thickness of $1/8$ inch (3 mm). • Use a 2-inch (5-cm) cookie cutter to cut out the cookies. Gather the dough scraps, re-roll, and continue cutting out cookies until all the dough is used. • Use a spatula to transfer the cookies to the cookie sheets, placing them 2 inches (5 cm) apart. • Filling: Mix the almonds, brown sugar, and orange zest and juice in a small bowl. • Drop $1/2$ teaspoon of the filling onto one half of each cookie. • Fold half of the cookie over the filling to make a crescent-shaped pocket. • Use a fork to seal the edges together and brush with a little milk. • Set aside for 30 minutes. • Preheat the oven to 350°F/180°C/gas 4. • Bake for 8–10 minutes, or until just golden at the edges. • Transfer to racks to cool. • Orange Glaze: Mix the confectioners' sugar with the orange juice. Add enough water to make a runny glaze. Drizzle over the cookies.

Zesty and tongue-tingling, these heavenly cookies are ideal for every occasion.

Makes: 30–35 cookies

Preparation: 40' + 60' to chill and rest

Cooking: 8–10'

Level of difficulty: 2

- 1⅓ cups/200 g all-purpose/plain flour
- ⅓ cup/50 g cornstarch/cornflour
- ½ tsp baking powder
- ⅛ tsp salt
- ⅓ cup/70 g granulated sugar
- 1 tbsp vanilla sugar
- 1 tsp orange zest
- ¾ cup/180 g butter, cut up
- 1 large egg
- Milk, to brush

FILLING
- 1 cup/150 g finely ground almonds
- ⅓ cup/70 g brown sugar
- Grated zest and juice of 1 orange

ORANGE GLAZE
- ⅔ cup/100 g confectioners'/icing sugar
- 1 tbsp orange juice
- 2–3 tsp hot water

JAVA COOKIES

Preheat the oven to 300°F/150°C/gas 2. • Butter a cookie sheet. • Sift the flour, baking powder, and baking soda into a medium bowl. • Beat the butter and sugar in a large bowl with an electric mixer at high speed until creamy. • Add the egg, beating until just blended. • Mix in the dry ingredients, peanuts, corn flakes, and oats to make a stiff dough. • Drop teaspoons of the dough 1 inch (2.5 cm) apart onto the prepared cookie sheet. • Bake for 10–15 minutes, or until lightly browned. • Cool on the sheet until the cookies firm slightly. • Transfer to racks and let cool completely.

Makes: 14–16 cookies

Preparation: 20'

Cooking: 10–15'

Level of difficulty: 1

- 1 cup/150 g all-purpose/plain flour
- ½ tsp baking powder
- ½ tsp baking soda
- ½ cup/125 g butter, softened
- 1 cup/200 g granulated sugar
- 1 large egg, lightly beaten
- ½ cup/75 g salted peanuts
- 1 cup/100 g corn flakes
- 2¼ cups/330 g old-fashioned rolled oats

APRICOT BRANDY MACAROONS

Makes: 20 cookies

Preparation: 55'

Cooking: 20–25'

Level of difficulty: 2

- $^1/_3$ cup/50 g all-purpose/plain flour
- 2 cups/300 g finely ground walnuts
- 3 large egg whites
- $^1/_4$ tsp salt
- $^3/_4$ cup/150 g granulated sugar

FILLING

- 7 oz/200 g white chocolate, coarsely chopped
- 4 tbsp light/double cream
- 2 tbsp apricot brandy
- 1–2 tbsp finely chopped pistachios

Preheat the oven to 275°F/140°C/gas 1. • Butter two cookie sheets. • Sift the flour into a medium bowl. Stir in the walnuts. • Beat the egg whites and salt in a large bowl until frothy. • Beat in the sugar, beating until stiff peaks form. • Fold in the dry ingredients. • Fit a pastry bag with a $^3/_4$-inch (2-cm) plain tip. Fill the pastry bag, twist the opening tightly closed, and squeeze out mounds the size of walnuts spacing them 1 inch (2.5 cm) apart on the sheets. • Bake for 20–25 minutes, or until the cookies are set and lightly browned. • Transfer the macaroons to racks and let cool completely. • Filling: Melt the chocolate with the cream in a double boiler over barely simmering water. • Stir in the brandy. • Plunge the pan into a bowl of ice water and stir until the mixture has cooled. • With mixer at high speed, beat until creamy. • Stick the macaroons together in pairs with the filling. Roll in the pistachios.

Makes: 35–40 cookies

Preparation: 50' + 60' to chill and set

Cooking: 12–15'

Level of difficulty: 2

- 2 cups/300 g all-purpose/plain flour
- 1 tsp baking powder
- 1 tsp ground cinnamon
- 1/2 tsp allspice
- 1/4 tsp ground cloves
- 1/8 tsp salt
- 3 large eggs
- 1 1/2 cups/300 g granulated sugar
- 2 1/2 cups/350 g ground almonds
- 4 oz/125 g semisweet/dark chocolate, grated
- 1/2 cup/50 g finely chopped candied lemon peel
- 1/2 cup/50 g finely chopped candied orange peel
- 1 tsp finely grated lemon zest

CHOCOLATE GLAZE

- 7 oz/200 g semisweet/dark chocolate, coarsely chopped
- 3 tbsp warm water
- 2 tbsp butter

SPICED ALMOND COOKIES

Sift the flour, baking powder, cinnamon, allspice, cloves, and salt into a medium bowl. • Beat the eggs and sugar in a large bowl with an electric mixer at high speed until very pale and thick. • Mix in the dry ingredients, almonds, chocolate, candied lemon and orange peel, and lemon zest to form a smooth dough. • Press the dough into a disk, wrap in plastic wrap, and refrigerate for 30 minutes. • Preheat the oven to 325°F/170°C/gas 3. • Line three cookie sheets with parchment paper. • Roll out the dough on a lightly floured surface to a thickness of 1/4 inch (5 mm). • Cut into 2-inch (5 cm) squares and triangles. Gather the dough scraps, re-roll, and continue cutting out cookies until all the dough is used. • Use a spatula to transfer the cookies to the prepared cookie sheets, placing them 1 inch (2.5 cm) apart. • Bake, one sheet at a time, for 12–15 minutes, or until the edges are firm and the bottoms are lightly browned. • Transfer to racks to cool. • Chocolate Glaze: Melt the chocolate with the water in a double boiler over barely simmering water. • Stir in the butter until smooth. • Drizzle the glaze over the cookies and let stand on parchment paper for 30 minutes until completely set.

ALMOND SQUARES

Toast the whole almonds in a skillet over medium heat for 5–7 minutes, or until lightly golden. • Transfer the almonds to a food processor, add 2 tablespoons of the superfine sugar, and process until finely ground. • Beat the egg whites and salt in a large bowl with an electric mixer at medium speed until frothy. • With mixer at high speed, gradually add the remaining superfine sugar, beating until stiff, glossy peaks form. • Use a large rubber spatula to fold in the toasted ground almond mixture, 2 cups (300 g) finely ground almonds, cashews, and lemon and orange zests to form a stiff dough. • Press the dough into a disk, wrap in plastic wrap, and refrigerate for 30 minutes. • Preheat the oven to 300°F/150°C/ gas 2. • Line four cookie sheets with parchment paper. • Discard the plastic wrap. Roll out the dough on a surface lightly dusted with raw sugar to a thickness of $1/8$ inch (3 mm). • Use a sharp knife to cut the dough into $1^1/2$-inch (4-cm) squares. Gather the dough scraps, re-roll, and continue cutting out cookies until all the dough is used. • Transfer the cookies to the prepared cookie sheets, placing them 1 inch (2.5 cm) apart. • Bake, one sheet at a time, for 12–15 minutes, or until just golden around the edges. • Cool on the sheets until the cookies firm slightly. Transfer to racks to finish cooling. • Mix the confectioners' sugar and water in a small bowl and spread over the cookies. Sprinkle with the sugar crystals.

Makes: 60 cookies

Preparation: 50' + 30' to chill

Cooking: 12–15'

Level of difficulty: 1

- 1 cup/150 g whole almonds
- 1 cup/200 g superfine/caster sugar
- 2 large egg whites
- $1/8$ tsp salt
- 2 cups/300 g finely ground almonds
- $1/2$ cup/50 g coarsely chopped cashew nuts
- 1 tsp finely grated lemon zest
- 1 tsp finely grated orange zest
- 2–3 tbsp raw sugar (such as Barbados or Demerara), for rolling out
- sugar crystals, to decorate
- $1/2$ cup/75 g confectioners'/ icing sugar
- 2 tbsp hot water

HONEY FILLED COOKIES

Makes: 30 cookies

Preparation: 55' + 30' to chill

Cooking: 10–12'

Level of difficulty: 2

- 2¼ cups/330 g all-purpose/plain flour
- ⅔ cup/100 g confectioners'/icing sugar
- ⅛ tsp salt
- 1 cup/250 g butter, softened
- 1 tbsp warm water + more as needed

SPICE HONEY

- 2 cups/400 g firmly packed dark brown sugar
- 1 stick cinnamon
- 2 cloves
- zest of 1 orange, in one piece
- 1 cup/250 ml water
- ¼ tsp white vinegar

Sift the flour, confectioners' sugar, and salt into a large bowl. Use a pastry blender to cut in the butter until the mixture resembles coarse crumbs. Add the water to form a stiff dough. • Press the dough into a disk, wrap in plastic wrap, and refrigerate for 30 minutes. • Preheat the oven to 375°F/190°C/gas 5. • Line two cookie sheets with parchment paper. • Roll out the dough on a lightly floured surface to a thickness of ⅛ inch (3 mm). • Use a 2½-inch (6-cm) cookie cutter to cut out the cookies. Gather the dough scraps, re-roll, and continue cutting out cookies until all the dough is used. • Use a spatula to transfer the cookies to the prepared cookie sheets, spacing them 1 inch (2.5 cm) apart. • Bake for 10–12 minutes, or until just golden. • Transfer to racks and let cool completely. • Spice Honey: Place the brown sugar, cinnamon, cloves, orange zest, and water in a medium saucepan. • Wash down the sides of the pan with a pastry brush dipped in cold water to prevent sugar crystals from forming. Cook, without stirring, until the mixture reaches 238°F (114°C), or the soft-ball stage. • Stir in the vinegar, discard the cloves, cinnamon stick, and orange zest, and remove from the heat. • Let cool completely. • Stick the cookies together in pairs with the spice honey.

GLAZED ALMOND COOKIES

Beat the whole egg and yolk, granulated and vanilla sugars, and salt in a large bowl with an electric mixer at high speed until creamy. • Melt the chocolate in a double boiler over barely simmering water. • Mix in the coffee. • Beat the chocolate mixture into the batter. • Mix in the almonds and baking powder to form a stiff dough, adding more almonds if needed. • Divide the dough in half. Press the dough into two disks, wrap each in plastic wrap, and refrigerate for 30 minutes. • Preheat the oven to 350°F/180°C/ gas 4. • Butter three cookie sheets. • Roll out each dough disk between sheets of waxed paper into an 8 x 5-inch (20 x 13-cm) rectangle. • Cut into 2¹/₂ x ³/₄-inch (6 x 2-cm) strips. • Use a spatula to transfer the cookies to the prepared cookie sheets, placing them 1 inch (2.5 cm) apart. • Glaze: With mixer at medium speed, beat the egg white and salt in a small bowl until frothy. • With mixer at high speed, gradually add the confectioners' sugar until stiff, glossy peaks form. • Spread the glaze evenly over the tops of the cookies. • Bake, one sheet at a time, for 10–12 minutes, or until golden at the edges and the bottoms are lightly browned. • Transfer to racks to cool.

Makes: 30–35 cookies

Preparation: 45' + 30' to chill

Cooking: 10–12'

Level of difficulty: 1

- 1 large egg + 1 large egg yolk
- ²/₃ cup/140 g granulated sugar
- 1 tbsp vanilla sugar
- 1 tsp freeze-dried coffee granules dissolved in 1 tsp warm water
- ¹/₈ tsp salt
- 2 oz/60 g semisweet/dark chocolate, coarsely chopped
- 2 cups/300 g finely ground almonds + more as needed
- ¹/₄ tsp baking powder

GLAZE
- 1 large egg white
- ¹/₈ tsp salt
- ¹/₃ cup/50 g confectioners'/ icing sugar

Makes: 50 cookies
Preparation: 45'
Cooking: 15–20'
Level of difficulty: 2

- 4 cups/600 g all-purpose/plain flour
- 1 tsp baking soda
- 1/8 tsp salt
- 1 cup/250 ml honey
- 1 1/2 cups/300 g granulated sugar
- 1 tbsp ground cinnamon
- 1 tsp cloves, very finely chopped
- 1 1/2 cups/150 g chopped blanched almonds
- 1 1/2 cups/150 g chopped unblanched almonds
- 2/3 cup/70 g chopped candied lemon peel
- 2/3 cup/70 g chopped candied orange peel
- 6 tbsp kirsch

GLAZE

- 1 1/3 cups/200 g confectioners'/icing sugar or more as needed
- 1 tbsp hot water or more as needed
- 1 tbsp fresh lemon juice
- 1 tbsp dark rum

RUM GLAZED ALMOND SQUARES

Preheat the oven to 350°F/180°C/gas 4. • Butter and flour two cookie sheets. • Sift the flour, baking soda, and salt into a large bowl. • Heat the honey in a medium saucepan over low heat until liquid. Stir in the sugar, cinnamon, cloves, both almonds, and the candied lemon and orange peel. • Remove from the heat. • Mix in the dry ingredients and kirsch. • Shape the warm mixture into a ball and knead on a lightly floured surface until smooth. • If it is sticky, add more flour. • Roll out the dough to a thickness of 1/4 inch (5 mm). Use a sharp knife to cut into 2-inch (5-cm) rectangles. • Place the rectangles closely together on the prepared baking sheets. • Bake for 15–20 minutes, or until lightly browned. Transfer the cookies to racks and let cool to warm. • Glaze: Mix the confectioners' sugar with the water in a small bowl. Add lemon juice and rum to make a pouring consistency. Add more water if needed. • Thinly brush the glaze on the hot cookies and let cool completely.

VANILLA-GLAZED STARS

Line two cookie sheets with parchment paper. •
Beat the egg whites in a large bowl with an
electric mixer at medium speed until frothy. With
mixer at high speed, gradually add the
confectioners' sugar and lemon juice until stiff,
glossy peaks form. • Spoon 1 cup (250 ml) beaten
whites into a small bowl and set aside in the
refrigerator as a glaze. • Use a large rubber
spatula to fold 3 cups (450 g) almonds, the vanilla
sugar, and vanilla into the large bowl of beaten
whites. Cover with plastic wrap and refrigerate for
30 minutes. • Preheat the oven to 275°F/140°C/
gas 1. • Sprinkle a lightly floured surface with the
remaining ground almonds. Roll out the dough in
small portions to a thickness of $1/2$ inch (1 cm).
• Dip a star cutter into cold water and stamp out
star shapes. Gather the dough scraps, re-roll, and
continue cutting out cookies until all the dough is
used. Use a spatula to transfer the cookies to the
cookie sheets, placing them 1 inch (2.5 cm) apart.
Brush a thin layer of reserved chilled egg white
over each star. • Bake for 25–30 minutes, or until
firm to the touch. • Cool completely on the
cookie sheets.

Makes: 40 cookies

*Preparation: 60' + 30'
to chill*

Cooking: 25–30'

Level of difficulty: 2

- **3 large egg whites**
- **1½ cups/225 g
  confectioners'/
  icing sugar**
- **⅛ tsp cream of
  tartar**
- **4 cups/600 g finely
  ground almonds**
- **2 tsp vanilla sugar**
- **¼ tsp vanilla
  extract/essence**

372

MARZIPAN FILLED HONEY DROPS

Sweet Honey Dough: Sift the all-purpose and rye flours, the baking soda, cinnamon, aniseeds, nutmeg, ginger, and salt into a large bowl. • Heat the honey and sugar in a small saucepan over low heat until the sugar has dissolved completely. Cool for 15 minutes. • Use a wooden spoon to work the honey mixture into the dry ingredients to form a smooth dough. • Cover with a clean kitchen towel and let rest at room temperature for 3 days. • Preheat the oven to 350°F/180°C/gas 4. • Line two cookie sheets with parchment paper. • Marzipan Filling: Knead the marzipan, confectioners' sugar, and lemon juice and zest until smooth. • Roll the honey dough out on a lightly floured surface into three 12 x 4-inch (30 x 10-cm) strips. • Shape the marzipan filling into logs of the same length as the dough strips. • Place the marzipan logs on top of the dough strips and fold over the dough to seal. • Slice the filled dough 1 inch (2.5 cm) thick and place cut-side up 1 inch (2.5 cm) apart on the prepared cookie sheets. • Bake for 12–15 minutes, or until just golden at the edges. • Transfer to racks. • Toast the cornstarch in a frying pan for 3–4 minutes, or until lightly golden, shaking the pan constantly. Add the confectioners' sugar and water and bring to a boil, stirring constantly. • Remove from the heat and drizzle over the cookies while warm.

The addition of a marzipan filling in these sweet honey drops makes them simply sublime.

Makes: 35–40 cookies

Preparation: 1 h + 3 days to rest

Cooking: 12–15'

Level of difficulty: 3

Sweet Honey Dough
- 1 cup/150 g all-purpose/plain flour
- ⅔ cup/100 g rye flour
- 1 tsp baking soda
- 1 tsp ground cinnamon
- 1 tsp aniseeds
- ½ tsp finely grated nutmeg
- ¼ tsp ground ginger
- ¼ tsp salt
- 1 cup/250 ml honey
- ¼ cup/50 g granulated sugar

Marzipan Filling
- 14 oz/400 g marzipan, softened
- ⅔ cup/100 g confectioners'/icing sugar
- ½ tsp lemon juice
- 1 tsp finely grated lemon zest
- 1 tbsp cornstarch/cornflour
- 1 tbsp confectioners'/icing sugar
- ¾ cup/180 ml hot water

CRISPY TOP SQUARES

Makes: 25 squares

Preparation: 30'

Cooking: 30–35'

Level of difficulty: 1

- 2/3 cup/100 g all-purpose/plain flour
- 1/2 cup/75 g confectioners'/icing sugar
- 1/8 tsp salt
- 6 tbsp butter, softened
- 1 large egg + 2 large egg whites
- 2/3 cup/220 g raspberry preserves
- 1/2 cup/100 g superfine/caster sugar
- 1 tsp ground cinnamon

Preheat the oven to 350°F/190°C/gas 5. • Butter a 10-inch (25-cm) square baking pan. • Sift the flour, confectioners' sugar, and salt into a large bowl. • With an electric mixer at medium speed, beat in the butter and whole egg until well blended. • Firmly press the mixture into the prepared pan to form a smooth, even layer. • Bake for 10 minutes. • Reduce the oven temperature to 300°F/150°C/gas 2. • Warm the preserves in a small saucepan over low heat until liquid. • Spread the preserves over the base. • With mixer at medium speed, beat the egg whites in a large bowl until soft peaks form. • With mixer at high speed, gradually add the superfine sugar and cinnamon, beating until stiff, glossy peaks form. • Spread the meringue on top of preserves. • Bake for 20–25 minutes, or until the meringue is lightly browned. • Cool in the pan for 15 minutes. • Cut into squares and let cool.

CINNAMON ROSETTES

Makes: 30 cookies

Preparation: 30'

Cooking: 12–15'

Level of difficulty: 2

- 1 cup/150 g all-purpose/plain flour
- ½ tsp ground cinnamon
- ¼ tsp salt
- ½ cup/125 g butter, softened
- 4 tbsp cream cheese, softened
- ½ cup/100 g granulated sugar
- ½ tsp vanilla extract/essence
- 1 large egg yolk

Preheat the oven to 350°F/180°C/gas 4. • Set out two cookie sheets. • Sift the flour, cinnamon, and salt into a medium bowl. • Beat the butter, cream cheese, and sugar in a large bowl with an electric mixer at high speed until creamy. • Add the vanilla and egg yolk, beating until just blended. • Mix in the dry ingredients until well blended. • Insert the chosen design plate into the press by sliding it into the head and locking in place. • Press out the cookies, spacing 1 inch (2.5 cm) apart on the cookie sheets. • Bake for 12–15 minutes, or until just golden. • Transfer to racks to cool.

CHERRY PETITS FOURS

D ust two cookie sheets with rice flour. • Mix the almonds, confectioners' sugar, egg whites, and salt in a large bowl until smooth. • Fit a pastry bag with a $1/2$-inch (1-cm) star tip. Fill the pastry bag, twist the opening tightly closed, and squeeze out rosettes, spacing 1 inch (2.5 cm) apart on the prepared cookie sheets. • Place a piece of candied cherry on top of each cookie. • Refrigerate for 30 minutes. • Preheat the oven to 475°F/250°C/gas 9. • Bake for 3–5 minutes, or until lightly browned at the edges. • Transfer to racks to cool.

Makes: 25 cookies

Preparation: 25' + 30' to chill

Cooking: 3–5'

Level of difficulty: 2

- $1^1/4$ cups/125 g finely ground almonds
- $3/4$ cup/125 g confectioners'/icing sugar
- 2 large egg whites
- $1/8$ tsp salt
- 6 candied cherries, finely chopped

HAZELNUT HORSESHOES

Preheat the oven to 375°F/190°C/gas 5. • Set out four cookie sheets. • Sift the flour and salt into a medium bowl. • Beat the butter and granulated and vanilla sugars in a large bowl with an electric mixer at high speed until creamy. • Add the egg and almond extract, beating until just blended. • Mix in the dry ingredients and ground hazelnuts. • Fit a pastry bag with a $^1/_2$-inch (1-cm) star tip. Fill the pastry bag, twist the opening tightly closed, and squeeze out generous 1-inch (2.5-cm) tall arches (horseshoes), spacing 1 inch (2.5-cm) apart on the cookie sheets. • Bake, one sheet at a time, for 8–10 minutes, or until golden and firm at the edges. • Transfer to racks to cool and dust with confectioners' sugar.

Makes: 60–65 cookies

Preparation: 30'

Cooking: 8–10'

Level of difficulty: 2

- 2 cups/300 g all-purpose/plain flour
- $^1/_8$ tsp salt
- 1 cup/250 g butter, softened
- $^2/_3$ cup/140 g granulated sugar
- 2 tbsp vanilla sugar
- 1 large egg
- $^1/_4$ tsp almond extract/essence
- 1 cup/150 g finely ground hazelnuts or pecans
- 2 tbsp confectioners'/icing sugar, to dust

ALMOND MUNCHIES

Makes: 60 cookies

Preparation: 30'

Cooking: 10–15'

Level of difficulty: 2

- **3 cups/450 g all-purpose/plain flour**
- **½ tsp salt**
- **1½ cups/375 g butter, softened**
- **1¼ cups/250 g granulated sugar**
- **2 tbsp vanilla sugar**
- **1½ cups/200 g finely ground almonds**

Preheat the oven to 375°F/190°C/gas 5. • Butter four cookie sheets. • Sift the flour and salt into a medium bowl. • Beat the butter and granulated and vanilla sugars in a large bowl with an electric mixer at high speed until creamy. • Gradually mix in the dry ingredients and ground almonds to form a smooth dough. • Insert a flower or star design plate into a cookie press by sliding it into the head and locking in place. Press out the cookies, spacing about 1 inch (2.5 cm) apart on the prepared cookie sheets. • Bake, one batch at a time, for 10–15 minutes, or until golden brown and firm at the edges. • Transfer to racks to cool.

HAZELNUT CLOVE BISCOTTI

Preheat the oven to 325°F/170°C/gas 4. •
Spread the hazelnuts on a large baking sheet.
Toast for 7 minutes, or until lightly golden. •
Transfer to a large cotton kitchen towel. Fold the
towel over the nuts and rub them in the towel to
remove the thin inner skins. • Discard the skins and
coarsely chop the
nuts. • Butter a
cookie sheet. • Sift the flour, cinnamon, cloves,
and salt into a medium bowl. • Beat the eggs and
egg yolk and sugar in a large bowl with an electric
mixer at high speed until very pale and thick. • Mix
in the dry ingredients, hazelnuts, lemon zest, and
vanilla to form a smooth dough. • Divide the dough
in half. Form the dough into two 12-inch (30-cm)
long logs about 1¹/₂ inches (4 cm) in diameter and
place them 2 inches (5 cm) apart on the prepared
sheet. • Bake for 30–40 minutes, or until firm to
the touch. • Cool on the cookie sheet for 15
minutes. • Cut on the diagonal into 1¹/₂-inch (4-cm)
slices and transfer to racks to cool completely.

*Allow the dough to cool slightly after the first
baking: this will make it easier to slice.*

Makes: 16 cookies

Preparation: 35'

Cooking: 30–40'

Level of difficulty: 2

- 1¹/₄ cups/175 g whole hazelnuts
- 1²/₃ cups/250 g all-purpose/plain flour
- 1 tsp ground cinnamon
- ¹/₂ tsp ground cloves
- ¹/₈ tsp salt
- 2 large eggs + 1 egg yolk
- 1 cup/200 g granulated sugar
- grated zest of 1 lemon
- ¹/₂ tsp vanilla extract/essence

GINGER ROPES

Makes: 36–40 cookies

Preparation: 30' + 30' to chill

Cooking: 12–15'

Level of difficulty: 1

- 1 cup/150 g all-purpose/plain flour
- ½ cup/75 g whole-wheat flour
- 1 tbsp ground ginger
- 1 tsp baking powder
- ¼ tsp salt
- ½ cup/125 g butter, cut up
- ⅓ cup/70 g firmly packed light brown sugar
- ¼ cup/25 g finely chopped walnuts
- 1 large egg, lightly beaten

Sift the all-purpose and whole-wheat flours, ginger, baking powder, and salt into a large bowl. • Use a pastry blender to cut in the butter until the mixture resembles coarse crumbs. • Stir in the brown sugar and walnuts. • Mix in the egg to form a smooth dough. • Cover with plastic wrap and refrigerate for 30 minutes. • Preheat the oven to 350°F/180°C/gas 4. • Butter three cookie sheets. • Form tablespoons of the dough into 6-inch (15-cm) ropes and fold the ropes in half. • Twist the dough and place 1½ inches (4 cm) apart on the prepared cookie sheets. • Bake, one sheet at a time, for 12–15 minutes, or until lightly browned and firm to the touch. • Transfer to racks to cool.

GINGER AND LEMON CRISPS

Preheat the oven to 375°F/190°C/gas 5. •
Butter four cookie sheets. • Sift the flour,
ginger, cloves, and salt into a medium bowl. • Beat
the butter and granulated and vanilla sugars in a
large bowl with an electric mixer at high speed until
creamy. • Add the egg and lemon zest and juice,
beating until just blended. • Mix in the dry
ingredients to form a stiff dough. • Insert the
chosen design plate into a cookie press by sliding
it into the head and locking in place. Press out the
cookies, spacing about 1 inch (2.5 cm) apart on
the prepared cookie sheets. • Decorate each
cookie with crystallized ginger and sprinkle with
sugar crystals. • Bake, one sheet at a time, for
10–12 minutes, or until firm to the touch and
golden at the edges. • Transfer to racks to cool.

Makes: 60 cookies

Preparation: 30'

Cooking: 10–12'

Level of difficulty: 2

- 3 cups/450 g all-purpose/plain flour
- 2 tsp ground ginger
- ¼ tsp ground cloves
- ¼ tsp salt
- 1½ cups/375 g butter, softened
- 1¼ cups/250 g granulated sugar
- 2 tbsp vanilla sugar
- 1 large egg
- 1 tbsp finely grated lemon zest
- 1 tbsp fresh lemon juice
- 1 tbsp chopped crystallized ginger
- 1 tbsp colored sugar crystals

PECAN GINGER COOKIES

Makes: 36 cookies

Preparation: 20'

Cooking: 10–12'

Level of difficulty: 1

- **2⅓ cups/250 g all-purpose/plain flour**
- **2 tsp baking soda**
- **1 tbsp ground ginger**
- **¼ tsp salt**
- **1¼ cups/250 g firmly packed light brown sugar**
- **3 tbsp light corn syrup/golden syrup**
- **4 tbsp water**
- **1 large egg**
- **1 cup/100 g finely chopped pecans**

Preheat the oven to 375°F/190°C/gas 5. • Butter three cookie sheets. • Sift the flour, baking soda, ginger, and salt into a medium bowl. • Beat the brown sugar, corn syrup, water, and egg in a large bowl with an electric mixer at high speed until well blended. • Stir in the dry ingredients and pecans. • Drop teaspoons of the dough 2 inches (5 cm) apart onto the prepared cookie sheets. • Bake, one sheet at a time, for 10–12 minutes, or until just golden at the edges. • Transfer to racks to cool.

AFTER-DINNER COOKIES

Sift the flour and salt into a medium bowl. • Beat the butter and sugar in a large bowl with an electric mixer at high speed until creamy. • Add the egg and lemon zest, beating until just blended. • Mix in the dry ingredients to form a stiff dough. Press the dough into a disk, wrap in plastic wrap, and refrigerate for 30 minutes. • Preheat the oven to 350°F/180°C/gas 4. • Set out two cookie sheets. • Roll out the dough on a lightly floured surface to a thickness of $1/4$ inch (5 mm). • Use a sharp knife to cut into 2 x 3-inch (4 x 8-cm) rectangles. Gather the dough scraps, re-roll, and continue cutting out cookies until all the dough is used. • Sprinkle the cookies lightly with the water. • Arrange the almond halves on top of the cookies in a diagonal line. • Use a spatula to transfer the cookies to the cookie sheets, placing them 1 inch (2.5 cm) apart. • Bake for 20–25 minutes, or until pale gold and firm to the touch. • Cool completely on the sheets.

Makes: 20–25 cookies

Preparation: 40' + 30' to chill

Cooking: 20–25'

Level of difficulty: 1

- 1 1/3 cups/200 g all-purpose/plain flour
- 1/8 tsp salt
- 2/3 cup/150 g butter, softened
- 1/2 cup/100 g granulated sugar
- 1 large egg
- 1 tbsp finely grated lemon zest
- 1 tsp ice water
- 3/4 cup/125 g almond halves

ANISEED CORIANDER COOKIES

Preheat the oven to 350°F/180°C/gas 4. •
Butter two cookie sheets. • Sift the flour,
coriander, aniseeds, and salt into a large bowl. •
Beat the eggs and sugar in a medium bowl with an
electric mixer at high speed until pale and thick. •
Mix in the dry ingredients until well blended. • Drop
teaspoons of the cookie dough 3 inches (8 cm)
apart onto the prepared cookie sheets. • Bake for
8–12 minutes, or until faintly tinged with brown on
top and slightly darker at the edges. • Use a
spatula to turn the cookies over. • Bake for 3–5
minutes more, or until firm to the touch. • Transfer
to racks and let cool completely.

*Makes: 25–30
cookies*

Preparation: 20'

Cooking: 11–17'

Level of difficulty: 1

- ¾ cup/125 g all-purpose/plain flour
- 1 tsp ground coriander
- ½ tsp ground aniseeds
- ⅛ tsp salt
- 2 large eggs
- ⅔ cup/140 g granulated sugar

GOLDEN GINGER CRISPS

Makes: 20–24 cookies

Preparation: 25'

Cooking: 10–15'

Level of difficulty: 1

- 1½ cups/225 g all-purpose/plain flour
- 1 tbsp ground ginger
- 2 tsp baking powder
- 2 tsp baking soda
- 2 tsp ground allspice
- 1 tsp ground cinnamon
- ⅛ tsp salt
- ½ cup/125 g butter, cut up
- ½ cup/100 g granulated sugar
- 4 tbsp light corn syrup/golden syrup

Preheat the oven to 400°F/200°C/gas 6. • Butter two cookie sheets. • Sift the flour, ginger, baking powder, baking soda, allspice, cinnamon, and salt into a large bowl. • Use a pastry blender to cut in the butter until the mixture resembles fine crumbs. • Stir in the sugar and corn syrup until well blended. • Form the dough into balls the size of walnuts and place 2 inches (5 cm) apart on the prepared cookie sheets. • Bake for 10–15 minutes, or until just golden. • Watch them closely towards the end of the baking time as they darken very quickly. • Cool on the sheets until the cookies firm slightly. • Transfer to racks and let cool completely.

CASHEW SQUARES

Sift the flour and salt into a large bowl. • Use a pastry blender to cut in the butter until the mixture resembles coarse crumbs. • Add the egg yolks, granulated sugar, cashew nuts, lemon zest, and milk to form a stiff dough. • Press the dough into a disk, wrap in plastic wrap, and refrigerate for 30 minutes. • Preheat the oven to 325°F/170°C/gas 3. • Butter two cookie sheets. • Roll out the dough on a lightly floured surface to a thickness of $1/4$ inch (5 mm). • Cut into $1^1/2$-inch (4-cm) wide strips, then cut the strips into $2^1/2$-inch (6-cm) rectangles. • Use a spatula to transfer the cookies to the prepared cookie sheets, placing them 1 inch (2.5 cm) apart. • Bake for 12–15 minutes, or until just golden. • Transfer to racks to cool.

Makes: 30 cookies

Preparation: 40' + 30' to chill

Cooking: 12–15'

Level of difficulty: 1

- 1$^2/3$ cups/250 g all-purpose/plain flour
- $1/8$ tsp salt
- 4 tbsp butter, cut up
- 3 large egg yolks, lightly beaten
- $2/3$ cup/140 g granulated sugar
- $1/4$ cup/25 g coarsely chopped cashew nuts
- Grated zest of $1/2$ lemon
- 6 tbsp milk

COOL GINGER COOKIES

Makes: 64 cookies

Preparation: 40' + 30' to chill

Cooking: 15–20'

Level of difficulty: 2

- ⅔ cup/150 g butter, cut up
- 6 tbsp light corn syrup
- 6 tbsp dark molasses
- ¾ cup/150 g firmly packed dark brown sugar
- 2 tsp finely grated fresh ginger root
- 2⅔ cups/400 g all-purpose/plain flour
- 1½ tsp baking soda
- 1 tsp ground allspice
- ⅛ tsp salt
- 2 tbsp granulated sugar
- 2 large eggs, lightly beaten

Melt the butter with the corn syrup, molasses, and brown sugar in a small saucepan over low heat. • Mix in the ginger, remove from the heat, and let cool. • Sift the flour, baking powder, allspice, and salt into a large bowl. • Stir in the granulated sugar. Add the eggs, beating until just blended. • Mix in the corn syrup mixture to form a smooth dough. • Form the dough into four logs, each 8 inches (20-cm) long and 2 inches (5 cm) in diameter. • Wrap in plastic wrap and refrigerate for at least 30 minutes. • Preheat the oven to 325°F/170°C/gas 3. • Line two cookie sheets with parchment paper. • Slice the dough ¹/₂ inch (1-cm) thick and place 1 inch (2.5 cm) apart on the prepared cookie sheets. • Bake for 15–20 minutes, or until the edges are firm but the center still gives a little to the touch. • Cool on the sheets until the cookies firm slightly. • Transfer to racks to cool completely.

FAIRY GLEN COOKIES

Makes: 36 cookies

Preparation: 25'

Cooking: 10–15'

Level of difficulty: 2

- **3 large egg whites**
- **1/8 tsp salt**
- **1 3/4 cups/350 g granulated sugar**
- **3 1/3 cups/330 g finely ground almonds**
- **4 tbsp orange marmalade**
- **18 candied cherries, cut in half**

Preheat the oven to 350°F/180°C/gas 4. • Butter three cookie sheets. • Beat the egg whites and salt in a large bowl with an electric mixer at medium speed until soft peaks form. • With mixer at high speed, gradually add the sugar, beating until stiff, glossy peaks form. • Use a large rubber spatula to fold in the almonds. • Heat the marmalade in a small saucepan over low heat until liquid. Let cool slightly. • Carefully fold the marmalade into the batter. • Fit a pastry bag with a 1/2-inch (1-cm) star tip. Fill the pastry bag, twist the opening tightly closed. Squeeze out generous 1 1/2-inch (4-cm) stars spacing them 2 inches (5 cm) apart on the prepared cookie sheets. • Decorate with cherry halves. • Bake, one sheet at a time, for 10–15 minutes, or until just golden. • Transfer to racks to cool.

MONROE'S ALMOND DREAMS

Preheat the oven to 350°F/180°C/gas 4. • Line two cookie sheets with rice paper. • Beat the egg whites in a large bowl with an electric mixer at high speed until stiff peaks form. • Use a large rubber spatula to fold in the superfine sugar, almonds, and almond extract. • Fit a pastry bag with a $1/2$-inch (1-cm) plain tip. Fill the pastry bag, twist the opening tightly closed, and pipe out 3 inch (8-cm) long lines spacing $1^1/2$ inches (4 cm) apart on the prepared cookie sheets. • Bake for 15–20 minutes, or until golden brown. • Cool the cookies on the cookie sheets for 1 minute. • Transfer to racks to cool. • Tear away the excess rice paper from around the edges. • Melt the chocolate in a double boiler over barely simmering water. • Drizzle the chocolate in a zigzag pattern over the tops.

Makes: 20 cookies

Preparation: 30'

Cooking: 15–20'

Level of difficulty: 2

- **2 large egg whites**
- **1 cup/200 g superfine sugar**
- **1¾ cups/275 g finely ground almonds**
- **½ tsp almond extract/essence**
- **4 oz/125 g semisweet/dark chocolate, coarsely chopped**

MARZIPAN BITES

Makes: 40 cookies

Preparation: 25'

Cooking: 12–15'

Level of difficulty: 2

- 8 oz/250 g marzipan, grated
- 2 large eggs
- 2 tbsp cornstarch/cornflour
- 3 tbsp superfine/caster sugar
- 1 tbsp vanilla sugar
- ½ tsp almond extract/essence
- 5 tbsp slivered almonds, toasted

Preheat the oven to 350°F/180°C/gas 4. • Line two cookie sheets with parchment paper. • Beat the marzipan, eggs, cornstarch, superfine sugar, vanilla sugar, and almond extract in a large bowl with an electric mixer at medium speed until smooth. • Fit a pastry bag with a ³/4-inch (2-cm) plain tip. Fill the pastry bag, twist the opening tightly closed, and squeeze out 1¹/2-inch (4-cm) mounds spacing them 2 inches (5 cm) apart on the prepared cookie sheets. • Crush the almonds and sprinkle over the mounds. • Bake for 12–15 minutes, or until golden brown. • Cool on the cookie sheets for 15 minutes. • Transfer to racks and let cool completely.

ORANGE SPRITZ COOKIES

Preheat the oven to 300°F/150°C/gas 2. • Line two cookie sheets with parchment paper. • Sift the flour and salt into a small bowl. • Stir the hazelnuts, almonds, and egg in a large bowl. • Mix in the orange juice, orange zest, and 1 tablespoon of maple syrup. • Gradually mix in the dry ingredients, 1 tablespoon at a time, to form a soft, smooth dough. • Fit a pastry bag with a plain 1-inch (2.5-cm) tip. Spoon half the mixture into the pastry bag and squeeze out half moons and wreaths spacing 2 inches (5 cm) apart on the prepared cookie sheets. • Fit a second pastry bag with an 1-inch (2.5-cm) star tip. Spoon the remaining dough into the pastry bag and squeeze out ridged moons and wreaths. • Bake for 12–15 minutes, or until lightly golden. • Transfer to racks to cool. • Warm the preserves in a small saucepan over low heat until melted. • Brush over the warm cookies and sprinkle with the pistachios.

Ideal as a Christmas treat with a glass of full-bodied mulled wine.

Makes: 30 cookies

Preparation: 30'

Cooking: 12–15'

Level of difficulty: 2

- 3 tbsp all-purpose/ plain flour
- 1/8 tsp salt
- 1$\frac{1}{3}$ cups/200 g finely ground hazelnuts
- 2/3 cup/100 g finely ground almonds
- 1 large egg, lightly beaten
- 4 tbsp fresh orange juice
- 1 tbsp finely grated orange zest
- 1 tbsp maple or corn/golden syrup
- 3 tbsp apricot preserves
- 2 tbsp finely chopped pistachios or almonds

ALMOND-TOPPED WAVES

Makes: 24–26 cookies

Preparation: 25'

Cooking: 15–20'

Level of difficulty: 2

- 1⅓ cups/200 g all-purpose/plain flour
- ⅛ tsp salt
- ⅔ cup/150 g butter, softened
- ⅓ cup/70 g granulated sugar
- 1 large egg white
- grated zest of 1 lemon
- ½ tsp vanilla extract/essence
- 24–26 whole almonds

Preheat the oven to 350°F/180°C/gas 4. • Butter two cookie sheets. • Sift the flour and salt into a medium bowl. • Beat the butter and sugar in a large bowl with an electric mixer at high speed until creamy. • Add the egg white, lemon zest, and vanilla, beating until just blended. • Mix in the dry ingredients. • Fit a pastry bag with a ½-inch (1-cm) star tip. Fill the pastry bag and twist the opening tightly closed. Squeeze out 1½-inch (4-cm) wide heaps, dragging the cookies forward to finish in a thin point, spacing 2 inches (5 cm) apart on the prepared cookie sheets. • Press an almond onto the thin point of the cookie. • Bake for 15–20 minutes, or until just golden. • Cool on the sheets until the cookies firm slightly. Transfer to racks to finish cooling.

HEAVENLY ARCHES

Makes: 40 cookies

Preparation: 50'

Cooking: 12–15'

Level of difficulty: 1

- 7 oz/200 g marzipan, diced and softened
- 2 large eggs
- 2 tbsp superfine/ caster sugar
- 1 tbsp vanilla sugar
- $1/3$ cup/50 g cornstarch/ cornflour
- $1/2$ tsp baking powder
- $1/4$ tsp almond extract/essence
- $1/8$ tsp salt
- $1/2$ cup/50 g slivered almonds, toasted and coarsely chopped

Preheat the oven to 350°F/180°C/gas 4. • Line two cookie sheets with parchment paper. • Beat the marzipan, eggs, superfine and vanilla sugars, cornstarch, baking powder, almond extract, and salt in a large bowl with an electric mixer at low speed until smooth. • Fit a pastry bag with a plain $1/4$-inch (5-mm) tip. Fill the pastry bag, twist the opening tightly closed, and squeeze about forty small arches spacing them 1 inch (2.5 cm) apart on the prepared cookie sheets. Sprinkle with the almonds, pressing them lightly into the tops. • Bake for 12–15 minutes, or until golden brown. • Cool on the sheet for 5 minutes. • Transfer to racks and let cool completely.

ANISEED COOKIES

L ine two cookie sheets with parchment paper. •
Sift the flour, cornstarch, and aniseed into a
large bowl. • Beat the eggs, sugar, and salt in a
double boiler over barely simmering water with an
electric mixer at high speed until pale and thick.
Remove from the heat and continue beating until
the mixture has cooled. • Use a large rubber
spatula to fold the dry ingredients into the batter,
followed by the water. • Fit a pastry bag with a
$^1/_4$-inch (5-mm) plain tip. Fill the pastry bag, twist
the opening tightly closed, and squeeze about
$^3/_4$ inch (2-cm) round cookies, spacing $1^1/_2$ inches
(4 cm) apart on the prepared cookie sheets. • Set
aside, covered, at room temperature for about 12
hours, or until a thin crust has formed. • Preheat
the oven to 275°F/140°C/gas 1. • Bake for
25–30 minutes, or until lightly browned.
• Transfer to racks to cool.

Makes: 20–25
   cookies

Preparation: 60' + 12
   h to rest

Cooking: 25–30'

Level of difficulty: 2

• $^1/_2$ cup/75 g all-
  purpose/plain flour
• 2 tbsp cornstarch/
  cornflour
• 1 tbsp ground
  aniseeds
• 2 large eggs
• $^1/_2$ cup/100 g
  granulated sugar
• $^1/_4$ tsp salt
• 1 tsp water

GLAZED HAZELNUT COOKIES

Makes: 36 cookies
Preparation: 25'
Cooking: 10–15'
Level of difficulty: 2

- **3 large egg whites**
- **1/8 tsp salt**
- **1 3/4 cups/350 g granulated sugar**
- **3 1/3 cups/500 g finely ground hazelnuts**
- **4 tbsp orange marmalade**
- **18 candied cherries, cut in half**

Preheat the oven to 350°F/180°C/gas 4. • Butter three cookie sheets. • Beat the egg whites and salt in a large bowl with an electric mixer at medium speed until soft peaks form. • With mixer at high speed, gradually add the sugar, beating until stiff, glossy peaks form. • Fold in the hazelnuts. • Heat the marmalade in a small saucepan over low heat until liquid. Let cool slightly. • Carefully fold the marmalade into the batter. • Fit a pastry bag with a 1/2-inch (1-cm) star tip. Fill the pastry bag, twist the opening tightly closed. Squeeze out generous 1 1/2-inch (4-cm) stars spacing 2 inches (5 cm) apart on the prepared cookie sheets. • Decorate with cherry halves. • Bake, one sheet at a time, for 10–15 minutes, or until just golden. • Transfer to racks to cool.

NUTMEG COOKIES

Preheat the oven to 350°F/180°C/gas 4. • Set out two cookie sheets. • Sift the flour, nutmeg, and salt into a medium bowl. • Beat the butter, cream cheese, and sugar in a large bowl with an electric mixer at high speed until creamy. • Add the almond extract and egg yolk, beating until just blended. • Mix in the dry ingredients until well blended. • Insert the chosen design plate into the press by sliding it into the head and locking in place. • Press out the cookies, spacing 1 inch (2.5 cm) apart on the cookie sheets. • Bake for 12–15 minutes, or until just golden. • Transfer to racks to cool. • Dust with the ground nutmeg.

Makes: 48 cookies

Preparation: 40'

Cooking: 5–8'

Level of difficulty: 2

- **1 cup/250 g butter, softened**
- **²⁄₃ cup/140 g granulated sugar**
- **1½ tsp almond extract/essence**
- **1 large egg**
- **2 cups/300 g all-purpose/plain flour**
- **½ tsp freshly grated nutmeg**
- **⅛ tsp salt**
- **ground nutmeg, to dust**

SOUTHERN ITALIAN BISCOTTI

Preheat the oven to 350°F/180°C/gas 4. • Line a cookie sheet with parchment paper. • Sift the flour, allspice, and salt into a medium bowl. • Beat the egg whites, sugar, and honey in a large bowl with an electric mixer at high speed until frothy. • Mix in the dry ingredients and almonds. • Form the mixture into a 9-inch (23-cm) log. • Bake for 25–30 minutes, or until lightly browned and firm to the touch. • Let cool completely and wrap in aluminum foil. Let stand for 12 hours. • Re-heat the oven to 300°F/150°C/gas 2. • Discard the foil. Slice the dough $1/8$ inch (3 mm) thick and arrange on cookie sheets. • Bake for 15–20 minutes, or until golden and toasted. • Let cool completely.

Makes: 45 cookies

Preparation: 40' + 12 h to rest

Cooking: 40–50'

Level of difficulty: 2

- **1⅓ cups/200 g all-purpose/plain flour**
- **½ tsp allspice**
- **⅛ tsp salt**
- **2 large egg whites**
- **¼ cup/50 g granulated sugar**
- **1 tbsp honey**
- **½ cup/75 g blanched almonds, halved**

PACIFIC ISLAND BISCOTTI

Makes: 30 cookies

Preparation: 40'

Cooking: 40–50'

Level of difficulty: 1

- 1²/₃ cups/250 g all-purpose/plain flour
- 1 tsp baking powder
- ⅛ tsp salt
- 2 large eggs
- 1 cup/200 g superfine/caster sugar
- 1 tsp finely grated lemon zest
- ½ cup/60 g shredded/desiccated coconut
- 1 cup/150 g blanched almonds, halved

Preheat the oven to 350°F/180°C/gas 4. • Butter a cookie sheet. • Sift the flour, baking powder, and salt into a medium bowl. • Beat the eggs, sugar, and lemon zest in a large bowl with an electric mixer at high speed until frothy. • Mix in the dry ingredients, coconut, and almonds to form a stiff dough. • Divide the dough in two. Form into two 8-inch (20-cm) logs and place 4 inches (10-cm) apart on the prepared cookie sheet, flattening them slightly. • Bake for 30–35 minutes, or until firm to the touch. • Transfer to a chopping board and let cool completely. • Cut on the diagonal into 1-inch (2.5-cm) slices and arrange cut-side up on two cookie sheets. • Bake for 10–15 minutes, or until golden and toasted. • Transfer to racks to cool.

BOOZY ANISEED COOKIES

Makes: 48 cookies

Preparation: 40' + 12 h to rest

Cooking: 15–20'

Level of difficulty: 2

- 3 cups/450 g all-purpose/plain flour
- ⅛ tsp salt
- 4 large eggs
- 1½ cups/300 g granulated sugar
- ⅛ tsp anisette
- grated zest of 1 lemon
- 1 tbsp aniseeds

Butter four cookie sheets. • Sift the flour and salt into a medium bowl. • Beat the eggs and sugar in a large bowl with an electric mixer at high speed until pale and very thick. • Beat in the anisette, lemon zest, and aniseeds. • Mix in the dry ingredients. • Fit a pastry bag with a ¼-inch (5-mm) plain tip. Fill the pastry bag, twist the opening tightly closed, and squeeze out 1-inch (2.5-cm) mounds spacing 2 inches (5 cm) apart onto the prepared cookie sheets. • Set aside for 12 hours. • Preheat the oven to 300°F/150°C/gas 2. • Bake, one sheet at a time, for 15–20 minutes, or until puffed and just golden. • Transfer to racks and let cool completely.

SPICED BLACK PEPPER COOKIES

Sift the flour, baking powder, baking soda, cinnamon, allspice, and salt into a medium bowl. • Beat the butter and sugar in a large bowl with an electric mixer at high speed until creamy. • Beat in the cream. • Mix in the dry ingredients and black pepper to form a smooth dough. • Form the dough into a log 2^1/$_2$ inches (6 cm) in diameter. Wrap in plastic wrap and refrigerate for 30 minutes. • Preheat the oven to 375°F/190°C/ gas 5. • Butter four cookie sheets. • Slice the dough ^{1}/$_4$ inch (5 mm) thick and place the cookies 1 inch (2.5 cm) apart on the prepared cookie sheets. • Bake, one sheet at a time, for 5–7 minutes, or until just golden. • Transfer to racks and let cool completely.

Makes: 55 cookies

Preparation: 40' + 30' to chill

Cooking: 5–7'

Level of difficulty: 1

- **3 cups/450 g all-purpose/plain flour**
- **1 tsp baking powder**
- **1 tsp baking soda**
- **1 tsp ground cinnamon**
- **1 tsp ground allspice**
- **¼ tsp salt**
- **1 cup/250 g butter**
- **1 cup/200 g granulated sugar**
- **4 tbsp heavy/double cream**
- **1 tsp freshly ground black pepper**

CURRANT SPICE COOKIES

Makes: 36 cookies

Preparation: 40' + 30' to chill

Cooking: 5–8'

Level of difficulty: 1

- 1²/₃ cups/250 g all-purpose/plain flour
- 1 tsp baking soda
- 1 tsp ground cinnamon
- ¼ tsp ground nutmeg
- ⅛ tsp ground cloves
- ⅛ tsp salt
- ½ cup/125 g butter, softened
- 1 cup/200 g granulated sugar
- 2 tsp milk
- 1 large egg, lightly beaten
- ½ cup/90 g currants

Sift the flour, baking soda, cinnamon, nutmeg, and cloves into a medium bowl. • Beat the butter and ³/₄ cup (150 g) sugar in a large bowl with an electric mixer at high speed until creamy. • Add the milk and egg, beating until just blended. • Mix in the dry ingredients, followed by the currants. • Press the dough into a disk, wrap in plastic wrap, and refrigerate for 30 minutes. • Preheat the oven to 375°F/190°C/gas 5. • Set out three cookie sheets. • Roll out the dough on a lightly floured surface to a thickness of ¹/₈ inch (3 mm). • Sprinkle with the remaining sugar. • Use a 2-inch (5-cm) diamond-shaped cookie cutter to cut out the cookies. Gather the dough scraps, re-roll, and continue cutting out until all the dough is used. Transfer the cookies to the cookie sheets. • Bake for 5–8 minutes, or until lightly browned. • Transfer to racks to cool.

Makes: 35–40
cookies

Preparation: 50' + 30'
to set

Cooking: 15–20'

Level of difficulty: 2

- 10 cloves
- 1 piece (3-inch/
  8-cm) cinnamon
- seeds from 5
  cardamom pods
- 1 blade mace
- ½ tsp freshly
  grated nutmeg
- 2 cups/300 g
  whole almonds
- ½ cup/50 g finely
  chopped candied
  lemon peel
- ½ cup/50 g finely
  chopped candied
  orange peel
- grated zest of ½
  lemon
- 2⅓ cups/350 g all-
  purpose/plain flour
- 1 tsp baking powder
- ⅛ tsp salt
- 3 large eggs
- 1 cup/200 g sugar
- 2 tbsp honey
- 1 tsp kirsch

GLAZE

- 1 cup/150 g
  confectioners'/
  icing sugar
- 1 tbsp warm water
- ½ tsp white rum

LEBKUCHEN

Preheat the oven to 325°F/170°C/gas 3. •
Pound the cloves, cinnamon, cardamom seeds,
mace, and nutmeg in a pestle and mortar until
finely ground. • Spread the almonds on a large
baking sheet. Toast for 7 minutes, or until lightly
golden. • Finely chop the almonds. • Increase the
oven temperature to 350°F/180°C/gas 4. • Line
three cookie sheets with rice paper. • Let the
almonds cool completely and transfer to a medium
bowl. • Stir in the candied lemon and orange peel,
lemon zest, and ground spices. • Sift the flour,
baking powder, and salt into a medium bowl. •
Beat the eggs and sugar in a large bowl with an
electric mixer at high speed until pale and thick.
• Beat in the honey and almond mixture. • Add the
kirsch. • Mix in the dry ingredients. • Drop rounded
tablespoons of the mixture 2 inches (5 cm) apart
onto the prepared cookie sheets. • Bake, one
sheet at a time, for 15–20 minutes, or until lightly
browned. • Cool on the sheets until the cookies
firm slightly. • Transfer the cookies still on the rice
paper to racks and let cool completely. • Tear
away the excess rice paper from around the
cookies. • Light Rum Glaze: Mix the confectioners'
sugar, water, and rum in a small bowl until smooth.
• Spread the glaze over the cookies and let stand
for 30 minutes until set.

EASTERN DIAMONDS

Sift the flour and salt into a medium bowl. •
Beat the butter and granulated sugar in a large
bowl until creamy. • Add the egg, beating until just
blended. • Mix in the dry ingredients and caraway
seeds until stiff. Refrigerate for 30 minutes. •
Preheat the oven to 325°F/170°C/gas 3. • Butter
three cookie sheets. • Roll out the dough to a
thickness of ¹/₈ inch (3 mm). Cut the dough into
2-inch (5-cm) diamonds. Continue cutting out
cookies until all the dough is used. • Transfer the
cookies to the prepared cookie sheets, placing
them 1 inch (2.5 cm) apart. Sprinkle the tops of
the cookies with the sugar crystals. • Bake, one
sheet at a time, for 10–12
minutes, or until pale gold. •
Transfer to racks to cool.

Makes: 38–42
cookies

Preparation: 40' + 30'
to chill

Cooking: 10–12'

Level of difficulty: 1

- 1½ cups/225 g all-
  purpose/plain flour
- ⅛ tsp salt
- 4 tbsp butter,
  softened
- ¼ cup/50 g
  granulated sugar
- 1 large egg
- 1 tsp caraway
  seeds
- 2 tbsp colored
  sugar crystals

CHOCOLATE DIAMONDS

Makes: 32 cookies

Preparation: 40' + 30' to chill

Cooking: 15–20'

Level of difficulty: 1

- 4 tbsp milk
- 1 tsp baking soda
- 3⅓ cups/500 g all-purpose/plain flour
- 2 tsp baking powder
- ⅛ tsp salt
- 1 cup/200 g granulated sugar
- 1 tsp vanilla extract/essence
- 2 large eggs + 1 large egg white, lightly beaten
- 6 tbsp sunflower oil
- 7 oz/200 g semisweet/dark chocolate, finely grated

Heat the milk in a small saucepan. Remove from the heat and mix in the baking soda. • Sift the flour, baking powder, and salt into a large bowl. • Stir in the sugar. • Add the vanilla and 2 eggs. • Pour in the oil and baking soda mixture and mix until smooth. Press the dough into a disk, wrap in plastic wrap, and refrigerate for 30 minutes. • Preheat the oven to 350°F/180°C/gas 4. • Butter three cookie sheets. • Roll out the dough on a lightly floured surface to a thickness of ¼ inch (5 mm). • Use a 2½-inch (6-cm) diamond-shaped cookie cutter to cut out the cookies. Continue cutting out cookies until all the dough is used. • Transfer the cookies to the sheets, placing them 1 inch (2.5 cm) apart. • Brush with the egg white and sprinkle with chocolate. • Bake for 20 minutes, or until golden.

HEARTS OF SPICE

Makes: 30–35 cookies

Preparation: 40' + 30' to chill

Cooking: 7–10'

Level of difficulty: 1

- 1 3/4 cups/275 g all-purpose/plain flour
- 1/4 tsp ground allspice
- 1/4 tsp baking soda
- 1/4 tsp ground cinnamon
- 1/4 tsp ground cloves
- 1/4 tsp ground ginger
- 1/4 tsp freshly grated nutmeg
- 1/8 tsp salt
- 1/2 cup/125 g light molasses
- 1/2 cup/200 g firmly packed light brown sugar
- 4 tbsp butter, melted

Sift the flour, allspice, baking soda, cinnamon, cloves, ginger, nutmeg, and salt into a medium bowl. • Use a wooden spoon to beat the molasses, brown sugar, and butter in a large bowl until well blended. • Mix in the dry ingredients to form a stiff dough. • Press the dough into a disk, wrap in plastic wrap, and refrigerate for 30 minutes. • Preheat the oven to 375°F/190°C/gas 5. • Butter two cookie sheets. • Roll out the dough on a lightly floured surface to a thickness of 1/4 inch (5 mm). • Use a 1 1/2-inch (4-cm) heart-shaped cookie cutter to cut out the cookies. Gather the dough scraps, re-roll, and continue cutting out cookies until all the dough is used. • Use a spatula to transfer the cookies to the prepared cookie sheets, placing them 1 inch (2.5 cm) apart. • Bake for 7–10 minutes, or until golden brown. • Transfer to racks to cool.

DUTCH COOKIES

Sift the flour, baking powder, cocoa, ginger, and salt into a large bowl. Use a wooden spoon to mix in the raw sugar, egg, butter, milk, and vanilla to form a soft dough. • Press the dough into a disk, wrap in plastic wrap, and refrigerate for 30 minutes. • Preheat the oven to 350°F/180°C/gas 4. • Butter two cookie sheets. • Roll out the dough on a lightly floured surface to a thickness of ¹/₄ inch (5 mm). • Use Christmas cookie cutters to cut out the cookies. Use a spatula to transfer the cookies to the prepared cookie sheets, placing them 1 inch (2.5 cm) apart. Prick all over with a fork. • Bake for 8–10 minutes, or until just golden. • Transfer to racks and let cool completely.

Makes: 25 cookies

Preparation: 40' + 30' to chill

Cooking: 8–10'

Level of difficulty: 1

- 2¹/₃ cups/350 g all-purpose/plain flour
- 1 tsp baking powder
- 1 tsp unsweetened cocoa powder
- 1 tsp ground ginger
- 1 cup/200 g raw sugar (Demerara or Barbados)
- 1 large egg
- ¹/₂ cup/125 g butter, melted
- 2 tbsp milk
- ¹/₂ tsp vanilla extract/essence

TUSCAN BISCOTTI

Preheat the oven to 375°F/190°C/gas 5. • Set out a cookie sheet. • Sift the flour, baking powder, and salt into a medium bowl. Stir in the aniseeds. • Beat the butter and sugar in a large bowl with an electric mixer at high speed until creamy. • Add the lemon zest and eggs, beating until just blended. • Mix in the dry ingredients to form a stiff dough. • Divide the dough in half. Form the dough into two 11-inch (28-cm) logs and place 3 inches (8 cm) apart on the cookie sheet. • Bake for 25–35 minutes, or until firm to the touch. • Transfer to a cutting board to cool for 15 minutes. • Cut on the diagonal into 1-inch (2.5-cm) slices. • Arrange the slices cut-side up on two cookie sheets and bake for 5–7 minutes more, or until golden and toasted. • Transfer to racks to cool.

Makes: 25–30 cookies

Preparation: 40'

Cooking: 30–42'

Level of difficulty: 2

- **3 cups/450 g all-purpose/plain flour**
- **2 tsp baking powder**
- **⅛ tsp salt**
- **2 tsp ground aniseeds**
- **⅔ cup/150 g butter, softened**
- **1 cup/200 g granulated sugar**
- **grated zest of 2 lemons**
- **3 large eggs**

CARDAMOM BISCOTTI

Makes: 35 cookies

Preparation: 40'

Cooking: 33–40'

Level of difficulty: 2

- 2½ cups/375 g bread flour
- 1 tsp baking powder
- 1 tsp ground cardamom
- ¼ tsp ground allspice
- ¼ tsp salt
- 1¼ cups/250 g raw sugar (Barbados or Demerara)
- 2 large eggs + 1 egg white
- 1 tsp lemon extract/essence
- 2 tbsp finely chopped candied mixed peel
- 1 tbsp finely grated lemon zest
- 1 tbsp finely grated orange peel

GLAZE

- 1 large egg yolk
- 1 tbsp milk
- 1 tsp granulated sugar
- ¼ tsp ground cardamom

Preheat the oven to 350°F/180°C/gas 4. • Butter two cookie sheets. • Sift the flour, baking powder, cardamom, allspice, and salt into a medium bowl. • Stir in the sugar, candied peel, and lemon and orange zests. • Beat the eggs, egg white, and lemon extract until frothy. • Mix in the dry ingredients. • Form into three 10-inch (25-cm) logs and place 4 inches (10 cm) apart on the prepared cookie sheets. • Cardamom Glaze: Mix the egg yolk and milk and brush over the logs. Sprinkle with sugar and cardamom. • Bake for 25–30 minutes, or until firm. • Transfer to a cutting board. • Reduce the oven temperature to 300°F/150°C/gas 2. • Cut on the diagonal into 1-inch (2.5-cm) slices. • Bake for 8–10 minutes, or golden and toasted. • Transfer to racks to cool.

CHINESE BISCOTTI

Makes: 20 cookies	
Preparation: 40'	
Cooking: 30–45'	
Level of difficulty: 2	

- 2½ cups/375 g all-purpose/plain flour
- 2 tbsp unsweetened cocoa powder
- 1 tsp baking soda
- ½ tsp salt
- ¼ tsp ground cinnamon
- ¼ tsp ground cloves
- 1 cup/200 g granulated sugar
- 1¼ cups/125 g finely chopped almonds
- 3 large eggs, lightly beaten
- 2 tbsp freshly grated fresh ginger
- ½ tsp almond extract/essence

Preheat the oven to 350°F/180°C/gas 4. • Line a cookie sheet with parchment paper. • Sift the flour, cocoa, baking soda, salt, cinnamon, and cloves into a large bowl. • Stir in the sugar and almonds. • Mix in the eggs, ginger, and almond extract to form a stiff dough. • Divide the dough in half. • Form the dough into two 10-inch (25-cm) logs and place 3 inches (8 cm) apart on the prepared cookie sheet, flattening the tops. • Bake for 20–30 minutes, or until lightly browned and firm to the touch. • Transfer to a cutting board to cool for 15 minutes. • Reduce the oven temperature to 300°F/150°C/gas 2. • Cut on the diagonal into 1-inch (2.5-cm) slices. • Arrange the slices cut-side up on two cookie sheets and bake for 10–15 minutes, or until golden and toasted. • Transfer to racks to cool.

SAILOR'S BISCOTTI

Preheat the oven to 325°F/170°C/gas 3. •
Spread the blanched almonds on a large
baking sheet. Toast for 7 minutes, or until lightly
golden. • Let cool completely and cut the almonds
in half. • Increase the oven temperature to 350°F/
180°C/gas 4. • Line a cookie sheet with
parchment paper. • Toast the pine nuts in a frying
pan over medium heat for 5–7 minutes, or until
lightly golden. • Sift the flour, baking powder, and
salt into a large bowl. Stir in the sugar, dates,
apricots, prunes, halved and whole almonds, pine
nuts, and the orange and lemon zests. • Beat the
eggs in a medium bowl with an electric mixer at
high speed until frothy. • Add the beaten egg to
the dry ingredients, reserving 1 tablespoon.
• Divide the dough in half. Form the dough into
two long logs about 1^1/$_4$ inches (3-cm) in
diameter. • Transfer the logs to the prepared
cookie sheets, flattening them slightly. • Bake for
15–20 minutes, or firm to the touch. • Transfer to
a cutting board to cool for 10 minutes. • Lower
the oven temperature to 300°F/150°C/gas 2.
• Cut on the diagonal into ^{1}/$_2$ inch (1-cm) slices.
• Arrange the slices cut-side up on the cookie
sheet and bake for 7–10 minutes, or until golden
and toasted. • Transfer to racks to cool.

Makes: about 40 biscotti

Preparation: 40'

Cooking: 22–30'

Level of difficulty: 2

- ^{1}/$_4$ cup/40 g blanched almonds
- ^{1}/$_2$ cup/90 g pine nuts
- 2 cups/300 g all-purpose/plain flour
- 1 tsp baking powder
- ^{1}/$_4$ tsp salt
- 1^1/$_4$ cups/250 g granulated sugar
- ^{1}/$_2$ cup/50 g finely chopped pitted dates
- ^{1}/$_4$ cup/25 g finely chopped dried apricots
- ^{1}/$_4$ cup/50 g finely chopped pitted prunes
- ^{1}/$_4$ cup/40 g whole almonds with skins
- Grated zest of 1 orange
- 1 tsp grated lemon zest
- 3 large eggs, lightly beaten

COCONUT AND HONEY THINS

Preheat the oven to 375°F/190°C/gas 5. • Butter four cookie sheets. • Sift the flour, nutmeg, and salt into a medium bowl. • Beat the butter and brown sugar in a large bowl with an electric mixer at high speed until creamy. • Beat in the honey and egg, beating until just blended. • Mix in the dry ingredients and coconut. • Drop teaspoons of the batter 3 inches (8 cm) apart onto the prepared cookie sheets. Do not drop more than eight cookies onto each sheet. Spread the mixture out into thin circles. • Bake, one sheet at a time, for 8–10 minutes, or until faintly tinged with brown on top and slightly darker at the edges. • Working quickly, use a spatula to lift each cookie from the sheet. Transfer to racks to cool. • Butter the cookie sheets again and continue to bake in batches until all the batter has been used.

Makes: 32–36 cookies

Preparation: 20'

Cooking: 8–10'

Level of difficulty: 2

- 1/3 cup/50 g all-purpose/plain flour
- 1/4 tsp freshly ground nutmeg
- 1/8 tsp salt
- 4 tbsp butter, softened
- 1/4 cup/50 g firmly packed light brown sugar
- 3/4 cup/180 ml honey
- 1 large egg
- 1/2 cup/60 g shredded/desiccated coconut

ROSE WATER COOKIES

Makes: 16–20 cookies

Preparation: 20'

Cooking: 12–15'

Level of difficulty: 1

- 1 cup/150 g all-purpose/plain flour
- 1/8 tsp salt
- 1/2 cup/125 g butter, softened
- 2/3 cup/140 g granulated sugar
- 1/2 cup/50 g finely chopped almonds
- 1 tsp rose water

Preheat the oven to 350°F/180°C/gas 4. • Butter two cookie sheets. • Sift the flour and salt into a medium bowl. • Use a wooden spoon to beat the butter and sugar in a medium bowl until creamy. • Mix in the dry ingredients, almonds, and rose water to form a stiff dough. • Drop teaspoons of dough 1 inch (2.5 cm) apart onto the prepared cookie sheets. • Bake for 12–15 minutes, or until golden. • Transfer to racks to cool.

WAYFARER WAFERS

Makes: 10–15
  cookies

Preparation: 20'

Cooking: 10–15'

Level of difficulty: 1

- **4 tbsp butter,
  softened**
- **¼ cup/50 g
  granulated sugar**
- **1 tbsp freeze-dried
  coffee granules**
- **1 large egg, lightly
  beaten**
- **⅓ cup/50 g all-
  purpose/plain flour**
- **⅛ tsp salt**
- **¼ cup/25 g finely
  chopped pecans**
- **½ tsp vanilla
  extract/essence**

Preheat the oven to 350°F/180°C/gas 4. •
Butter a cookie sheet. • Beat the butter, sugar,
and coffee granules in a large bowl with an electric
mixer at high speed until creamy. • Add the egg,
beating until just blended. • Mix in the flour and salt
until well blended. • Stir in the pecans and vanilla.
• Drop rounded teaspoons of the cookie dough
1 inch (2.5 cm) apart onto the prepared cookie
sheets. • Bake for 10–15 minutes, or until just
golden. • Cool on the sheet until the cookies firm
slightly. Transfer to racks to finish cooling.

HAZELNUT ORANGE COOKIES

Makes: 36 cookies

Preparation: 25'

Cooking: 10–15'

Level of difficulty: 2

- **3 large egg whites**
- **⅛ tsp salt**
- **1¾ cups/350 g granulated sugar**
- **3⅓ cups/500 g finely ground hazelnuts**
- **4 tbsp orange marmalade**
- **18 candied cherries, cut in half**

Preheat the oven to 350°F/180°C/gas 4. • Butter three cookie sheets. • Beat the egg whites and salt in a large bowl with an electric mixer at medium speed until soft peaks form. • With mixer at high speed, gradually add the sugar, beating until stiff, glossy peaks form. • Fold in the hazelnuts. • Heat the marmalade in a small saucepan over low heat until liquid. Let cool slightly. • Carefully fold the marmalade into the batter. • Fit a pastry bag with a ½-inch (1-cm) star tip. Fill the pastry bag, twist the opening tightly closed. Squeeze out generous 1½-inch (4-cm) stars spacing 2 inches (5 cm) apart on the prepared cookie sheets. • Decorate with cherry halves. • Bake, one sheet at a time, for 10–15 minutes, or until just golden. • Transfer to racks to cool.

SPICE SQUARES

Sift the flour, ginger, cinnamon, cloves, baking soda, and salt into a medium bowl. • Mix the butter, brown sugar, and molasses in a medium saucepan over low heat. • Cook, stirring constantly, until the sugar has dissolved completely. • Remove from the heat and mix in the dry ingredients and lemon zest to form a stiff dough. • Divide the dough in half. Press the dough into two disks, wrap in plastic wrap, and refrigerate for 1 hour. • Preheat the oven to 350°F/180°C/ gas 4. • Butter two cookie sheets. • Roll half the dough out on a lightly floured surface to 10-inch (25-cm) square. • Cut into 2-inch (5-cm) squares. • Use a spatula to transfer the cookies to the prepared cookie sheets, placing them 1 inch (2.5 cm) apart. • Prick all over with a fork. • Repeat with the remaining dough. • Sprinkle with the granulated sugar. • Bake for 5–7 minutes, or until lightly browned. • Transfer to racks and let cool completely.

Makes: 30 cookies

Preparation: 40' + 60' to chill

Cooking: 5–7'

Level of difficulty: 1

- 1¼ cups/180 g all-purpose/plain flour
- 1 tsp ground ginger
- 1 tsp ground cinnamon
- ¼ tsp ground cloves
- ½ tsp baking soda
- ⅛ tsp salt
- 4 tbsp butter, cut up
- ¼ cup/50 g firmly packed dark brown sugar
- 2 tbsp dark molasses/treacle
- Grated zest of 1 lemon
- ¼ cup/50 g granulated sugar

PECAN MELTING MOMENTS

Makes: 25–30 cookies

Preparation: 25' + 30' to chill

Cooking: 10–12'

Level of difficulty: 1

- 1¼ cups/180 g all-purpose/plain flour
- ⅛ tsp salt
- ½ cup/125 g butter, softened
- ⅓ cup/50 g confectioners'/icing sugar
- ½ tsp vanilla extract/essence
- ½ cup/50 g finely chopped pecans

Preheat the oven to 400°F/200°C/gas 6. • Set out two cookie sheets. • Sift the flour and salt into a medium bowl. • Beat the butter, ¼ cup (30 g) confectioners' sugar, and vanilla in a large bowl with an electric mixer at high speed until creamy. • Mix in the dry ingredients and pecans to make a stiff dough. • Press the dough into a disk, wrap in plastic wrap, and refrigerate for 30 minutes. • Form the dough into balls the size of walnuts and place 1 inch (2.5 cm) apart on the cookie sheets. • Bake for 10–12 minutes, or until firm to the touch but not browned. • Transfer to racks to cool. • Dust with the remaining confectioners' sugar.

DATE PECAN SQUARES

Makes: 36–45 bars

Preparation: 20'

Cooking: 20–30'

Level of difficulty: 1

- ⅔ cup/100 g all-purpose/plain flour
- ⅔ cup/100 g cornstarch/cornflour
- ⅛ tsp salt
- ½ cup/125 g butter, softened
- ½ cup/100 g firmly packed light brown sugar
- 1 large egg
- ⅔ cup/60 g finely chopped pitted dates
- 1 cup/100 g coarsely chopped pecans
- 2 tbsp milk
- 2 tbsp granulated sugar

Preheat the oven to 375°F/190°C/gas 5. • Line a 13 x 9-inch (33 x 23-cm) baking pan with aluminum foil, letting the edges overhang. Butter the foil. • Sift the flour, cornstarch, and salt into a large bowl. • Beat the butter, brown sugar, and egg in a large bowl with an electric mixer at high speed until well blended. • Mix in the dry ingredients, dates, and pecans to form a stiff dough. • Firmly press the mixture into the prepared pan to form a smooth, even layer. • Brush with the milk and sprinkle with the granulated sugar. • Bake for 20–30 minutes, or until just golden. • Cool completely in the pan on a rack. • Using the foil as handles, lift onto a cutting board. Peel off the foil. Cut into squares.

PEPPER STARS

Melt the butter with the molasses in a small saucepan. Remove from the heat and set aside to cool. • Mix the peppercorns and cardamom in a small bowl. • Sift the flour, baking soda, cinnamon, ginger, and salt into a large bowl. Stir in the peppercorns and cardamom. • Use a wooden spoon to stir in the sugar, molasses mixture, and egg. • Turn out onto a lightly floured surface and knead lightly until smooth. • Shape into a disk, wrap in plastic wrap, and refrigerate for 30 minutes. • Preheat the oven to 325°F/170°C/ gas 3. • Line two cookie sheets with parchment paper. • Roll out the dough on a lightly floured surface to a thickness of $1/4$ inch (5 mm). • Use a star-shaped cutter to stamp into shapes. • Gather the dough scraps, re-roll, and continue cutting out cookies until all the dough is used. Use a metal spatula to transfer to the prepared cookie sheets, spacing 1 inch (2.5 cm) apart. • Bake for 10–15 minutes, or until firm to the touch. • Cool the cookies completely on the cookie sheets. Transfer to a rack. • Mix the confectioners' sugar an water in a small bowl. Drizzle over the cookies.

Makes: 35 cookies

Preparation: 50' + 30' to chill

Cooking: 10–15'

Level of difficulty: 1

- 6 tbsp butter, cut up
- 2 tbsp dark molasses/treacle
- 3 black peppercorns, crushed
- Seeds of 10 cardamom pods, crushed
- 1½ cups/225 g all-purpose/plain flour
- ½ tsp baking soda
- ½ tsp ground cinnamon
- ½ tsp ground ginger
- ½ tsp salt
- ¼ cup/50 g granulated sugar
- 1 large egg, lightly beaten
- 1 cup/150 g confectioners'/ icing sugar
- 2 tbsp warm water

454

ALMOND TOFFEE BARS

Makes: 15 bars

Preparation: 30'

Cooking: 30–35'

Level of difficulty: 1

TOPPING

- 6 tbsp butter
- ½ cup/100 g granulated sugar
- 2 tbsp firmly packed light brown sugar
- 2 tbsp milk
- 2½ cups/250 g flaked almonds

COOKIE BASE

- 1⅓ cups/200 g all-purpose/plain flour
- 1 tsp baking powder
- ¼ tsp salt
- ½ cup/125 g butter, softened
- ⅔ cup/140 g granulated sugar
- 1 large egg
- 1 tsp finely grated lemon zest

Preheat the oven to 350°F/180°C/gas 4. • Butter a 9-inch (23-cm) baking pan. • Almond-Toffee Topping: Melt the butter with the granulated and brown sugars in a small saucepan over low heat. • Add the milk and bring to a boil, stirring constantly. • Remove from the heat and stir in the almonds. • Cookie Base: Sift the flour, baking powder, and salt into a medium bowl. • Beat the butter and sugar in a large bowl with an electric mixer at high speed until creamy. • Add the egg, beating until just blended. • Mix in the dry ingredients and lemon zest. • Firmly press the mixture into the prepared pan to form a smooth, even layer. • Spread the almond-toffee topping evenly over the cookie base. • Bake for 30–35 minutes, or until just golden. • Cut into bars while the topping is still warm.

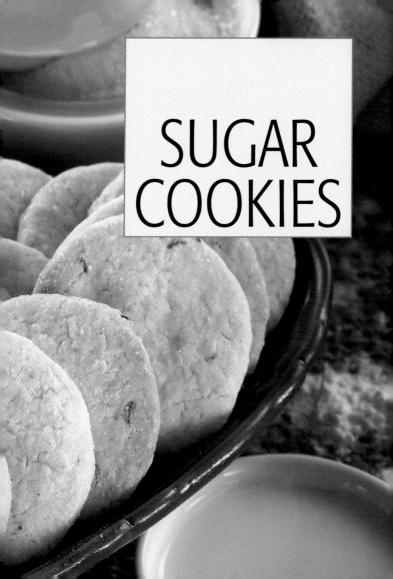

SUGAR
COOKIES

BLACK SUGAR COOKIES

Sift the flour, cocoa, and salt into a large bowl.
• Use a pastry blender to cut in the butter until
the mixture resembles coarse crumbs. • Mix in the
cream. • Press the dough into a disk, wrap in
plastic wrap, and refrigerate for 30 minutes.
• Preheat the oven to 375°F/190°C/gas 5.
• Line two cookie sheets with parchment paper.
• Roll out the dough on a lightly floured surface to
a thickness of $1/8$ inch (3 mm). • Use a $1^1/2$-inch
(4-cm) cookie cutter to cut out the cookies. Gather
the dough scraps, reroll, and continue cutting out
cookies until all the dough is used. • Use a spatula
to transfer the cookies to the cookie sheet,
spacing them $1^1/2$ inches (4-cm) apart. • Sprinkle
with the sugar. • Bake for 8–10 minutes, or until
just firm to the touch. • Transfer to racks to cool.
• Filling: Melt the chocolate in a double boiler over
barely simmering water. Remove from the heat and
mix in the confectioners' sugar and cream. • Stick
the cookies together in pairs with the filling. • Let
the cookies stand for 30 minutes to set.

*Makes: 12–14
cookies*

*Preparation: 40' + 60'
to chill and set*

Cooking: 8–10'

Level of difficulty: 2

- 1 cup/150 g all-
purpose/plain flour
- 4 tbsp unsweetened
cocoa powder
- $1/8$ tsp salt
- 6 tbsp butter, cut
up
- 5 tbsp light/single
cream
- $1/3$ cup/70 g
granulated sugar,
to sprinkle

FILLING

- 2 oz/60 g
semisweet/dark
chocolate,
coarsely chopped
- 1 cup/150 g
confectioners'/
icing sugar
- 1 tbsp light/single
cream

460

PRETTY PINK SUGAR COOKIES

Makes: 12–14 cookies

Preparation: 40' + 30' to chill

Cooking: 8–10'

Level of difficulty: 2

- 1 cup/150 g all-purpose/plain flour
- 1/8 tsp salt
- 6 tbsp butter, cut up
- 4 tbsp light/single cream
- 1/3 cup/50 g confectioners'/icing sugar, to dust

PINK FILLING
- 1 cup/150 g confectioners'/icing sugar
- 1 tbsp butter, softened
- 1 tbsp light/single cream
- 1/2 tsp vanilla extract/essence
- few drops red food coloring

Sift the flour and salt into a large bowl. • Use a pastry blender to cut in the butter until the mixture resembles coarse crumbs. • Mix in the cream. • Press the dough into a disk, wrap in plastic wrap, and refrigerate for 30 minutes.
• Preheat the oven to 375°F/190°C/gas 3.
• Line two cookie sheets with parchment paper. • Roll out the dough on a lightly floured surface to a thickness of 1/8 inch (3 mm).
• Use a 1 1/2-inch (4-cm) cookie cutter to cut out the cookies. Gather the dough scraps, reroll, and continue cutting out cookies until all the dough is used. • Use a spatula to transfer the cookies to the cookie sheet, spacing them 1 1/2 inches (4 cm) apart. • Bake for 8–10 minutes, or until just golden at the edges. • Transfer to racks to cool. • Pink Filling: Mix the confectioners' sugar, butter, cream, vanilla, and red food coloring in a small bowl.
• Stick the cookies together in pairs with the filling.
• Dust with the confectioners' sugar.

For a different look, change the food coloring to green or any other color you like.

CHOCOLATE DIPPED SUGAR HEARTS

Sift the flour, baking powder, and salt into a medium bowl. • Beat the butter and sugar in a large bowl with an electric mixer at high speed until creamy. • Add the vanilla and almond extracts and half-and-half. • Add the egg and egg yolk, beating until just blended. • Mix in the dry ingredients to form a soft dough. • Divide the dough in half. Press the dough into disks, wrap each in plastic wrap, and refrigerate for 30 minutes. • Preheat the oven to 350°F/180°C/gas 4. • Line three cookie sheets with parchment paper. • Roll out one of the disks of dough on a lightly floured surface to a thickness of $1/4$ inch (5 mm). • Use a $2^1/2$-inch (6-cm) heart cookie cutter to cut out the cookies. • Gather the dough scraps, re-roll, and continue cutting out cookies until all the dough is used. • Use a spatula to transfer the cookies to the prepared cookie sheets, placing them 2 inches (5 cm) apart.
• Repeat with the remaining dough. • Bake, one sheet at a time, for 12–15 minutes, or until just golden. • Transfer to racks and let cool completely.
• Melt the chocolate in a double boiler over barely simmering water. • Dip the hearts halfway into the chocolate and let stand for 30 minutes until set.

Makes: 40 cookies

Preparation: 40' + 60' to chill and set

Cooking: 12–15'

Level of difficulty: 1

- **3 cups/450 g all-purpose/plain flour**
- **$1/2$ tsp baking powder**
- **$1/2$ tsp salt**
- **1 cup/250 g butter, softened**
- **1 cup/250 g granulated sugar**
- **1 tsp vanilla extract/essence**
- **$1/4$ tsp almond extract/essence**
- **4 tbsp half-and-half**
- **1 large egg + 1 large egg yolk**
- **6 oz/180 g semisweet/dark chocolate, coarsely chopped**

464

SIMPLE BUTTERMILK COOKIES

Makes: 20–22 cookies

Preparation: 40'

Cooking: 10–15'

Level of difficulty: 1

- **1¹/₂ cups/225 g all-purpose/plain flour**
- **1 tsp baking powder**
- **¹/₂ tsp baking soda**
- **¹/₈ tsp salt**
- **6 tbsp butter, cut up**
- **6 tbsp granulated sugar**
- **³/₄ cup/180 ml buttermilk**

Preheat the oven to 350°F/180°C/gas 4. • Butter a cookie sheet. • Sift the flour, baking powder, baking soda, and salt into a large bowl. Stir in the sugar. • Use a pastry blender to cut in the butter until the mixture resembles fine crumbs. • Stir in the buttermilk to form a smooth dough. • Roll out the dough on a lightly floured surface to a thickness of ¹/₂ inch (1 cm). • Use a 2-inch (5-cm) cookie cutter to cut out the cookies. • Gather the dough scraps, re-roll, and continue cutting out cookies until all the dough is used. • Use a spatula to transfer the cookies to the prepared cookie sheet, placing them 1 inch (2.5 cm) apart. • Bake for 10–15 minutes, or until lightly browned. • Transfer to racks to cool.

RASPBERRY COOKIES

Sift the flour into a medium bowl. • Beat the butter and sugar in a large bowl until creamy. • Mix in the flour, almonds, and lemon zest and juice. • Divide the dough in half. Refrigerate for 30 minutes. • Roll out half the dough to a thickness of $1/8$ inch (3 mm). • Use a $1^1/2$-inch (4-cm) cookie cutter to cut out the cookies. • Place 1 inch (2.5 cm) apart on the sheets. • Use a $3/4$-inch (2-cm) fluted cutter to cut the centers out of half the cookies. • Repeat the cutting out procedure. • Refrigerate for 30 minutes. • Preheat the oven to 375°F/190°C/gas 5. • Bake for 6–8 minutes, or until just golden and the edges are firm. • Let cool. • Glaze: Mix the confectioners' sugar with enough lemon juice. • Spread the cookies with cut-out centers with the glaze. • Set aside until the glaze has dried. • Stick the cookies together in pairs with the preserves.

Makes: 25–30 cookies

Preparation: 45' + 60' to chill

Cooking: 6–8'

Level of difficulty: 2

- 1 cup/150 g all-purpose/plain flour
- $2/3$ cup/150 g butter, softened
- $1/2$ cup/100 g granulated sugar
- 1 cup/150 g finely ground almonds
- 1 tsp finely grated lemon zest
- 1 tsp lemon juice

Glaze

- $2/3$ cup/100 g confectioners'/icing sugar
- 1 tsp lemon juice, or more as needed
- 2 tbsp seedless red currant or raspberry preserves

ZESTY REFRIGERATOR COOKIES

Makes: 30–35 cookies

Preparation: 40' + 30' to chill

Cooking: 6–8'

Level of difficulty: 1

- 3 cups/450 g all-purpose/plain flour
- 1 tsp baking powder
- ½ tsp baking soda
- ½ tsp salt
- 1 cup/250 g butter, softened
- ¾ cup/150 g granulated sugar
- ⅔ cup/140 g firmly packed light brown sugar
- 2 tbsp vanilla sugar
- 2 large eggs, lightly beaten
- 1 tsp vanilla extract/essence
- 1 tsp finely grated lemon zest
- 1 tsp fresh lemon juice
- 2 tbsp milk or more as needed

Sift the flour, baking powder, baking soda, and salt into a medium bowl. • Beat the butter, granulated sugar, brown sugar, and vanilla sugar in a large bowl with an electric mixer at high speed until creamy. • Add the eggs, beating until just blended. • Stir in the vanilla and lemon zest and juice. • Mix in the dry ingredients until well blended. • Add enough milk to form a soft, but not sticky dough. • Turn the cookie dough onto a lightly floured surface and knead until smooth. • Divide the dough in half. Form each half into a 12-inch (30-cm) log, wrap in plastic wrap, and refrigerate for 30 minutes. • Preheat the oven to 400°F/200°C/gas 6. • Butter two cookie sheets • Slice the dough ¼ inch (5 mm) thick and place 1 inch (2.5 cm) apart on the prepared cookie sheets. • Bake for 6–8 minutes, or until lightly browned and firm around the edges. • Transfer to racks to cool.

CARAWAY ROSE COOKIES

Sift the flour and salt into a medium bowl. • Stir in the sugar and caraway seeds. • Beat in the egg yolk and egg whites and rose water to form a stiff dough. • Press the dough into a disk, wrap in plastic wrap, and refrigerate for 30 minutes. • Preheat the oven to 325°F/170°C/gas 3. • Butter two cookie sheets. • Roll out the dough on a lightly floured surface to a thickness of $1/8$ inch (3 mm). • Use a 2-inch (5-cm) cookie cutter to cut out the cookies. Gather the dough scraps, re-roll, and continue cutting out cookies until all the dough is used. • Use a spatula to transfer the cookies to the prepared cookie sheets, placing them 1 inch (2.5 cm) apart. • Bake for 10–15 minutes, or until golden brown. • Transfer to racks to cool.

Makes: 24–30 cookies

Preparation: 40' + 30' to chill

Cooking: 10–15'

Level of difficulty: 1

- 1½ cups/225 g all-purpose/plain flour
- ⅛ tsp salt
- 1 cup/200 g granulated sugar
- 1 tsp caraway seeds
- 1 large egg yolk + 3 large egg whites
- 1 tbsp rose water

SAINT REMY COOKIES

Makes: about 20 cookies

Preparation: 20'

Cooking: 10–12'

Level of difficulty: 1

- 1¼ cups/180 g all-purpose/plain flour
- 1 tsp baking powder
- ⅛ tsp salt
- 6 tbsp butter
- ¼ cup/50 g granulated sugar
- 1 large egg yolk
- 1 tbsp lavender flowers (heads only), rinsed and dried

Preheat the oven to 450°F/230°C/gas 8. • Line two cookie sheets with parchment paper. • Sift the flour, baking powder, and salt into a large bowl. • Beat the butter and sugar in a large bowl with an electric mixer at high speed until creamy. • Add the egg yolk, beating until just blended. • Mix in the dry ingredients and lavender leaves. •

Aromatic and fragrant, these cookies are best eaten with homemade lemonade.

473

Turn the dough out onto a lightly floured surface and knead to form a soft dough. • Roll out the dough to a thickness of ¼ inch (5 mm). • Sprinkle the dough with the lavender flowers, pressing in the heads with a rolling pin. • Use 2-inch (5-cm) cookie cutters to cut out the cookies. Gather the dough scraps, re-roll, and continue cutting out cookies until all the dough is used. • Use a spatula to transfer the cookies to the prepared cookie sheets. • Bake for 10–12 minutes, or until firm to the touch and lightly browned. • Transfer to racks to cool.

VANILLA HONEY COOKIES

Use a wooden spoon to mix the flour, sugar, egg, butter, water, baking soda, honey, vanilla, and salt in a large bowl to form a smooth dough. Press the dough into a disk, wrap in plastic wrap, and refrigerate for 30 minutes. • Preheat the oven to 350°F/180°C/gas 4. • Butter two cookie sheets. • Roll out the dough on a lightly floured surface to a thickness of $^1/_4$ inch (5 mm). • Use a knife to cut out squares. Gather the dough scraps, re-roll, and continue cutting out cookies until all the dough is used. • Use a spatula to transfer the cookies to the prepared cookie sheets, placing them 1 inch (2.5 cm) apart. • Brush with the milk. • Bake for 10–15 minutes, or until just golden at the edges. • Transfer to racks to cool.

Makes: 25 cookies

Preparation: 35' + 30' to chill

Cooking: 10–15'

Level of difficulty: 1

- 2$^1/_3$ cups/350 g all-purpose/plain flour
- $^1/_2$ cup/100 g granulated sugar
- 1 large egg
- 6 tbsp butter, softened
- 2 tbsp water
- 1 tsp baking soda
- 2 tbsp honey
- 1 tsp vanilla extract/essence
- $^1/_4$ tsp salt
- 1 tbsp milk

ALMOND CRISPS

Makes: 25 cookies

Preparation: 20'

Cooking: 5–7'

Level of difficulty: 1

- **1⅓ cups/150 g coarsely chopped almonds**
- **¾ cup/150 g granulated sugar**
- **5 tbsp all-purpose/ plain flour**
- **1 tbsp cornstarch/ cornflour**
- **⅛ tsp salt**
- **3 tbsp butter, melted**
- **½ tsp almond extract/essence**
- **1 tsp ground cinnamon**
- **3 large egg whites, lightly beaten**

Stir together the almonds, sugar, flour, cornstarch, and salt in a large bowl. • Add the butter, almond extract, and cinnamon. • Stir in the egg whites. • Refrigerate for 30 minutes. • Preheat the oven to 400°F/200°C/gas 6. • Line two cookie sheets with aluminum foil. • Drop ½ tablespoons of the dough 2 inches (5 cm) apart onto the prepared cookie sheets. • Bake for 5–7 minutes, or until golden brown. • Transfer to racks to cool.

ICED MACE COOKIES

Makes: about 36 cookies

Preparation: 30'+ 2 h to chill

Cooking: 10–12'

Level of difficulty: 1

Stir together the flour, baking powder, and mace in a medium bowl. • Beat the butter, sugar, and vanilla in a large bowl with an electric mixer at high speed until pale and creamy. • With mixer at medium speed, add the eggs, one at a time, and beat until just combined. • With mixer at low speed, gradually beat in the mixed dry ingredients. • Wrap in plastic wrap and refrigerate for at least 2 hours. • Preheat oven to 350°F/180°C/gas 4. • Grease and lightly flour a baking sheet. • Roll out the dough on a lightly floured work surface to $^1/8$ inch (3-mm) thick. Cut with cookie cutters in round or other shapes. Carefully transfer the cookies to the prepared trays. • Bake for 10–12 minutes, or until golden. Transfer to racks to cool. • Mix the confectioners' sugar with the water and spread over the cookies.

- 1$^3/4$ cups/275 g all-purpose/plain flour
- 2 tsp baking powder
- $^1/2$ tsp ground mace
- $^1/2$ cup/125 g butter
- 1 cup/200 g granulated sugar
- 1 tsp vanilla extract/essence
- 2 large eggs
- 1 cup/150 g confectioners'/icing sugar
- 2–3 tbsp warm water

Makes: 35 cookies

Preparation: 40' + 30' to chill

Cooking: 8–10'

Level of difficulty: 1

- 2¹/₃ cups/350 g all-purpose/plain flour
- ¹/₄ tsp salt
- 1 cup/250 g butter, softened
- 1¹/₄ cups/250 g granulated sugar
- ¹/₂ tsp vanilla extract/essence
- 1 large egg + 1 large egg white, lightly beaten
- 1 cup/100 g finely chopped pecans

PECAN VANILLA ROUNDS

Sift the flour and salt into a medium bowl. • Beat the butter and sugar in a large bowl with an electric mixer at high speed until creamy. • Add the egg, beating until just blended. • Mix in the dry ingredients. • Press the dough into four disks, wrap each in plastic wrap, and refrigerate for 30 minutes. • Preheat the oven to 350°F/180°C/ gas 4. • Butter three cookie sheets. • Roll out the dough on a lightly floured surface to a thickness of ¹/₄ inch (5 mm). • Use a 2-inch (5-cm) cookie cutter to cut out the cookies. Gather the dough scraps, re-roll, and continue cutting out cookies until all the dough is used. • Use a spatula to transfer the cookies to the prepared cookie sheets, placing them 1 inch (2.5 cm) apart. • Brush with the beaten egg white and sprinkle with the pecans. • Bake, one sheet at a time, for 8–10 minutes, or until just golden. • Cool on the sheets until the cookies firm slightly. • Transfer to racks to cool completely.

SHERRY CARAWAY CRISPS

Makes: 18–22 cookies

Preparation: 40' + 1 h to chill

Cooking: 10–15'

Level of difficulty: 1

- ½ cup/125 g butter, cut up
- 1 tbsp half-and-half
- 1²/₃ cups/250 g all-purpose/plain flour
- ²/₃ cup/140 g granulated sugar
- 1½ tsp caraway seeds
- ½ tsp freshly grated nutmeg
- ⅛ tsp salt
- 1 large egg yolk
- 1 tbsp sweet sherry

Melt the butter with the cream in a small saucepan over low heat. • Transfer to a large bowl. • Mix in the flour, sugar, caraway seeds, nutmeg, and salt. • Beat the egg yolk and sherry in a small bowl until frothy. • Stir the egg mixture into the dry ingredients to form a stiff dough. • Press the dough into a disk, wrap in plastic wrap, and refrigerate for 1 hour. • Preheat the oven to 325°F/170°C/gas 3. • Butter two cookie sheets. • Roll out the dough on a lightly floured surface to a thickness of ¹/₄ inch (5 mm). • Use a 2-inch (5-cm) cookie cutter to cut out the cookies. • Gather the dough scraps, re-roll, and continue cutting out cookies until all the dough is used. • Use a spatula to transfer the cookies to the cookie sheets, placing them 1 inch (2.5 cm) apart. • Bake for 10–15 minutes, or until just golden. • Transfer to racks to cool.

STRAWBERRY CINNAMON CRISPS

Preheat the oven to 400°F/200°C/gas 6. • Butter three cookie sheets. • Sift the flour, baking powder, cinnamon, and salt into a medium bowl. • Beat the butter and sugar in a large bowl with an electric mixer at high speed until creamy. • Add the eggs and vanilla, beating until just blended. • Mix in the dry ingredients. • Fit the pastry bag with a 1/2-inch (1-cm) plain tip. Fill the pastry bag, twist the opening tightly closed, and squeeze out 2-inch (5-cm) rounds, spacing 1 inch (2.5 cm) apart on the prepared cookie sheets. • Press your thumb into each cookie to make a small hollow. • Bake, one sheet at a time, for 8–10 minutes, or until just golden. • Transfer to racks to cool. • Heat the preserves in a small saucepan over low heat until liquid. • Fill each hollow with a little preserves and let stand for 20 minutes until set.

Makes: 50 cookies

Preparation: 25'+ 20' to stand

Cooking: 8–10'

Level of difficulty: 2

- 2 1/3 cups/350 g all-purpose/plain flour
- 1 tsp baking powder
- 1 tsp ground cinnamon
- 1/8 tsp salt
- 6 tbsp butter, softened
- 1/2 cup/100 g granulated sugar
- 2 large eggs
- 1/2 tsp vanilla extract/essence
- 1/2 cup/160 g strawberry preserves

ROSE WATER FINGERS

Makes: about 30
  cookies

Preparation: 25'

Cooking: 8–10'

Level of difficulty: 2

- 1 cup/150 g all-
  purpose/plain flour
- 1/8 tsp salt
- 3 large eggs,
  separated
- 1/2 cup/75 g
  confectioners'/
  icing sugar
- 1 tsp rose water

Preheat the oven to 350°F/180°C/gas 4. • Line two cookie sheets with parchment paper. • Sift the flour and salt into a large bowl. • Beat the egg whites in a large bowl with an electric mixer at medium speed until soft peaks form. • With mixer at high speed, gradually add the confectioners' sugar, beating until stiff, glossy peaks form. • With mixer at medium speed, beat the egg yolks and rose water in a medium bowl until well blended. • Use a large rubber spatula to fold the beaten yolks into the beaten whites. • Fold in the dry ingredients. • Fit a pastry bag with a 1/2-inch (1-cm) plain tip. Fill the pastry bag, twist the opening tightly closed, and squeeze out 3-inch (8-cm) fingers, spacing 2 inches (5-cm) apart on the prepared cookie sheets. • Bake for 8–10 minutes, or until lightly browned. • Cool on the sheets until the cookies firm slightly. • Transfer to racks and let cool.

SAVOY LADYFINGERS

Preheat the oven to 325°F/170°C/gas 3 • Line two cookie sheets with parchment paper. • Sift the flour and salt into a medium bowl. • Beat the eggs, $^1/_2$ cup (100 g) superfine sugar, and vanilla in a double boiler over barely simmering water. Beat until the batter falls off the beaters in ribbons.

A classic recipe from the leading London hotel, famed for its afternoon dinner dances.

486

• Use a large rubber spatula to fold in the dry ingredients. • Fit a pastry bag with a $^1/_2$-inch (1-cm) star tip. Fill the pastry bag, twist the opening tightly closed, and squeeze out 3 x $^3/_4$-inch (8 x 2-cm) lengths spacing them 1 inch (2.5 cm) apart on the prepared cookie sheets.

• Sprinkle with the remaining superfine sugar.
• Bake for 10–15 minutes, or until crisp and dry to the touch. • Cool on the sheets until the cookies firm slightly. • Transfer to racks to finish cooling.

Makes: 30–35 fingers

Preparation: 30'

Cooking: 10–15'

Level of difficulty: 2

- $^2/_3$ cup/100 g all-purpose/plain flour
- $^1/_8$ tsp salt
- 3 large eggs
- $^2/_3$ cup/140 g superfine sugar
- $^1/_2$ tsp vanilla extract/essence

CRIMSON COOKIES

Makes: 35–40 cookies

Preparation: 40'

Cooking: 5–8'

Level of difficulty: 1

- ¾ cup/180 ml pure maple syrup
- ⅔ cup/150 g butter, cut up
- 1 cup/150 g all-purpose/plain flour
- ¼ tsp baking soda
- ⅛ tsp salt
- ¼ cup/50 g granulated sugar
- 1 tsp vanilla extract/essence
- 1 large egg

FROSTING

- 1 cup/150 g confectioners'/icing sugar
- 2–3 tbsp water
- few drops red food coloring

Preheat the oven to 375°F/190°C/gas 5. • Butter four cookie sheets. • Bring the maple syrup to a boil in a small saucepan over medium heat and boil for 5 minutes. • Add the butter and boil for 2 minutes. • Let cool for 10 minutes. • Sift the flour, baking soda, and salt into a large bowl. Stir in the sugar. • Add the vanilla and egg to the maple syrup mixture, beating until just blended. • Pour into the dry ingredients and mix well. • Drop teaspoons of the batter 3 inches (8 cm) apart onto the prepared cookie sheets. Do not drop more than four cookies onto each cookie sheet. • Bake, one sheet at a time, for 5–8 minutes, or until faintly tinged with brown on top and slightly darker at the edges. • Cool on the sheets until the cookies firm slightly. • Transfer to racks to finish cooling.

• Butter the cookie sheets again and continue to bake in batches until all the batter has been used.

• Frosting: Mix the confectioners' sugar, water, and food coloring in a small bowl to make a thin glaze. Drizzle over the tops of the cookies in a decorative manner.

BROWN SUGAR PECAN SNAPS

Makes: about 20 cookies

Preparation: 40'

Cooking: 5–7'

Level of difficulty: 3

- ½ cup/75 g all-purpose/plain flour
- ¼ tsp baking powder
- ⅛ tsp salt
- 4 tbsp butter, cut up
- 6 tbsp light corn syrup
- ¼ cup/50 g firmly packed dark brown sugar
- ½ cup/50 g finely chopped pecans
- ½ cup/125 ml heavy/double cream
- ¼ tsp vanilla extract/essence
- 2 tbsp confectioners'/icing sugar

Preheat the oven to 375°F/190°C/gas 5. • Line three cookie sheets with parchment paper. Butter two rolling pins. • Sift the flour, baking powder, and salt into a medium bowl. • Melt the butter with the corn syrup and brown sugar in a medium saucepan. Remove from heat and let cool slightly. • Mix in the dry ingredients and pecans. • Drop teaspoons of the dough 3 inches (8 cm) apart onto the sheets. Do not drop more than six cookies onto each sheet. • Bake for 5–7 minutes, or until lightly browned. • Lift each cookie from the sheet and drape it over a rolling pin. Slide each cookie off the pin and onto racks to finish cooling. • Butter the cookie sheets again and continue to bake in batches until all the batter has been used. • Beat the cream with the vanilla and confectioners' sugar until stiff. Fit a pastry bag with a 1½-inch star tip. Fill the pastry bag, twist the opening tightly closed, and squeeze out cream rosettes into the cookies.

ORANGE SESAME THINS

Toast the sesame seeds in a frying pan over medium heat for 5–7 minutes until lightly browned. • Sift the flour and salt into a medium bowl. • Beat the butter, confectioners' sugar, and orange zest in a large bowl with an electric mixer at high speed until creamy. • Gradually beat in the egg whites. • Mix in the dry ingredients and sesame seeds. Refrigerate for 1 hour. • Preheat the oven to 350°F/180°C/gas 4. • Butter four cookie sheets. • Butter two rolling pins. • Drop teaspoons of the mixture 2 inches (5 cm) apart onto the prepared cookie sheets. Use a thin spatula to spread out the mixture to about 3 inches (8 cm) in diameter. • Do not place more than five cookies on one sheet. • Bake, one sheet at a time, for 5–6 minutes, or until the edges are lightly golden. • Working quickly, use a spatula to place the cookies over a rolling pin. • Slide each cookie off the pin onto a rack to finish cooling. • Butter the cookie sheets again and continue to bake in batches until all the batter has been used.

Makes: about 26 cookies

Preparation: 50' + 1 h to chill

Cooking: 5–6'

Level of difficulty: 3

- 1 cup/100 g sesame seeds
- 2/3 cup/100 g all-purpose/plain flour
- 1/8 tsp salt
- 6 tbsp butter, softened
- 2/3 cup/100 g confectioners'/ icing sugar
- 2 tbsp vanilla sugar
- grated zest of 1 orange
- 3 large egg whites, lightly beaten

BEST SUGAR COOKIES

Makes: about 18
  cookies

Preparation: 40' + 30'
  to chill

Cooking: 15–20'

Level of difficulty: 1

- 1½ cups/225 g all-purpose/plain flour
- ½ tsp ground cinnamon
- ⅛ tsp salt
- ½ cup/125 g butter, softened
- 3 tbsp confectioners'/icing sugar

Sift the flour, cinnamon, and salt into a medium bowl. • Use a wooden spoon to beat the butter and sugar in a medium bowl until creamy. • Mix in the dry ingredients to form a smooth dough. Press the dough into a disk, wrap in plastic wrap, and refrigerate for 30 minutes. • Preheat the oven to 400°F/200°C/gas 6. • Butter a cookie sheet. • Roll out the dough on a lightly floured surface to a thickness of ¼ inch (5 mm). • Use a 3-inch (8-cm) cookie cutter to cut out the cookies. Gather the dough scraps, re-roll, and continue cutting out cookies until all the dough is used. Use a spatula to transfer the cookies to the prepared cookie sheet, placing them 2 inches (5 cm) apart. • Bake for 15–20 minutes, or until just golden. • Transfer to racks to cool.

GOLDEN CRISPS

Sift the flour and arrowroot into a large bowl. •
Use a pastry blender to cut in the butter until
the mixture resembles fine crumbs. • Stir in the
sugar. • Add the egg and egg yolk to form a stiff
dough. • Press the dough into a disk, wrap in
plastic wrap, and refrigerate for 30 minutes. •
Preheat the oven to 425°F/220°C/gas 7. • Butter
two cookie sheets. • Roll out the dough on a lightly
floured surface to a thickness of $^1/_4$ inch (5 mm).
• Use a 2-inch (5-cm) cookie cutter to cut out the
cookies. • Gather the dough scraps, re-roll, and
continue cutting out cookies until all the dough is
used. • Use a spatula to transfer the cookies to the
cookie sheets, placing them 1 inch (2.5 cm) apart.
• Bake for 10–15 minutes, or until pale golden
brown. • Transfer to racks to cool. Sprinkle with
the extra sugar.

496

*Makes: 20–25
cookies*

*Preparation: 40' + 30'
to chill*

Cooking: 10–15'

Level of difficulty: 1

- 1$^1/_3$ cups/200 g all-
purpose/plain flour
- 2 tbsp arrowroot
starch
- $^1/_2$ cup/125 g
butter, softened
- $^2/_3$ cup/140 g
granulated sugar +
2 tbsp, to sprinkle
- 1 large egg + 1
large egg yolk,
lightly beaten

GINGER MOLASSES COOKIES

Makes: 25–30
cookies

Preparation: 40' + 1 h
to chill

Cooking: 10–15'

Level of difficulty: 1

- 1 1/4 cups/180 g all-purpose/plain flour
- 1 tsp ground ginger
- 1/2 tsp baking powder
- 1/8 tsp salt
- 4 tbsp butter, cut up
- 1/4 cup/50 g firmly packed light brown sugar
- 4 tbsp light molasses

Sift the flour, ginger, baking powder, and salt into a medium bowl. • Melt the butter with the brown sugar and molasses in a medium saucepan over low heat. • Remove from the heat and mix in the dry ingredients to form a stiff dough. • Press the dough into a disk, wrap in plastic wrap, and refrigerate for 1 hour. • Preheat the oven to 325°F/170°C/gas 3. • Butter two cookie sheets. • Roll out the dough on a lightly floured surface to a thickness of 1/4 inch (5 mm). • Use a 2-inch (5-cm) cookie cutter to cut out the cookies. • Gather the dough scraps, re-roll, and continue cutting out cookies until all the dough is used. • Use a spatula to transfer the cookies to the prepared cookie sheets, placing them 1 inch (2.5 cm) apart. • Bake for 10–15 minutes, or until firm to the touch and just golden. • Transfer to racks to cool.

GLUTEN-FREE COOKIES

Makes: 18–22 cookies

Preparation: 40' + 30' to chill

Cooking: 10–15'

Level of difficulty: 1

- ½ cup/125 g butter, softened
- ⅔ cup/140 g granulated sugar
- 1½ cups/225 g rice flour
- 2 large eggs, lightly beaten

Beat the butter and sugar in a large bowl with an electric mixer at high speed until creamy. • Mix in the rice flour. • Add the eggs, beating to form a smooth dough. • Press the dough into a disk, wrap in plastic wrap, and refrigerate for 30 minutes. • Preheat the oven to 300°F/150°C/gas 2. • Butter two cookie sheets. • Roll out the dough on a surface lightly dusted with rice flour to a thickness of ¼ inch (5 mm). • Use a 2-inch (5-cm) cookie cutter to cut out the cookies. • Gather the dough scraps, re-roll, and continue cutting out cookies until all the dough is used. • Use a spatula to transfer the cookies to the cookie sheets, placing them 1 inch (2.5 cm) apart. • Bake for 15–20 minutes, or until just golden.
• Transfer to racks to cool.

EASY HONEY COOKIES

Sift the flour and salt into a medium bowl. • Use a pastry blender to cut in the butter until the mixture resembles fine crumbs. • Mix in the cream and honey to form a stiff dough. • Press the dough into a disk, wrap in plastic wrap, and refrigerate for 30 minutes. • Preheat the oven to 300°F/150°C/gas 2. • Butter two cookie sheets. • Roll out the dough on a lightly floured surface to a thickness of $1/8$ inch (3 mm). Use a 2-inch (5-cm) cookie cutter to cut out the cookies. • Gather the dough scraps, re-roll, and continue cutting out cookies until all the dough is used. • Use a spatula to transfer the cookies to the prepared cookie sheets, placing them 2 inches (5 cm) apart. • Bake for 15–20 minutes, or until golden. • Transfer to racks to cool.

Makes: 20–24 cookies

Preparation: 40' + 30' to chill

Cooking: 15–20'

Level of difficulty: 1

- 1$2/3$ cups/250 g all-purpose/plain flour
- $1/8$ tsp salt
- $1/2$ cup/125 g butter, cut up
- 2 tbsp heavy/double cream
- 2 tbsp honey

PECAN WAFERS

Makes: 20–25 cookies

Preparation: 30'

Cooking: 8–10'

Level of difficulty: 3

- ½ cup/50 g finely chopped pecans
- ½ cup/100 g granulated sugar
- 2 tbsp all-purpose/ plain flour
- 4 tbsp butter, melted
- 2 large egg whites, lightly beaten
- ½ tsp vanilla extract/essence
- ⅛ tsp salt

Preheat the oven to 350°F/180°C/gas 4. • Butter four cookie sheets. • Butter two rolling pins. • Process the pecans and sugar in a food processor or blender until finely ground. • Transfer to a large bowl and stir in the flour, butter, egg whites, vanilla, and salt. • Drop teaspoons of the batter 3 inches (8 cm) apart onto the prepared cookie sheets. • Do not place more than five cookies on one sheet. Spread the mixture out into thin circles. • Bake, one sheet at a time, for 8–10 minutes, or until just golden at the edges. • Use a spatula to lift each cookie off the sheet. Working quickly, drape it over a rolling pin to give it a rounded finish. • Let cool completely.

NORTHERN LIGHTS COOKIES

Makes: 20 cookies

Preparation: 40' +
    12 h to chill

Cooking: 15–20'

Level of difficulty: 1

- ⅔ cup/100 g all-purpose/plain flour
- 1 tsp baking powder
- ½ tsp ground ginger
- ¼ tsp ground cinnamon
- ⅛ tsp salt
- ¼ tsp baking soda
- 1 tbsp warm water
- 3 tbsp butter
- 4 tbsp light corn syrup/golden syrup
- 2 tbsp granulated sugar

Sift the flour, baking powder, ginger, cinnamon, and salt into a large bowl. • Dissolve the baking soda in the water. • Melt the butter with the corn syrup and sugar in a small saucepan over medium heat. • Mix in the baking soda mixture. • Mix the butter mixture into the dry ingredients. • Cover with plastic wrap and refrigerate for 12 hours. • Preheat the oven to 300°F/150°C/gas 2. • Butter two cookie sheets. • Roll out the dough on a lightly floured surface to a thickness of ¼ inch (5 mm). • Use 1-inch (2.5-cm) cookie cutters to cut out the cookies. • Gather the dough scraps, re-roll, and continue cutting out the cookies until all the dough is used. • Use a spatula to transfer the cookies to the prepared cookie sheets, placing them 1 inch (2.5 cm) apart. • Bake for 15–20 minutes, or until lightly browned. • Transfer to racks to cool.

HIGHLAND COOKIES

Makes: 20 cookies

Preparation: 40'

Cooking: 8–10'

Level of difficulty: 1

- 2 cups/300 g all-purpose/plain flour
- 1½ tsp baking powder
- ⅛ tsp salt
- 1 cup/250 g butter, softened
- 1½ cups/300 g granulated sugar
- 1 large egg
- ½ tsp vanilla extract/essence
- ½ cup/160 ml raspberry preserves
- ⅓ cup/50 g confectioners'/ icing sugar
- 1 tbsp water or more as needed
- 10 candied cherries, cut in half

Sift the flour, baking powder, and salt into a large bowl. • Beat the butter and sugar in a large bowl with an electric mixer at high speed until creamy. • Add the egg and vanilla, beating until just blended. • Turn the dough out onto a lightly floured surface and knead until smooth. • Press the dough into a disk, wrap in plastic wrap, and refrigerate for 30 minutes. • Preheat the oven to 350°F/180°C/ gas 4. • Butter two cookie sheets. • Roll out the dough to a thickness of ¼ inch (5 mm). • Use a 1½-inch (4-cm) cookie cutter to cut out the cookies. • Gather the dough scraps, re-roll, and continue cutting out cookies until all the dough is used. • Use a spatula to transfer the cookies to a cookie sheet, placing them 1 inch (2.5 cm) apart. • Bake for 8–10 minutes, or until lightly browned. • Cool on the sheets until the cookies firm slightly. Transfer to racks to finish cooling. • Warm the raspberry preserves in a small saucepan over low heat until liquid. • Stick the cookies together in pairs with the preserves. • Mix the confectioners' sugar with enough water to make a spreadable frosting. • Spread the tops of the cookies with the frosting and decorate with a half cherry.

CEREAL
& SEED
COOKIES

SCOTTISH COOKIES

Preheat the oven to 350°F/180°C/gas 4. • Line two cookie sheets with parchment paper. • Sift the flour, baking soda, and salt into a large bowl. • Beat the butter and brown sugar in a large bowl with an electric mixer at high speed until creamy. • Add the egg, beating until just blended. Add the vanilla. • Mix in the dry ingredients, oats, and water. • Roll teaspoons of the mixture into balls and place on the prepared cookie sheets, about 1 1/2 inches (4 cm) apart, flattening them slightly. • Bake for 12–15 minutes, or until golden brown. • Transfer to racks to cool.

Makes: 35–40 cookies

Preparation: 30'

Cooking: 12–15'

Level of difficulty: 1

- 1 cup/150 g all-purpose/plain flour
- 1/2 tsp baking soda
- 1/8 tsp salt
- 2/3 cup/150 g butter, softened
- 1 1/4 cups/250 g firmly packed dark brown sugar
- 1 large egg
- 1 tsp vanilla extract/essence
- 1 cup/150 g old-fashioned rolled oats
- 1 tbsp water or more as needed

GEORDIE COOKIES

Preheat the oven to 350°F/180°C/gas 4. • Butter three cookie sheets. • Sift the flour, baking soda, and salt into a large bowl. • Beat the butter and granulated and brown sugars in a large bowl with an electric mixer at high speed until creamy. • Add the vanilla and egg, beating until just blended. • Mix in the dry ingredients, oats, raisins, and peanuts. • Drop heaping teaspoons of the dough 2 inches (5 cm) apart onto the prepared cookie sheets. • Bake, one sheet at a time, for 12–15 minutes, or until lightly browned. • Transfer to racks and let cool completely

- 1¼ cups/180 g all-purpose/plain flour
- ½ tsp baking soda
- ½ tsp salt
- ½ cup/125 g butter, softened
- ½ cup/100 g granulated sugar
- ½ cup/100 g firmly packed dark brown sugar
- ½ tsp vanilla extract/essence
- 1 large egg, lightly beaten
- ⅓ cup/50 g old-fashioned rolled oats
- ½ cup/90 g raisins
- ⅔ cup/60 g coarsely chopped walnuts

FIRST DATE COOKIES

- 1½ cups/225 g all-purpose/plain flour
- ½ tsp baking powder
- ⅛ tsp salt
- ½ cup/125 g butter, cut up
- 1 large egg, lightly beaten
- 1 cup/200 g granulated sugar
- ½ cup/75 g old-fashioned rolled oats
- ½ cup/50 g coarsely chopped dates

Preheat the oven to 350°F/180°C/gas 4. • Butter two cookie sheets. • Sift the flour, baking powder, and salt into a large bowl. • Use a pastry blender to cut in the butter until the mixture resembles fine crumbs. • Add the egg, beating until just blended. • Mix in the sugar, oats, and dates. • Drop tablespoons of the dough 2 inches (5 cm) apart onto the prepared cookie sheets.
- Bake for 12–15 minutes, or until lightly browned.
- Cool on the sheets until the cookies firm slightly.
- Transfer to racks to cool.

515

DOWNUNDER OAT SQUARES

Preheat the oven to 325°F/170°C/gas 3. •
Butter a 9-inch (23-cm) square baking pan. •
Melt the butter, sugar, and corn syrup in a small
saucepan over medium heat. • Remove from the
heat and stir in the flour and oats until well blended.
• Spoon the mixture evenly into the prepared pan,
pressing down lightly. • Bake for 15–20 minutes,
or until golden brown. • Cool completely before
cutting into bars.

Makes: 16–25 bars
Preparation: 15'
Cooking: 15–20'
Level of difficulty: 1

- ½ cup/125 g butter, cut up
- 1 cup/200 g granulated sugar
- 1 tbsp light corn syrup/golden syrup
- 1 tbsp all-purpose/plain flour
- ½ cup/75 g old-fashioned rolled oats

DIGESTIVE BISCUITS

Makes: about 20 cookies

Preparation: 40' + 30' to chill

Cooking: 10–15'

Level of difficulty: 1

- 1 cup/150 g whole-wheat flour
- ½ tsp baking soda
- ¼ tsp salt
- ¾ cup/180 g butter, cut up
- 1 cup/150 g oat bran
- ½ cup/100 g granulated sugar
- 1 large egg, lightly beaten

Sift the whole-wheat flour, baking soda, and salt into a large bowl. • Cut in the butter until the mixture resembles fine crumbs. • Stir in the oat bran and sugar. • Mix in enough beaten egg. Press the dough into a disk, wrap in plastic wrap, and refrigerate for 30 minutes. • Preheat the oven to 375°F/190°C/gas 5. • Butter a cookie sheet.
• Roll out the dough on a surface lightly dusted with oat bran to a thickness of ¼ inch (5 mm).
• Use a 2-inch (5-cm) cookie cutter to cut out the cookies. Gather the dough scraps, re-roll, and continue cutting out cookies until all the dough is used. • Transfer the cookies to the prepared cookie sheet, placing them 1 inch (2.5 cm) apart.
• Bake for 10–15 minutes, or until browned.
• Transfer to racks and let cool.

LIGHT BROWN CHERRY OATIES

Makes: 20 cookies

Preparation: 15'

Cooking: 15–20'

Level of difficulty: 1

- 2 cups/300 g all-purpose/plain flour
- 1 tbsp baking powder
- ½ tsp salt
- ¾ cup/180 g butter, softened
- ¾ cup/150 g firmly packed light brown sugar
- 1 tsp vanilla extract/essence
- 1 large egg, lightly beaten
- 2 tbsp old-fashioned rolled oats
- 10 candied cherries, halved, to decorate

Preheat the oven to 350°F/180°C/gas 4. • Butter two cookie sheets. • Sift the flour, baking powder, and salt into a medium bowl. • Beat the butter, brown sugar, and vanilla in a large bowl with an electric mixer at high speed until creamy. • Add the egg, beating until just blended. • Mix in the dry ingredients and oats until well blended. • Form into balls the size of walnuts and place 2 inches (5 cm) apart on the prepared cookie sheets, flattening them slightly. • Place half a cherry in the center of each cookie. • Bake for 15–20 minutes, or until lightly browned. • Cool completely on the cookie sheets.

BREAKFAST COOKIES

Preheat the oven to 350°F/180°C/gas 4. • Line two cookie sheets with parchment paper. • Sift the flour and baking powder into a large bowl. • Beat the butter and brown sugar in a large bowl with an electric mixer at high speed until creamy. • Add the eggs, beating until just blended. • Mix in the dry ingredients, followed by the corn flakes, apricots, and coconut. • Drop heaping teaspoons of the mixture 1 1/2 inches (4 cm) apart onto the prepared cookie sheets. • Bake for 10–12 minutes, or until lightly browned. • Transfer the cookies on the parchment paper to racks to cool.

Makes: 35 cookies

Preparation: 30'

Cooking: 10–12'

Level of difficulty: 2

- **2/3 cup/100 g all-purpose/plain flour**
- **1 tsp baking powder**
- **6 tbsp butter, softened**
- **2/3 cup/140 g firmly packed light brown sugar**
- **2 large eggs**
- **2 tbsp corn flakes**
- **1/2 cup/50 g finely chopped dried apricots**
- **3 tbsp shredded/ desiccated coconut**

MINI CORN FLAKE COOKIES

Makes: 20–24 cookies

Preparation: 20'

Cooking: 10–15'

Level of difficulty: 1

- 1 cup/150 g all-purpose/plain flour
- ½ tsp baking powder
- 4 tbsp butter, softened
- 4 tbsp vegetable shortening
- ½ cup/100 g granulated sugar
- 1 large egg, lightly beaten
- 1 cup/150 g corn flakes

Preheat the oven to 350°F/180°C/gas 4. • Butter two cookie sheets. • Sift the flour and baking powder into a medium bowl. • Beat the butter, shortening, and sugar in a large bowl with an electric mixer at high speed until creamy. • Mix in the dry ingredients. • Add the egg, beating until just blended. • Sprinkle the corn flakes onto a cookie sheet. • Drop tablespoons of the batter onto the corn flakes. • Use a spatula to flatten the cookies and turn until completely coated. • Transfer the cookies to the prepared cookie sheets, placing 1 inch (2.5 cm) apart. • Bake for 10–15 minutes, or until just golden. • Transfer to racks to cool.

SUNFLOWER SEED DRIZZLERS

Makes: 20 cookies

Preparation: 25' + 30' to set

Cooking: 8–10'

Level of difficulty: 1

- 2 cups/300 g all-purpose/plain flour
- 1 tsp ground allspice
- 1 tsp baking soda
- $1/4$ tsp salt
- $1^1/2$ cups/225 g sunflower seeds
- 1 cup/150 g old-fashioned rolled oats
- 2 tbsp sesame seeds
- 1 cup/250 g butter, cut up
- 2 tbsp firmly packed dark brown sugar
- 1 tbsp dark molasses
- $1^1/2$ cups/250 g carob chips

Preheat the oven to 375°F/190°C/gas 5. • Butter two cookie sheets. • Sift the flour, allspice, baking soda, and salt into a large bowl. • Stir in the sunflower seeds, oats, and sesame seeds. • Melt the butter with the brown sugar and molasses in a small saucepan over low heat until the sugar has dissolved completely. • Pour the melted butter mixture into the dry ingredients and mix well. • Drop tablespoons of the mixture $1^1/2$ inches (4 cm) apart onto the prepared cookie sheets, flattening with a fork. • Bake for 8–10 minutes, or until just golden. • Transfer to racks to cool. • Melt the carob in a double boiler over barely simmering water. • Drizzle the carob over the cookies and let stand for 30 minutes.

Carob is a healthy alternative to chocolate and is readily available in health food stores.

APRICOT CRUNCH

Makes: 30 bars

Preparation: 20'

Cooking: 25–30'

Level of difficulty: 1

Preheat the oven to 350°F/180°C/gas 4. • Butter a 10^1/$_2$ x 15^1/$_2$-inch (26 x 36-cm) jelly-roll pan. • Crunchy Topping: Melt the butter in a small saucepan over medium heat. Stir in the brown sugar and oats until well blended. • Cookie Base: Sift the flour, baking powder, and salt into a large bowl and stir in the sugar. Make a well in the center. Use a pastry blender to cut in the butter until the mixture resembles fine crumbs. • Firmly press the mixture into the prepared pan. • Heat the preserves in a small saucepan over medium heat until liquid. Spread over the cookie base. • Sprinkle with the topping. • Bake for 25–30 minutes, or until lightly browned. • Cool completely before cutting into bars.

CRUNCHY TOPPING
- ^{1}/$_2$ cup/125 g butter, cut up
- 1 cup/200 g firmly packed dark brown sugar
- ^{1}/$_2$ cup/75 g old-fashioned rolled oats

COOKIE BASE
- 3^2/$_3$ cups/550 g all-purpose/plain flour
- 2 tsp baking powder
- ^{1}/$_4$ tsp salt
- ^{3}/$_4$ cup/150 g granulated sugar
- 1 cup/250 g butter, cut up
- ^{1}/$_2$ cup/125 g apricot preserves

Makes: 28 cookies

Preparation: 40' + 30' to chill

Cooking: 10–15'

Level of difficulty: 2

- 2/3 cup/100 g all-purpose/plain flour
- 1/2 tsp baking powder
- 1/4 tsp ground cinnamon
- 1/8 tsp salt
- 4 tbsp butter, softened
- 1/4 cup/50 g firmly packed light brown sugar
- 1 large egg
- 1/2 cup/90 g finely chopped raisins
- 1/4 cup/50 g finely chopped dried apricots
- 1/2 cup/50 g finely chopped almonds
- 1/4 cup/50 g finely chopped sunflower seeds

GLAZE
- 1/2 cup/160 g ginger preserves
- 2 tbsp butter

SUNFLOWER SEED GINGER COOKIES

Sift the flour, baking powder, cinnamon, and salt into a medium bowl. • Beat the butter and brown sugar in a large bowl with an electric mixer at high speed until creamy. • Add the egg, beating until just blended. • Mix in the raisins, apricots, almonds, and sunflower seeds. • Mix in the dry ingredients to form a soft dough. • Form the dough into a 14-inch (35-cm) log, wrap in plastic wrap, and refrigerate for at least 30 minutes. • Preheat the oven to 350°F/180°C/gas 4. • Line two cookie sheets with parchment paper. • Slice the dough 1/2 inch (1 cm) thick and place 1 inch (2.5 cm) apart on the prepared cookie sheets. • Bake for 10–15 minutes, or until just golden. • Transfer to racks and let cool completely. • Glaze: Heat the preserves and butter in a small saucepan over low heat and simmer for 2 minutes. • Drizzle the glaze over the cookies.

PEANUT MUNCHIES

Preheat the oven to 300°F/150°C/gas 2. •
Butter a cookie sheet. • Sift the flour, baking
powder, and baking soda into a medium bowl.
• Beat the butter and sugar in a large bowl with an
electric mixer at high speed until creamy. • Add the
egg, beating until just blended. • Mix in the dry
ingredients, peanuts, corn flakes, and oats to make
a stiff dough. • Drop teaspoons of the dough
1 inch (2.5 cm) apart onto the prepared cookie
sheet. • Bake for 10–15 minutes, or until lightly
browned. • Cool on the sheet until the cookies firm
slightly. • Transfer to racks and let cool completely.

Makes: about 25 cookies

Preparation: 20'

Cooking: 10–15'

Level of difficulty: 1

- 1 cup/150 g all-purpose/plain flour
- ½ tsp baking powder
- ½ tsp baking soda
- ½ cup/125 g butter, softened
- 1 cup/200 g granulated sugar
- 1 large egg, lightly beaten
- ½ cup/50 g salted peanuts
- 1 cup/150 g corn flakes
- 2¼ cups/330 g old-fashioned rolled oats

PEANUT BUTTER BRAN COOKIES

Makes: 20–25 cookies

Preparation: 20'

Cooking: 8–10'

Level of difficulty: 1

- 1 cup/150 g whole-wheat flour
- ½ tsp baking powder
- ⅛ tsp salt
- ½ cup/125 g butter, softened
- ½ cup/100 g firmly packed dark brown sugar
- 1 cup/250 ml smooth peanut butter
- 1 large egg
- ½ tsp vanilla extract/essence
- 1 cup/150 g bran

Preheat the oven to 375°F/190°C/gas 5. • Butter two cookie sheets. • Sift the flour, baking powder, and salt into a medium bowl. • Beat the butter and brown sugar in a large bowl with an electric mixer at high speed until creamy. • Beat in the peanut butter, egg, and vanilla. • Mix in the dry ingredients and bran. • Form the dough into balls the size of walnuts and place 1½ inches (4 cm) apart on the prepared cookie sheets, flattening them slightly. • Bake for 8–10 minutes, or until just golden. • Transfer to racks to cool.

WALNUT CRISPS

Makes: 36 cookies

Preparation: 20'

Cooking: 12–15'

Level of difficulty: 1

- ²⁄₃ cup/100 g all-purpose/plain flour
- ½ tsp baking soda
- ⅛ tsp salt
- ½ cup/125 g butter, softened
- ¼ cup/50 g granulated sugar
- ²⁄₃ cup/70 g firmly packed light brown sugar
- ½ tsp vanilla extract/essence
- 1 large egg, lightly beaten
- ⅓ cup/50 g corn flakes
- ²⁄₃ cup/70 g coarsely chopped walnuts

Preheat the oven to 375°F/190°C/gas 5. • Butter three cookie sheets. • Sift the flour, baking soda, and salt into a large bowl. • Beat the butter and granulated and brown sugars in a large bowl with an electric mixer at high speed until creamy. • Add the vanilla and egg, beating until just blended. • Mix in the dry ingredients, followed by the corn flakes and walnuts. • Drop teaspoons of the dough 1 inch (2.5 cm) apart onto the prepared cookie sheets. • Bake, one sheet at a time, for 12–15 minutes, or until lightly browned. • Cool on the sheets until the cookies firm slightly. • Transfer to racks to finish cooling.

SUMMERTIME DROPS

Preheat the oven to 350°F/180°C/gas 4. •
Butter three cookie sheets. • Sift the flour,
baking soda, and salt into a medium bowl. • Beat
the butter and brown and granulated sugars in a
large bowl with an electric mixer at high speed until
creamy. • Add the eggs and vanilla, beating until
just blended. • Mix in the dry ingredients, oats, and
sunflower seeds. • Drop tablespoons of the dough
2 inches (5 cm) apart onto the prepared cookie
sheets. • Bake, one batch at a time, for 10–15
minutes, or until golden brown. • Cool on the
sheets until the cookies firm slightly. Transfer to
racks to finish cooling.

*Makes: 36–40
  cookies*

Preparation: 20'

Cooking: 10–15'

Level of difficulty: 1

- 1½ cups/225 g all-
  purpose/plain flour
- 1 tsp baking soda
- ¼ tsp salt
- 1 cup/250 g butter,
  softened
- 1 cup/200 g firmly
  packed light brown
  sugar
- 1 cup/200 g
  granulated sugar
- 2 large eggs, lightly
  beaten
- ½ tsp vanilla
  extract/essence
- 2 cups/300 g old-
  fashioned rolled
  oats
- 1 cup/100 g
  sunflower seeds

MINSTREL COOKIES

Makes: 35 cookies

Preparation: 25'

Cooking: 20–25'

Level of difficulty: 1

- 1½ cups/225 g all-purpose/plain flour
- 1 cup/150 g finely ground yellow cornmeal
- 1 tsp baking powder
- ⅛ tsp salt
- ½ cup/125 g butter, cut up
- 2 large eggs, lightly beaten
- ⅔ cup/140 g firmly packed dark brown sugar

Preheat the oven to 325°F/170°C/gas 3. • Butter two cookie sheets. • Sift the flour, cornmeal, baking powder, and salt into a large bowl. • Use a pastry blender to cut in the butter until the mixture resembles coarse crumbs. • Mix in the eggs and brown sugar to form a soft dough. • Form the dough into balls the size of walnuts and place 1½ inches (4 cm) apart on the prepared cookie sheets. • Bake for 20–25 minutes, or until lightly browned. • Transfer to racks to cool.

533

SUNFLOWER COCONUT SQUARES

Preheat the oven to 350°F/180°C/gas 4. • Oil an 11 x 7-inch (28 x 18-cm) baking pan. • Process the cashew nuts and oil in a food processor or blender until smooth. (If you don't have a food processor or blender, grind the nuts with a pestle and mortar.) • Stir together the cashew nut mixture, sunflower seeds, apple juice, coconut, vanilla, and salt in a large bowl until well blended. • Press the mixture into the prepared pan, smoothing the top. • Bake for 25–30 minutes, or until golden brown. • Cool completely before cutting into bars.

Crisp and healthy, these easy cookies are great for school lunchboxes and afterschool snacks.

Makes: 22–33 bars
Preparation: 15'
Cooking: 25–30'
Level of difficulty: 1

- ¾ cup/125 g cashew nuts, shelled
- 1 tsp vegetable or sesame oil
- 4 cups/600 g sunflower seeds
- 6 tbsp apple juice concentrate or maple syrup
- 1 cup/125 g shredded/desiccated coconut
- ½ tsp vanilla extract/essence
- ¼ tsp salt

CARAWAY MOMENTS

Preheat the oven to 375°F/190°C/gas 5. • Set out two cookie sheets. • Sift the flour, baking powder, and salt into a medium bowl. • Beat the butter and $^1/_4$ cup (50 g) sugar in a large bowl with an electric mixer at high speed until creamy. • Mix in the dry ingredients, followed by the milk to make a soft dough. • Form the dough into balls the size of walnuts and place 2 inches (5 cm) apart on the cookie sheets. • Sprinkle with the caraway seeds and remaining sugar. • Bake for 12–15 minutes, or until lightly browned. • Cool on the sheets until the cookies firm slightly. • Transfer to racks to finish cooling.

Makes: 20 cookies

Preparation: 30'

Cooking: 12–15'

Level of difficulty: 1

- **1 cup/150 g all-purpose/plain flour**
- **1 tsp baking powder**
- **$^1/_8$ tsp salt**
- **7 tbsp butter, softened**
- **$^1/_4$ cup/50 g + 1 tsp granulated sugar**
- **1 tsp milk**
- **1 tsp caraway seeds**

EASY ANISEED COOKIES

Makes: 16 cookies

Preparation: 40' + 30'
to chill

Cooking: 12–15'

Level of difficulty: 1

- 2 cups/300 g all-purpose/plain flour
- 1 cup/200 g granulated sugar
- $1/8$ tsp salt
- 4 tbsp extra-virgin olive oil
- 4 tbsp Muscatel wine
- 2 tbsp anisette
- 1 tbsp aniseeds
- 1 large egg, lightly beaten
- 1 tbsp vanilla sugar

Stir together the flour, sugar, and salt in a large bowl. • Gradually mix in the oil and wine. • Add the anisette and aniseeds and knead until smooth. • Refrigerate for 30 minutes. • Preheat the oven to 350°F/180°C/gas 4. • Butter and flour a cookie sheet. • Roll out the dough to a thickness of $1/8$ inch (3 mm). • Use a 2-inch (5-cm) cookie cutter to cut out the cookies. • Continue cutting out cookies until all the dough is used. • Transfer the cookies to the prepared cookie sheet. Prick all over with a fork. • Brush the cookies with the beaten egg and sprinkle with the vanilla sugar. • Bake for 12–15 minutes, or until just golden. • Transfer to racks and let cool.

SWISS SQUARES

Makes: 36–45 bars

Preparation: 20'

Cooking: 15–20'

Level of difficulty: 1

- ½ cup/125 g
  butter, softened
- ⅔ cup/140 ml
  smooth peanut
  butter
- 6 tbsp honey
- ½ cup/60 g
  shredded/
  desiccated coconut
- ½ cup/75 g muesli
- 2 cups/300 g old-
  fashioned rolled
  oats
- ⅛ tsp salt

Preheat the oven to 350°F/180°C/gas 4. • Set out 13 x 9-inch (33 x 23-cm) baking pan. • Mix the butter, peanut butter, and honey in a medium saucepan over low heat until well blended. • Stir in the coconut, muesli, oats, and salt. • Spoon the mixture onto the baking sheet and level with a spoon. • Bake for 15–20 minutes, or until just golden. • Cool completely before cutting into bars.

POLENTA AND POPPY SEED COOKIES

Sift the cornmeal, flour, baking powder, and salt into a large bowl. • Stir in the sugar, butter, and 2 eggs. • Add the wine and mix to form a smooth dough. • Press the dough into a disk, wrap in plastic wrap, and refrigerate for 30 minutes. • Preheat the oven to 400°F/200°C/gas 6. • Butter two cookie sheets. • Roll out the dough on a lightly floured surface to a thickness of ¹/₄ inch (5 mm). • Cut into 2-inch (5-cm) triangles and place 1 inch (2.5 cm) apart on the prepared cookie sheets. • Beat the remaining egg with the milk in a small bowl. • Brush over the cookies. • Sprinkle with the poppy seeds and confectioners' sugar. • Bake for 15–20 minutes, or until just golden. • Transfer to racks to cool.

Makes: 36 cookies

Preparation: 40' + 30' to chill

Cooking: 15–20'

Level of difficulty: 1

- 1¹/₃ cups/200 g finely ground yellow cornmeal
- 1¹/₃ cups/200 g all-purpose/plain flour
- 2 tsp baking powder
- ¹/₈ tsp salt
- ²/₃ cup/140 g granulated sugar
- ²/₃ cup/150 g butter, softened
- 3 large eggs, lightly beaten
- 2 tsp dry white wine
- 1 tbsp milk
- ¹/₃ cup/40 g poppy seeds
- ¹/₃ cup/50 g confectioners'/icing sugar

HEALTHY BREAKFAST COOKIES

Makes: 30–35 cookies

Preparation: 20' + 30' to chill

Cooking: 12–15'

Level of difficulty: 1

- 1 cup/150 g all-purpose/plain flour
- 1 tsp baking powder
- ⅛ tsp salt
- ½ cup/125 g butter, softened
- ⅓ cup/70 g granulated sugar
- 1 large egg
- 1 cup/150 g bran flakes or sticks
- 1 cup/150 g whole-wheat flour

Sift the all-purpose flour, baking powder, and salt into a large bowl. • Beat the butter and sugar in a large bowl with an electric mixer at high speed until creamy. • Add the egg, beating until just blended. • Mix in the dry ingredients, followed by the bran flakes and whole-wheat flour. • Preheat the oven to 350°F/180°C/gas 4. • Set out two cookie sheets. • Press the dough into a disk, wrap in plastic wrap, and refrigerate for 30 minutes. • Roll out the dough on a lightly floured surface. Use a 2-inch (5-cm) cookie cutter to cut out the cookies. Gather the dough scraps, re-roll, and continue cutting out cookies until all the dough is used. • Use a spatula to transfer the cookies to the cookie sheets, placing them 1 inch (2.5 cm) apart. • Bake for 12–15 minutes, or until lightly browned. • Transfer to racks to cool.

SPICY CRISPS

Preheat the oven to 350°F/180°C/gas 4. •
Butter two cookie sheets. • Stir together the
wheat germ, baking soda, cinnamon, nutmeg, and
salt in a large bowl. Stir in the oats and sugar. •
Melt the butter with the corn syrup and milk in a
small saucepan over low heat. • Pour into the dry
ingredients and mix until smooth. • Form into balls
the size of walnuts and place 2 inches (5 cm) apart
on the prepared cookie sheets, flattening them
slightly. • Bake for 12–15 minutes, or until golden
brown. • Cool the cookies completely on the
cookie sheets.

Makes: 25 cookies

Preparation: 15'

Cooking: 12–15'

Level of difficulty: 1

- ¾ cup/125 g wheatgerm, toasted
- ½ tsp baking soda
- 1 tsp ground cinnamon
- ¹/2 tsp ground nutmeg
- ⅛ tsp salt
- ½ cup/75 g old-fashioned rolled oats
- ⅓ cup/70 g granulated sugar
- 6 tbsp butter, cut up
- 1 tbsp light corn syrup
- 1 tbsp milk

OAT AND SEED BARS

Makes: 22–33 bars

Preparation: 20'

Cooking: 30–35'

Level of difficulty: 1

- 6 tbsp butter, softened
- 6 tbsp honey
- ½ cup/100 g raw sugar (Demerara or Barbados)
- 1½ cups/225 g old-fashioned rolled oats
- ½ cup/50 g coarsely chopped walnuts
- ½ cup/90 g raisins
- 2 tbsp pumpkin seeds
- 2 tbsp sunflower seeds
- 2 tbsp sesame seeds
- 2 tbsp shredded/ desiccated coconut
- ¾ tsp ground cinnamon
- ⅛ tsp salt

Preheat the oven to 375°F/190°C/gas 5. • Butter an 11 x 7-inch (28 x 18-cm) baking pan. • Melt the butter with the honey and raw sugar in a large saucepan over low heat, stirring constantly. • Bring to a boil and cook until the sugar has dissolved completely. • Stir in the oats, walnuts, raisins, pumpkin seeds, sunflower seeds, sesame seeds, coconut, cinnamon, and salt. • Spoon the mixture evenly into the prepared pan. • Bake for 30–35 minutes, or until just golden. • Cool completely before cutting into bars.

MAPLE BISCOTTI

Preheat the oven to 350°F/180°C/gas 4. • Butter two cookie sheets. • Sift the flour, cornmeal, baking powder, and salt into a medium bowl. • Beat the eggs, egg yolk, and vanilla in a large bowl until frothy. • Mix in the dry ingredients, pecans, and maple syrup until stiff. • Form into four logs about 1 inch (2.5 cm) in diameter and place 2 inches (5 cm) apart on the prepared cookie sheets, flattening them slightly. • Bake for 25–30 minutes, or until firm to the touch. • Transfer to a cutting board to cool for 15 minutes. • Reduce the oven temperature to 300°F/150°C/gas 2. • Cut on the diagonal into 1-inch (2.5-cm) slices. • Arrange the slices cut-side down on the cookie sheets and bake for 15–20 minutes, or until golden and toasted. • Transfer to racks to cool.

Makes: 35 cookies

Preparation: 40'

Cooking: 40–50'

Level of difficulty: 2

- 1 2/3 cups/250 g bread flour
- 2/3 cup/100 g finely ground cornmeal
- 1 tsp baking powder
- 1/4 tsp salt
- 2 large eggs + 1 large egg yolk
- 1/2 tsp vanilla extract/essence
- 1 cup/100 g coarsely chopped pecans
- 1/2 cup/125 ml pure maple syrup

CORN FLAKE SQUARES

Makes: about 16 squares

Preparation: 10'

Cooking: 25–30'

Level of difficulty: 1

- ½ cup/60 g corn flakes
- 7 tbsp butter, melted
- ½ cup/100 g firmly packed dark brown sugar
- ½ cup/50 g candied green cherries
- ¹/₂ tsp ground ginger
- ⅛ tsp salt

Preheat the oven to 350°F/180°C/gas 4. • Butter an 8-inch (20-cm) square baking pan. • Mix the corn flakes, butter, sugar, cherries, ginger, and salt in a medium bowl . • Firmly press the mixture into the pan. • Bake for 25–30 minutes, or until golden brown. • Let cool before cutting into squares.

SUNFLOWER BUTTER COOKIES

Preheat the oven to 350°F/180°C/gas 4. • Line two cookie sheets with parchment paper. • Sift the flour and salt into a medium bowl. • Beat the butter and granulated and vanilla sugars until creamy. • Add the ground sunflower seeds and vanilla. • Mix in the dry ingredients and milk to form a stiff dough. • Divide the dough in half. Form the dough into two 8-inch (20-cm) logs and roll in the finely chopped sunflower seeds. Wrap each in plastic wrap, and refrigerate for at least 30 minutes. • Slice the dough $^{1}/_{2}$ inch (1 cm) thick and place 1 inch (2.5 cm) apart on the prepared cookie sheets. • Bake for 10–15 minutes, or until golden and the edges are firm. • Cool on the sheet until the cookies firm slightly. • Transfer to racks and let cool completely. Dust with the confectioners' sugar.

Makes: 32 cookies

Preparation: 50' + 30' to chill

Cooking: 10–15'

Level of difficulty: 2

- 1$^{2}/_{3}$ cups/250 g all-purpose/plain flour
- $^{1}/_{8}$ tsp salt
- $^{3}/_{4}$ cup/180 g butter, softened
- $^{1}/_{4}$ cup/50 g granulated sugar
- 2 tbsp vanilla sugar
- 1 cup/150 g ground sunflower seeds
- $^{1}/_{2}$ tsp vanilla extract/essence
- 2 tbsp milk
- 4 tbsp finely chopped sunflower seeds
- $^{1}/_{3}$ cup/50 g confectioners'/ icing sugar

OPEN SESAME COOKIES

Makes: 35 cookies

Preparation: 55' + 30' to chill

Cooking: 15–20'

Level of difficulty: 1

- $^1/_3$ cup/60 g golden raisins
- $^1/_2$ cup/125 ml brandy
- 1 cup/150 g all-purpose/plain flour
- 1 cup/150 g cornstarch/cornflour
- $^2/_3$ cup/140 g granulated sugar
- 1 tsp baking powder
- $^1/_4$ tsp ground cinnamon
- $^1/_8$ tsp salt
- 2 tbsp extra-virgin olive oil
- $^2/_3$ cup/150 g butter, softened
- 1$^1/_4$ cups/125 g sesame seeds, toasted
- $^1/_2$ cup/125 ml water or more as needed

Plump the raisins in the brandy in a small bowl for 15 minutes. Drain and pat dry with paper towels. • Mix the flour, cornstarch, sugar, baking powder, cinnamon, and salt in a large bowl. • Stir in the oil, butter, sesame seeds, and raisins. • Add enough water to form a smooth dough. • Form the dough into a log 1 inch (2.5 cm) in diameter, wrap in plastic wrap, and refrigerate for at least 30 minutes. • Preheat the oven to 350°F/180°C/gas 4. • Butter two cookie sheets. • Slice the dough $^1/_2$ inch (1 cm) thick and place 1 inch (2.5 cm) apart on the prepared cookie sheets. • Bake for 15–20 minutes, or until golden. • Transfer to racks and let cool completely.

CITRUS CORN FLAKE COOKIES

Sift the flour, baking powder, and salt into a medium bowl. • Beat the butter and sugar in a large bowl with an electric mixer at high speed until creamy. • Add the egg, beating until just blended. • Stir in the cornflakes and lemon zest. • Mix in the dry ingredients to form a stiff dough. • Form the dough into a 12 x 2-inch (30 x 5-cm) log, wrap in plastic wrap, and refrigerate for at least 30 minutes. • Preheat the oven to 425°F/220°C/gas 7. • Butter three cookie sheets. • Slice the dough 1/4 inch (5 mm) thick and place 1 inch (2.5 cm) apart on the prepared cookie sheets. • Bake, one sheet at a time, for 8–10 minutes, or until just golden. • Transfer to racks and let cool completely.

Makes: 48 cookies

Preparation: 40' + 30' to chill

Cooking: 8–10'

Level of difficulty: 1

- 1 1/2 cups/225 g all-purpose/plain flour
- 1 tsp baking powder
- 1/8 tsp salt
- 1/2 cup/125 g butter, softened
- 3/4 cup/150 g granulated sugar
- 1 large egg
- 2 cups/300 g cornflakes, lightly crushed
- 2 tsp grated lemon zest

MUESLI ROSETTES

Makes: 20–25
  cookies

Preparation: 15'

Cooking: 20–25'

Level of difficulty: 1

- 2 large egg whites
- ⅛ tsp salt
- ¾ cup/150 g granulated sugar
- 1 tsp vanilla sugar
- 1 tbsp all-purpose/plain flour
- 2 tsp cornstarch/cornflour
- ½ cup/75 g fine oat flakes or wheat flakes
- finely chopped dates, nuts, and dried fruit (muesli or granola)

Preheat the oven to 275°F/140°C/gas 1. • Line two cookie sheets with parchment or rice paper. • Beat the egg whites and salt in a large bowl with an electric mixer at medium speed until frothy. With mixer at high speed, gradually beat in the granulated and vanilla sugars, beating until stiff, glossy peaks form. • Mix in the flour, cornstarch, and oat flakes. • Fit a pastry bag with an 1-inch (2.5-cm) tip. Fill the pastry bag, twist the opening tightly closed, and squeeze out small rounds spacing them 1 inch (2.5 cm) apart on the prepared cookie sheets. • Sprinkle with the dates, nuts, and dried fruit. • Bake for 20–25 minutes, or until lightly golden. • Transfer on the parchment paper to racks and let cool completely.

DATE AND CORN FLAKE COOKIES

Makes: 64 cookies

Preparation: 45' + 30' to chill

Cooking: 10–12'

Level of difficulty: 2

- 1 cup/150 g all-purpose/plain flour
- ½ tsp baking soda
- ½ tsp salt
- ½ cup/125 g vegetable shortening
- ½ cup/100 g firmly packed light brown sugar
- ½ cup/100 g granulated sugar
- 2 large eggs
- 1 cup/150 g old-fashioned rolled oats
- ½ cup/50 g corn flakes
- ½ cup/50 g finely chopped dates
- ½ cup/90 g semisweet/dark chocolate chips

Sift the flour, baking soda, and salt into a large bowl. • Beat the shortening and brown and granulated sugars in a large bowl with an electric mixer at high speed until creamy. • Add the eggs, beating until just blended. • Mix in the dry ingredients, oats, corn flakes, dates, and chocolate chips to form a stiff dough. • Divide the dough in half. Form into two 8-inch (20-cm) logs, wrap in plastic wrap, and refrigerate for at least 30 minutes. • Preheat the oven to 375°F/190°C/ gas 5. • Butter two cookie sheets. • Slice the dough ¼ inch (5 mm) thick and place 2 inches (5 cm) apart on the prepared cookie sheets. • Bake for 10–12 minutes, or until lightly golden. • Cool on the sheets until the cookies firm slightly. • Transfer to racks to cool completely.

555

SEEDY S-SHAPES

Sift the flour, baking powder, and salt into a medium bowl. • Beat the butter and sugar in a large bowl with an electric mixer at high speed until creamy. • Add the aniseeds and lemon zest. • With mixer at high speed, beat the whole egg and egg yolk and 2 tablespoons milk until frothy in a large bowl. • Beat the egg mixture into the batter. • Mix in the dry ingredients to form a smooth dough. • Divide the dough in half. • Form into 8-inch (20-cm) logs, wrap in plastic wrap, and refrigerate for at least 30 minutes. • Preheat the oven to 375°F/190°C/gas 5. • Line two cookie sheets with parchment paper. • Slice the dough $1/2$ inch (1 cm) thick. • Roll each slice into a 6-inch (15-cm) log and form into an S-shape, flattening it slightly. • Place the cookies 1 inch (2.5 cm) apart on the prepared cookie sheets. • Mix the egg white and remaining milk in a small bowl. • Brush over the cookies and sprinkle with poppy seeds. • Bake for 8–10 minutes, or until just golden at the edges.
• Transfer to racks to cool.

Makes: 32 cookies

Preparation: 40' + 30' to chill

Cooking: 8–10'

Level of difficulty: 2

- 1⅓ cups/200 g all-purpose/plain flour
- 1 tsp baking powder
- ⅛ tsp salt
- ½ cup/125 g butter, softened
- ½ cup/100 g granulated sugar
- 1 tsp ground aniseeds
- 1 tsp finely grated lemon zest
- 1 large egg + 1 large egg yolk + 1 large egg white
- 2 tbsp + 1 tsp milk
- 2 tbsp poppy seeds

OATMEAL COCONUT COOKIES

Makes: 20 cookies	
Preparation: 20'	
Cooking: 15–20'	
Level of difficulty: 1	

- 1 cup/150 g all-purpose/plain flour
- ½ tsp baking soda
- ⅛ tsp salt
- 1 cup/150 g shredded/desiccated coconut
- 1 cup/150 g old-fashioned rolled oats
- ½ cup/125 g butter, cut up
- ¾ cup/150 g granulated sugar
- 2 tbsp light corn syrup/golden syrup

Preheat the oven to 350°F/180°C/gas 4. • Butter two cookie sheets. • Sift the flour, baking soda, and salt into a large bowl. Stir in the coconut and oats. • Melt the butter with the sugar and corn syrup in a small saucepan over medium heat. • Mix in the dry ingredients until well blended. • Roll into balls the size of walnuts and place 1 inch (2.5 cm) apart on the prepared cookie sheets, flattening them slightly with a fork. • Bake for 15–20 minutes, or until golden brown. • Cool on the sheets until the cookies firm slightly. Transfer to racks to cool.

NO-BAKE SESAME CRISPS

Place the sesame seeds in a medium frying pan over high heat and stir until nicely roasted. Set aside. • Grease an 8-inch (20-cm) square baking pan with the tahini. • Place the honey in a medium saucepan over medium heat and bring to the boil. • Stir in the lemon zest, sesame seeds, and nuts. Boil for 1–2 minutes. • Spoon the honey mixture into the pan, spreading evenly with the back of the spoon. Set aside to cool then refrigerate until set. • Cut into small squares or bars to serve.

Serves 4–6

Preparation: 10' + 2 h to cool

Level of difficulty: 1

- 1⅓ cups/130 g sesame seeds
- 1 tbsp tahini (sesame seed paste)
- 1 cup/250 ml honey
- 1 tbsp finely grated lemon zest
- ¾ cup/75 g coarsely chopped walnuts

SESAME SNAPS

Makes 20 cookies

Preparation: 10'

Cooking: 10–15'

Level of difficulty: 1

- 1 cup/250 g butter
- 1 cup/200 g sugar
- 1 tbsp finely grated lemon zest
- 2 cups/300 g all-purpose/plain flour
- 1 large egg white, lightly beaten
- 2 tbsp honey
- 1⅓ cups/130 g sesame seeds

Preheat the oven to 400°F/200°C/gas 6. • Butter and flour two cookie sheets. • Beat the butter, sugar, and lemon zest in a large bowl with an electric mixer at high speed until pale and creamy. • With mixer at low speed, gradually beat in the flour. • Place the egg white, honey, and sesame seeds in a small bowl and mix well. The mixture should be dense and dry. • Scoop out 1 heaping tablespoon of dough and shape into a ball about the size of a walnut. • Place over the sesame mixture and press down with your fingers until 3 inches (8 cm) in diameter. Repeat until all the dough and filling are used up. • Place the cookies, sesame seed-side up, on the sheet. • Bake for 10–15 minutes, or until golden brown. • Let cool completely.

OAT AND CHOCOLATE CHIP COOKIES

Preheat the oven to 350°F/180°C/gas 5. • Set out two cookie sheets. • Stir together the oats, brown and granulated sugars, flour, and salt in a large bowl. • Make a well in the center and stir in the butter, egg, and vanilla. • Stir in the chocolate chips. • Drop teaspoons of the dough 3 inches (8 cm) apart onto the cookie sheets. • Bake for 5–8 minutes, or until lightly browned and the centers are bubbling. • Transfer to racks and let cool completely.

Makes: 24 cookies

Preparation: 20'

Cooking: 5–8'

Level of difficulty: 1

- 2¼ cups/330 g old-fashioned rolled oats
- 1 cup/200 g firmly packed light brown sugar
- ½ cup/100 g granulated sugar
- 2 tbsp all-purpose/plain flour
- ¼ tsp salt
- 1⅓ cups/330 g butter, melted
- 1 large egg
- 1 tsp vanilla extract/essence
- ½ cup/90 g semisweet/dark chocolate chips

JOHN'S COOKIES

Makes: 36–40 cookies

Preparation: 20'

Cooking: 10–15'

Level of difficulty: 1

- 1½ cups/225 g all-purpose/plain flour
- 1 tsp baking soda
- ¼ tsp salt
- 1 cup/250 g butter, softened
- 1 cup/200 g firmly packed light brown sugar
- 1 cup/200 g granulated sugar
- 2 large eggs, lightly beaten
- ½ tsp vanilla extract/essence
- 2 cups/200 g corn flakes
- 1 cup/100 g sunflower seeds

Preheat the oven to 350°F/180°C/gas 4. • Butter two cookie sheets. • Sift the flour, baking soda, and salt into a medium bowl. • Beat the butter and both sugars in a large bowl with an electric mixer at high speed until creamy. • Add the eggs and vanilla, beating until just blended. • Mix in the dry ingredients, corn flakes, and sunflower seeds. • Drop tablespoons of the dough 2 inches (5 cm) apart onto the prepared cookie sheets.
- Bake for 10–15 minutes, or until golden brown.
- Cool on the sheets until the cookies firm slightly.
- Transfer to racks to cool.

ITALIAN RICE COOKIES

Preheat the oven to 350°F/180°C/gas 4. • Butter two cookie sheets. • Sift the flour, baking powder, baking soda, and salt into a large bowl. • Stir in the sugar. • Mix in the olive oil and enough water to form a stiff dough. • Form the dough into balls the size of walnuts and place 1 inch (2.5 cm) apart on the prepared cookie sheets, flattening them slightly. • Bake for 20–25 minutes, or until just golden. • Transfer to racks and let cool completely.

Makes: 24 cookies

Preparation: 20'

Cooking: 20–25'

Level of difficulty: 1

- 1²⁄₃ cups/250 g rice flour
- ½ tsp baking powder
- ⅛ tsp baking soda
- ⅛ tsp salt
- ⅓ cup/70 g granulated sugar
- 4 tbsp best-quality extra-virgin olive oil
- ⅓–²⁄₃ cup/ 80–150 ml water

POLENTA BISCOTTI

Makes: 40 biscotti

Preparation: 15'

Cooking: 32–40'

Level of difficulty: 2

- 1½ cups/225 g all-purpose/plain flour
- 1 tsp baking soda
- ⅛ tsp salt
- 2 large eggs
- 1 cup/200 g granulated sugar
- 2 tbsp anisette
- ⅓ cup/50 g finely ground yellow cornmeal
- Grated zest of 1 lemon
- 1 tsp coriander seeds
- ¼ cup/45 g almonds

GLAZE
- 1 egg yolk
- 2 tbsp milk
- 1 tbsp granulated sugar

Preheat the oven to 300°F/150°C/gas 2. • Line two cookie sheets with parchment paper. • Sift the flour, baking soda, and salt into a medium bowl. • Beat the eggs and sugar in a large bowl with an electric mixer at high speed until thick and creamy. • Beat in the anisette, polenta flour, lemon zest, and coriander seed. • Mix in the dry ingredients and nuts to form a sticky dough. • Form the dough into 3 flat logs, about 2½ inches (6 cm) wide. • Transfer the logs to the prepared cookie sheets. • Glaze: Mix the egg yolk and milk in a small bowl and brush it over the logs. Sprinkle them with sugar. • Bake for 25–30 minutes, or until firm to the touch. • Transfer to a cutting board to cool for 10 minutes. • Cut on the diagonal into ½-inch (1-cm) slices. • Arrange the slices cut-side up on three cookie sheets and bake for 7–10 minutes, or until golden and toasted. • Transfer to racks to cool.

569

BRAN SQUARES

Preheat the oven to 350°F/180°C/gas 4. •
Butter an 8-inch (20-cm) square baking pan.
• Mix the bran flakes, butter, sugar, dates, and salt
in a medium bowl . • Firmly press the mixture into
the pan. • Bake for 25–30 minutes, or until
golden brown. • Cool completely before cutting
into squares.

Makes: 16–25 squares

Preparation: 10'

Cooking: 25–30'

Level of difficulty: 1

- **1 cup/100 g bran flake cereal**
- **½ cup/125 g butter, melted**
- **½ cup/100 g firmly packed dark brown sugar**
- **½ cup/50 g coarsely chopped pitted dates**
- **⅛ tsp salt**

POPPY SEED ALMOND COOKIES

Makes: about 24 cookies

Preparation: 20'

Cooking: 6–8'

Level of difficulty: 1

- **4 large egg whites**
- **2 tbsp all-purpose/ plain flour**
- **¼ cup/50 g superfine/caster sugar**
- **2 cups/300 g finely ground almonds**
- **2 tbsp poppy seeds**
- **1 tbsp almond oil**

Preheat the oven to 350°F/180°C/gas 4. • Line two cookie sheets with parchment paper. • Beat the egg whites in a large bowl with an electric mixer at high speed until soft peaks form. • Use a large rubber spatula to fold in the flour, superfine sugar, almonds, poppy seeds, and almond oil until smooth. • Drop teaspoons of the cookie dough 1 inch (2.5 cm) apart onto the prepared cookie sheets. • Bake for 6–8 minutes, or until golden brown around the edges. • Cool the cookies on the cookie sheet for 1 minute. Transfer to racks to finish cooling.

BUTTER
COOKIES

BUTTER COOKIES WITH MINT FROSTING

Sift the flour, confectioners' sugar, cocoa, baking powder, and salt into a large bowl. • Mix in the butter, egg, and vanilla sugar to form a smooth dough. • Divide the dough in half. • Press the dough into disks, wrap in plastic wrap, and refrigerate for 30 minutes. • Preheat the oven to 350°F/180°C/gas 4. • Butter four cookie sheets. • Roll out the dough on a lightly floured surface to a thickness of $1/8$ inch (3 mm). • Use a $1^1/2$-inch (4-cm) cookie cutter to cut out the cookies. Gather the dough scraps, re-roll, and continue cutting out cookies until the dough is used. • Use a spatula to transfer the cookies to the prepared cookie sheets, placing them 1 inch (2.5 cm) apart. • Bake, one sheet at a time, for 10–15 minutes, or until the edges are firm and the bottoms are lightly browned. • Transfer on the parchment paper to racks and let cool completely. • Frosting: Mix the confectioners' sugar, corn syrup, lemon juice, peppermint extract, and green food coloring in a medium bowl until a smooth dough has formed. • Roll the mint paste out on a surface lightly dusted with confectioners' sugar to a thickness of $1/8$ inch (3 mm). • Use $1^1/2$-inch (4-cm) petit four cutters to cut out green shapes. • Melt the chocolate in a double boiler over barely simmering water. • Spoon the melted chocolate into a small freezer bag and cut off a tiny corner. • Pipe chocolate dots on top of the cookies and top with the mint shapes.

Makes: 60 cookies

Preparation: 60' + 30' to chill

Cooking: 10–15'

Level of difficulty: 3

- 1²/₃ cups/250 g all-purpose/plain flour
- ²/₃ cup/100 g confectioners'/icing sugar
- 1 tbsp unsweetened cocoa powder
- 1 tsp baking powder
- ¹/₈ tsp salt
- ²/₃ cup/150 g butter, softened
- 1 large egg
- 1 tbsp vanilla sugar

FROSTING

- 1²/₃ cups/250 g confectioners'/icing sugar
- 3 tbsp light corn syrup/golden syrup
- 1 tbsp lemon juice
- ¹/₂ tsp peppermint extract/essence
- 2–3 drops green food coloring
- 2 oz/60 g semisweet/dark chocolate, chopped

AFTERNOON TEA COOKIES

Makes 80–90 cookies

Preparation: 30' + 30' to chill

Cooking: 10–15'

Level of difficulty: 2

- 2²/₃ cups/400 g all-purpose/plain flour
- ²/₃ cup/100 g cornstarch
- ¹/₈ tsp salt
- ³/₄ cup/150 g granulated sugar
- 1 tbsp vanilla sugar
- ¹/₄ tsp vanilla extract/essence
- 3 oz/90 g marzipan, cut up and softened
- 1 cup/250 g cold butter, cut up
- 1 large egg, lightly beaten + 1 egg yolk, mixed with ¹/₂ cup/125 ml water

Sift the flour, cornstarch, and salt into a bowl. Stir in the granulated sugar, vanilla sugar, and vanilla. • Dot the butter and marzipan evenly over the dry ingredients. Use a pastry blender to cut in the ingredients until the mixture resembles coarse crumbs. • Make a well in the center and add the egg. • Work the dough until combined and knead once or twice on a lightly floured surface into a smooth dough. • Wrap in plastic wrap and refrigerate for 30 minutes, or until firm. • Preheat the oven to 350°F/180°C/gas 4. • Butter two cookie sheets. • Roll out the dough on a lightly floured surface to a thickness of about ¹/₈ inch (3 mm). Use small cookie cutters to stamp out different shapes. • Gather the dough scraps, re-roll, and continue cutting out cookies until all the dough is used. • Arrange on the prepared cookie sheets, spacing 1 inch (2.5 cm) apart. • Brush with the egg glaze. • Bake for 10–15 minutes, or until golden brown. • Cool on the cookie sheets for 5 minutes. • Transfer to racks to cool.

BUTTER KNOTS

Makes: 20 cookies

Preparation: 40' + 30' to chill

Cooking: 15–20'

Level of difficulty: 1

- 2 cups/300 g all-purpose/plain flour
- 1 tsp baking powder
- ¼ tsp ground allspice
- ⅛ tsp salt
- ½ cup/125 g butter, softened
- ⅓ cup/70 g granulated sugar
- ½ tsp vanilla extract/essence
- 1 large egg + 1 large egg yolk
- 4 tbsp milk
- Grated zest of ½ lemon
- 1 tbsp confectioners'/ icing sugar

Sift the flour, baking powder, allspice, and salt into a large bowl. • Beat the butter and sugar in a large bowl with an electric mixer at high speed until creamy. • Add the vanilla and egg and egg yolk, beating until just blended. • Stir in the milk and lemon zest. • Mix in the dry ingredients to form a smooth dough. Press the dough into a disk, wrap in plastic wrap, and refrigerate for 30 minutes. • Preheat the oven to 350°F/180°C/ gas 4. • Butter a cookie sheet. • Roll out the dough on a lightly floured surface to a thickness of ⅛ inch (3 mm). Cut into 12 x ½-inch (30 x 1-cm) long strips. • Carefully tie the dough strips into knots. • Place the cookies ½ inch (1 cm) apart on the prepared cookie sheet. • Bake for 15–20 minutes, or until lightly browned. • Transfer to racks and let cool completely. • Dust with the confectioners' sugar.

BUTTERCREAM SANDWICHES

Sift the flour and salt into a medium bowl. • Beat the butter and sugar in a large bowl with an electric mixer at high speed until creamy. • Add the milk, vanilla, and egg yolks, beating until just blended. • Mix in the dry ingredients to form a smooth dough. • Press the dough into a disk, wrap in plastic wrap, and refrigerate for 30 minutes. • Preheat the oven to 375°F/190°C/gas 5. • Butter three cookie sheets. • Roll out the dough on a lightly floured surface to a thickness of $^1/_8$ inch (3 mm). • Use a $2^1/_2$-inch (6-cm) cookie cutter to cut out the cookies. Cut the centers from half the cookies with a $^1/_2$-inch (1-cm) cutter. Gather the dough scraps, re-roll, and continue cutting out cookies until all the dough is used. • Use a spatula to transfer the cookies to the cookie sheets, placing them $^1/_2$ inch (1 cm) apart. • Bake, one sheet at a time, for 8–10 minutes, or until lightly browned. • Transfer to racks and let cool completely. • Filling: With mixer at high speed, beat the butter in a medium bowl until creamy. • Beat in the confectioners' sugar and milk to make a spreadable consistency. • Divide the filling among three small bowls and add a different color of food coloring to each one, stirring until well blended. • Spread the fillings over the whole cookies and place a ring cookie on top.

Makes: 36 cookies

Preparation: 45' + 30' to chill

Cooking: 8–10'

Level of difficulty: 2

- 1²/₃ cups/250 g all-purpose/plain flour
- ¹/₄ tsp salt
- ³/₄ cup/180 g butter, softened
- 1 cup/200 g granulated sugar
- 2 tbsp milk
- 1 tsp vanilla extract/essence
- 2 large egg yolks, lightly beaten

FILLING

- 4 tbsp butter, softened
- 1²/₃ cups/250 g confectioners'/icing sugar
- 2 tbsp milk
- 3 drops each red, green, and yellow food coloring

YELLOW COOKIES

Makes: 25 cookies

Preparation: 40'

Cooking: 12–15'

Level of difficulty: 1

- 2 cups/300 g finely ground yellow cornmeal
- 1 cup/150 g all-purpose/plain flour
- 1 cup/150 g confectioners'/icing sugar
- 1 tsp baking powder
- 1/8 tsp salt
- 1 large egg + 1 egg yolk
- 2/3 cup/150 g butter, cut up
- 4 tbsp lard or vegetable shortening
- Grated zest of 1 lemon

Preheat the oven to 375°F/190°C/gas 5. • Butter two cookie sheets. • Sift the cornmeal, flour, confectioners' sugar, baking powder, and salt onto a work surface and make a well in the center. • Add the egg and egg yolk, butter, lard, and lemon zest. • Use your hands to knead the mixture into a smooth dough. • Roll out the dough on a lightly floured surface to a thickness of 1/8 inch (3 mm). • Use a 2-inch (5-cm) fluted cookie cutter to cut out the cookies. Gather the dough scraps, re-roll, and continue cutting out cookies until all the dough is used. • Use a spatula to transfer the cookies to the prepared cookie sheets. • Bake for 12–15 minutes, or until just golden. • Transfer to racks and let cool completely.

BUTTER COOKIES WITH CHOCOLATE FLECKS

Sift the flour and salt into a large bowl. • Use a wooden spoon to mix in the sugar, butter, egg and egg yolks, and chocolate to form a smooth dough. Press the dough into a disk, wrap in plastic wrap, and refrigerate for 30 minutes. • Preheat the oven to 350°F/180°C/gas 4. • Butter three cookie sheets. • Roll out the dough on a lightly floured surface to a thickness of $1/4$ inch (5 mm). • Use a 2-inch (5-cm) cookie cutter to cut out the cookies. Gather the dough scraps, re-roll, and continue cutting out cookies until all the dough is used. • Use a spatula to transfer the cookies to the prepared cookie sheets, placing them 1 inch (2.5 cm) apart. • Bake, one sheet at a time, for 10–15 minutes, or until just golden. • Transfer the cookies to racks to cool.

Makes: 34 cookies

Preparation: 40' + 30' to chill

Cooking: 10–15'

Level of difficulty: 1

- 2$\frac{2}{3}$ cups/400 g all-purpose/plain flour
- $\frac{1}{8}$ tsp salt
- 1$\frac{1}{4}$ cups/250 g granulated sugar
- $\frac{3}{4}$ cup/180 g butter, softened
- 1 large egg + 2 large egg yolks
- 3 oz/90 g semisweet/dark chocolate, coarsely grated

GINGER AND BUTTER SQUARES

Makes: 30 bars

Preparation: 20'

Cooking: 30–35'

Level of difficulty: 1

- 2 cups/300 g all-purpose/plain flour
- 2 tsp baking powder
- 2 tsp ground ginger
- ⅛ tsp salt
- 1 cup/250 g butter, softened
- 1 cup/200 g granulated sugar

GINGER FROSTING
- ½ cup/125 g butter, cut up
- 1 cup/150 g confectioners'/icing sugar
- 1½ tsp ground ginger
- 1½ tbsp light corn syrup/golden syrup

Preheat the oven to 375°F/190°C/gas 5. • Butter a 10½ x 15½-inch (26 x 36-cm) jelly-roll pan. • Sift the flour, baking powder, ginger, and salt into a medium bowl. Beat the butter and sugar in a large bowl with an electric mixer at high speed until creamy. • Mix in the dry ingredients. • Spoon the mixture evenly into the prepared pan, pressing down lightly. • Bake for 30–35 minutes, or until golden brown. • Cool completely in the pan on a rack. • Ginger Frosting: Melt the butter with the confectioners' sugar, ginger, and corn syrup in a small saucepan over low heat, stirring constantly. • Remove from the heat and stir until smooth. • Pour the frosting evenly over the shortbread and let stand for 15 minutes. • Use a sharp knife to cut into 30 bars.

VIRGINIA SHORTBREAD

Makes: 16 cookies

Preparation: 30'

Cooking: 25–30'

Level of difficulty: 1

SHORTBREAD BASE

- 2⅓ cups/350 g all-purpose/plain flour
- ⅛ tsp salt
- 1 cup/250 g butter, softened
- ½ cup/100 g granulated sugar

PEANUT TOPPING

- 6 tbsp butter, softened
- ⅓ cup/70 g granulated sugar
- 1 cup/150 g finely ground peanuts
- ½ cup/75 g all-purpose/plain flour
- 3 tbsp coarsely chopped peanuts

Preheat the oven to 350°F/180°C/gas 4. • Line a 9-inch (23-cm) round cake pan with parchment paper. • Shortbread Base: Sift the flour and salt into a medium bowl. • Beat the butter and sugar in a large bowl with an electric mixer at high speed until creamy. • Mix in the dry ingredients. • Firmly press the dough into the prepared pan to form a smooth, even layer, pressing back the edges to make them thick. • Peanut Topping: With mixer at high speed, beat the butter and sugar in a medium bowl until creamy. • Mix in the ground peanuts and flour. • Spread the topping over the shortbread base and sprinkle with the chopped peanuts. • Press the peanuts in slightly with a knife and score the round into 16 wedges. • Bake for 25–30 minutes, or until pale gold. • Cool completely before cutting along the scored lines.

LEMON BUTTER BARS

Preheat the oven to 350°F/180°C/gas 4. •
Butter two cookie sheets. • Sift the flour and
salt into a large bowl. Stir in the brown sugar. •
Use a pastry blender to cut in the butter until the
mixture resembles fine crumbs. • Turn out onto a
lightly floured surface, add the lemon zest and
extract, and knead into a smooth dough. • Roll out
the dough to a $1/4$-inch (5-mm) thick rectangle. Use
a sharp knife to cut the dough into three $3/4$ x
1-inch (2 x 2.5-cm) bars. • Transfer the bars to the
prepared cookie sheets, spacing them $1/2$ inch
(1 cm) apart. • Prick all over with a fork. • Bake for
15–20 minutes, or until golden. • Cool the
shortbread completely on the cookie sheets.

Makes: 25–30 bars

Preparation: 40'

Cooking: 15–20'

Level of difficulty: 1

- 1$1/4$ cups/180 g all-purpose/plain flour
- $1/8$ tsp salt
- $1/4$ cup/50 g firmly packed light brown sugar
- $1/2$ cup/125 g cold butter, cut up
- 2 tsp finely grated lemon zest
- $1/4$ tsp lemon extract

RICH BUTTER COOKIES

Makes: 24 cookies
Preparation: 40'
Cooking: 12–15'
Level of difficulty: 1

- 1 cup/150 g all-purpose/plain flour
- 1/3 cup/50 g semolina flour
- 1/8 tsp salt
- 1/2 cup/125 g butter, softened
- 1/3 cup/70 g granulated sugar

Preheat the oven to 375°F/190°C/gas 5. • Butter two cookie sheets. • Sift the all-purpose and semolina flours and salt into a medium bowl. • Beat the butter and 1/4 cup (50 g) sugar in a large bowl with an electric mixer at high speed until creamy. • Mix in the dry ingredients to form a soft dough. • Turn the dough out onto a lightly floured surface and knead until smooth. • Roll out the dough to a thickness of 1/4 inch (5 mm). • Use a 2-inch (5-cm) cookie cutter to cut out the cookies. Gather the dough scraps, reroll, and continue cutting out cookies until all the dough is used. Use a spatula to transfer the cookies to the prepared cookie sheets, placing them 1 inch (2.5 cm) apart. • Bake for 15–20 minutes, or until just golden. • Sprinkle with the remaining sugar. • Cool the cookies completely on the sheets.

PASSIONFRUIT BUTTER DIAMONDS

Butter cookie base: Sift the all-purpose and rice flours and salt into a medium bowl. • Beat the butter and sugar in a large bowl with an electric mixer at high speed until creamy. • Mix in the dry ingredients to form a soft dough. • Turn the dough out onto a lightly floured surface and knead until smooth. • Press the dough into a disk, wrap in plastic wrap, and refrigerate for 30 minutes. • Preheat the oven to 300°F/150°C/gas 2. • Line four cookie sheets with parchment paper. • Roll out the dough on a lightly floured surface to a thickness of $1/4$ inch (5 mm). • Cut into $1^1/2$-inch (4-cm) diamonds. • Use a spatula to transfer the cookies to the prepared cookie sheets, placing them 1 inch (2.5 cm) apart. • Bake for 12–15 minutes, or until just golden at the edges. • Transfer to racks to cool. • Passionfruit Drizzle: Mix the confectioners' sugar, passionfruit pulp, butter, and water in a double boiler over barely simmering water until smooth. • Drizzle the tops of the cookies with the icing. • Let stand for 30 minutes until set. • Melt the white chocolate in a double boiler over barely simmering water and drizzle over the cookies. Let stand for 30 minutes.

Elegant and luxurious, this white chocolate and passionfruit combination is divine.

594

Makes: 35–40 cookies

Preparation: 40' + 90' to chill and set

Cooking: 12–15'

Level of difficulty: 2

BUTTER COOKIE BASE
- $2^1/4$ cups/330 g all-purpose/plain flour
- 2 tbsp rice flour
- $1/8$ tsp salt
- 1 cup/250 g butter, softened
- $1/3$ cup/70 g granulated sugar

PASSIONFRUIT DRIZZLE
- 1 cup/150 g confectioners'/icing sugar
- 2 tbsp passionfruit pulp
- 1 tbsp butter, softened
- 1 tbsp cold water
- 2 oz/60 g white chocolate, coarsely chopped

BUTTER WREATHS

Preheat the oven to 375°F/190°C/gas 5. • Set out four cookie sheets. • Sift the flour, baking powder, and salt into a medium bowl. • Beat the butter and sugar in a large bowl with an electric mixer at high speed until creamy. • Add the vanilla and egg, beating until just blended. • Mix in the dry ingredients. • Fit a pastry bag with a ³/₄-inch (2-cm) plain tip. Fill the pastry bag, twist the opening tightly closed, and squeeze out 1¹/₂-inch (4-cm) wreaths, spacing 1 inch (2.5 cm) apart on the cookie sheets. • Press the sugar strands and balls in a decorative manner into the tops of the cookies. • Bake, one batch at a time, for 8–10 minutes, or until the edges are just golden. • Transfer to racks to cool.

596

Makes: 35–40 cookies

Preparation: 25'

Cooking: 8–10'

Level of difficulty: 2

- 1¹/₄ cups/180 g all-purpose/plain flour
- ¹/₂ tsp baking powder
- ¹/₈ tsp salt
- ¹/₂ cup/125 g butter, softened
- ²/₃ cup/140 g granulated sugar
- ¹/₂ tsp vanilla extract/essence
- 1 large egg
- Silver and colored balls, to decorate
- 2 tbsp sugar strands, to decorate

GINGER SHORTBREAD

Makes: about 25
squares

Preparation: 30'

Cooking: 35–40'

Level of difficulty: 1

- 2½ cups/375 g all-purpose/plain flour
- ½ tsp baking powder
- ⅛ tsp salt
- 1 cup/250 g butter, softened
- ⅔ cup/140 g + 2 tbsp granulated sugar
- 2 large egg yolks
- 1 tbsp light corn syrup/golden syrup
- 1 tbsp brandy
- ½ cup/50 g finely chopped crystallized ginger

Preheat the oven to 325°F/170°C/gas 3. • Butter an 11 x 7-inch (28 x 18-cm) baking pan. • Sift the flour, baking powder, and salt into a medium bowl. • Beat the butter and ⅔ cup (140 g) sugar in a large bowl with an electric mixer at high speed until creamy. • Add the egg yolks, beating until just blended. • Beat in the corn syrup and brandy. • Mix in the dry ingredients to form a stiff dough. • Divide the dough in half. Firmly press one half into the prepared pan to form a smooth, even layer. Sprinkle with the ginger. • Roll out the remaining dough on a lightly floured surface into an 11 x 7-inch (28 x 18-cm) rectangle. Place the dough on top of the ginger. • Sprinkle with the remaining sugar. • Bake for 35–40 minutes, or until pale gold. • Cool completely before cutting into squares.

597

ITALIAN ALMOND WEDGES

Makes: 16 cookies

Preparation: 35'

Cooking: 40–45'

Level of difficulty: 1

- ²/₃ cup/100 g all-purpose/plain flour
- ²/₃ cup/100 g finely ground yellow cornmeal
- ⅛ tsp salt
- ½ cup/125 g butter, cut up
- 1 cup/150 g finely ground almonds
- ½ cup/100 g granulated sugar
- 2 large egg yolks, lightly beaten
- grated zest and juice of 1 lemon
- ½ tsp almond extract/essence
- 2 tbsp finely chopped almonds
- 2 tbsp raw sugar (Barbados or Demerara)

Preheat the oven to 350°F/180°C/gas 4. • Butter a 9-inch (23-cm) springform pan. • Sift the flour, cornmeal, and salt into a medium bowl. • Use a pastry blender to cut in the butter until the mixture resembles coarse crumbs. • Stir in the ground almonds and granulated sugar. • Mix in the egg yolks, lemon zest and juice, and almond extract to form a stiff dough. • Firmly press the dough into the prepared pan to form a smooth, even layer. Sprinkle with the chopped almonds and raw sugar. • Use a sharp knife to score the cookie into 16 wedges. • Bake for 20 minutes. • Reduce the oven temperature to 300°F/150°C/ gas 2. • Bake for 20–25 minutes more, or until pale gold and firm to the touch. • Use a sharp knife to cut into 16 wedges along the scored lines. • Loosen and remove the pan sides and bottom. Transfer to racks and let cool completely.

COCONUT AND WALNUT SHORTBREAD

Preheat the oven to 325°F/170°C/gas 2. • Set out a 9-inch (23-cm) springform pan. • Process the walnuts and granulated sugar in a food processor or blender until very finely ground. • Sift the flour, baking powder, and salt into a medium bowl. • Beat the butter and confectioners' sugar in a large bowl with an electric mixer at high speed until creamy. • Mix in the dry ingredients and 2 tablespoons of coconut to form a stiff dough. • Firmly press the dough into the pan to form a smooth, even layer. Sprinkle with the remaining coconut. Use a sharp knife to score the shortbread into 16 wedges. • Bake for 25–30 minutes, or until golden brown. • Cool in the pan for 15 minutes. • Use a sharp knife to cut into wedges along the scored lines. • Loosen and remove the pan sides and let cool completely.

Makes: 16 cookies

Preparation: 25'

Cooking: 25–30'

Level of difficulty: 1

- ½ cup/75 g walnuts
- 2 tbsp granulated sugar
- 1 cup/150 g all-purpose/plain flour
- ½ tsp baking powder
- ¼ tsp salt
- 6 tbsp butter, softened
- 2 tbsp confectioners'/ icing sugar
- ½ cup/60 g shredded/ desiccated coconut

CITRUS SHORTBREAD

Makes: 16 cookies

Preparation: 20'

Cooking: 35–40'

Level of difficulty: 1

- 1 cup/150 g all-purpose/plain flour
- 1 tbsp semolina flour
- 1/8 tsp salt
- 1/2 cup/125 g butter, softened
- 1/4 cup/50 g granulated sugar
- 1 tsp finely grated lemon zest
- 1 tsp finely grated orange zest
- 1/4 cup/50 g superfine/caster sugar, to dust

Preheat the oven to 325°F/170°C/gas 3. • Butter an 8-inch (20-cm) springform pan. • Sift the all-purpose and semolina flours and salt into a medium bowl. • Beat the butter and granulated sugar in a large bowl with an electric mixer at high speed until creamy. • Mix in the dry ingredients and lemon and orange zests. • Firmly press the mixture into the prepared pan, pinching the edges to make a decorative pattern. Use a sharp knife to score the shortbread into 16 wedges. • Bake for 35–40 minutes, or until firm to the touch. • Dust with the superfine sugar. Use a sharp knife to cut into 16 wedges along the scored lines. • Loosen and remove the pan sides and bottom. Transfer to racks and let cool completely.

CHERRY SHORTBREAD SQUARES

P reheat the oven to 325°F/170°C/gas 3. •
Butter an 11 x 7-inch (28 x 18-cm) baking pan.
• Sift the flour, baking powder, and salt into a
medium bowl. • Beat the butter and ²/₃ cup
(140 g) sugar in a large bowl with an electric mixer
at high speed until creamy. • Add the egg yolks,
beating until just blended. • Beat in the corn syrup
and rum. • Mix in the dry ingredients to form a stiff
dough. • Divide the dough in half. Firmly press one
half into the prepared pan to form a smooth, even
layer. Sprinkle with the cherries. • Roll out the
remaining dough on a lightly floured surface into an
11 x 7-inch (28 x 18-cm) rectangle. Place the
dough on top of the cherries. • Sprinkle with the
remaining sugar. • Bake for 35–40 minutes, or
until pale gold. • Cool completely before cutting
into squares.

Makes: about 25
  squares

Preparation: 30'

Cooking: 35–40'

Level of difficulty: 1

- 2½ cups/375 g all-purpose/plain flour
- ½ tsp baking powder
- ⅛ tsp salt
- 1 cup/250 ml butter, softened
- ²/₃ cup/140 g + 2 tbsp granulated sugar
- 2 large egg yolks
- 1 tbsp light corn syrup/golden syrup
- 1 tbsp dark rum
- ½ cup/50 g finely chopped candied cherries

DUTCH SHORTBREAD

Sift the flour, cocoa, and salt into a medium bowl. • Beat the butter, confectioners' sugar, vanilla sugar, and vanilla in a large bowl until creamy. • Gradually beat in the dry ingredients. • Spread out a large sheet of plastic wrap and turn the dough onto it. • Place a sheet of plastic wrap on top and roll out the dough to a thickness of about $2/3$ inch (1.5 cm). • Refrigerate for 2 hours. • Preheat the oven to 325°F/170°C/gas 3. • Butter two cookie sheets and line with parchment paper. • Remove the dough from the refrigerator and peel off the top sheet of plastic wrap. • Use a 2-inch (5-cm) cookie cutter to cut out cookies. • Transfer to the prepared baking sheets, spacing $1/2$ inch (1 cm) apart. • Bake for 10–15 minutes, or until firm to the touch. • Let cool completely. • Dust with the confectioners' sugar.

Makes: 30 cookies

Preparation: 40' + 2 h to chill

Cooking: 15–20'

Level of difficulty: 2

- $1\,2/3$ cups/250 g all-purpose/plain flour
- 2 tbsp unsweetened cocoa powder
- $1/4$ tsp salt
- 1 cup/250 ml butter, softened
- 1 cup/150 g confectioners'/icing sugar
- 1 tsp vanilla sugar
- $1/2$ tsp vanilla extract/essence
- 1 tbsp confectioners'/icing sugar, to dust

BROWN BUTTER COOKIES

Makes: 12–15 cookies

Preparation: 40' + 30' to chill

Cooking: 12–15'

Level of difficulty: 1

- 2¼ cups/330 g all-purpose/plain flour
- ½ cup/75 g unsweetened cocoa powder
- ¼ tsp salt
- 1 cup/250 g butter, softened
- ¾ cup/125 g confectioners'/icing sugar
- ½ tsp vanilla extract/essence
- 2 tbsp 24-carat gold dust or metallic luster dust (optional)

Sift the flour, cocoa, and salt into a medium bowl. • Beat the butter, confectioners' sugar, and vanilla in a large bowl with an electric mixer at high speed until creamy. • Mix in the dry ingredients to form a smooth dough. • Press the dough into a disk, wrap in plastic wrap, and refrigerate for 30 minutes. • Preheat the oven to 300°F/150°C/gas 2. • Set out a cookie sheet. • Lightly dust a work surface with confectioners' sugar and roll out the dough to a thickness of ¼ inch (5 mm). • Use a 3-inch (8-cm) cookie cutter to cut out the cookies. Gather the dough scraps, re-roll, and continue cutting out cookies until all the dough is used. • Use a spatula to transfer the cookies to the cookie sheet. • Lightly brush the tops with the gold dust. • Bake for 12–15 minutes, or until firm to the touch. • Transfer to racks to cool.

CHOCOLATE CARAMEL SQUARES

Makes: 40–45 bars

Preparation: 40' + 60'
to set and cool

Cooking: 20–25'

Level of difficulty: 2

BASE

- 3 cups/450 g all-purpose/plain flour
- 1/8 tsp salt
- 1 cup/250 g butter, softened
- 1/2 cup/100 g granulated sugar
- 2 tbsp water + more as needed

TOPPING

- 1/2 cup/125 g butter, cut up
- 2 tbsp light molasses/treacle
- 2/3 cup/140 g granulated sugar
- 1 can (14 oz/ 400 ml) sweetened condensed milk
- 7 oz/200 g semisweet/dark chocolate, coarsely chopped

Base: Preheat the oven to 350°F/180°C/ gas 4. • Butter a cookie sheet and dust lightly with flour. • Sift the flour and salt into a medium bowl. • Beat the butter and sugar in a large bowl with an electric mixer at high speed until creamy. • Mix in the dry ingredients and enough water to form a soft dough. Transfer to the prepared cookie sheet and use your hands to press the dough to a thickness of 1/2 inch (1 cm). Prick all over with a fork. • Bake for 20–25 minutes, or until just golden. • Cool completely on the sheet. • Topping: Melt the butter with the molasses, sugar, and condensed milk in a medium saucepan over low heat. Bring the mixture to the boil, stirring constantly. Boil for 10 minutes, until it darkens and thickens. • Use a spatula to spread the topping over the shortbread. Let cool completely. • Melt the chocolate in a double boiler over barely simmering water. Spread the melted chocolate evenly over the topping and let stand for 30 minutes, or until set. • Cut into squares.

HAZELNUT BUTTER COOKIES

Process the raw sugar, hazelnuts, flour, and salt in a food processor until well blended. • Add the butter and process briefly until the mixture resembles fine crumbs. • Add the egg and process briefly to mix. • Gather the dough together and press into a disk. Wrap in plastic wrap and refrigerate for 30 minutes. • Preheat the oven to 350°F/180°C/gas 4. • Line two cookie sheets with parchment paper. • Roll out the dough on a lightly floured surface to a thickness of $^1/_8$ inch (3 mm). • Use a $2^1/_2$-inch (6-cm) cookie cutter to cut out the cookies. Gather the dough scraps, re-roll, and continue cutting out cookies until all the dough is used. • Use a spatula to transfer the cookies to the prepared cookie sheets, spacing them 1 inch (2.5 cm) apart. • Bake for 12–15 minutes, or until lightly browned. • Transfer to racks to cool.

Makes: 32–36 cookies

Preparation: 40' + 30' to chill

Cooking: 12–15'

Level of difficulty: 1

- $^1/_2$ cup/100 g raw sugar (Demerara or Barbados)
- $1^2/_3$ cups/250 g finely ground hazelnuts
- $1^1/_2$ cups/225 g all-purpose/plain flour
- $^1/_8$ tsp salt
- $^2/_3$ cup/150 g butter, cut up
- 1 large egg yolk, lightly beaten

608

CHERRY-TOPPED SHORTBREAD

Makes: 12 cookies

Preparation: 25'

Cooking: 20–25'

Level of difficulty: 1

- 1¼ cups/180 g all-purpose/plain flour
- ⅛ tsp salt
- ¾ cup/180 g butter, softened
- ¼ cup/50 g granulated sugar
- ½ tsp vanilla extract/essence
- 2 tsp milk
- 2 tbsp finely chopped candied cherries

Preheat the oven to 325°F/170°C/gas 3. • Set out twelve mini paper liners on a baking sheet. • Sift the flour and salt into a medium bowl. • Beat the butter, granulated sugar, and vanilla in a large bowl with an electric mixer at high speed until creamy. • Mix in the dry ingredients and milk. • Fit a pastry bag with a ½-inch (1-cm) star tip. Fill the pastry bag, twist the opening tightly closed, and squeeze rosettes into the paper liners. Press a piece of cherry into the top of each cookie. • Bake for 20–25 minutes, or until firm to the touch. • Transfer the cookies still in the liners to racks to cool.

609

BALMORAL SHORTBREAD

Sift the flour and salt into a medium bowl. • Beat the butter and sugar in a large bowl until creamy. • Mix in the dry ingredients until well blended. • Press the dough into a disk, wrap in plastic wrap, and refrigerate for 30 minutes. • Preheat the oven to 350°F/180°C/gas 4. • Butter a cookie sheet. • Roll out the dough on a lightly floured surface to a thickness of $1/8$ inch (5 mm). • Use a 2-inch (5-cm) cookie cutter to cut out the cookies. Gather the dough scraps, re-roll, and continue cutting out cookies until all the dough is used. • Use a skewer to prick each cookie with three rows of three dots. • Use a spatula to transfer the cookies to the prepared cookie sheets, placing them 1 inch (2.5 cm) apart. • Bake for 12–15 minutes, or until pale golden. • Transfer to racks to cool.

Balmoral is the official Scottish home of Queen Elizabeth II.

610

Makes: 16–20 cookies

Preparation: 40' + 30' to chill

Cooking: 12–15'

Level of difficulty: 1

- 1⅓ cups/200 g all-purpose/plain flour
- ⅛ tsp salt
- ⅓ cup/70 g granulated sugar
- ½ cup/125 g butter, softened

ALMOND BUTTER WEDGES

Preheat the oven to 325°F/170°C/gas 3. •
Butter a 9-inch (23-cm) round cake pan. • Sift
the all-purpose and rice flours and salt into a
medium bowl. Use a pastry blender to cut in the
butter until the mixture resembles coarse crumbs.
• Stir in the granulated sugar. • Mix in the candied
peel and almonds. • Firmly press the dough into
the prepared pan to form a smooth, even layer,
using your thumb to press the dough into a raised,
decorative edge. • Prick all over with a fork and
sprinkle with superfine sugar. Use a sharp knife to
score the shortbread into 16 wedges. • Bake for
35–40 minutes, or until pale gold. • Cool
completely before cutting along the scored lines.

Makes: 16 cookies

Preparation: 30'

Cooking: 35–40'

Level of difficulty: 1

- 1½ cups/225 g all-
  purpose/plain flour
- 2 tbsp rice flour
- ⅛ tsp salt
- ¾ cup/180 g
  butter, cut up
- ⅓ cup/70 g
  granulated sugar
- 2 tbsp finely
  chopped mixed
  candied peel
- 1 tbsp coarsely
  chopped almonds
- 1 tbsp superfine/
  caster sugar, to
  dust

BRANDY WEDGES

Makes: 16 cookies

Preparation: 20'

Cooking: 20–25'

Level of difficulty: 1

- ¾ cup/125 g all-purpose/plain flour
- ½ cup/75 g rice flour
- ⅛ tsp salt
- ½ cup/125 g butter, softened
- ⅔ cup/140 g + 1 tbsp granulated sugar
- 1 tbsp brandy

Preheat the oven to 350°F/180°C/gas 4. • Set out a 9-inch (23-cm) springform pan. • Sift the all-purpose and rice flours and salt into a medium bowl. • Beat the butter and ⅔ cup (140 g) sugar in a large bowl with an electric mixer at high speed until creamy. • Mix in the dry ingredients and brandy. • Firmly press the mixture into the pan to form a smooth, even layer. Prick all over with a fork and sprinkle with the remaining sugar. • Use a sharp knife to score the shortbread into 16 wedges. • Bake for 20–25 minutes, or until pale gold. • Use a sharp knife to cut into 16 wedges along the scored lines. • Loosen and remove the pan sides and bottom. Transfer to racks to cool.

613

CRISPY BUTTER COOKIES

Makes: 12–16
cookies

Preparation: 40' + 30'
to chill

Cooking: 5–8'

Level of difficulty: 1

- 1 large egg yolk
- 2 tbsp milk
- 1¼ cups/180 g all-purpose/plain flour
- ⅓ cup/70 g granulated sugar
- 2 tbsp butter, melted
- ⅛ tsp salt

Beat the egg yolk and milk in a small bowl until frothy. • Stir together the flour, sugar, butter, and salt in a medium bowl. • Use a wooden spoon to stir in the beaten egg mixture until well blended. Press the dough into a disk, wrap in plastic wrap, and refrigerate for 30 minutes. • Preheat the oven to 400°F/200°C/gas 6. • Butter a cookie sheet. • Roll out the dough on a lightly floured surface to a thickness of ¹/₈ inch (3 mm). • Use a 2-inch (5-cm) cookie cutter to cut out the cookies. Gather the dough scraps, re-roll, and continue cutting out cookies until all the dough is used. • Use a spatula to transfer the cookies to the prepared cookie sheet, placing them 1 inch (2.5 cm) apart. • Bake for 5–8 minutes, or until lightly browned. • Cool on the sheet until the cookies firm slightly. • Transfer to a rack and let cool completely.

CHOCOLATE CHIP BUTTER WEDGES

Preheat the oven to 325°F/170°C/gas 3. •
Butter two 9-inch (23-cm) springform pans. •
Sift the flour, confectioners' sugar, cornstarch, and
salt into a large bowl. • Use a pastry blender to cut
in the butter until the mixture resembles coarse
crumbs. • Stir in the chocolate chips. • Firmly
press the mixture evenly into the prepared pans to
form smooth, even layers. • Bake for 15–20
minutes, or until just golden. • Cool for 5 minutes
in the pan. • Loosen and remove the springform
sides. Let cool completely. • Cut each round into
sixteen wedges.

Makes: 32 cookies

Preparation: 20' + 30'
to set

Cooking: 15–20'

Level of difficulty: 1

- 1¾ cups/275 g all-
  purpose/plain flour
- ½ cup/75 g
  confectioners'/
  icing sugar
- 2 tbsp cornstarch/
  cornflour
- ¼ tsp salt
- 1 cup/250 g butter,
  cut up
- 2 cups/260 g
  semisweet/dark
  chocolate chips

Makes: 16 cookies	
Preparation: 30'	
Cooking: 40–45'	
Level of difficulty: 1	

- 1½ cups/225 g all-purpose/plain flour
- ⅛ tsp salt
- 1 cup/250 g butter, cut up
- 1 cup/150 g finely ground hazelnuts
- ⅓ cup/70 g granulated sugar
- 2 large egg yolks, lightly beaten
- ¾ cup/180 ml honey
- 2¼ cups/225 g finely chopped hazelnuts

HONEY AND NUT SHORTBREAD

Preheat the oven to 325°F/170°C/gas 3. • Butter a 9-inch (23-cm) springform pan. • Sift the flour and salt into a large bowl. • Use a pastry blender to cut in ¾ cup (180 g) butter until the mixture resembles fine crumbs. • Mix in the ground hazelnuts, sugar, and egg yolks to form a stiff dough. • Firmly press the mixture into the prepared pan to form a smooth, even layer. • Melt the remaining butter with the honey in a small saucepan over low heat. • Stir in the chopped hazelnuts and cook for 5 minutes, or until the hazelnuts are well coated. • Remove from the heat and spread evenly over the shortbread base. • Use a sharp knife to score the shortbread into 16 wedges. • Bake for 40–45 minutes, or until the topping is golden brown. • Use a sharp knife to cut into 16 wedges along the scored lines. • Loosen and remove the pan sides and bottom. Transfer to racks to cool.

COCONUT BUTTER THINS

Preheat the oven to 375°F/190°C/gas 5. • Set out a cookie sheet. • Sift the flour and salt into a medium bowl. • Beat the butter, sugar, and vanilla in a large bowl with an electric mixer at high speed until creamy. • Mix in the dry ingredients and coconut to form a smooth dough. • Form the dough into balls the size of walnuts and place 2 inches (5 cm) apart on the cookie sheet. • Press a half-cherry into each cookie. • Bake for 12–15 minutes, or until just golden at the edges. • Transfer to racks to cool.

618

Makes: 16–18 cookies

Preparation: 20'

Cooking: 12–15'

Level of difficulty: 1

- ⅔ cup/100 g all-purpose/plain flour
- ⅛ tsp salt
- ½ cup/125 g butter, softened
- ¼ cup/50 g granulated sugar
- ½ tsp vanilla extract/essence
- 2 tbsp shredded/desiccated coconut
- 8 candied cherries, cut in half

WALNUT SHORTBREAD

Sift the flour and salt into a medium bowl. •
Beat the butter and brown sugar in a large
bowl with an electric mixer at high speed until
creamy. • Add the egg yolk, beating until just
blended. • Mix in the dry ingredients, cherries, and
walnuts to form a smooth dough. • Divide the
dough in half. Form into two 4-inch (10-cm) logs,
wrap each in plastic wrap, and refrigerate for 30
minutes. • Preheat the oven to 375°F/190°C/
gas 5. • Butter two cookie sheets. • Slice the
dough 1/4 inch (5 mm) thick and place 1 inch
(2.5 cm) apart on the prepared cookie sheets. •
Bake for 10–12 minutes, or until just golden at the
edges. • Transfer to racks to cool.

Makes: 32 cookies

*Preparation: 25' + 30'
    to chill*

Cooking: 10–12'

Level of difficulty: 1

- **2 cups/300 g all-
  purpose/plain flour**
- **1/8 tsp salt**
- **1 cup/250 g butter,
  softened**
- **1 cup/200 g firmly
  packed dark brown
  sugar**
- **1 large egg yolk**
- **1/2 cup/50 g
  candied cherries,
  cut in half**
- **1/2 cup/50 g finely
  chopped walnuts**

PEREGRINE BUTTER COOKIES

Makes: 12–16 cookies

Preparation: 40' + 30' to chill

Cooking: 25–35'

Level of difficulty: 1

- 1¼ cups/225 g all-purpose/plain flour
- ⅛ tsp salt
- ½ cup/125 g butter, softened
- ¼ cup/50 g granulated sugar
- ¼ cup/50 g superfine/caster sugar, to dust

Sift the flour and salt into a medium bowl. • Beat the butter and granulated sugar in a large bowl with an electric mixer at high speed until creamy. • Mix in the dry ingredients to form a smooth dough. • Press the dough into a disk, wrap in plastic wrap, and refrigerate for 30 minutes. • Preheat the oven to 300°F/150°C/gas 2. • Butter a cookie sheet. • Roll out the dough on a lightly floured surface to a thickness of ¼-inch (5-mm). • Use a 3-inch (8-cm) fluted cookie cutter to cut out the cookies. Gather the dough scraps, reroll, and continue cutting out cookies until all the dough is used. • Use a spatula to transfer the cookies to the prepared cookie sheet, placing them 1 inch (2.5 cm) apart. • Bake for 25–35 minutes, or until just golden at the edges. • Transfer to racks to cool and dust with the superfine sugar.

SICILIAN CRISPS

Makes: 25–30 cookies

Preparation: 40' + 30' to chill

Cooking: 10–15' per batch

Level of difficulty: 1

- 1 cup/150 g all-purpose/plain flour
- 1 cup/150 g finely ground cornmeal
- $^1/_8$ tsp salt
- $^2/_3$ cup/150 g butter, cut up
- $^3/_4$ cup/150 g granulated sugar
- 3 large egg yolks, lightly beaten
- 1 tbsp Marsala
- Grated zest of 1 orange

Sift the flour, cornmeal, and salt into a large bowl. • Use a pastry blender to cut in the butter until the mixture resembles fine crumbs. • Stir in the sugar, egg yolks, Marsala, and orange zest to form a stiff dough. • Press the dough into a disk, wrap in plastic wrap, and refrigerate for 30 minutes. • Preheat the oven to 350°F/180°C/ gas 4. • Butter two cookie sheets. • Roll out the dough on a lightly floured surface to a thickness of $^1/_4$ inch (5 mm). • Use a fluted 2-inch (5-cm) cookie cutter to cut out the cookies. Gather the dough scraps, re-roll, and continue cutting out cookies until all the dough is used. • Use a spatula to transfer the cookies to the prepared cookie sheets, placing them 1 inch (2.5 cm) apart. • Bake for 15–20 minutes, or until just golden. • Transfer to racks to cool.

CHRISTMAS SHORTBREAD

Sift the flour and salt into a medium bowl. • Use a wooden spoon to beat the butter and marzipan in a large bowl until well blended. • Beat in the brown sugar. • Mix in the dry ingredients to form a stiff dough. • Press the dough into a disk, wrap in plastic wrap, and refrigerate for 30 minutes. • Preheat the oven to 350°F/180°C/ gas 4. • Line two cookie sheets with parchment paper. • Discard the plastic wrap. Roll out the dough on a lightly floured surface to a thickness of $^1/_4$ inch (5 mm). • Cut into $^3/_4$ x $2^1/_2$-inch (2 x 6-cm) strips. Gather the dough scraps, re-roll, and continue cutting out cookies until all the dough is used. • Use a spatula to transfer the cookies to the prepared cookie sheets, placing them 1 inch (2.5 cm) apart. • Sprinkle with the raw sugar. • Bake for 10–12 minutes, or until golden brown. • Transfer to racks to cool.

Makes: 25–30 cookies

Preparation: 40' + 30' to chill

Cooking: 10–12'

Level of difficulty: 1

- 1$^2/_3$ cups/400 g all-purpose/plain flour
- $^1/_8$ tsp salt
- 1 cup/250 g butter, softened
- 3$^1/_2$ oz/100 g marzipan, softened
- $^1/_2$ cup/100 g firmly packed light brown sugar
- 1 tbsp raw sugar (Demerara or Barbados)

Makes: 30 cookies
Preparation: 20'
Cooking: 15–20'
Level of difficulty: 1

- ¾ cup/75 g finely chopped pine nuts
- 2 tbsp granulated sugar
- 1 cup/250 g butter, softened
- 1⅓ cups/200 g confectioners'/icing sugar
- 1⅔ cups/400 g all-purpose/plain flour
- ⅛ tsp salt

NEVERLAND SHORTBREAD

Preheat the oven to 350°F/180°C/gas 4. • Butter and flour two cookie sheets. • Stir together the pine nuts and granulated sugar in a small bowl. • Beat the butter and confectioners' sugar in a large bowl with an electric mixer at high speed until creamy. • With mixer at low speed, gradually beat in the flour and salt. • Scoop out a heaping tablespoon of dough and shape into a ball the size of a walnut. • Place the cookies on the prepared cookie sheets, spacing them 1 inch (2.5 cm) apart. • Sprinkle with the pine nut mixture. • Bake for 15–20 minutes, or until golden brown. • Cool the cookies completely on the cookie sheets.

FRENCH SHORTBREAD

Preheat the oven to 325°F/170°C/gas 3. • Set out a 9-inch (23-cm) springform pan. • Sift the flour, cornstarch, and salt into a medium bowl. Stir in the lavender. • Beat the butter, sugar, and vanilla in a large bowl with an electric mixer at high speed until creamy. • Mix in the dry ingredients. • Firmly press the dough into the pan to form a smooth, even layer. Use a sharp knife to score the shortbread into 16 wedges. • Bake for 25–30 minutes, or until lightly browned. • Use a sharp knife to cut the shortbread into wedges along the scored lines. • Loosen and remove the pan sides and bottom. Transfer to racks to cool.

Makes: 16 cookies

Preparation: 25'

Cooking: 25–30'

Level of difficulty: 1

- 1 cup/150 g all-purpose/plain flour
- 2 tbsp cornstarch/cornflour
- ⅛ tsp salt
- 1 tsp lavender flowers (heads only), rinsed and dried
- ½ cup/125 g butter, softened
- ¼ cup/50 g granulated sugar
- ½ tsp vanilla extract/essence

LEMON DROPS

Makes: 35–40
cookies

Preparation: 20' + 30'
to chill

Cooking: 20–25' per
batch

Level of difficulty: 1

- 1¾ cups/275 g all-purpose/plain flour
- ⅓ cup/50 g cornstarch/cornflour
- ⅛ tsp salt
- 1 cup/250 g butter, softened
- ¼ cup/50 g granulated sugar
- 1 tbsp fresh lemon juice
- 1 large egg yolk
- ⅓ cup/80 ml lemon curd
- Confectioners' sugar, to dust

Sift the flour, cornstarch, and salt into a medium bowl. • Beat the butter and granulated sugar in a large bowl with an electric mixer at high speed until creamy. • Add the lemon juice and egg yolk, beating until just blended. • Mix in the dry ingredients to make a soft, sticky dough. • Cover with plastic wrap and refrigerate for 30 minutes. • Preheat the oven to 350°F/180°C/gas 4. • Line three cookie sheets with parchment paper. • Form the dough into balls the size of walnuts and place 1 inch (2.5 cm) apart on the prepared cookie sheets. Make a slight hollow in each center and fill with a small amount of Lemon Curd • Bake, one batch at a time, for 20–25 minutes, or until just golden. • Transfer to racks to cool. • Dust with the confectioners' sugar.

CHERRY TOPPED BUTTER WHIRLS

Makes: 16–18 cookies

Preparation: 25'

Cooking: 15–20'

Level of difficulty: 2

- 1¼ cups/180 g all-purpose/plain flour
- ½ tsp baking powder
- ⅛ tsp salt
- ¾ cup/180 g butter, softened
- ⅓ cup/50 g confectioners'/icing sugar
- ½ tsp vanilla extract/essence
- 8–9 candied cherries, cut in half

Preheat the oven to 325°F/170°C/gas 3. • Butter a cookie sheet. • Sift the flour, baking powder, and salt into a medium bowl. • Beat the butter, confectioners' sugar, and vanilla in a large bowl with an electric mixer at high speed until creamy. • Mix in the dry ingredients until well blended. • Fit a pastry bag with a ½-inch (1-cm) star tip. Fill the pastry bag, twist the opening tightly closed, and squeeze out flat whirls, spacing 1 inch (2.5 cm) apart on the prepared cookie sheet. • Place a half cherry on top of each whirl. • Bake for 15–20 minutes, or until lightly browned. • Cool on the sheet until the cookies firm slightly. • Transfer to racks and let cool completely.

SWEET SUMMER KISSES

Makes: 12 cookies

Preparation: 20'

Cooking: 15–20'

Level of difficulty: 1

- ¾ cup/180 g butter, softened
- ½ cup/75 g confectioners'/icing sugar
- 1 tsp vanilla extract/essence
- 2 cups/300 g all-purpose/plain flour
- ⅛ tsp salt
- ½ cup/160 g apricot preserves or jam

Preheat the oven to 350°F/180°C/gas 4. • Butter two cookie sheets. • Beat the butter, confectioners' sugar, and vanilla in a large bowl with an electric mixer at high speed until creamy. • Mix in the flour and salt. • Drop tablespoons of the dough 2 inches (5 cm) apart onto the prepared cookie sheets, flattening them slightly with a fork. • Bake for 15–20 minutes, or until just golden at the edges. • Transfer to racks to cool. • Warm the preserves in a small saucepan over low heat until liquid. • Stick the cookies together in pairs with the preserves.

BUTTER AND CHOCOLATE PIPED COOKIES

Makes: about 26 cookies

Preparation: 25'

Cooking: 10–15'

Level of difficulty: 2

- 1⅓ cups/200 g all-purpose/plain flour
- ⅓ cup/50 g cornstarch/cornflour
- 1 cup/250 g butter, softened
- ⅔ cup/100 g confectioners'/icing sugar
- 1 large egg
- ¼ tsp vanilla extract/essence
- ¼ tsp lemon extract/essence
- 2 tbsp unsweetened cocoa powder
- 1 tsp vegetable oil

Preheat the oven to 350°F/180°C/gas 4. • Butter three cookie sheets. • Sift the flour and cornstarch into a medium bowl. • Beat the butter and confectioners' sugar in a large bowl with an electric mixer at high speed until creamy. • Add the egg, beating until just blended. Stir in the vanilla and lemon extracts. Continue beating until pale and fluffy. • Mix in the dry ingredients. • Divide the dough evenly between two bowls. • Mix the cocoa and oil in a small bowl. Stir the cocoa mixture into one bowl of the dough. • Fit a pastry bag with a ¼-inch (5-mm) star tip. Fill the pastry bag with the plain batter, twist the opening tightly closed, and pipe out small rings, hearts, circles, and swirls spacing 1½ inches (4 cm) apart on the prepared cookie sheets. • Repeat with the chocolate batter. • Bake, one sheet at a time, for 10–15 minutes, or until the plain cookies are golden brown. • Cool the cookies on the cookie sheets for 2 minutes. • Transfer to racks to cool. • Dust some of the dark cookies with the confectioners' sugar.

BROWN SUGAR DROPS

Preheat the oven to 375°F/190°C/gas 5. •
Butter three cookie sheets. • Sift the flour,
baking soda, and salt into a medium bowl. • Beat
the butter and brown and granulated sugars in a
large bowl with an electric mixer at high speed until
creamy. • Add the egg and vanilla extract, beating
until just blended. • Mix in the dry ingredients. •
Drop teaspoons of the dough 2 inches (5 cm) apart
onto the prepared cookie sheets. • Bake, one
sheet at a time, for 7–10 minutes, or until golden.
• Transfer to racks to cool.

Makes: 40–45 cookies

Preparation: 20'

Cooking: 7–10'

Level of difficulty: 1

- 1¼ cups/180 g all-purpose/plain flour
- ½ tsp baking soda
- ⅛ tsp salt
- ½ cup/125 g butter, softened
- 3 tbsp firmly packed light brown sugar
- 3 tbsp granulated sugar
- 1 large egg, lightly beaten
- ½ tsp vanilla extract/essence

PIPED VANILLA COOKIES

Makes: 48 cookies	
Preparation: 40'	
Cooking: 5–8'	
Level of difficulty: 2	

- 1 cup/250 g butter, softened
- ½ cup/100 g + 2 tbsp granulated sugar
- 1½ tsp vanilla extract/essence
- 1 large egg
- 2 cups/300 g all-purpose/plain flour
- ⅛ tsp salt

Preheat the oven to 375°F/190°C/gas 5. • Set out four cookie sheets. • Beat the butter and ½ cup (100 g) sugar in a large bowl with an electric mixer at high speed until creamy. • Add the vanilla and egg, beating until just blended. • Mix in the flour and salt to form a soft dough. • Insert the chosen design plate into the press by sliding it into the head and locking it in place. Press out the cookies, spacing 1 inch (2.5 cm) apart on the cookie sheets. • Sprinkle with the remaining sugar. • Bake, one sheet at a time, for 5–8 minutes, or until just golden at the edges. • Transfer to racks and let cool completely.

ORANGE BUTTER COOKIES

B eat the butter and sugar in a large bowl with an electric mixer at high speed until creamy. • Add the egg yolk, beating until just blended. • Mix in the flour, salt, and orange juice until well blended. • Refrigerate for 1 hour. • Preheat the oven to 375°F/190°C/gas 5. • Butter two cookie sheets. • Fit a pastry bag with a 1-inch (2.5-cm) star tip. Fill the pastry bag, twist the opening tightly closed, and squeeze out four long strips on each sheet, spacing them at least 1 inch apart on the prepared cookie sheets. • Use a sharp knife to score each strip at 2$\frac{1}{2}$-inch (6-cm) intervals. • Bake, one sheet at a time, for 8–10 minutes, or until just golden. • Cut up the cookies along the scored lines. • Cool on the sheet until the cookies firm slightly. • Transfer to racks to finish cooling.

Makes: 36 cookies

Preparation: 40' + 60' to chill

Cooking: 8–10'

Level of difficulty: 2

- $\frac{2}{3}$ cup/150 g butter, softened
- $\frac{1}{2}$ cup/100 g granulated sugar
- 1 large egg yolk, lightly beaten
- 1$\frac{2}{3}$ cups/400 g all-purpose/plain flour
- $\frac{1}{8}$ tsp salt
- 2 tbsp fresh orange juice

ORANGE-GLAZED BUTTER COOKIES

Makes: 27 cookies	
Preparation: 45'	
Cooking: 13–15'	
Level of difficulty: 2	

BUTTER COOKIES
- 1 cup/150 g all-purpose/plain flour
- $1/8$ tsp salt
- 6 tbsp butter, softened
- $1/4$ cup/50 g granulated sugar
- 1 large egg yolk, lightly beaten
- 2 tbsp sour cream
- $1/4$ tsp almond extract/essence

ORANGE GLAZE
- 6 tbsp confectioners'/icing sugar
- 2 tbsp fresh orange juice
- $1/4$ cup/60 g apricot preserves

Butter Cookies: Preheat the oven to 375°F/190°C/gas 5. • Set out two cookie sheets. • Sift the flour and salt into a medium bowl. • Beat the butter and sugar in a large bowl with an electric mixer at high speed until creamy. • Add the egg yolk, beating until just blended. • Beat in the sour cream and almond extract. • Mix in the dry ingredients to form a smooth dough. • Insert a Christmas tree design plate into a cookie press by sliding it into the head and locking in place. Press out the cookies, spacing about $1/2$ inch (1 cm) apart on the cookie sheets. • Bake for 8–10 minutes, or until lightly browned. • Orange Glaze: Mix the confectioners' sugar and orange juice in a small bowl. • Warm the apricot preserves in a small saucepan over low heat until liquid. • Brush the cookies with a little preserves, followed by the orange glaze. • Bake for 5 minutes more, or until the glaze begins to crystallize. • Cool on the sheets until the cookies firm slightly. • Transfer to racks to finish cooling.

LEMON GLAZED S-SHAPES

Use a wooden spoon to mix the flour, egg yolks, butter, sugar, and salt in a large bowl to form a smooth dough. • Press the dough into a disk, wrap in plastic wrap, and refrigerate for 30 minutes. • Preheat the oven to 350°F/180°C/gas 4. • Butter two cookie sheets. • Form the dough into 1-inch (2.5-cm) long logs and place 1 inch (2.5 cm) apart on the prepared cookie sheets. • Shape the logs into S-shapes. • Bake for 8–10 minutes, or until just golden. • Lemon Glaze: Put the confectioners' sugar in a medium bowl. Beat in 4 tablespoons lemon juice and zest until smooth, adding the additional tablespoon of lemon juice as needed to make a good spreading consistency. • Drizzle the glaze over the cookies.

Makes: 25 cookies

Preparation: 35' + 30' to chill

Cooking: 8–10'

Level of difficulty: 1

- 1²/₃ cups/400 g all-purpose/plain flour
- 3 large egg yolks
- ½ cup/125 g butter, softened
- ²/₃ cup/140 g granulated sugar
- ⅛ tsp salt

LEMON GLAZE

- 1 cup/150 g confectioners'/ icing sugar
- 4–5 tbsp fresh lemon juice
- 1½ tsp finely grated lemon zest

VANILLA SHORTBREAD

Makes: 16 cookies

Preparation: 25'

Cooking: 10–12'

Level of difficulty: 1

- 1⅓ cups/200 g all-purpose/plain flour
- ⅛ tsp salt
- ⅔ cup/150 g butter, cut up
- ⅓ cup/70 g granulated sugar
- 1 large egg yolk, lightly beaten
- ½ tsp vanilla extract/essence
- Grated zest of 1 lemon
- ⅓ cup/50 g confectioners'/icing sugar

Preheat the oven to 350°F/180°C/gas 4. • Line a cookie sheet with parchment paper. • Sift the flour and salt into a large bowl. • Use a pastry blender to cut in the butter until the mixture resembles coarse crumbs. • Mix in the granulated sugar, egg yolk, vanilla, and grated lemon zest to form a smooth dough. • Form the dough into 1½ x ½-inch (4 x 1-cm) logs and place 1 inch (2.5 cm) apart on the prepared cookie sheet, flattening them slightly. • Bake for 10–12 minutes, or until just golden. • Transfer to racks to cool. • Dust with the confectioners' sugar.

PERFECT PARTY COOKIES

Preheat the oven to 350°F/180°C/gas 4. •
Lightly oil two cookie sheets. • Beat the butter
and confectioners' sugar in a large bowl with an
electric mixer at high speed until creamy. • With
mixer at low speed, gradually beat in the flour and
salt. • Continue beating for 2–3 minutes until
smooth and light. • Fit a pastry bag with a $^3/_4$-inch
(2-cm) star tip. Fill the pastry bag, twist the opening
tightly closed, and squeeze 2-inch (5-cm) lines and
rosettes spacing them 2 inches (5 cm) apart on
the prepared cookie sheets. • Bake for 6–8
minutes, or until lightly browned. • Cool the
cookies on the sheet for 1 minute. Transfer to
racks to cool. • Lemon Glaze: Sift the
confectioners' sugar into a small bowl and mix with
the lemon juice until smooth. • Drizzle over the
cookies. • Sprinkle with the confetti.

Makes: 35 cookies

Preparation: 25'

Cooking: 6–8'

Level of difficulty: 1

- 1 cup/250 g butter,
  softened
- $^1/_2$ cup/75 g
  confectioners'/
  icing sugar
- 1$^1/_4$ cups/180 g all-
  purpose flour
- $^1/_8$ tsp salt

LEMON GLAZE
- $^1/_3$ cup/50 g
  confectioners'/
  icing sugar
- 2–3 tsp fresh lemon
  juice
- 1 tbsp sugar
  confetti (available
  from Maid of
  Scandinavia and
  other specialty
  baking stores)

BUTTER S-SHAPES

Makes: 60 cookies

Preparation: 40'

Cooking: 7–10' + 90' to chill

Level of difficulty: 2

- 2²/₃ cups/400 g all-purpose/plain flour
- ¹/₈ tsp salt
- 1 cup/250 g butter, softened
- 1¼ cups/250 g granulated sugar
- 3 large eggs
- Grated zest of ½ lemon
- 1¼ cups/125 g finely ground hazelnuts or almonds
- 5 tbsp vanilla sugar

Sift the flour and salt into a medium bowl. • Beat the butter and granulated sugar in a large bowl with an electric mixer at high speed until creamy. • Add the eggs and lemon zest, beating until just blended. • Mix in the dry ingredients and hazelnuts to form a smooth, not sticky, dough. • Refrigerate for 30 minutes. • Set out four cookie sheets. • Fit a pastry bag with a ¹/₂-inch (1-cm) round or star tip, twist the opening tightly closed, and squeeze out long strips of dough onto a sheet of parchment paper. • Cut into 3-inch (8-cm) lengths and press into S-shapes with your fingers . Use a long spatula to transfer to the prepared cookie sheets, spacing 2 inches (5 cm) apart. • Refrigerate for 1 hour. • Preheat the oven to 375°F/190°C/gas 5. • Bake, one sheet at a time, for 7–10 minutes, or until golden and the edges are firm. • Cool on the sheets for 2 minutes until slightly firm. Dip in the vanilla sugar while still warm. • Transfer to racks and let cool completely.

RASPBERRY PINWHEELS

Sift the flour and salt into a large bowl. Stir in the almonds and sugar. • Use a pastry blender to cut in the butter until the mixture resembles fine crumbs. • Mix in the egg mixture to form a firm dough. • Turn the dough out onto a lightly floured surface and knead until smooth. • Transfer to a large sheet of parchment paper and roll out to a 10 x 14-inch (25 x 35-cm) rectangle. Spread evenly with the preserves and tightly roll up the dough from the long side. • Wrap in plastic wrap and refrigerate for at least 30 minutes. • Preheat the oven to 350°F/180°C/gas 4. • Line two cookie sheets with parchment paper. • Slice the dough $1/2$ inch (1-cm) thick and place $1/2$ inch (1-cm) apart on the prepared cookie sheets. • Bake for 12–15 minutes, or until just golden at the edges. • Transfer to racks to cool.

Makes 28 cookies

Preparation: 60'+ 30' to chill

Cooking: 12–15'

Level of difficulty: 2

- **2 cups/300 g all-purpose flour**
- **$1/8$ tsp salt**
- **$1/2$ cup/75 g finely ground almonds**
- **$1/2$ cup/100 g granulated sugar**
- **6 tbsp butter, cut up**
- **1 large egg, lightly beaten with 2 tbsp cold water**
- **$1/4$ cup/90 g raspberry preserves**

VANILLA SHORTS

Sift the flour, cornstarch, baking powder, and salt into a large bowl. • Use a pastry blender to cut in the butter until the mixture resembles fine crumbs. • Mix in the sugar, eggs, and vanilla to form a smooth dough. • Wrap in plastic wrap and refrigerate for 30 minutes. • Preheat the oven to 375°F/190°C/gas 5. • Set out two cookie sheets. • Roll out the dough on a lightly floured surface to a thickness of $1/4$ inch (5 mm). • Use a 2-inch (5-cm) cookie cutter to cut out the cookies. Gather the dough scraps, re-roll, and continue cutting out cookies until all the dough is used. • Use a spatula to transfer the cookies to the cookie sheets, placing them 1 inch (2.5 cm) apart. • Prick the cookies all over with a fork. • Bake, one sheet at a time, for 10–15 minutes, or until just golden at the edges. • Transfer to racks and let cool completely.

Makes 40–45 cookies

Preparation: 40' + 30' to chill

Cooking: 10–15' per batch

Level of difficulty: 1

- $1^2/3$ cups/250 g all-purpose/plain flour
- $3/4$ cup/125 g cornstarch/cornflour
- 1 tsp baking powder
- $1/2$ cup/125 g butter, cut up
- $1/8$ tsp salt
- $3/4$ cup/150 g granulated sugar
- **2 large eggs, lightly beaten**
- 1 tsp vanilla extract/essence

654

BUTTER RINGS

Makes: 36 cookies

Preparation: 30' + 1 h 45' to rise

Cooking: 12–15'

Level of difficulty: 2

- 1½ tsp active dry yeast
- 2 tbsp granulated sugar
- 4 tbsp warm water (105°–115°F)
- 1⅔ cups/250 g all-purpose/plain flour
- ⅛ tsp salt
- 6 tbsp butter, softened

Stir together the yeast, 1 tablespoon of the sugar, and water. Set aside for 10 minutes. • Sift the flour and salt into a large bowl. • Stir in the yeast mixture to make a smooth dough. • Cover with plastic wrap and let rise in a warm place for 1 hour, or until doubled in bulk. • Punch down the dough and let rise for 30 minutes more. • Preheat the oven to 350°F/180°C/gas 4. • Butter three cookie sheets. • Break off small pieces of dough and form into 2½-inch (6-cm) long ropes, about ⅛ inch (3 mm) in diameter. Bend into rings, pressing the ends together, and sprinkle with the remaining sugar. • Transfer to the prepared cookie sheets, placing 1 inch (2.5 cm) apart. • Cover with a kitchen towel and let rest for 15 minutes. • Bake, one sheet at a time, for 12–15 minutes, or until crisp and golden. • Transfer to racks to cool.

FRESH
FRUIT
COOKIES

FROSTED PINEAPPLE BITES

Preheat the oven to 400°F/200°C/gas 6. •
Butter three cookie sheets. • Sift the flour,
baking powder, and salt into a medium bowl. •
Beat the shortening and brown sugar in a large
bowl with an electric mixer at high speed until
creamy. • Add the egg and vanilla, beating until just
blended. • Mix in the pineapple, reserving a few
pieces for decoration, and the dry ingredients. •
Drop teaspoons of the dough 2 inches (5 cm) apart
onto the prepared cookie sheets. • Bake, one
sheet at a time, for 8–10 minutes, or until just
golden at the edges. • Transfer to racks to cool. •
Pineapple Glaze: Mix the confectioners' sugar and
pineapple juice in a small bowl. • Spread the glaze
over the tops of the cookies and top with the
reserved pineapple. Let set for 30 minutes.

Makes: 32–36
  cookies

Preparation: 25' + 30'
to set

Cooking: 8–10'

Level of difficulty: 1

- **2 cups/300 g all-purpose/plain flour**
- **1½ tsp baking powder**
- **¼ tsp salt**
- **½ cup/125 g vegetable shortening**
- **1 cup/200 g firmly packed light brown sugar**
- **1 large egg**
- **½ tsp vanilla extract/essence**
- **1 can (8 oz/250 g) crushed pineapple, drained (reserve the juice**

PINEAPPLE GLAZE

- **3 cups/450 g confectioners'/icing sugar**
- **4 tbsp pineapple juice (see above)**

TROPICAL BASKETS

Makes: 6–8 cookies

Preparation: 20'

Cooking: 8–10'

Level of difficulty: 1

- ½ cup/125 g butter
- 8 tbsp corn/golden syrup
- ¼ cup/50 g sugar
- ½ tsp cream of tartar
- ¾ cup/125 g all-purpose/plain flour
- 2 tsp ground ginger
- fresh fruit salad, made with fruits of the season, sliced and marinated with lemon juice and sugar

Preheat the oven to 350°F/180°C/gas 4. • Butter a large baking sheet. • Heat the butter, corn syrup, and sugar over low heat in a small saucepan until melted. • Remove from heat and stir in the cream of tartar, flour, and ginger. • Drop tablespoons of the mixture onto the prepared baking sheet. Shape into 2-inch (5-cm) rounds, spacing well apart. • Bake for 8–10 minutes, or until golden brown. • Cool the cookies on the sheet for 5 minutes, or until pliable. • Use a thin metal spatula to remove them from the sheet. • Shape into small baskets, fluting the edges with your fingertips. • Let cool completely, then fill with fresh fruit salad just before serving.

| Makes: 45–48 cookies |
| Preparation: 20' |
| Cooking: 15–20' |
| Level of difficulty: 1 |

- 2 cups/300 g all-purpose/plain flour
- ½ tsp baking powder
- ½ tsp baking soda
- ½ tsp ground cinnamon
- ¼ tsp salt
- ½ cup/125 g butter, softened
- ½ cup/100 g granulated sugar
- ¼ cup/50 g firmly packed dark brown sugar
- 1 large egg
- 1 cup/250 ml applesauce
- 1 tart apple, such as Granny Smith, peeled, cored, and finely chopped
- 1 cup/100 g finely chopped walnuts

FIVE SISTERS COOKIES

Preheat the oven to 375°F/170°C/gas 3. • Butter three cookie sheets. • Sift the flour, baking powder, baking soda, cinnamon, and salt into a medium bowl. • Beat the butter and granulated and brown sugars in a large bowl with an electric mixer at high speed until creamy. • Add the egg and applesauce, beating until just blended. • Mix in the dry ingredients, apple, and walnuts. • Drop tablespoons of the dough 2 inches (5 cm) apart onto the prepared cookie sheets. • Bake, one sheet at a time, for 15–20 minutes, or until just golden at the edges. • Transfer to racks to cool.

APPLE COOKIES

Makes: 40–45 cookies

Preparation: 30'

Cooking: 10–15'

Level of difficulty: 1

- 2 medium sweet cooking apples, peeled, cored, and finely chopped
- ¾ cup/150 g granulated sugar
- 2 cups/300 g all-purpose/plain flour
- 1 tsp baking powder
- 1 tsp ground cinnamon
- ⅛ tsp salt
- ¾ cup/180 g butter, softened
- 1 large egg
- ¾ cup/120 g raisins
- 1 cup/100 g corn flakes

Cook the apples with 1 tablespoon of sugar in a small saucepan over low heat, stirring often, until the apples have softened. Remove from the heat and let cool completely. • Preheat the oven to 400°F/200°C/gas 6. • Butter three cookie sheets. • Sift the flour, baking powder, cinnamon, and salt into a medium bowl. • Beat the butter and remaining sugar in a large bowl with an electric mixer at high speed until creamy. • Add the egg, beating until just blended. • Mix in alternating tablespoons of the dry ingredients and the cooked apples until well blended. • Stir in the raisins and corn flakes. • Drop teaspoons of the dough 1 inch (2.5 cm) apart onto the prepared cookie sheets. • Bake, one sheet at a time, for 10–15 minutes, or until golden brown. • Transfer to racks to cool.

HEALTHY BANANA COOKIES

Preheat the oven to 350°F/180°C/gas 4. • Butter a cookie sheet. • Finely grind the sunflower seed and oats with a pestle and mortar or in a blender until they resemble flour. • Heat the honey and oil in a small saucepan over low heat. • Mix the honey mixture with the sunflower seed mixture in a medium bowl. • Add the egg, beating until just blended. Stir in the banana. • Drop teaspoons of the mixture 1 inch (2.5 cm) apart onto the prepared cookie sheet. • Bake for 12–15 minutes, or until golden brown. • Cool the cookies completely on the cookie sheets. • Sprinkle with the remaining sunflower seeds.

Makes: 20 cookies

Preparation: 20'

Cooking: 12–15'

Level of difficulty: 1

- 1/3 cup/30 g sunflower seeds
- 1/3 cup/50 g old-fashioned rolled oats
- 1/3 cup/50 g all-purpose/plain flour
- 2 tbsp honey
- 1 tbsp sunflower oil
- 1 large egg, lightly beaten
- 1 large ripe banana, mashed
- 1 tbsp sunflower seeds, to decorate

BLIMEY LIME COOKIES

667

Makes: 36 cookies

Preparation: 25'

Cooking: 10–12'

Level of difficulty: 1

- **3½ cups/535 g all-purpose/plain flour**
- **1 tsp baking soda**
- **½ tsp salt**
- **½ cup/50 g sunflower seeds, toasted**
- **½ cup/125 g butter, softened**
- **2¼ cups/450 g granulated sugar**
- **2 tbsp extra-virgin olive oil**
- **grated zest of 2 limes**
- **2 large eggs**
- **3 tbsp fresh lime juice**

Preheat the oven to 350°F/180°C/gas 4. • Line three cookie sheets with parchment paper. • Sift the flour, baking soda, and salt into a medium bowl. • Stir in the sunflower seeds. • Beat the butter, 2 cups (400 g) of sugar, oil, and grated zest of 1 lime in a large bowl with an electric mixer at high speed until creamy. • Add the eggs, beating until just blended. • Mix in the dry ingredients and lime juice. • Mix the remaining sugar and lime zest in a small bowl. • Form the dough into balls the size of walnuts and roll in the lime sugar. • Place the cookies 2 inches (5 cm) apart on the prepared cookie sheets, flattening them slightly. • Bake, one sheet at a time, for 10–12 minutes, or until just golden at the edges. • Transfer to racks and let cool completely.

CARROT AND ORANGE COOKIES

Preheat the oven to 375°F/190°C/gas 5. • Oil four cookie sheets. • Sift the flour, baking soda, cinnamon, allspice, nutmeg, ginger, and salt into a medium bowl. • Beat the butter and brown sugar in a large bowl with an electric mixer at high speed until creamy. • Add the orange zest and vanilla. • Add the eggs, carrots, raisins, coconut, and oats. • Mix in the dry ingredients. • Drop teaspoons of the dough 2 inches (5 cm) apart on the prepared cookie sheets. • Bake, one sheet at a time, for 8–10 minutes, or until golden brown. • Transfer to racks and let cool completely.

Makes: about 60 cookies

Preparation: 20'

Cooking: 8–10'

Level of difficulty: 1

- 1⅓ cups/200 g all-purpose/plain flour
- 1 tsp baking soda
- 1 tsp ground cinnamon
- ½ tsp ground allspice
- ½ tsp freshly grated nutmeg
- ¼ tsp ground ginger
- ¼ tsp salt
- 1 cup/250 g butter, softened
- 1 cup/200 g firmly packed light brown sugar
- 1 tsp finely grated orange zest
- 1 tsp vanilla extract/essence
- 2 large eggs
- 1½ cups/185 g finely shredded carrots
- ½ cup/90 g raisins
- ½ cup/60 g shredded/desiccated coconut
- ¼ cup/30 g old-fashioned rolled oats

LEMON CARROT COOKIES

Makes: 16 cookies

Preparation: 40'

Cooking: 15–20'

Level of difficulty: 1

Preheat the oven to 350°F/180°C/gas 4. • Butter a cookie sheet. • Sift the flour, baking powder, and salt into a medium bowl. • Reserve 2 teaspoons of the sugar. • Beat the margarine and remaining sugar with the lemon zest in a medium bowl with an electric mixer at high speed until creamy. • Use a wooden spoon to mix in the shredded carrot, followed by the dry ingredients to make a soft dough. • If the dough is stiff, add the water. • Drop tablespoons of the dough 2 inches (5 cm) apart onto the prepared cookie sheet. Sprinkle the tops of the cookies with the reserved sugar. • Bake for 15–20 minutes, or until golden and firm to the touch.

- ½ cup/75 g all-purpose/plain flour
- 1 tsp baking powder
- ⅛ tsp salt
- ¼ cup/50 g granulated sugar
- 2 tbsp finely grated lemon zest
- 2 tbsp margarine or butter, softened
- 1⅔ cups/200 g very finely shredded carrots or grated carrots
- 1 tbsp cold water (optional)

Makes: 12–15
cookies

Preparation: 45' + 30'
to chill

Cooking: 6–8'

Level of difficulty: 1

- 1½ cups/225 g all-
  purpose/plain flour
- ⅛ tsp salt
- ⅔ cup/150 g
  butter, cut up
- ⅓ cup/70 g
  granulated sugar
- 1 tbsp finely grated
  lemon zest
- 2 tbsp fresh lemon
  juice
- 2 large egg yolks
- 1 cup/250 ml
  lemon curd
- 1 tbsp
  confectioners'/
  icing sugar

LEMON CURD COOKIES

Sift the flour and salt into a large bowl. • Cut in the butter until the mixture resembles fine crumbs. • Stir in the granulated sugar, lemon zest and juice, and egg yolks to form a stiff dough. • Press the dough into a disk, wrap in plastic wrap, and refrigerate for 30 minutes. • Preheat the oven to 350°F/180°C/gas 4. • Butter two cookie sheets. • Roll out the dough to a thickness of ⅛ inch (3 mm). • Use a 3-inch (8-cm) fluted cookie cutter to cut out the cookies. • Use a 1-inch (2.5-cm) crescent-shaped cookie cutter to cut out the centers from half the cookies. Gather the dough scraps, re-roll, and continue cutting out cookies until all the dough is used. • Transfer the cookies to the sheets. • Bake for 6–8 minutes, or until golden brown. • Transfer to racks to cool. • Spread the whole cookies with the lemon curd and place the cookies with holes on top. Dust with the confectioners' sugar.

APPLE SMILES

Makes: 12–15 cookies

Preparation: 60'

Cooking: 20–30'

Level of difficulty: 2

Dough

- 1 cup/250 g quark or 1⅓ cups/310 g ricotta cheese
- 2 cups/300 g all-purpose/plain flour
- 1 tsp baking powder
- ⅛ tsp salt
- 6 tbsp vegetable oil
- 1–2 tbsp milk
- ⅓ cup/70 g granulated sugar
- 1 large egg
- 1 tsp finely grated lemon zest
- ¼ tsp vanilla extract/essence
- 6 tbsp butter

Filling

- 3 tbsp golden raisins/sultanas
- 3 medium apples, peeled, cored, and cubed
- 1 tbsp butter
- ⅓ cup/70 g granulated sugar
- Zest of 1 lemon
- 1 tsp lemon juice
- 1 large egg
- Confectioners'/icing sugar, to dust

Quark Dough: Mix all the ingredients for the quark dough in a large bowl to form a stiff dough. • Filling: Plump the raisins in hot water for 10 minutes. Drain well and pat dry with paper towels. • Preheat the oven to 350°F/180°C/gas 4. • Set out a cookie sheet. • Mix the apples, butter, sugar, and lemon zest and juice in a large saucepan over low heat and stew for about 5 minutes, or until the apples begin to soften. • Stir in the raisins and let cool completely. • Discard the lemon zest. • Roll out to a thickness of ¼ inch (5 mm). • Use a round cookie cutter to stamp out 3-inch (8-cm) circles. • Spread with a heaping teaspoonful of the apple filling, leaving a ½-inch (1-cm) border around the edge. • Brush the border with the beaten egg and fold over, pressing down firmly. • Brush the tops with the remaining egg. • Arrange on the cookie sheet about 1 inch (2.5 cm) apart. • Bake for 20–30 minutes, or until golden brown. • Cool on the sheet for 2 minutes. Transfer to racks to cool. • Dust with confectioners' sugar.

FEBRUARY HEARTS

S ift the flour, baking powder, cinnamon, and salt into a medium bowl. • Beat the butter and granulated and brown sugars in a large bowl with an electric mixer at high speed until creamy. • Add the egg, vanilla, and lemon zest, beating until just blended. • Mix in the dry ingredients to form a smooth dough. •

674

A gift for your loved one on Valentine's Day.

Press the dough into a disk, wrap in plastic wrap, and refrigerate for 30 minutes. • Preheat the oven to 350°F/180°C/ gas 4. • Butter two cookie sheets. • Roll out one-third of the dough on a lightly floured surface to a thickness of $1/4$ inch (5 mm). • Use a $3^1/2$-inch (9-cm) heart-shaped cookie cutter to cut out the cookies. • Gather the dough scraps, re-roll, and continue cutting out cookies until all the dough is used. • Use a spatula to transfer the cookies to the prepared cookie sheets, placing them $1/2$ inch (1 cm) apart. • Bake for 8–10 minutes, or until just golden. • Transfer to racks to cool. • Cranberry Topping: Process the cranberries, granulated sugar, and preserves in a food processor or blender until pureed. • Transfer to a saucepan and cook over medium heat for 8 minutes, or until reduced to 1 cup (250 ml). • Remove from the heat and let cool for 15 minutes. • Use a thin metal spatula to spread the topping over the tops of the cookies. Dust with the confectioners' sugar just before serving.

- 2¼ cups/330 g all-purpose/plain flour
- 1½ tsp baking powder
- ½ tsp ground cinnamon
- ¼ tsp salt
- ¾ cup/180 g butter, softened
- ½ cup/100 g granulated sugar
- ½ cup/100 g firmly packed dark brown sugar
- 1 large egg
- ½ tsp vanilla extract/essence
- Grated zest of 1 lemon

CRANBERRY TOPPING

- 1 cup/250 g fresh or frozen cranberries
- ¼ cup/50 g granulated sugar
- ¾ cup/210 g raspberry preserves
- ¾ cup/125 g confectioners'/ icing sugar, to dust

CITRUS MOONS

677

Makes: 20–25 cookies

Preparation: 45' + 30' to chill

Cooking: 8–10'

Level of difficulty: 1

- 1²/₃ cups/250 g all-purpose/plain flour
- ¹/₈ tsp salt
- ¹/₂ cup/125 g butter, softened
- ³/₄ cup/125 g confectioners'/icing sugar
- 1 tbsp vanilla sugar
- 1 large egg + 1 large egg yolk
- ¹/₂ tsp vanilla extract/essence
- Grated zest of 1 orange
- Grated zest of ¹/₂ lemon

TOPPING

- 1 large egg yolk
- 1 tbsp water
- 2 tbsp flaked almonds

Sift the flour and salt into a medium bowl. • Beat the butter and confectioners' and vanilla sugars in a large bowl with an electric mixer at high speed until creamy. • Add the whole egg and egg yolk and vanilla, beating until just blended. • Mix in the dry ingredients to form a stiff dough. • Divide the dough in half. Knead the orange zest into one half and lemon zest into the other. • Press each dough into a disk, wrap in plastic wrap, and refrigerate for 30 minutes. • Preheat the oven to 350°F/180°C/gas 4. • Set out three cookie sheets. • Roll out each dough half on a lightly floured surface to a thickness of ¹/₄ inch (5 mm). • Use 2-inch (5-cm) crescent-shaped cookie cutters to cut out the cookies. Gather the dough scraps, re-roll, and continue cutting out cookies until all the dough is used. • Use a spatula to transfer the cookies to the prepared cookie sheets, placing them 1 inch (2.5 cm) apart. • Topping: Beat the egg yolk with the water in a small bowl. Brush over the tops of the cookies and decorate with almonds. • Bake, one sheet at a time, for 8–10 minutes, or until firm to the touch and the edges are lightly golden. • Transfer to racks to cool.

CHERRY COOKIES

Sift the flour, baking powder, and salt into a large bowl. • Use a pastry blender to cut in the butter until the mixture resembles fine crumbs. • Add the egg, beating until just blended. • Stir in the sugar, cherries, and vanilla to form a soft dough. • Turn the dough out onto a lightly floured surface and knead until smooth. • Form the dough into a long log 2 inches (5 cm) in diameter, wrap in plastic wrap, and refrigerate for at least 30 minutes. • Preheat the oven to 375°F/190°C/gas 5. • Butter three cookie sheets. • Slice the dough ¹/₂ inch (1 cm) thick and place 1 inch (2.5 cm) apart on the prepared cookie sheets. • Bake, one sheet at a time, for 8–10 minutes, or until just golden. • Transfer to racks to cool.

Makes: 35 cookies

Preparation: 40' + 30' to chill

Cooking: 8–10'

Level of difficulty: 1

- 1²/₃ cups/250 g all-purpose/plain flour
- 1 tsp baking powder
- ¹/₈ tsp salt
- ¹/₂ cup/125 g butter, cut up
- 1 large egg, lightly beaten
- ³/₄ cup/150 g granulated sugar
- ¹/₂ cup/50 g finely chopped candied cherries
- 1 tsp vanilla extract/essence

CREAM CHEESE SQUARES

Makes: 24 bars

Preparation: 30'

Cooking: 25–30'

Level of difficulty: 1

COOKIE BASE
- 1¼ cups/155 g graham cracker crumbs
- 6 tbsp butter, melted

TOPPING
- 1 cup/250 g cream cheese, softened
- ½ cup/100 g granulated sugar
- 3 tbsp lemon curd
- 3 tbsp cornstarch/cornflour
- 1 large egg, lightly beaten

Preheat the oven to 375°F/190°C/gas 5. • Butter a 13 x 9-inch (33 x 23-cm) baking pan. • Cookie Base: Mix the graham cracker crumbs and butter in a large bowl until well blended. • Firmly press the mixture into the prepared pan to form a smooth, even layer. • Topping: Beat the cream cheese and sugar in a large bowl with an electric mixer at low speed until smooth. • Beat in the lemon curd, cornstarch, and egg. • Spoon the topping over the cookie base. • Bake for 25–30 minutes, or until firm to the touch. • Cool completely before cutting into bars.

FRESH FRUIT SQUARES

Preheat the oven to 350°F/180°C/gas 4. •
Butter an 11 x 7-inch (28 x 18-cm) baking pan.
• Sift the flour, baking powder, and salt into a
medium bowl. • Process the apples, butter,
granulated and vanilla sugars, corn syrup, and
orange-flower water in a food processor until
pureed. • Add the egg, processing until just
blended. • Mix in the dry ingredients. • Firmly
press the mixture into the baking pan to form a
smooth, even layer. • Bake for 15–20 minutes, or
until firm to the touch. • Cool completely in the
pan. • Orange Glaze: Mix the confectioners' sugar
with enough orange juice and water to form a
runny glaze. • Drizzle over the cake and sprinkle
with the orange zest. Cut into bars.

Makes: 22–33 bars

Preparation: 30'

Cooking: 15–20'

Level of difficulty: 2

- 2⅔ cups/400 g all-purpose/plain flour
- 1 tsp baking powder
- ½ tsp salt
- ½ cup/50 g finely chopped dried apples
- ¾ cup/180 g butter, cut up
- ⅓ cup/70 g granulated sugar
- 2 tbsp vanilla sugar
- 6 tbsp light corn syrup/golden syrup
- 1 tbsp orange-flower water or orange juice
- 1 large egg

Orange Glaze
- 1 cup/150 g confectioners'/icing sugar
- 1–2 tbsp orange juice
- 1 tbsp warm water
- Grated zest of 1 orange

PINEAPPLE GINGER SQUARES

Makes: 36–45 bars

Preparation: 30'

Cooking: 45–50'

Level of difficulty: 1

- 2 cups/300 g all-purpose/plain flour
- 1 tsp ground ginger
- 1/8 tsp salt
- 1 cup/250 g butter, softened
- 2/3 cup/140 g firmly packed soft brown sugar
- 1 large egg, lightly beaten
- 1 cup/150 g chopped crystallized pineapple
- 1/2 cup/50 g finely chopped crystallized ginger

Preheat the oven to 350°F/180°C/gas 4. • Butter a 13 x 9-inch (33 x 23-cm) baking pan. • Sift the flour, ground ginger, and salt into a medium bowl. • Beat the butter and brown sugar in a large bowl with an electric mixer at high speed until creamy. • Use a wooden spoon to mix in the dry ingredients until the mixture resembles coarse crumbs. Transfer half the mixture to a small bowl and set aside. • Add the egg to the remaining mixture and mix to form a smooth dough. • Firmly press the dough into the prepared pan to form a smooth, even layer. • Sprinkle the crystallized pineapple and ginger on top. Sprinkle with the reserved crumb mixture. • Bake for 45–50 minutes, or until golden. • Cool in the pan for 15 minutes and cut into bars. • Serve warm.

ORANGE LADYFINGERS

Preheat the oven to 375°F/190°C/gas 5. • Line two cookie sheets with parchment paper. • Sift the flour and salt into a medium bowl. • Beat the eggs, superfine sugar, and orange zest in a large bowl with an electric mixer at high speed until pale and very thick. • Use a large rubber spatula to gradually fold in the dry ingredients. • Fit a pastry bag with a $^1/_2$-inch (1-cm) star tip. Fill the pastry bag, twist the opening tightly closed, and squeeze out 2-inch (5-cm) lines, spacing them 3 inches (8 cm) apart on the prepared cookie sheets. • Bake, one sheet at a time, for 5–10 minutes, or until just golden. • Transfer to racks to cool.

Makes: 20 cookies
Preparation: 15'
Cooking: 5–10'
Level of difficulty: 2

- $^1/_3$ cup/50 g all-purpose/plain flour
- $^1/_8$ tsp salt
- 2 large eggs
- $^1/_3$ cup/70 g superfine/caster sugar
- grated zest of 1 orange

CRISP ORANGE COOKIES

Makes: 25 cookies

Preparation: 25'

Cooking: 12–15'

Level of difficulty: 1

- 1½ cups/225 g all-purpose/plain flour
- 1 tbsp cornstarch/cornflour
- ½ tsp baking powder
- ⅛ tsp salt
- 1 cup/250 g butter, softened
- ⅔ cup/100 g confectioners'/icing sugar + extra, to dust
- grated zest of 2 oranges

Preheat the oven to 350°F/180°C/gas 4. • Butter two cookie sheets. • Sift the flour, cornstarch, baking powder, and salt into a large bowl. • Beat the butter and ⅔ cup (100 g) confectioners' sugar in a large bowl with an electric mixer at high speed until creamy. • Mix in the dry ingredients and orange zest. • Drop teaspoons of the mixture 2 inches (5 cm) apart onto the prepared cookie sheets. • Bake for 12–15 minutes, or until golden brown. • Cool completely on the sheets.

LEMON STARS

Makes: 25 cookies

Preparation: 25'

Cooking: 10–15'

Level of difficulty: 2

- 1²/₃ cups/250 g all-purpose/plain flour
- ½ tsp baking powder
- ⅛ tsp salt
- ½ cup/100 g granulated sugar
- 1 large egg
- 6 tbsp sunflower oil
- 4 tbsp light/single cream
- 1 tsp honey
- Grated zest of 1 lemon
- 1 tbsp lemon curd
- 1 tbsp candied lemon zest

Preheat the oven to 350°F/180°C/gas 4. • Butter two cookie sheets. • Sift the flour, baking powder, and salt into a large bowl. • Stir in the sugar. • Add the egg, beating until just blended. • Stir in the oil, cream, honey, and lemon zest. • Fit a pastry bag with a ½-inch (1-cm) star tip. Fill the pastry bag, twist the opening tightly closed, and squeeze out generous 1½-inch (4-cm) stars, spacing 1 inch (2.5 cm) apart onto the prepared cookie sheets. • Bake for 10–15 minutes, or until just golden at the edges. • Transfer to racks to cool. • Dot the tops of the cookies with lemon curd and decorate with the candied lemon zest.

TANGY PINEAPPLE COOKIES

Preheat the oven to 400°F/200°C/gas 6. • Set out two cookie sheets. • Sift the flour, baking powder, and salt into a medium bowl. • Beat the butter and sugar in a large bowl with an electric mixer at high speed until creamy. • Add the egg, beating until just blended. • Mix in the dry ingredients, followed by the pineapple juice. • Insert a star-shaped design plate into a cookie press by sliding it into the head and locking it in place. Press out the cookies, spacing about 1 inch (2.5 cm) apart on the prepared cookie sheets. • Bake for 8–10 minutes, or until just golden at the edges. • Cool on the sheets until the cookies firm slightly. • Transfer to racks and let cool completely.

Makes: 32–36 cookies

Preparation: 25'

Cooking: 8–10'

Level of difficulty: 2

- 2¼ cups/330 g all-purpose/plain flour
- ½ tsp baking powder
- ¼ tsp salt
- 1 cup/250 g butter, softened
- ⅔ cup/140 g granulated sugar
- 1 large egg
- 1 tbsp fresh or canned pineapple juice

LEMON CRUNCHIES

Makes: 48 cookies

Preparation: 25' + 30' to chill

Cooking: 10–15'

Level of difficulty: 1

Line a cookie sheet with parchment paper. • Mix the flour, sugar, egg whites, almonds, candied lemon peel, lemon zest, baking soda, and salt in a large bowl to form a stiff dough. Press the dough into a disk, wrap in plastic wrap, and refrigerate for 30 minutes. • Roll out the dough on a lightly floured surface to a 12 x 3-inch (30 x 8-cm) rectangle. • Transfer to the prepared cookie sheet and refrigerate for 30 minutes. • Preheat the oven to 300°F/150°C/gas 2. • Cut the dough in half lengthwise and slice into $^1/_2$-inch (1-cm) strips. • Bake for 10–15 minutes, or until just golden. • Transfer to racks to cool.

- 2$^1/_4$ cups/330 g all-purpose/plain flour
- 1$^3/_4$ cups/350 g granulated sugar
- 4 large egg whites, lightly beaten
- 1$^1/_3$ cups/200 g finely ground almonds
- $^2/_3$ cup/60 g finely chopped candied lemon peel
- Grated zest of 1 lemon
- 1 tsp baking soda
- $^1/_8$ tsp salt

Makes: 20 cookies	
Preparation: 40' + 30' to chill	
Cooking: 8–10'	
Level of difficulty: 1	

- **6 tbsp butter, softened**
- **3 tbsp granulated sugar**
- **1 large egg yolk**
- **Finely grated zest of 1 orange**
- **1¼ cups/180 g all-purpose/plain flour**

GLAZE
- **⅔ cup/100 g confectioners'/icing sugar**
- **1 tbsp fresh orange juice + more as needed**

GLAZED ORANGE COOKIES

Beat the butter and sugar in a large bowl until creamy. • Add the egg yolk and orange zest. • Mix in the flour to form a stiff dough. Refrigerate for 30 minutes. • Preheat the oven to 350°F/180°C/gas 4. • Butter and flour a cookie sheet. • Roll out the dough to a thickness of ¹/₈ inch (3 mm). • Use a fluted cutter to stamp out small rounds. Continue cutting out cookies until all the dough is used. • Use a spatula to transfer the cookies to the prepared cookie sheet. • Bake for 8–10 minutes, or until golden around the edges. • Cool the cookies on the sheet for 5 minutes. Transfer to racks to cool. • Glaze: Mix the confectioners' sugar with enough orange juice to make a pourable consistency. • Drizzle the glaze in a decorative zigzag over the cookies.

ORANGE THINS

Preheat the oven to 375°F/190°C/gas 5. • Line two baking sheets with parchment paper. • Sift the flour, cornstarch, and salt into a medium bowl. • Use a whisk to beat the eggs, superfine sugar, and orange zest in a double boiler over barely simmering water until pale and very thick. • Transfer to a medium bowl. • Use a large rubber spatula to fold in the dry ingredients. • Fit a pastry bag with a $1/2$-inch (1-cm) plain tip. Fill the pastry bag, twist the opening tightly closed, and squeeze out 3-inch (8-cm) lines, spacing 2 inches (5 cm) apart on the prepared cookie sheets. • Sprinkle with the sugar crystals. • Bake for 8–10 minutes, or until just golden. • Cool the cookies on the cookie sheets for 5 minutes. • Transfer to racks and let cool completely.

Makes: 30–35 cookies

Preparation: 40'

Cooking: 8–10'

Level of difficulty: 1

- 1¼ cups/180 g all-purpose/plain flour
- ½ cup/75 g cornstarch/cornflour
- ⅛ tsp salt
- 3 large eggs, lightly beaten
- 1 cup/200 g superfine/caster sugar
- 2 tsp grated orange zest
- 2 tbsp sugar crystals

ORANGE ESSES

Sift the flour and salt into a large bowl. • Stir in the ground almonds, sugar, and orange zest. • Use a pastry blender to cut in the butter until the mixture resembles fine crumbs. • Mix in the egg whites to form a stiff dough. • Divide the dough in half. Form the dough into two disks, wrap in plastic wrap, and refrigerate for 30 minutes. • Preheat the oven to 350°F/180°C/gas 4. • Butter three cookie sheets. • Pinch off balls of dough the size of walnuts and shape into rounded S-shape cookies. • Use a spatula to transfer the cookies to the prepared cookie sheets, placing them 1 inch (2.5 cm) apart. • Bake, one sheet at a time, for 12–15 minutes, or until golden brown. • Transfer to racks to cool.

Makes: 40 cookies

Preparation: 25' + 30' to chill

Cooking: 12–15' per batch

Level of difficulty: 1

- ¾ cup/125 g all-purpose/plain flour
- ⅛ tsp salt
- 1⅓ cups/200 g finely ground almonds
- 1 cup/200 g granulated sugar
- 1 tbsp finely grated orange zest
- ½ cup/125 g butter, cut up
- 2 large egg whites, lightly beaten

LIME ESSES

Sift the flour and salt into a large bowl. • Stir in the ground almonds, sugar, and lime zest. • Use a pastry blender to cut in the butter until the mixture resembles fine crumbs. • Mix in the egg whites to form a stiff dough. • Divide the dough in half. Form the dough into two disks, wrap in plastic wrap, and refrigerate for 30 minutes. • Preheat the oven to 350°F/180°C/gas 4. • Butter three cookie sheets. • Pinch off balls of dough the size of walnuts and shape into rounded S-shape cookies. • Use a spatula to transfer the cookies to the prepared cookie sheets, placing them 1 inch (2.5 cm) apart. • Bake, one sheet at a time, for 12–15 minutes, or until golden brown. • Transfer to racks to cool.

Makes: 40 cookies

Preparation: 25' + 30' to chill

Cooking: 12–15' per batch

Level of difficulty: 1

- ¾ cup/125 g all-purpose/plain flour
- ⅛ tsp salt
- 1⅓ cups/200 g finely ground almonds
- 1 cup/200 g granulated sugar
- 1 tbsp finely grated lime zest
- ½ cup/125 g butter, cut up
- 2 large egg whites, lightly beaten

LADY LEMON COOKIES

Makes: 38 cookies

Preparation: 25'

Cooking: 15–20' per batch

Level of difficulty: 1

- 3⅓ cups/500 g all-purpose/plain flour
- ¾ cup/150 g granulated sugar
- 2 large eggs
- ½ cup/125 ml milk
- 1 tsp vanilla extract/essence
- 6 tbsp butter, softened
- Grated zest of 1 lemon
- ⅛ tsp salt

Preheat the oven to 350°F/180°C/gas 4. • Line three cookie sheets with parchment paper. • Use a wooden spoon to mix the flour, sugar, eggs, milk, vanilla, butter, lemon zest, and salt in a large bowl to make a smooth dough. • Break off balls of dough the size of walnuts and form into 4-inch (10-cm) ropes. Form the ropes into 1½-inch (4-cm) rings and place 1 inch (2.5 cm) apart on the prepared cookie sheets. • Bake, one sheet at a time, for 15–20 minutes, or until just golden. • Cool the cookies completely on the cookie sheets.

FRITTERS

CARDAMOM FRITTERS

Sift the flour and salt into a large bowl. • Beat the egg yolks and egg white, rose water, milk, and cardamom in a large bowl with an electric mixer at high speed until well blended. • Mix in the dry ingredients to form a smooth dough. • Turn the dough out onto a lightly floured surface and knead until smooth. • Cover with a clean kitchen towel and let stand for 2 hours. • Form into balls the size of walnuts. • Roll the balls out to a thickness of $1/8$ inch (3 mm) and a diameter of 3 inches (8 cm) . • Carefully fold the dough over, using a fork to press down the edges. • Cover with a kitchen towel and let stand for 5 minutes. • Heat the corn oil to 325°F (170°C) in a large deep frying pan. • Fry the cookies in batches for 1 minute, or until lightly browned all over. • Drain well on paper towels. • Dust with the confectioners' sugar.

Makes: 10 cookies

Preparation: 30' + 2 h 5' to stand

Cooking: 1'

Level of difficulty: 3

- **2²/₃ cups/400 g all-purpose/plain flour**
- **1/8 tsp salt**
- **3 large egg yolks + 1 large egg white**
- **4 tbsp rose water**
- **1/2 cup/125 ml milk**
- **1/2 tsp ground cardamom**
- **2 cups/500 ml corn oil, for frying**
- **1/3 cup/50 g confectioners'/icing sugar, to dust**

CURRENT FRITTERS

Sift the flour, baking powder, and salt into a large bowl. • Use a pastry blender to cut in the shortening until the mixture resembles fine crumbs. • Stir in the $1/4$ cup (50 g) sugar and the currants. • Mix in 2 tablespoons water to form a smooth dough, adding more water as needed. • Press the dough into a disk, wrap in plastic wrap, and refrigerate for 30 minutes. • Roll out the dough on a lightly floured surface to a thickness of $1/2$ inch (1 cm). • Use a 2-inch (5-cm) cookie cutter to cut out the cookies. • Heat the oil in a large deep frying pan until very hot (365°F/185°C). • Fry the cookies in small batches for 5–7 minutes, or until golden brown. • Drain well on paper towels. • Sprinkle with the remaining sugar and serve hot.

Makes: 12–15 cookies

Preparation: 40' + 30' to chill

Cooking: 3–4'

Level of difficulty: 3

- $1^1/2$ cups/225 g all-purpose/flour flour
- $1/2$ tsp baking powder
- $1/8$ tsp salt
- 4 tbsp vegetable shortening
- $1/3$ cup/70 g granulated sugar
- $1/2$ cup/90 g dried currants
- 2 tbsp water + more as needed
- 1 cup/250 ml peanut oil, for frying

ITALIAN CHRISTMAS FRITTERS

Serves: 10

Preparation: 1 h + 2 h
to rest the batter

Cooking: 30'

Level of difficulty: 2

- 3½ cups/525 all-
  purpose/plain flour
- 4 eggs
- 2 tbsp superfine/
  caster sugar
- ½ cup/125 ml
  anisette
- ⅛ tsp salt
- 2 cups/500 ml oil,
  for frying
- ¾ cup/180 ml
  honey
- 1 cup/100 g diced
  candied orange
  peel
- 1 cup/100 g diced
  candied lemon
  peel
- 4 tbsp colored
  sprinkles

Mix the flour with the eggs, sugar, liqueur, and salt in a large bowl and beat until smooth. Set aside to rest for 2 hours. • Scoop out tablespoonfuls of the dough and roll them into sticks about the thickness of a pencil. Cut into pieces about $1/2$ inch (1-cm) long. • Heat the oil to very hot in a large frying pan and fry in small batches until light golden brown. Scoop the fritters out of the oil with a slotted spoon and drain on paper towels. • Heat the honey in a large, heavy-bottomed saucepan until thoroughly melted. Add the cookies and the candied orange and lemon peels. Stir carefully until they are all coated with honey. • Place the cookies on a serving dish and decorate with the sprinkles. Serve.

These tiny fritters come from southern Italy.

BATTERED FRESH FRUIT

B eat the eggs in a large bowl with an electric mixer at high speed until pale. • With mixer at medium speed, beat in 2 tablespoons of flour and the milk. • Cover with a clean cloth and let stand in a warm place for 1 hour. • Peel the pineapple and cut the flesh into ¹/₂-inch (1-cm) thick slices. Cut each slice in 4. • Peel the bananas and cut in 4. • Stir the baking powder and vanilla into the batter. • Dip the pineapple, bananas, and apples in the batter, turning to coat well. • Heat the oil in a deep fryer or frying pan until very hot. • Fry the fruit in batches for 5–7 minutes, or until crisp golden brown all over. • Drain well on paper towels. • Dust with the confectioners' sugar and serve hot.

708

Makes: 16–20 fritters

Preparation: 20' + 1 h to rest the batter

Cooking: 5–7'

Level of difficulty: 1

- **3 eggs**
- **4 tbsp all-purpose/ plain flour**
- **1 quart/1 liter milk**
- **1 small pineapple**
- **2 firm-ripe bananas**
- **2 tart apples, cut into wedges**
- **¹/₂ tsp baking powder**
- **1 tsp vanilla extract/essence**
- **2 cups/500 ml olive oil, for frying**
- **¹/₃ cup/50 g confectioners'/ icing sugar, to dust**

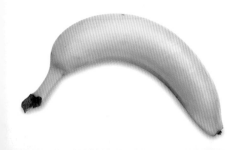

SLICED APPLE FRITTERS

B eat the egg yolks in a large bowl with an electric mixer at high speed until pale. • With mixer at medium speed, beat in the flour, wine, extra-virgin oil, and salt. • Cover with a clean cloth and let stand for 1 hour. • Slice the apples and slice crosswise. Drizzle with the lemon juice to prevent them from turning brown. • With mixer at high speed, beat the egg whites in a large bowl until stiff peaks form. Use a large rubber spatula to fold them into the batter. • Dip the apple slices in the batter, turning to coat well. • Heat the oil in a deep fryer or frying pan until very hot. • Fry the apple slices in batches for 5–7 minutes, or until lightly browned all over. • Drain well on paper towels. • Dust with the confectioners' sugar and serve hot.

Makes: 16–20 fritters

Preparation: 20' + 1 h to rest the batter

Cooking: 5–7'

Level of difficulty: 1

- 2 eggs, separated
- ¾ cup/125 g all-purpose/plain flour
- ½ cup/125 ml dry white wine
- 2 tbsp extra-virgin olive oil
- ⅛ tsp salt
- 6 tart apples, peeled and cored
- juice of 1 lemon
- 2 cups/500 ml olive oil, for frying
- ⅓ cup/50 g confectioners'/icing sugar, to dust

Makes: 16–20 fritters
Preparation: 20' + 30' to stand
Cooking: 1 h
Level of difficulty: 1

- 2 cups/500 ml milk
- 1¼ cups/310 ml water
- 1 cup/200 g short-grain rice
- ⅛ tsp salt
- 3 egg yolks
- ¾ cup/150 g sugar
- ¾ cup/125 g all-purpose/plain flour
- 6 oz/180 g oranges, cut into small pieces
- 1 tsp vanilla extract/essence
- 1 tbsp orange liqueur
- 2 cups/500 ml olive oil, for frying

ORANGE RICE FRITTERS

Mix the milk and water in a large saucepan. Add the rice and salt. • Bring to a boil over medium heat and simmer until all the liquid has been absorbed, about 40 minutes. • Remove from heat and stir in the egg yolks, ½ cup (100 g) of sugar, the flour, orange, vanilla, and orange liqueur until well blended. • Let stand for 30 minutes. • Heat the oil in a deep fryer or frying pan until very hot. • Drop scant tablespoons of the batter into the oil and fry in batches for 5–7 minutes, or until crisp and golden brown all over. • Drain well on paper towels. • Dust with the remaining sugar and serve.

FRUIT AND NUT FRITTERS

Makes: 20 fritters

Preparation: 15' + 1 h
to rest the batter

Cooking: 25–30'

Level of difficulty: 2

- 1²/₃ cups/250 g all-purpose/plain flour
- ³/₄ cup/180 ml milk
- ¹/₃ cup/70 g sugar
- 3 tbsp butter, melted
- 3 egg yolks
- 1 tsp baking powder
- 1 tbsp Marsala wine
- 1 tsp ground cinnamon
- ¹/₈ tsp salt
- 10 oz/300 g dried fruit and nuts, such as prunes, pineapple, papaya, pear, apricots, peanuts, hazelnuts, pecans, walnuts, or figs
- 2 cups/500 ml olive oil, for frying
- ¹/₃ cup/50 g confectioners'/icing sugar, to dust

Beat the flour, milk, sugar, butter, egg yolks, baking powder, Marsala, cinnamon, and salt in a large bowl with an electric mixer at medium speed until smooth. • Cover with a clean cloth and let stand in a warm place for 1 hour. • Chop the dried fruit and nuts in a food processor or until very finely chopped. • Shape the fruit and nut mixture into balls the size of walnuts. • Dip the balls into the batter, turning to coat well. • Heat the oil in a deep fryer or frying pan until very hot. • Fry the gnocchi in batches for 5–7 minutes, or until crisp and golden brown all over. • Drain well on paper towels. • Dust with the confectioners' sugar and serve hot.

APPLE FRITTERS

Sift the flour, baking powder, and salt into a large bowl. Beat in the sugar, lemon zest, orange juice, rum, and eggs. Add the milk gradually and stir until smooth. • Stir in the raisins and apples. • Heat the oil in a deep fryer or frying pan until very hot. • Drop scant tablespoons of the batter into the oil and fry in batches for 5–7 minutes, or until crisp and golden brown all over. • Drain well on paper towels. • Dust with the confectioners' sugar and serve hot.

- 2²/₃ cups/400 g all-purpose/plain flour
- 1 tsp baking powder
- ¹/₈ tsp salt
- ²/₃ cup/140 g superfine/caster sugar
- Grated zest of 1 lemon
- Juice of ½ orange
- 2 tsp dark rum
- 2 eggs
- ²/₃ cup/150 ml milk
- ½ cup/90 g golden raisins/sultanas
- 1½ lb/750 g apples, peeled, cored, and cut into small sticks
- 2 cups/500 ml olive oil, for frying
- ¹/₃ cup/50 g confectioners'/icing sugar

BANANA FRITTERS

Makes: 16–20 fritters

Preparation: 15'

Cooking: 25'

Level of difficulty: 1

- **6 firm-ripe bananas, peeled**
- **1 tbsp sugar**
- **1 tbsp all-purpose/ plain flour**
- **1 tsp ground ginger**
- **½ tsp ground cinnamon**
- **2 cups/500 ml olive oil, for frying**

Mash the bananas in a medium bowl. • Stir in the sugar, flour, ginger, and cinnamon, mixing well. • Heat the oil in a deep fryer or frying pan until very hot. • Drop tablespoons of the batter into the oil and fry the fritters in batches for 5–7 minutes, or until crisp and golden brown all over. • Drain well on paper towels. • Serve hot.

PUMPKIN FRITTERS

Peel the pumpkin and remove the seeds and fibrous matter. Slice the flesh and place in a saucepan with sufficient cold water to cover. • Cook until the flesh is just tender (not too long, about 20 minutes). Drain well and press in a cloth to absorb any excess moisture. • Place in a bowl, add the drained raisins, the sugar, the flour and baking powder sifted together, the lemon zest, and salt. Mix thoroughly with a spoon and then shape into little balls about the size of a walnut. • Fry in batches in plenty of very hot oil, removing with a slotted spoon when golden brown all over. Drain on paper towels. • Sprinkle with sugar and serve hot.

Makes: 20 fritters

Preparation: 30'

Cooking: 35'

Level of difficulty: 1

- 2 lb/1 kg pumpkin
- 1 cup/180 g seedless white raisins/sultanas, soaked
- ¹⁄₄ cup/50 g sugar
- ²⁄₃ cup/100 g all-purpose/plain flour
- 1 tbsp baking powder
- grated zest of 1 lemon
- ¹⁄₈ tsp salt
- 1 cup/250 ml sunflower oil, for frying
- sugar, to sprinkle

FRIED EGG CREAM

Makes: 10 fritters

Preparation: 20'

Cooking: 25'

Level of difficulty: 1

- 5 eggs, separated
- ¾ cup/150 g sugar
- 1⅓ cups/200 g all-purpose/plain flour
- 1 quart/1 liter milk, warmed
- grated zest of 1 lemon
- 1¾ cups/100 g fresh bread crumbs
- 1 cup/250 ml sunflower oil, for frying

Place the egg yolks and sugar in a fairly small or double boiler and beat well until they are pale and frothy. • Sift in the flour a little at a time and mix well. Keep stirring as you add the tepid milk and the lemon zest (without any of the white pith). • Place the saucepan over a very low heat and cook the custard while stirring slowly and continuously with a wooden spoon until it becomes very thick. • Turn the custard out onto a lightly oiled marble slab or into a shallow container and leave to cool. • Cut the custard diagonally to produce diamond shapes. Lightly whisk the egg whites. Dip the custard into the egg whites and coat with bread crumbs. • Fry in batches in plenty of very hot oil until they are a good golden brown.

Makes: 15 fritters

Preparation: 15' + 1 h
to rest

Cooking: 20'

Level of difficulty: 1

- 1²/₃ cups/400 g
  Ricotta cheese
- 3 eggs
- ¹/₃ cup/70 g
  granulated sugar
- grated zest of 1
  orange
- ¹/₈ tsp salt
- ¹/₈ tsp baking soda
- ¹/₄ cup/40 g
  raisins, soaked in
  rum overnight
- 1¹/₂ cups/225 g all-
  purpose/plain flour
- 2 cups/500 ml oil,
  for frying
- ³/₄ cup/120 g
  confectioners'/
  icing sugar

SWEET RICOTTA FRITTERS

Sieve the Ricotta into a mixing bowl. • Add the eggs, sugar, orange zest, salt, baking soda, and drained raisins. Lastly, stir in the sifted flour. Mix until smooth. Leave to rest for 1 hour. • Heat the oil to very hot in a large frying pan. Scoop out tablespoonfuls of the batter and fry in batches of 6–8 until golden brown. • Drain on paper towels. • Sprinkle with the confectioners' sugar and serve hot.

BRANDY-FLAVORED FRITTERS

Sift the flour into a bowl and mix well with the sugar and salt. • Turn out onto a pastry board and shape into a mound. Make a well in the center and add the butter, eggs, and brandy (or white wine or lemon zest). Combine all the ingredients, gradually working in the flour to form a smooth, well-blended dough. • Cover with a clean cloth and leave to rest in a warm place for 2 hours. • Roll out the dough to make a very thin sheet about $1/8$ inch (3 mm). • Use a fluted pastry wheel to cut the pastry into strips $1^1/4$ inch (3 cm) wide and 8 inch (20 cm) long. • Tie each strip loosely into a knot and deep fry a few at a time in very hot oil until pale golden brown. • Drain on paper towels. • Dust with the confectioners' sugar before serving.

Makes: 15–20 fritters

Preparation: 20' + 2 h to rest

Cooking: 15'

Level of difficulty: 1

- $3^1/3$ cups/500 g all-purpose/plain flour
- 2 tbsp superfine/caster sugar
- $1/8$ tsp salt
- 2 tbsp butter, cut into small pieces
- 4 eggs
- 3 tbsp Cognac (or other grape brandy) or white wine or finely grated lemon zest
- 1 cup/250 ml oil, for frying
- confectioners'/icing sugar, to dust

LEMON AND EGG FRITTERS

Makes: 20 fritters

Preparation: 25' + 1 h to rest

Cooking: 25'

Level of difficulty: 1

- 1 cup/250 ml water
- ⅛ tsp salt
- ½ cup/125 g butter
- ¼ cup/50 g superfine/caster sugar
- grated zest of 1 lemon
- 1⅔ cups/250 g all-purpose/plain flour
- 8 eggs
- 1–2 cups/ 250–500 ml olive oil for frying
- confectioners'/ icing sugar, to dust

Place the water, salt, butter, sugar, and lemon zest in a heavy-bottomed saucepan and bring to a boil. • When the water is boiling, add the flour and stir with a wooden spoon. Continue cooking, stirring continuously, until the dough is thick and comes away from the sides of the saucepan. Remove from the heat and set aside to cool.
• When cool, stir in the eggs one at a time. The dough should be soft, but not runny. • Set aside to rest for at least 1 hour. • Heat the oil in a deep-sided frying pan until very hot, but not smoking.
• Use a teaspoon to scoop up the dough and drop it into the hot oil. Fry the fritters, a few at a time, until they are plump and golden brown. • Remove the fritters from the oil with a slotted spoon and drain on paper towels. Keep warm. Repeat until all the dough has been used up. • Sprinkle with confectioners' sugar and serve hot.

FRIED CARNIVAL COOKIES WITH CONFECTIONERS' SUGAR

Sift the flour onto a surface and make a well in the center. Add the butter, eggs, sugar, dessert wine, salt, and orange zest. Gradually combine with the flour and knead well. The dough should be soft but hold its shape well. • Cover with a clean cloth and leave to rest for 30 minutes. • Roll out into a thin sheet using a lightly floured rolling pin. • Cut into diamonds, rectangles, and into broad rectangular strips which can be tied loosely into a knot if wished. • Heat the oil to very hot and fry a few at a time until pale golden brown all over. • Remove with a slotted spoon and drain on paper towels. • Serve at once, sprinkled with confectioners' sugar.

Makes: 30 cookies

Preparation: 20' + 30' to stand

Cooking: 20'

Level of difficulty: 1

- 1²/₃ cups/250 g all-purpose/plain flour + ¹/₃ cup/ 50 g extra
- 2 tbsp butter, softened
- 2 eggs
- ¹/₄ cup/50 g superfine/caster sugar
- 1¹/₂ tbsp Vin Santo or other good quality sweet dessert wine
- ¹/₈ tsp salt
- 1¹/₂ tbsp grated orange zest
- 1¹/₄ cups/310 ml olive oil, for frying
- ¹/₃ cup/50 g confectioners'/icing sugar, to dust

LEMON RICE FRITTERS

Makes: 20 fritters

Preparation: 20' + 1 h to chill

Cooking: 1¼ h

Level of difficulty: 1

- 1 cup/200 g short-grain, pudding rice (or sticky rice)
- 2 cups/500 ml milk
- 1 tbsp butter
- 3 tbsp granulated sugar
- grated zest of ½ lemon or orange
- 2 eggs
- ⅛ tsp salt
- ⅓ cup/50 g all-purpose/plain flour
- ⅓ cup/50 g golden raisins/sultanas, soaked in warm water for 15 minutes, drained and squeezed
- 3 tbsp rum
- scant 1 cup/200 ml olive oil for frying
- ⅔ cup/100 g confectioners'/icing sugar

Cook the rice in the milk for about 1 hour or until the grains have almost disintegrated. • Stir the butter into this very thick mixture and remove from the heat. • Add the sugar and the zest. Stir in the eggs one at a time, then add the salt, flour, raisins, and rum. Stir thoroughly and refrigerate for about 1 hour. • Heat the oil in a nonstick frying pan until very hot. To test, drop a tiny piece of fritter into the oil. If bubbles form around it immediately, it is hot enough. • Scoop the fritter mixture up in tablespoonful-size lots and place in the hot oil. Fry 5–6 fritters together until they are golden brown all over. This should take about 4 minutes for each fritter. • Drain on paper towels. Dust with sugar and transfer to a serving dish. • Serve at once.

GOOD FRIDAY FRITTERS

B ring the milk, 3 tablespoons of sugar, and
anise to a boil in a medium saucepan. • Sift the
flour into a large bowl. • Stir in the lemon zest,
cinnamon, and vanilla and make a well in the
center. • Pour in the boiling milk mixture and stir
until smooth. • Add the eggs, one at a time, until
just blended after each addition. • Add the apples.
• Heat the oil in a large frying pan to very hot. •
Scoop out tablespoonfuls of the batter and fry in
batches for 5–7 minutes, or until golden brown all
over. • Drain well on paper towels. • Dust with the
sugar and anise.

Makes: 20 fritters

Preparation: 15'

Cooking: 20'

Level of difficulty: 1

- **1³⁄₄ cups/430 ml
  milk**
- **¹⁄₂ cup/100 g sugar**
- **1 tsp anise + extra
  to dust**
- **1¹⁄₂ cups/225 g all-
  purpose/plain flour**
- **grated zest of 1
  lemon**
- **¹⁄₂ tsp ground
  cinnamon**
- **¹⁄₂ tsp vanilla
  extract/essence**
- **4 large eggs**
- **4 apples, peeled,
  cored, and finely
  chopped**
- **2 cups/500 ml
  olive oil, for frying**

MERINGUES

CHOCOLATE-GLAZED MACAROONS

Sift the flour, baking powder, and salt into a large bowl. • Beat the egg whites in a large bowl with an electric mixer at medium speed until frothy. • With mixer at high speed, gradually add the superfine sugar, beating until stiff, glossy peaks form. • Use a large rubber spatula to fold in the almonds, grated chocolate, and candied peel, followed by the dry ingredients until well blended. • Drop spoonfuls of the mixture onto the rice paper circles. Use a thin metal spatula to spread the mixture to $1/2$ inch (1 cm) thick and place on a baking sheet. • Refrigerate for at least 2 hours. • Preheat the oven to 300°F/150°C/gas 2. • Bake for 20–25 minutes, or until firm to the touch. • Transfer to racks to cool. • Tear off any extra paper from around the cookies. • Melt each chopped chocolate in a separate double boiler over barely simmering water. • Drizzle the chocolates over the top of the macaroons, swirling with a knife to create a marbled effect.

Makes: 15 cookies

Preparation: 50' + 2 h to chill

Cooking: 20–25'

Level of difficulty: 2

- 2 tbsp all-purpose/plain flour
- 1 tsp baking powder
- $1/8$ tsp salt
- 4 large egg whites
- $1^1/2$ cups/300 g superfine/caster sugar
- $2^1/2$ cups/250 g finely ground almonds
- 3 oz/90 g semisweet/dark chocolate, coarsely grated
- 1 cup/100 g mixed candied peel, finely chopped
- Rice paper, cut into 2-inch/5-cm rounds
- 3 oz/90 g semisweet/dark chocolate, coarsely chopped
- 3 oz/90 g white chocolate, coarsely chopped

MUDDY MACAROONS

Makes: 20 cookies

Preparation: 20'

Cooking: 10–12'

Level of difficulty: 1

- 1¼ lb/575 g bittersweet/plain chocolate, coarsely chopped
- 1⅓ cups/200 g finely ground almonds
- ⅔ cup/140 g granulated sugar
- ¼ tsp almond extract/essence
- ¼ tsp vanilla extract/essence
- 1 tbsp unsweetened cocoa powder
- 2 large egg whites, lightly beaten
- 1 tsp water
- 2 tbsp confectioners'/ icing sugar, to dust

Preheat the oven to 350°F/180°C/gas 4. • Line two cookie sheets with parchment paper. • Melt the chocolate in a double boiler over barely simmering water. • Remove from the heat and let cool for 5 minutes. • Stir together the almonds, granulated sugar, almond and vanilla extract, and cocoa in a large bowl. • Make a well in the center and pour in the melted chocolate and three-quarters of the beaten whites. Mix well to make a smooth dough, adding more whites if the dough is too stiff to mold. • Dust your hands with a little confectioners' sugar. • Shape the dough into balls the size of walnuts. • Place 2 inches (5 cm) apart on the prepared cookie sheets. Use a fork to flatten them slightly. Brush with a little water. Dust with confectioners' sugar. • Bake for 10–12 minutes, or until firm to the touch. Cool the macaroons on the sheet for 1 minute. • Transfer to racks and let cool completely.

733

SPICED AND GLAZED MACAROONS

Preheat the oven to 325°F/170°C/gas 3. • Line two baking sheets with rice paper. • Sprinkle the nuts on a large baking sheet. Toast for 7 minutes, or until lightly golden. • Chop finely in a food processor. • Sift the flour, cinnamon, cloves, and nutmeg into a medium bowl. • Beat the egg whites in a large bowl with an electric mixer at medium speed until frothy. With mixer at high speed, gradually add the confectioners' sugar and cream of tartar, beating until stiff, glossy peaks form. • Mix the baking soda and water in a small bowl. • Use a large rubber spatula to fold the baking soda mixture into the egg whites, followed by the dry ingredients and lemon and orange peels. Fold in the almonds. • Drop heaped spoonfuls 1 inch (2.5 cm) apart onto the paper. Use the back of a wooden spoon to flatten them slightly. • Refrigerate for at least 2 hours. • Preheat the oven to 300°F/150°C/gas 2. • Bake for 20–25 minutes, or until golden brown. • Cool the macaroons on the baking sheets for 5 minutes. Transfer to racks to cool. • Tear away any excess paper from around the edges. • Lemon Glaze: Sift the confectioners' sugar into a medium bowl. Beat in the lemon juice and hot water, a teaspoon at a time, until thick. • Drizzle with the glaze.

Makes: 30–35 cookies

Preparation: 45' + 2 h to chill

Cooking: 20–25'

Level of difficulty: 2

- 1½ cups/225 g blanched whole almonds
- ¾ cup/125 g all-purpose/plain flour
- 1 tsp ground cinnamon
- ⅛ tsp ground cloves
- ⅛ tsp freshly grated nutmeg
- 5 large egg whites
- 2 cups/300 g confectioners'/icing sugar
- ⅛ tsp cream of tartar
- ½ tsp baking soda
- 1 tsp hot water
- ½ cup/50 g finely chopped candied lemon peel
- ½ cup/50 g finely chopped candied orange peel

LEMON GLAZE
- 1⅓ cups/200 g confectioners'/icing sugar
- 2 tbsp fresh lemon juice
- 1–2 tbsp hot water

SICILIAN MACAROONS

Makes: 12–15 cookies

Preparation: 40'

Cooking: 15–20'

Level of difficulty: 2

- 1 cup/150 g blanched almonds, toasted and finely ground
- ½ cup/100 g vanilla sugar
- 4 tbsp orange-flavored sugar
- 2 large egg whites
- ¼ tsp almond extract/essence
- 15 blanched almonds or almond halves
- 1 tsp water
- 3 tbsp confectioners'/icing sugar, to dust

Preheat the oven to 375°F/190°C/gas 5. • Line a cookie sheet with parchment paper. • Mix the almonds with the egg white in a food processor to form a smooth paste. • Mix the vanilla and orange sugars and gradually work the sugars into the almond paste until the mixture is soft. • Add the almond extract. • Form the mixture into balls the size of walnuts. • Place 2 inches (5 cm) apart on the prepared cookie sheet, flattening them slightly. • Lightly press an almond into the top of each cookie. Brush with the water and dust with the confectioners' sugar. • Bake for 15–20 minutes, or until golden and slightly firm to the touch. • Transfer the cookies on their parchment to racks and cool until they firm slightly. • Peel from the paper and let cool completely.

HAZELNUT MOMENTS

Preheat the oven to 300°F/150°C/gas 2. • Line a cookie sheet with parchment paper. • Beat the egg whites in a medium bowl with an electric mixer at medium speed in a bowl over barely simmering water. With mixer at high speed, gradually beat in the granulated and vanilla sugars. • Mix in the ground hazelnuts, nutmeg, and lemon juice and beat until frothy. The mixture should remain just warm to the touch. • Remove from the water and beat with an electric mixer until stiff and glossy. • Mix in the nuts. • Fill a pastry bag fitted with a $^1/_2$-inch (1-cm) plain tip and squeeze out 1-inch (2.5-cm) rounds onto the prepared cookie sheets. Press a hazelnut into the center of each cookie. • Brush lightly with water and dust with the confectioners' sugar. • Bake for 15–20 minutes, or until lightly golden around the edges and just firm to the touch. • Transfer on their parchment to racks and cool until the cookies firm slightly. • Peel from the paper and let cool completely.

Makes: 25–30 cookies

Preparation: 50'

Cooking: 18–20'

Level of difficulty: 2

- **2 large egg whites**
- **$^1/_2$ cup/100 g granulated sugar**
- **2 tbsp vanilla sugar**
- **1 cup/150 g finely ground shelled hazelnuts, toasted + 25–30 hazelnuts**
- **$^1/_8$ tsp freshly grated nutmeg**
- **1 tsp fresh lemon juice**
- **1 tsp water**
- **3 tbsp confectioners'/ icing sugar, to dust**

738

GIANDUIA KISSES

Makes: 18–22
cookies

Preparation: 30'

Cooking: 8–10'

Level of difficulty: 2

- **2 large egg whites**
- **1/8 tsp salt**
- **2 tbsp superfine/ caster sugar**
- **1/3 cup/50 g confectioners'/ icing sugar**
- **1 1/4 cups/125 g finely chopped hazelnuts**
- **6 tbsp Nutella (chocolate hazelnut cream)**

Preheat the oven to 375°F/190°C/gas 5. • Line two cookie sheets with parchment paper. • Beat the egg whites and salt in a large bowl with an electric mixer at medium speed until frothy. • With mixer at medium speed, gradually add the superfine sugar, beating until stiff, glossy peaks form. • Use a large rubber spatula to fold in the confectioners' sugar and hazelnuts. • Fit a pastry bag with a 1-inch (2.5-cm) star tip. Fill the pastry bag, twist the opening tightly closed, and squeeze out 1-inch (2.5-cm) stars spacing 1 inch (2.5 cm) apart onto the prepared cookie sheets. • Bake for 8–10 minutes, or until pale gold. • Transfer to racks to cool. • Stick the cookies together in pairs with the chocolate hazelnut cream.

Gianduia is an Italian word for chocolate hazelnut flavoring. These cookies come from Piedmont.

ALMOND LEMON MERINGUES

Preheat the oven to 250°F/130°C/gas ¹/₂. •
Line two cookie sheets with parchment paper.
• Beat the egg whites and salt in a large bowl with
an electric mixer at medium speed until soft peaks
form. With mixer at high speed, gradually add the
superfine sugar and lemon juice, beating until stiff,
glossy peaks form. • Stir together the finely
ground nuts and cornstarch and fold it into the
mixture. • Fit a pastry bag with a ¹/₂-inch (1-cm)
star tip. Fill the pastry bag, twist the opening tightly
closed, and squeeze out small stars and shells,
spacing 1 inch (2.5 cm) apart on the prepared
cookie sheets. • Sprinkle with the flaked almonds
and dust with the confectioners' sugar. • Bake for
50–60 minutes, or until the meringues are dry to
the touch. • Turn off the oven. Leave in the warm
oven for 30 minutes more. • Using the parchment
paper as handles, lift the meringues onto a rack.
Carefully peel off the paper and let cool completely.

Makes: 20–25
  meringues

Preparation: 30'

Cooking: 50–60' +
  30' to rest

Level of difficulty: 2

- 2 large egg whites
- ¹/₈ tsp salt
- ¹/₂ cup/100 g
  superfine/caster
  sugar
- 1 tsp fresh lemon
  juice
- 3 tbsp finely ground
  almonds, toasted
- 1 tsp cornstarch/
  cornflour
- 2 tbsp flaked
  almonds, to
  sprinkle
- 2 tbsp
  confectioners'/
  icing sugar, to dust

MOCHA MERINGUES

Makes: 15 cookies

Preparation: 30'

Cooking: 80–90'

Level of difficulty: 2

- **2 large egg whites**
- **$1/8$ tsp salt**
- **1 cup/200 g superfine/caster sugar**
- **1 tsp coffee extract/essence**
- **$1/2$ cup/50 g coarsely chopped pecans**
- **1 tbsp cornstarch/ cornflour**
- **$1/2$ cup/125 ml heavy/double cream, whipped**

Preheat the oven to 300°F/150°C/gas 2. • Line a cookie sheet with waxed paper. • Beat the egg whites and salt in a large bowl with an electric mixer at medium speed until frothy. • With mixer at high speed, gradually beat in the superfine sugar, beating until stiff, glossy peaks form. • Use a large rubber spatula to fold in the coffee extract, pecans, and cornstarch. • Fit a pastry bag with a $1/2$-inch (1-cm) star tip. Fill the pastry bag, twist the opening tightly closed, and squeeze out 2-inch (5-cm) stars, spacing 2 inches (5-cm) apart on the prepared cookie sheet. • Bake for 80–90 minutes, or until the meringues are crisp and lightly browned. • Cool the meringues completely in the oven with the door ajar. • Fill with whipped cream just before serving.

MISSISSIPPI MERINGUES

Preheat the oven to 300°F/150°C/gas 2. • Line two cookie sheets with parchment paper. • Stir together the superfine sugar, confectioners' sugar, and cocoa in a medium bowl. • Beat the egg whites and salt in a large bowl with an electric mixer at medium speed until soft peaks form. • With mixer at high speed, gradually beat in half the sugar mixture, beating until stiff, glossy peaks form. • Use a large rubber spatula to fold in the remaining sugar mixture. • Fit a pastry bag with a $1/2$-inch (1-cm) star tip. Fill the pastry bag, twist the opening tightly closed, and squeeze out small stars, spacing 1 inch (2.5 cm) apart on the prepared cookie sheets. • Bake for 40–50 minutes, or until the meringues are dry to the touch. • Turn off the oven. Leave in the warm oven for 30 minutes. • Using the parchment paper as handles, lift the meringues onto a rack. Carefully peel off the paper and let cool completely.

Makes: 48 cookies

Preparation: 25' + 30' to cool

Cooking: 40–50'

Level of difficulty: 2

- ½ cup/100 g superfine/caster sugar
- ⅔ cup/100 g confectioners'/icing sugar
- 2 tbsp unsweetened cocoa powder
- 4 large egg whites
- ⅛ tsp salt

PISTACHIO ORANGE MACAROONS

Makes: 25–30 cookies

Preparation: 20'

Cooking: 10–12'

Level of difficulty: 1

- ⅓ cup/50 g all-purpose/plain flour
- ⅛ tsp salt
- ⅔ cup/100 g + 2 tbsp pistachios
- ⅔ cup/140 g granulated sugar
- 3 tbsp finely chopped orange candied peel
- 1 tbsp finely grated orange zest
- 3 large egg whites
- ¼ cup/50 g superfine/caster sugar
- 2 tbsp confectioners'/icing sugar, to dust

Preheat the oven to 350°F/180°C/gas 4. • Line two cookie sheets with parchment paper and grease them with almond oil. • Sift the flour and salt into a medium bowl. • Process ⅔ cup (100 g) of pistachios in a food processor until finely chopped. • Transfer to a large bowl and mix in the granulated sugar, candied peel, and orange zest. • Mix in the dry ingredients. • Beat the egg whites in a large bowl with an electric mixer at medium speed until frothy. With mixer at high speed, gradually beat in the superfine sugar, beating until stiff, glossy peaks form. • Mix in the pistachios. • Drop teaspoons of the mixture 1½ inches (4 cm) apart onto the prepared cookie sheets. • Sprinkle with the remaining pistachios. • Bake for 10–12 minutes, or until the cookies are lightly golden and the bottoms are firm and just browned. • Dust with the confectioners' sugar and let cool on the parchment. • Transfer to racks to cool completely.

> Replace the pistachios with almonds, hazelnuts, or other nuts, depending what you have on hand.

749

COFFEE HAZELNUT MERINGUES

Preheat the oven to 300°F/150°C/gas 2. • Line a cookie sheet with waxed paper. • Beat the egg whites and salt in a large bowl with an electric mixer at medium speed until frothy. • With mixer at high speed, gradually add the superfine sugar, beating until stiff, glossy peaks form. • Use a large rubber spatula to fold in the coffee extract, hazelnuts, and cornstarch. • Fit a pastry bag with a $^1/_2$-inch (1-cm) star tip. Fill the pastry bag, twist the opening tightly closed, and squeeze out 2-inch (5-cm) stars, spacing 2 inches (5 cm) apart on the prepared cookie sheet. • Bake for 80–90 minutes, or until the meringues are crisp and lightly browned. • Cool in the oven with the door ajar.

Makes: 20 cookies

Preparation: 30'

Cooking: 80–90'

Level of difficulty: 2

- **2 large egg whites**
- **$^1/_8$ tsp salt**
- **1 cup/200 g superfine/caster sugar**
- **1 tsp coffee extract/essence**
- **$^1/_2$ cup/50 g coarsely chopped hazelnuts**
- **1 tbsp cornstarch/ cornflour**

HAZELNUT MACAROONS

Preheat the oven to 325°F/170°C/gas 3. •
Spread the 4 cups hazelnuts on a large baking
sheet. Toast for 7 minutes, or until lightly golden.
• Transfer to a large cotton kitchen towel. Fold the
towel over the nuts and rub them to remove the
thin inner skins. • Discard the skins and process
with $1/2$ cup (100 g) of granulated sugar in a food
processor or blender until finely ground. • Line
three cookie sheets with rice paper. • Beat the
eggs and remaining granulated sugar and vanilla
sugar in a large bowl with an electric mixer until
very pale and thick. • Mix in the ground hazelnuts
to form a smooth dough. • Moisten your hands
with water and form the dough into balls the size
of walnuts. • Place 2 inches (5 cm) apart on the
rice paper, flattening each ball slightly and
pressing a hazelnut half into the center. • Bake,
one sheet at a time, for 10–12 minutes, or until
firm to the touch. Transfer on the rice paper to
racks to cool. • Tear away the excess rice paper
from around the cookies

*Makes: 60–70
cookies*

Preparation: 45'

Cooking: 10–12'

Level of difficulty: 2

- **4 cups/600 g
  hazelnuts + 40
  hazelnuts, halved**
- **1½ cups/300 g
  granulated sugar**
- **4 large eggs**
- **1 cup/200 g vanilla
  sugar**

ANNIE'S MACAROONS

Makes: 20–22
  cookies

Preparation: 20'

Cooking: 15–20'

Level of difficulty: 1

- 3 large egg whites
- 1/8 tsp salt
- 1 cup/150 g
  confectioners'/
  icing sugar
- 1 cup/100 g
  toasted, finely
  chopped hazelnuts

Preheat the oven to 300°F/150°C/gas 2. •
Butter a cookie sheet. • Beat the egg whites
and salt in a large bowl with an electric mixer at
high speed until stiff peaks form. • Use a large
rubber spatula to gradually fold in the
confectioners' sugar, followed by the hazelnuts.
• Place the bowl over barely simmering water and
cook, stirring constantly with a wooden spoon, until
the mixture starts to shrink from the sides. • Drop
heaping teaspoons of the mixture $1/2$ inch (1 cm)
apart onto the prepared cookie sheet. • Bake for
15–20 minutes, or until just golden. • Transfer to
racks and let cool completely.

LIGHT LEMON COOKIES

Preheat the oven to 350°F/150°C/gas 2. • Butter two cookie sheets. • Beat the egg whites in a large bowl with an electric mixer at high speed until stiff peaks form. • Use a large rubber spatula to fold the almonds, sugar, flour, lemon zest, vanilla, and salt into the beaten whites. • Fit a pastry bag with a $^1/_2$-inch (1-cm) plain tip. Fill the pastry bag, twist the opening tightly closed, and squeeze out dots, spacing 1 inch (2.5 cm) apart on the prepared cookie sheets. • Bake for 20–25 minutes, or until lightly golden. • Cool on the sheets for 5 minutes. • Transfer to racks and let cool completely.

Makes: 25 cookies

Preparation: 25'

Cooking: 20–25'

Level of difficulty: 2

- **2 large egg whites**
- **2$^1/_2$ cups/250 g finely chopped almonds**
- **1$^1/_4$ cups/250 g granulated sugar**
- **1 tbsp whole-wheat flour**
- **grated zest of 1 lemon**
- **$^1/_2$ tsp vanilla extract/essence**
- **$^1/_8$ tsp salt**

ORANGE WHISPIES

Makes: 25–30 cookies

Preparation: 20'

Cooking: 20–25'

Level of difficulty: 1

- **3 large egg whites**
- **¼ tsp cream of tartar**
- **⅛ tsp salt**
- **½ tsp fresh orange juice**
- **¾ cup/150 g granulated sugar**
- **½ cup/50 g finely chopped peanuts**

Preheat the oven to 300°F/150°C/gas 2. • Line two cookie sheets with parchment paper. • Beat the egg whites, cream of tartar, and salt in a large bowl with an electric mixer at medium speed until frothy. • Add the orange juice. • With mixer at high speed, gradually add the sugar, beating until stiff, glossy peaks form. • Use a large rubber spatula to fold in the peanuts. • Drop teaspoons of the mixture 1 inch (2.5 cm) apart onto the prepared cookie sheets. • Bake for 20–25 minutes, or until the meringues are dry and crisp. • Transfer to racks to cool.

ALMOND CHOCOLATE MACAROONS

Preheat the oven to 325°F/170°C/gas 3. • Line three cookie sheets with rice paper. • Sprinkle the almonds onto a large baking sheet. Toast for 7 minutes, or until lightly golden. • Set aside to cool completely. Lower the oven to 275°F/140°C/gas 1. • Beat the egg whites in a large bowl with an electric mixer at medium speed until frothy. • With mixer at high speed, gradually add the sugar, cream of tartar, vanilla, and salt, until stiff, glossy peaks form. • Use a large rubber spatula to fold in the chocolate and almonds. • Drop teaspoons of the batter 1 1/2 inches (4 cm) apart onto the rice paper. • Bake, one sheet at a time, for 20–25 minutes, or until lightly browned. • Cool the cookies completely on the cookie sheets. Tear away the excess paper from around the nests.

Makes: 40 cookies

Preparation: 40'

Cooking: 20–25'

Level of difficulty: 1

- 2 cups/200 g slivered almonds
- 3 large egg whites
- 1 cup/200 g superfine/caster sugar
- 1/8 tsp cream of tartar
- 1/4 tsp vanilla extract/essence
- 1/8 tsp salt
- 4 oz/125 g semisweet/dark chocolate, finely grated

NUTTY RAW SUGAR MACAROONS

Makes: 15–18 cookies

Preparation: 35'

Cooking 20–25'

Level of difficulty: 1

- ⅔ cup/100 g blanched almonds
- ½ cup/100 g raw sugar (Barbados or Demerara)
- ½ tsp ground aniseeds
- ¼ tsp almond extract/essence
- 1 large egg white, lightly beaten
- 1 tbsp finely chopped pine nuts

Preheat the oven to 325°F/170°C/gas 3. • Line a cookie sheet with parchment paper. • Spread the almonds on a large baking sheet. Toast for 7 minutes, or until lightly browned. • Transfer the nuts to a food processor, add the raw sugar, and process until finely ground. • Transfer to a large bowl and stir in the aniseeds. • Beat the egg white and almond extract in a medium bowl until frothy. • Use a large spatula to fold in the nut mixture. • Form the dough into balls the size of walnuts and place 1 inch (2.5 cm) apart on the prepared cookie sheet, flattening them slightly. • Sprinkle the tops of the cookies with the pine nuts, pressing them into the dough. • Bake for 20–25 minutes, or until golden and dry to the touch. • Transfer to racks to cool.

CHOCOLATE AMARETTI COOKIES

Preheat the oven to 350°F/180°C/gas 4. •
Butter two cookie sheets. • Mix the sugar,
almonds, cornstarch, egg whites, cocoa, and salt
in a large bowl until well blended. • Drop heaping
teaspoons of the dough 1 inch (2.5 cm) apart onto
the prepared cookie sheets. • Bake for 10–12
minutes, or until firm to the touch. • Transfer to
racks and let cool completely.

Makes: 30 cookies

Preparation: 20'

Cooking: 10–12'

Level of difficulty: 1

- 1 cup/200 g
  granulated sugar
- 1¼ cups/180 g
  finely ground
  almonds
- 1 tbsp cornstarch/
  cornflour
- 2 large egg whites
- 1 tsp unsweetened
  cocoa powder
- ⅛ tsp salt

CRISPY ALMOND MACAROONS

Preheat the oven to 325°F/170°C/gas 4. • Butter and flour a large cookie sheet. • Spread the almonds out on a separate baking sheet. Toast in the oven for 7 minutes, or until lightly golden. Increase the temperature to 350°F/180°C/gas 4. • Use a kitchen towel to rub off the skins. Transfer the nuts to a food processor, add 1 cup (200 g) of superfine sugar, and process until finely chopped. • Beat the egg whites and salt in a large bowl until soft peaks form. • Fold in the ground almonds and remaining superfine sugar. • Transfer to a large bowl over barely simmering water. Cook, covered, for 20 minutes, or until very thick. • Drop heaped tablespoons 2 inches (5 cm) apart onto the prepared cookie sheet. Top with almonds. • Bake for 40–45 minutes, or until golden brown. • Cool completely on the cookie sheets.

Makes: 25 cookies
Preparation: 40'
Cooking: 40–45'
Level of difficulty: 1

- **6 cups/900 g whole almonds**
- **2¼ cups/450 g superfine sugar**
- **6 large egg whites**
- **⅛ tsp salt**
- **Slivered almonds, to decorate**

Makes: 45–50 cookies	
Preparation: 30'	
Cooking: 20–25'	
Level of difficulty: 2	

- 1¼ cups/180 g finely ground almonds
- 1 tbsp confectioners'/ icing sugar
- 1 tsp cornstarch/ cornflour
- 3 large egg whites
- ⅛ tsp salt
- ⅔ cup/140 g superfine/caster sugar
- 1 tbsp vanilla sugar
- ½ tsp almond extract/essence
- Chopped candied cherries, angelica, and chopped nuts, to decorate

ASSORTED MACAROONS

Preheat the oven to 275°F/140°C/gas 1. • Line three cookie sheets with parchment paper. • Mix the almonds, confectioners' sugar, and cornstarch in a medium bowl. • Beat the egg whites and salt in a large bowl with an electric mixer at medium speed until frothy. • With mixer at high speed, gradually add the superfine and vanilla sugars until stiff, glossy peaks form. • Use a large rubber spatula to fold in the dry ingredients and almond extract. • Fit a pastry bag with a 1½-inch (4-cm) plain tip. Fill the pastry bag, twist the opening tightly closed, and squeeze out small lengths and rings, spacing them 1 inch (2.5 cm) apart on the prepared cookie sheets. • Top with the candied cherries, angelica, and nuts. • Bake, one sheet at a time, for 20–25 minutes, or until golden brown. • Transfer to racks to cool.

WALNUT CRISPIES

Makes: 35–40
  cookies

Preparation: 20'

Cooking: 12–15'

Level of difficulty: 2

- 2¹/₃ cups/350 g
  walnut halves
- 1¹/₃ cups/270 g
  granulated sugar
- 3 large eggs
- grated zest and
  juice of ½ lemon

Preheat the oven to 325°F/170°C/gas 3. • Line three cookie sheets first with parchment paper and then rice paper. • Spread the walnuts on a large baking sheet. Toast for 7 minutes, or until lightly golden. • Process in a food processor or blender with ¹/₃ cup (50 g) of sugar until finely ground. • Beat the eggs and the remaining sugar in a large bowl with an electric mixer at high speed until pale and thick. • Mix in the lemon zest and juice and ground walnuts. • Drop rounded teaspoons of the mixture onto the prepared cookie sheets, spacing them 1¹/₂ inches (4 cm) apart. • Bake, one sheet at a time, for 12–15 minutes, or until lightly browned. • Transfer the cookies still on the parchment paper to racks to cool. • Tear away the excess rice paper from around the cookies.

ORANGE MACAROON DRIZZLERS

Preheat the oven to 325°F/170°C/gas 3. • Line three cookie sheets with parchment paper. • Sprinkle the almonds on a large baking sheet. Toast for 7 minutes, or until lightly golden. Lower the oven temperature to 275°F/140°C/gas 1. • Process the almonds in a food processor until very finely chopped. • Beat the egg whites, superfine sugar, and vanilla sugar in a double boiler over barely simmering water with an electric mixer at high speed until stiff peaks form. • Add the orange zest and juice. • Remove from the heat. Use a rubber spatula to fold the almonds and bread crumbs into the batter. • Drop teaspoons of the batter 1 inch (2.5 cm) apart onto the prepared cookie sheets. • Bake, one sheet at a time, for 20–25 minutes, or until pale golden. The macaroons should still be soft but will harden while cooling. • Transfer to racks to cool. • Glaze: Heat the marmalade in a small saucepan and drizzle over the cooled macaroons. Set aside. • Melt the chocolate in a double boiler over barely simmering water. • Drizzle the chocolate over the tops.

Makes: 50 cookies

Preparation: 50'

Cooking: 20–25'

Level of difficulty: 2

- 1¼ cups/180 g blanched almonds
- 3 large egg whites
- ¾ cup/150 g superfine/caster sugar
- 1 tbsp vanilla sugar
- grated zest of 1 orange
- 1 tbsp orange juice
- 1 cup/60 g fresh bread crumbs

GLAZE
- 2 tbsp orange marmalade
- 2 oz/60 g semisweet/dark chocolate, coarsely chopped

HAZELNUT MERINGUES

Makes: 30–35 cookies

Preparation: 20'

Cooking: 50–60'

Level of difficulty: 1

- 2 cups/300 g hazelnuts
- 1 cup/200 g superfine sugar
- 4 large egg whites
- 1/4 tsp salt

Preheat the oven to 325°F/170°C/gas 3. • Line two cookie sheets with parchment paper. • Spread the hazelnuts on a large baking sheet. Toast for 7 minutes, or until lightly golden. • Reduce the oven temperature to 250°F/130°C/gas 1/2. • Transfer the nuts to a food processor with 1/2 cup (100 g) of superfine sugar and process until finely ground. • Beat the egg whites and salt in a large bowl with an electric mixer at medium speed until soft peaks form. With mixer at high speed, gradually add the remaining superfine sugar, beating until stiff, glossy peaks form. • Use a large rubber spatula to fold in the hazelnuts. • Drop teaspoons of the meringue 2 inches (5 cm) apart on the prepared cookie sheets. • Bake for 50–60 minutes, or until the meringues are dry and crisp. • Transfer while still on the parchment paper to a rack to cool.

CANDIED COCONUT MERINGUES

Preheat the oven to 325°F/170°C/gas 3. • Line a cookie sheet with parchment paper. • Beat the egg whites and salt in a large bowl with an electric mixer at medium speed until frothy. With mixer at high speed, gradually add the sugar, beating until stiff, glossy peaks form. • Use a large rubber spatula to fold in the coconut. • Drop teaspoons of the meringue 2 inches (5 cm) apart onto the prepared cookie sheet. • Decorate with the cherries. • Bake for 35–45 minutes, or until dry and crisp. • Turn the oven off and let the meringues cool in the oven with the door ajar.

| Makes: 15–20 cookies |
| Preparation: 20' |
| Cooking: 35–45' |
| Level of difficulty: 1 |

- **2 large egg whites**
- **⅛ tsp salt**
- **½ cup/100 g superfine/caster sugar**
- **1 cup/125 g shredded/desiccated coconut**
- **candied cherries, to decorate**

COFFEE MERINGUES

Makes: 18 cookies

Preparation: 25' + 30'
to cool

Cooking: 50–60'

Level of difficulty: 2

- 1 tbsp + 1 cup/
  150 g
  confectioners'/
  icing sugar
- 1 tsp unsweetened
  cocoa powder
- ½ tsp freeze-dried
  coffee granules
- 2 large egg whites
- ⅛ tsp salt
- ½ tsp vanilla
  extract/essence

Preheat the oven to 250°F/130°C/gas ½. •
Line two cookie sheets with parchment paper.
• Sift 1 tablespoon of confectioners' sugar and the
cocoa into a small bowl. Stir in the coffee granules.
• Beat the egg whites and salt in a large bowl with
an electric mixer at medium speed until soft peaks
form. • With mixer
at high speed,
gradually add the remaining confectioners' sugar,
beating until stiff, glossy peaks form. • Fold in the
cocoa mixture and vanilla. • Fit a pastry bag with a
½-inch (1-cm) star tip. Fill the pastry bag, twist the
opening tightly closed, and squeeze out 2½-inch
(6-cm) rosettes, spacing 2 inches (5-cm) apart on
the prepared cookie sheets. • Bake for 50–60
minutes, or until the meringues are dry to the
touch. • Turn the oven off. Carefully lift the
meringues off the paper, press in the bottoms
slightly, and return to the warm oven for 30
minutes more. • Transfer the meringues to racks
to cool completely.

Use good quality espresso granules for best results.

CHOCOLATE MERINGUE DROPS

Preheat the oven to 250°F/130°C/gas $^1/_2$. •
Line two cookie sheets with parchment paper.
• Beat the egg whites and salt in a large bowl with
an electric mixer at medium speed until frothy. •
With mixer at high speed, gradually add the
superfine sugar, beating until stiff, glossy peaks
form. • Fold in the cocoa, cinnamon, and almond
extract. • Fit a pastry bag with a $1^1/_2$-inch (4-cm)
star tip. Fill the pastry bag, twist the opening tightly
closed, and squeeze out generous rosettes
spacing 1 inch (2.5 cm) apart on the prepared
cookie sheets. • Bake for 50–60 minutes, or until
crisp and dry to the touch. • Cool completely on
the sheets.

778

Makes: 25–30 cookies

Preparation: 25'

Cooking: 50–60'

Level of difficulty: 2

- **2 large egg whites**
- **$^1/_8$ tsp salt**
- **$^2/_3$ cup/140 g superfine/caster sugar**
- **$^1/_3$ cup/50 g unsweetened cocoa powder**
- **$^1/_2$ tsp ground cinnamon**
- **$^1/_2$ tsp almond extract/essence**

CHOCOLATE CINNAMON MACAROONS

Makes: 20–24 cookies

Preparation: 40'+ 60' to chill and set

Cooking: 10–12'

Level of difficulty: 2

- 1 cup/150 g blanched almonds
- 6 oz/180 g milk chocolate, coarsely chopped
- ½ cup/100 g granulated sugar
- 1 tbsp unsweetened cocoa powder
- ¼ tsp ground cinnamon
- 2 large egg whites, lightly beaten
- 1 tsp water
- 2 tbsp confectioners'/ icing sugar

Preheat the oven to 325°F/170°C/gas 3. • Spread the almonds on a large baking sheet. Toast for 7 minutes, or until lightly golden. • Let cool completely. • Transfer the nuts to a food processor and process until finely ground. • Melt 3 oz (90 g) of chocolate in a double boiler over barely simmering water. • Mix the ground almonds, sugar, cocoa, and cinnamon in a large bowl and make a well in the center. • Mix in the melted chocolate and enough egg white to form a soft, but not sticky paste. • Refrigerate for 30 minutes. • Line two cookie sheets with parchment paper. • Spoon scant tablespoons of the mixture 1 inch (2.5 cm) apart onto the prepared cookie sheets, flattening them slightly. • Brush the tops with a little water and sprinkle with the confectioners' sugar. • Bake for 10–12 minutes, or until just firm to the touch. • Transfer to racks to cool. • Melt the remaining chocolate in a double boiler over barely simmering water. • Dip the macaroons halfway into the melted chocolate. • Let dry on parchment paper for 30 minutes.

GREAT BARRIER REEF MERINGUES

Preheat the oven to 300°F/150°C/gas 2. • Line two cookie sheets with parchment paper. • Mix the egg whites and brown sugar in a large bowl over barely simmering water, stirring until the sugar has dissolved and the mixture has become warm to the touch. • Remove the bowl from the heat and whisk with an electric mixer until thick and cool, about 15–20 minutes. • Fold in 1 tablespoon of nuts. • Drop tablespoons of the mixture 2 inches (5 cm) apart onto the prepared cookie sheets. • Sprinkle with the remaining 1 tablespoon nuts. • Bake for 12–15 minutes, or until crisp and dry to the touch. • Cool completely in the oven.

Makes: 12 cookies

Preparation: 40'

Cooking: 15'

Level of difficulty: 2

- 3½ oz/100 g egg whites (3½ large egg whites)
- 1 cup/200 g soft dark brown sugar
- 2 tbsp coarsely chopped hazelnuts

ANGELICA-TOPPED MOMENTS

Makes: 13–18
  cookies

Preparation: 20'

Cooking: 20–25'

Level of difficulty: 1

- **1 large egg white**
- **⅛ tsp salt**
- **1 cup/200 g granulated sugar**
- **⅓ cup/30 g finely chopped crystallized ginger**
- **⅓ cup/30 g finely chopped candied cherries**
- **⅓ cup/30 g finely chopped seedless raisins**
- **⅔ cup/70 g finely chopped almonds**
- **⅓ cup/30 g finely chopped angelica**

Preheat the oven to 325°F/170°C/gas 3. • Line a cookie sheet with parchment paper. • Beat the egg white and salt in a medium bowl with an electric mixer at medium speed until frothy. • With mixer at high speed, gradually add the sugar, beating until stiff, glossy peaks form. • Fold in the ginger, candied cherries, raisins, and almonds. • Drop teaspoons of the batter 2 inches (5 cm) apart onto the prepared cookie sheets. • Bake for 10 minutes. • Remove from the oven and top with angelica. • Bake for 10–15 minutes more, or until firm to the touch. • Transfer to racks to cool.

LEMON BITES

Preheat the oven to 325°F/170°C/gas 3. • Line a cookie sheet with rice paper. • Spread the almonds out on a large baking sheet. Toast in the oven for 7 minutes, or until lightly golden. Transfer to a food processor, add the superfine sugar, and process until finely chopped. • Transfer to a large bowl. Stir in the confectioners' sugar, lemon peel, and lemon extract. • Beat the egg white in a small bowl with an electric mixer at high speed until stiff peaks form. • Fold the beaten white into the almond mixture. • Spread the mixture into 1-inch (2.5-cm) squares on the prepared cookie sheet. • Cover with a clean kitchen towel and let stand in a cool place overnight. • Preheat the oven to 300°F/150°C/gas 2. • Bake for 55–65 minutes, or until set. Cool completely on the cookie sheet. • Tear off any excess paper and dust with the confectioners' sugar.

Makes: about 15 cookies

Preparation: 25' + 12 h to rest

Cooking: 55–65'

Level of difficulty: 2

- 1¾ cups/275 g whole almonds
- 1 cup/200 g superfine/caster sugar
- 1 cup/150 g confectioners'/icing sugar + extra to dust
- 2 tbsp chopped candied lemon peel
- ½ tsp lemon extract/essence
- 1 large egg white

LINDA'S BROWN SUGAR MERINGUES

Makes: 12 cookies

Preparation: 40'

Cooking: 15'

Level of difficulty: 2

- 3½ oz/100 g egg whites (3½ large egg whites)
- 1 cup/200 g soft dark brown sugar
- 2 tbsp coarsely chopped almonds

Preheat the oven to 300°F/150°C/gas 2. • Line two cookie sheets with parchment paper. • Mix the egg whites and brown sugar in a large bowl over barely simmering water, stirring until the sugar has dissolved and the mixture is warm to the touch. • Remove the bowl from the heat and whisk with an electric mixer until thick and cool, about 15–20 minutes. • Fold in 1 tablespoon of almonds. • Drop tablespoons of the mixture 2 inches (5 cm) apart onto the prepared cookie sheets. • Sprinkle with the remaining almonds. • Bake for 12–15 minutes, or until crisp and dry to the touch. • Cool completely in the oven.

CANDIED MERINGUES

Makes: 30 cookies

Preparation: 30' + 1 h
to soak

Cooking: 8–10'

Level of difficulty: 2

- 2 tbsp finely chopped mixed candied peel
- 2 tbsp orange liqueur
- 1 cup/150 g all-purpose/plain flour
- $1/4$ tsp baking powder
- $1/8$ tsp salt
- $1/2$ cup/125 g butter, softened
- $2/3$ cup/140 g granulated sugar
- $1/2$ tsp lemon extract/essence
- 2 egg whites, lightly beaten

Soak the candied peel in the orange liqueur for 1 hour. • Drain, reserving the liqueur. • Preheat the oven to 375°F/190°C/gas 5. • Line two cookie sheets with parchment paper. • Sift the flour, baking powder, and salt into a medium bowl. • Beat the butter and sugar in a large bowl with an electric mixer at high speed until creamy. • Add the lemon extract. • With mixer at high speed, beat in the egg whites and the reserved orange liqueur. • Mix in the dry ingredients. • Fit a pastry bag with a $1/2$-inch (1-cm) plain tip. Fill the pastry bag, twist the opening tightly closed, and squeeze out $1 1/2$-inch (4-cm) mounds, spacing 2 inches (5 cm) apart on the prepared cookie sheets. • Lightly press a piece of candied peel into the top of each cookie. • Bake for 8–10 minutes, or until golden brown. • Cool on the sheets until the cookies firm slightly. • Transfer to racks and let cool completely.

AUSTRALIAN MACAROONS

Preheat the oven to 350°F/180°C/gas 4. •
Butter a cookie sheet. • Beat the egg whites
and salt in a large bowl with an electric mixer at
medium speed until frothy. • With mixer at high
speed, gradually add the sugar, beating until stiff,
glossy peaks form. • Use a large rubber spatula to
fold in the coconut and macadamia nuts. • Drop
teaspoons of the mixture 1 inch (2.5 cm) apart
onto the prepared cookie sheet. • Bake for 10–15
minutes, or until lightly golden. • Transfer to racks
to cool.

Makes: 15 cookies

Preparation: 20'

Cooking: 10–15'

Level of difficulty: 1

- **2 large egg whites**
- **⅛ tsp salt**
- **¾ cup/150 g granulated sugar**
- **1½ cups/185 g shredded coconut**
- **1 cup/100 g coarsely chopped macadamia nuts**

OVERLAND MACAROONS

Makes: 35–40 cookies

Preparation: 25'

Cooking: 12–15'

Level of difficulty: 1

- 1¼ cups/310 g butter, softened
- 2 cups/250 g old-fashioned rolled oats
- 1⅓ cups/200 g all-purpose/plain flour
- 1 tsp baking powder
- ¼ tsp salt
- ½ cup/100 g firmly packed light brown sugar
- ½ cup/100 g raw sugar (Barbados or Demerara)
- 2 large eggs
- 1¼ cups/150 g shredded/desiccated coconut
- 3 tbsp heavy/double cream
- 1 tsp vanilla extract/essence

Preheat the oven to 350°F/180°C/gas 4. • Line two cookie sheets with parchment paper. • Melt 6 tablespoons of butter in a large skillet and toast the oats until lightly golden. • Sift the flour, baking powder, and salt into a large bowl. • Beat the remaining butter and the sugars in a large bowl with an electric mixer at high speed until creamy. • Add the eggs, coconut, cream, and vanilla, beating until just blended. • Mix in the dry ingredients. • Form into balls the size of walnuts and place 2 inches (5 cm) apart on the prepared cookie sheets, flattening them slightly. • Bake for 12–15 minutes, until firm to the touch and golden brown. • Cool on the sheets until the cookies firm slightly. • Transfer to racks and let cool completely.

PINE NUT CRISPIES

Line a cookie sheet with parchment paper. •
Place small heaps of pine nuts (about 10 pine
nuts per heap) on the prepared cookie sheet. • Mix
the almonds, sugar, and vanilla in a large bowl. •
Beat the egg whites in a large bowl with an electric
mixer at high speed until stiff peaks form. • Use a
large rubber spatula to fold the beaten whites into
the almond mixture. • Drop teaspoons of the
mixture on top of the pine nuts to cover them
completely. • Refrigerate for 30 minutes. • Preheat
the oven to 300°F/150°C/gas 2. • Bake for
18–20 minutes, or until set. • Turn off the oven.
Cool the meringues completely in the oven with the
door ajar.

Makes: 16 cookies

Preparation: 20'+ 30' to chill

Cooking: 18–20'

Level of difficulty: 1

- ³/₄ cup/150 g pine nuts
- 1¹/₂ cups/150 g finely chopped almonds
- 1¹/₄ cups/250 g granulated sugar
- ¹/₂ tsp vanilla extract/essence
- 2 large egg whites

MARY POPPINS MACAROONS

Makes: 14–16 cookies

Preparation: 30'

Cooking: 12–15'

Level of difficulty: 2

- ¾ cup/120 g blanched almonds
- 1 cup/200 g granulated sugar
- 2 tbsp all-purpose/plain flour
- 2 large egg whites
- ⅛ tsp salt
- ¼ tsp vanilla extract/essence
- 1 tbsp poppy seeds

Preheat the oven to 325°F/170°C/gas 3. • Line a cookie sheet with rice paper. • Spread the nuts on a large baking sheet. • Toast for 7 minutes, or until lightly golden. • Increase the oven temperature to 375°F/190°C/gas 5. • Transfer the almonds to a food processor, add the sugar, and process until finely ground. • Stir together the almond mixture and flour in a medium bowl. • Beat the egg whites and salt in a large bowl with an electric mixer at high speed until stiff peaks form. • Use a large rubber spatula to fold in the dry ingredients and vanilla. • Fit a pastry bag with a 1-inch (2.5-cm) star tip. Fill the pastry bag, twist the opening tightly closed, and squeeze out 1-inch (2.5-cm) stars 1 inch (2.5-cm) apart on the prepared cookie sheet. Sprinkle with the poppy seeds. • Bake for 12–15 minutes, or until pale gold. • Cool on the sheets until the cookies firm slightly. • Transfer to racks on the rice paper, tearing away the excess paper, and let cool completely.

MINI MERINGUES

Preheat the oven to 300°F/150°C/gas 4. • Line two cookie sheets with aluminum foil. • Process the almonds in a food processor or blender until finely chopped. • Beat the egg whites, confectioners' sugar, and salt in a large bowl placed over barely simmering water with an electric mixer at high speed until stiff peaks form. • Remove the bowl from the water. Stir in the almond extract and chopped almonds. • Drop teaspoons of the mixture 1 inch (2.5 cm) apart onto the prepared cookie sheets. • Bake for 20–30 minutes, or until crisp. • Transfer the meringues on the foil to racks and let cool.

Makes: 25 cookies

Preparation: 20'

Cooking: 20–30'

Level of difficulty: 1

- 1¼ cups/175 g blanched almonds
- 4 large egg whites
- ⅛ tsp salt
- 2 cups/300 g confectioners'/ icing sugar
- ¼ tsp almond extract/essence

NO-BAKE COOKIES

PEANUT BUTTER SQUARES

Butter an 11 x 7-inch (28 x 18-cm) baking pan.
• Bring the corn syrup to a boil with the peanut butter in a medium saucepan over low heat, stirring constantly. • Remove from the heat and mix in the bran flakes and peanuts until well coated. • Spoon the mixture into the prepared pan. • Refrigerate for at least 1 hour, or until set.
• Melt the chocolate in a double boiler over barely simmering water. • Drizzle the melted chocolate over the peanut base and let stand for 30 minutes until set. • Cut into squares.

Makes: 22–33 squares

Preparation: 25' + 90' to chill and set

Level of difficulty: 1

- 1¼ cups/310 ml light corn syrup/ golden syrup
- 1 cup/250 ml smooth peanut butter
- 1 cup/100 g bran flakes or corn flakes
- 2 cups/200 g coarsely chopped peanuts
- 8 oz/250 g semisweet/dark chocolate, coarsely chopped

MOCHA NUT WEDGES

Makes: 16 cookies

Preparation: 20' + 60'
to chill

Level of difficulty: 1

- **6 tbsp butter, cut up**
- **2 tbsp granulated sugar**
- **1¾ cups/215 g graham cracker crumbs/crushed digestive biscuits**
- **1 cup/100 g coarsely chopped pecans**
- **1 tbsp freeze-dried coffee granules dissolved in 1 tbsp hot water**
- **2 tbsp plain yogurt**

Set out an 8-inch (20-cm) springform pan. • Melt the butter with the sugar in a small saucepan over low heat until the sugar has dissolved completely. • Remove from the heat and mix in the graham cracker crumbs, pecans, coffee, and yogurt. • Firmly press the mixture into the prepared pan to form a smooth, even layer. • Refrigerate for at least 1 hour, or until set. • Loosen and remove the pan sides and cut into wedges.

PRALINE SQUARES

Line a large baking sheet with aluminum foil. Oil the foil. • Melt both sugars in a medium saucepan over low heat. Stir in the butter, honey, and marzipan. • Add the hazelnuts, almonds, candied cherries, lemon peel, pistachios, and salt. Cook, stirring constantly, for 3–5 minutes until well mixed. • Pour the mixture onto the foil. • Flatten the mixture and spread it out to a thickness of $^1/_2$ inch (1-cm). • Set aside to cool. • Melt the chocolate in a double boiler over barely simmering water. • Spread over the cookie. • Use a sharp knife to cut into squares.

Beautifully textured and delicious, these squares will become a favorite.

Makes: 50–60 squares

Preparation: 60'

Level of difficulty: 1

- $^3/_4$ cup/150 g granulated sugar
- 1 tbsp vanilla sugar
- 6 tbsp butter
- 1 tbsp honey
- 2 oz/60 g marzipan, grated
- $^3/_4$ cup/125 g toasted hazelnuts, finely chopped
- 1 cup/150 g toasted almonds, coarsely chopped
- $^2/_3$ cup/70 g candied cherries, finely chopped
- 3 tbsp candied lemon peel, finely chopped
- 1 tbsp pistachios, crushed
- $^1/_8$ tsp salt
- 3 oz/90 g semisweet/dark chocolate, coarsely chopped

CHOCOLATE HAZELNUT SQUARES

Makes: 16–25
squares

Preparation: 25' + 60'
to chill

Level of difficulty: 1

- ½ cup/75 g whole hazelnuts
- 5 oz/150 g semisweet/dark chocolate, coarsely chopped
- ⅔ cup/150 g butter, cut up
- ⅛ tsp salt
- 1¼ cups/150 g graham cracker crumbs/crushed digestive biscuits

Preheat the oven to 325°F/170°C/gas 3. • Butter an 8-inch (20-cm) square baking pan. • Spread the nuts on a large baking sheet. Toast for 7 minutes, or until lightly golden. • Transfer to a large cotton kitchen towel. Fold the towel over the nuts and rub these through the towel to remove the thin inner skins. Pick out the nuts and chop coarsely. • Melt the chocolate with the butter and salt in a double boiler over barely simmering water. • Remove from the heat and mix in the graham cracker crumbs and chopped hazelnuts until well coated. • Firmly press the mixture into the prepared pan to form a smooth, even layer. • Refrigerate for at least 1 hour, or until set. • Cut into squares.

ORANGE RICE CRISP SQUARES

Makes: 16–25 squares

Preparation: 20' + 30' to set

Level of difficulty: 1

- 4 tbsp butter, cut up
- ¼ cup/50 g granulated sugar
- 3 tbsp honey
- 4 tbsp smooth peanut butter
- 3 oz/90 g semisweet/dark chocolate, grated
- grated zest of 1 orange
- 1 cup/100 g rice krispies

Butter an 8-inch (20-cm) square baking pan. • Melt the butter with the sugar, honey, peanut butter, and grated chocolate in a large saucepan over low heat until the sugar has dissolved completely. • Remove from the heat and mix in the orange zest and rice krispies until well coated. • Press the mixture lightly into the prepared pan. • Let set for 30 minutes before cutting into squares.

HALLOWEEN SPOOKIES

Mix the graham cracker crumbs, sugar, cocoa, and almonds in a large bowl. • Stir in the melted butter and enough milk to form a stiff dough. • Divide the mixture into 15 pieces and form into balls the size of walnuts. • Flatten into 1-inch (2.5-cm) thick rounds. • Colored Butter Icing: Beat the butter,

With no cooking involved, these great Halloween cookies can be made safely by quite young children.

812

confectioners' sugar, and vanilla in a large bowl with an electric mixer at high speed until creamy. • Divide into three small bowls. Add the food coloring to each bowl. Mix pale colors for smiley faces and deep blue and red icing for a spooky design. • Spread the icing over the tops of the cookies. • Decorate with candies or candied cherries to resemble eyes and noses. • Cut up the licorice whips into short lengths to resemble smiley mouths, hair, and other decorative details.

Makes: 15 cookies

Preparation: 25'

Level of difficulty: 1

- 1¾ cups/215 g graham cracker crumbs/crushed digestive biscuits
- ¾ cup/150 g granulated sugar
- 2 tbsp unsweetened cocoa powder
- ½ cup/75 g finely ground almonds
- 6 tbsp butter, melted
- 2 tbsp milk + more as needed

COLORED BUTTER ICING

- ½ cup/125 g butter, softened
- 1⅔ cups/250 g confectioners'/ icing sugar
- ½ tsp vanilla extract/essence
- Few drops each blue, yellow, or red food coloring
- Small candies, licorice whips, and candied cherries, to decorate

NO-BAKE DOUBLE CHOCOLATE COOKIES

Makes: 45–50 cookies

Preparation: 25' + 60' to chill and set

Level of difficulty: 1

- 2 oz/60 g semisweet/dark chocolate, coarsely chopped
- 2½ cups/310 g vanilla wafer crumbs
- ½ cup/50 g finely chopped pecans
- 1 can (14 oz/ 400 g) sweetened condensed milk
- 10 oz/300 g white chocolate, coarsely chopped
- ½ cup/90 g semisweet/dark chocolate chips

Line four cookie sheets with parchment paper. • Melt the semisweet chocolate in a double boiler over barely simmering water. • Mix the vanilla wafer crumbs, pecans, condensed milk, and melted semisweet chocolate in a large bowl until well blended. • Form the mixture into balls the size of walnuts and place 1 inch (2.5 cm) apart on the prepared cookie sheets, flattening them slightly.
• Refrigerate for 30 minutes until firm to the touch.
• Melt the white chocolate in the double boiler over barely simmering water. • Spread the white chocolate over the tops of the cookies. Decorate with the chocolate chips. • Let stand for 30 minutes until set.

CHOCOLATE MARSHMALLOW BITES

Line a cookie sheet with waxed paper. • Melt the white chocolate in a double boiler over barely simmering water. • Remove from the heat and mix in the vanilla wafers, pecans, apricots, marshmallows, and candied cherries until well coated. • Drop heaped teaspoons onto the cookie sheet. • Refrigerate for 1 hour, or until set. • Melt the semisweet chocolate in a double boiler over barely simmering water. Remove from the heat and dip the cookies halfway into the semisweet chocolate. • Decorate with the silver balls or sprinkle with sugar strands. • Let stand for 30 minutes until set.

Makes: 18–20 cookies

Preparation: 20' + 90' to chill and set

Level of difficulty: 1

- 5 oz/150 g white chocolate, coarsely chopped
- 2 tbsp lightly crushed vanilla wafers
- ½ cup/50 g coarsely chopped pecans
- ½ cup/50 g coarsely chopped dried apricots
- ½ cup/50 g mini marshmallows
- 4 candied cherries, coarsely chopped
- 3 oz/90 g semisweet/dark chocolate, coarsely chopped
- silver balls or sugar strands, jimmies, sprills, or sprinkles, to decorate

ALMOND BRITTLE

Makes: 12–16 bars

Preparation: 10' +
  12 h to set

Level of difficulty: 1

- 1 cup/200 g
  granulated sugar
- 2 cups/300 g
  unpeeled almonds
- 1 tsp vanilla
  extract/essence
- 2 tbsp almond oil

Place the sugar in a large heavy-bottomed saucepan over medium-low heat. Stir in the almonds and vanilla. • Cook, stirring constantly with a wooden spoon, until the sugar begins to stick to the almonds. The mixture should become semi-liquid and the almonds will begin to stick together. • Grease a marble surface with the almond oil. • Pour the mixture onto the surface and let cool to warm. • Use a metal spatula to work the mixture until it is about $1/2$-inch (1-cm) thick. • Leave until almost, but not completely, cool. • Use a long sharp knife to cut the nougat into bars. • Set aside for 12 hours in a cool place before serving.

MINT MOMENTS

Mix the wafer crumbs, walnuts, 1 cup (150 g) confectioners' sugar, corn syrup, and mint liqueur in a large bowl to form a stiff dough. • Form the dough into balls the size of walnuts and roll in the remaining confectioners' sugar. • Arrange in mini paper liners and serve.

Makes: 24–28 cookies

Preparation: 20'

Level of difficulty: 1

- 1 cup/125 g vanilla wafer crumbs
- ¾ cup/75 g finely chopped walnuts
- 1¼ cups/180 g confectioners'/ icing sugar
- 2 tbsp light corn syrup/golden syrup
- 6 tbsp green- colored mint liqueur

CHOCOLATE WEDGES

Makes: 8 cookies

Preparation: 15' + 3 h to chill

Level of difficulty: 1

- 4 tbsp butter, cut up
- 4 oz/125 g semisweet/dark chocolate, coarsely chopped
- 4 tbsp light corn syrup/golden syrup
- 1/3 cup/40 g corn flakes
- 2 tbsp shredded/ desiccated coconut

Butter an 8-inch (20-cm) round cake pan and line with waxed paper. • Melt the butter and chocolate with the corn syrup in a medium saucepan over low heat. • Stir in the corn flakes and coconut until well blended. • Spoon into the prepared pan, pressing down lightly. • Refrigerate for 3 hours. • Use a sharp knife to cut into wedges.

GLAZED CHOCOLATE COOKIE CAKE

Makes: 15 bars

Preparation: 20'

Level of difficulty: 1

- ½ cup/125 g butter, cut up
- 1½ tbsp light corn syrup/golden syrup
- 2 tbsp unsweetened cocoa powder
- 1 cup/180 g golden raisins/sultanas
- 2 cups/250 g graham cracker crumbs/crushed digestive biscuits
- 6 oz/180 g semisweet/dark chocolate, coarsely chopped

Set out a 10½ x 15½-inch (26 x 36-cm) jelly-roll pan. • Melt the butter with the corn syrup and cocoa in a medium saucepan over low heat. • Remove from the heat and stir in the raisins and graham cracker crumbs. • Firmly press the mixture onto the baking pan. • Melt the chocolate in a double boiler over barely simmering water. • Pour the melted chocolate evenly over the cookie base. • Let stand until set and cut into small bars.

823

CHOCOLATE WALNUT SQUARES

L ine an 8-inch (20-cm) baking pan with waxed paper. • Melt the butter and chocolate with the corn syrup in a double boiler over barely simmering water. • Stir in the graham cracker crumbs and walnuts and mix until well blended. • Firmly press the mixture into the prepared pan. • Refrigerate for 3 hours. • Use a sharp knife to cut into squares, peeling off the paper.

Makes: 16–25 squares

Preparation: 15' + 3 h to chill

Level of difficulty: 1

- 4 tbsp butter, cut up
- 7 oz/200 g semisweet/dark chocolate, coarsely chopped
- 3 tbsp light corn syrup/golden syrup
- 2 cups/250 g graham cracker crumbs
- 1 cup/100 g coarsely chopped walnuts

NO-BAKE CHOCOLATE CHERRY DROPS

Makes: 15–18
  cookies

Level of difficulty: 1

Preparation: 25' + 60'
  to chill

- 3 oz/90 g
  semisweet/dark
  chocolate,
  coarsely chopped
- 4 tbsp butter, cut
  up
- 1 tbsp dark rum
- 1½ cups/250 g
  cake crumbs
- ¾ cup/75 g
  coarsely chopped
  red and green
  candied cherries
- ¼ cup/45 g golden
  raisins/sultanas

Line a cookie sheet with parchment paper. •
Melt the chocolate with the butter and rum in a
double boiler over barely simmering water. • Mix
in the cake crumbs, candied cherries, and golden
raisins to form a soft dough. • Drop tablespoons
of the mixture onto the prepared cookie sheet.
• Refrigerate for at least 1 hour, or until firm to
the touch.

MARSHMALLOW BITES

S et out 15–20 mini paper cases on a cookie sheet. • Melt the semisweet and milk chocolates with the butter and corn syrup in a double boiler over barely simmering water. • Remove from the heat and mix in the marshmallows and rice krispies until well coated. • Spoon evenly into the paper cases. • Refrigerate for 2 hours, or until set.

Makes: 15–20 cookies

Preparation: 20' + 2 h to set

Level of difficulty: 1

- 2 oz/60 g semisweet/dark chocolate, coarsely chopped
- 2 oz/60 g milk chocolate, coarsely chopped
- 2 tbsp butter, cut up
- 2 tbsp light corn syrup/golden syrup
- ½ cup/50 g mini marshmallows
- ½ cup/50 g rice krispies

BANANA SQUARES

Makes: 16–25
  squares

Preparation: 50–55'

Level of difficulty: 1

- **2 tbsp fresh lemon juice**
- **2 tbsp honey**
- **²⁄₃ cup/150 ml water**
- **2¼ cups/225 g coarsely chopped dried apricots**
- **2¼ cups/225 g coarsely chopped bananas**
- **6 tbsp butter, cut up**
- **1 cup/200 g firmly packed light brown sugar**
- **1¼ cups/125 g corn flakes**

Bring the lemon juice, honey, and water to a boil with the apricots and bananas in a medium saucepan over medium heat. • Reduce the heat and simmer over low heat for 25–30 minutes, or until the fruit has softened. • Remove from the heat and let cool for 15 minutes. • Butter an 8-inch (20-cm) baking pan. • Melt the butter with the brown sugar in a medium saucepan over low heat until the sugar has dissolved completely. • Mix in the corn flakes until well coated. • Firmly press half the corn flake mixture into the prepared pan to form a smooth, even layer. Spoon the apricot mixture evenly over the base and cover with the remaining corn flake mixture. • Cool completely before cutting into squares.

TEA
CAKES

OLD-FASHIONED MADELEINES WITH LAVENDER HONEY

Preheat the oven to 425°F/220°C/gas 7. • Butter two madeleine pans (for 20–24 madeleines). • Sift the flour and salt into a large bowl. • Beat the eggs and lemon zest in a large bowl with an electric mixer at high speed until pale and thick. Add the honey and beat until creamy.

Madeleine pans are available from specialist baking stores.

• Fold in the dry ingredients, followed by the butter. • Spoon the batter evenly into the prepared pans. • Bake for 15–20 minutes, or until a toothpick inserted into one comes out clean. • Cool the madeleines in the pans for 15 minutes. Transfer to racks to cool completely. • Dust with the confectioners' sugar.

834

Makes: 20–22 cookies

Preparation: 20'

Cooking: 15–20'

Level of difficulty: 1

- ⅓ cup/50 g all-purpose/plain flour
- ⅛ tsp salt
- 3 large eggs
- grated zest of 1 lemon
- 2 tbsp lavender honey
- ½ cup/125 g butter, melted
- confectioners'/icing sugar, to dust

EGG CUSTARD TARTS

Preheat the oven to 300°F/150°C/gas 2. • Mix the egg yolks and whole eggs in a jug or bowl. Beat slowly with the whisk. Add the sugar and beat until it is dissolved. • Pour in the milk and cream, and beat well until foamy. • Roll out the pastry and cut it into circles large enough to line the inside of the baking pans. Press the pastry pieces into the baking pans. Make sure the bottom and sides of the tin are evenly covered. Fill each tart case with the egg mixture. • Place the tarts on a baking sheet and bake for 45 minutes, or until the tarts are golden brown. • Let the tarts cool for 10 minutes. • Remove from the pans and place them on a rack to cool completely. • Serve the tarts at room temperature.

Makes: 20 cookies
Preparation: 30'
Cooking: 45'
Level of difficulty: 2

- **2 large eggs + 3 egg yolks**
- **1 cup/250 ml milk**
- **2 tbsp single/light cream**
- **1 packet ready-made frozen pastry (flaky or shortcrust)**

PINK AND PRETTY JEWELS

Makes: 25 cookies

Preparation: 20'

Cooking: 15–20'

Level of difficulty: 1

- 1²/₃ cups/250 g all-purpose/plain flour
- 1 tsp baking powder
- ¹/₈ tsp salt
- 6 tbsp butter
- ¹/₂ cup/100 g granulated sugar
- ¹/₂ tsp Alchermes liqueur or red food coloring
- 1 large egg, lightly beaten
- 1 tbsp milk
- 2 tbsp sugar crystals

Preheat the oven to 375°F/190°C/gas 5. • Line two cookie sheets with parchment paper. • Sift the flour, baking powder, and salt into a large bowl. • Use a pastry blender to cut in the butter until the mixture resembles coarse crumbs. • Stir in the granulated sugar, Alchermes, and egg to form a soft dough. • Form the dough into balls the size of walnuts and place 2 inches (5 cm) apart on the prepared cookie sheets, flattening them slightly. • Brush with the milk and sprinkle with sugar crystals. • Bake for 15–20 minutes, or until just golden. • Transfer to racks to cool.

NEAPOLITAN RUM CAKES

Serves: 6

Preparation: 20'

Cooking: 15'

Level of difficulty: 2

- 1 oz fresh yeast or 2 (¼ oz/7 g) packages active dry yeast
- 4 tbsp warm water
- 5 eggs
- 3 tbsp sugar
- ½ cup/125 ml extra-virgin olive oil
- 2 tbsp butter, melted and cooled,
- 3 cups/450 g all-purpose/plain flour
- ⅛ tsp salt
- 1⅓ cups/240 g granulated sugar
- 2 cups/500 ml water
- 1 lemon, sliced
- ½ cup/125 ml rum

Put the yeast in a small bowl with ½ cup (125 ml) warm water. Stir until dissolved then set aside for 10 minutes. • Beat the eggs and 3 tablespoons of sugar until pale and creamy. • Gradually beat in the oil, butter, and yeast mixture. • Lastly, add the sifted flour and salt. • Knead the dough thoroughly by hand until it is soft and elastic. • Fill the babà molds just under half full, cover, and leave in a warm place to rise. • When the dough has risen to just below the rim of each mold, bake in a preheated oven at 350°F/180°C/gas 4 for about 15 minutes. • Meanwhile, boil the 1⅓ cups (330 ml) sugar and water for 10 minutes, or until the mixture becomes syrupy. • Add the lemon slices and the rum and leave to cool. • When the babàs are cooked, set aside to cool before soaking them in the rum syrup. Leave on a wire rack to drain, then serve.

CREAM CAKES

Makes: 40 cookies

Preparation: 50' + 90'
to rise

Cooking: 15–20'

Level of difficulty: 2

Dissolve the yeast in 1 cup (250 ml) of water. Let stand until foamy. • Sift 2 cups (300 g) of flour into a large bowl. Pour in the yeast mixture and enough warm water to form a dough. • Place the dough in a bowl. Cover with a cloth and let rise in a warm place until doubled in bulk. • Sift the remaining flour onto a surface. Knead in the oil, eggs, and egg yolks, sugar, lemon zest, and vanilla. Add the remaining water to form a dough. • Knead in the dough that has doubled in bulk. • Shape into small oval loaves. Arrange on baking sheets and let rest until doubled in bulk. • Preheat the oven to 350°F/180°C/gas 4. • Brush the loaves with the egg. • Bake for 15–20 minutes, or until golden. • Beat the cream in a medium bowl until stiff. • Slice the loaves and fill with the cream. Sprinkle with the confectioners' sugar.

- 1 oz/25 g fresh yeast or 2 packages (½ oz/7 g) active dry yeast
- 2⅔ cups/650 ml warm water
- 6 cups/900 g all-purpose/plain flour
- 6 tbsp extra-virgin olive oil
- 6 large eggs + 4 large egg yolks, lightly beaten
- 1 cup/200 g sugar
- Grated zest of 1 lemon
- ½ tsp vanilla extract/essence
- 1 large egg, lightly beaten, to brush
- 2 cups/500 ml light/single cream
- 4 tbsp confectioners'/icing sugar

Makes: about 36 pastries

Preparation: 30'

Cooking: 8–10'

Level of difficulty: 2

- **6 large eggs**
- **4 cups/800 g sugar**
- **2 cups/500 ml milk**
- **Grated zest of 1 lemon**
- **1 cup/250 ml Sambuca**
- **3 lb/1.5 kg flour, or more as needed**
- **1 cup/250 ml Alchermes liqueur**
- **raw sugar, to roll**

VANILLA PASTRY CREAM
- **8 large egg yolks**
- **½ cup/125 g sugar**
- **¾ cup/125 g all-purpose/plain flour**
- **1 quart/1 liter boiling milk**
- **1 tsp vanilla extract/essence**

ITALIAN PASTRY CREAM KISSES

Preheat the oven to 325°F/170°C/gas 3. • Butter 2–3 baking sheets. • Beat the eggs and sugar in a large bowl until pale and thick. • Fold in the lemon zest, and flour, alternating with the Sambuca and milk. Make a fairly soft dough and shape into balls the size of walnuts. • Place on the prepared sheets, 1 inch (2 cm) apart. • Bake for 8–10 minutes, or until lightly browned. • Cool on a rack. • Vanilla Pastry Cream: Beat the egg yolks and sugar until pale and creamy. Stir in the flour, then gradually add the milk and vanilla. Cook over medium heat until thick. Let cool. • Poke a hole in the flat bottom of each one to make room for the filling. Let cool completely. • Brush with a little milk and fill with the cream, sticking them together in pairs. • Dip in the liqueur to color. Roll in the sugar.

CITRUS MADELEINES

Preheat the oven to 350°F/180°C/gas 4. •
Butter a madeleine pan (for 12 cookies). • Sift
the flour, baking powder, and salt into a medium
bowl. • Beat the butter and vanilla sugar in a large
bowl with an electric mixer at high speed until
creamy. • Add the egg yolk and lemon zest and
juice, beating until just blended. • Mix in the dry
ingredients. • With mixer at high speed, beat the
egg white in a medium bowl until stiff peaks form.
• Use a large rubber spatula to fold in the beaten
white. • Spoon the batter into prepared pan, filling
each cup three-quarters full. • Bake for 10–12
minutes, or until springy to the touch. • Cool the
madeleines in the pan for 15 minutes. • Transfer to
racks and let cool completely. • Lemon drizzle:
Melt the butter with the lemon juice in a small
saucepan over low heat. • Remove from the heat
and beat in the confectioners' sugar. • Drizzle the
frosting over the cookies and let stand for 30
minutes until set.

Makes: 12 cookies

*Preparation: 20' + 30'
to set*

Cooking: 10–12'

Level of difficulty: 1

- ½ cup/75 g all-
  purpose/plain flour
- 1 tsp baking
  powder
- ⅛ tsp salt
- 6 tbsp butter,
  softened
- ⅓ cup/70 g vanilla
  sugar
- 1 large egg,
  separated
- Grated zest and
  juice of 1 lemon

LEMON DRIZZLE
- 1 tsp butter
- 2–3 tbsp fresh
  lemon juice
- ⅓ cup/50 g
  confectioners'/
  icing sugar

MINI MAPLE SYRUP PIES

Makes: 24 cookies

Preparation: 45' + 30'
  to chill

Cooking: 15–20'

Level of difficulty: 2

PASTRY
- 1¼ cups/180 g all-purpose/plain flour
- ⅛ tsp salt
- ½ cup/125 g butter, cut up
- 1–2 tbsp milk

SYRUP FILLING
- ½ cup/125 ml pure maple syrup
- ⅔ cup/100 g all-purpose/plain flour
- ½ tsp baking powder
- 4 tbsp butter, softened
- ¼ cup/50 g firmly packed light brown sugar
- 1 large egg, lightly beaten
- ½ tsp vanilla extract/essence
- 1 tbsp milk

Pastry: Sift the flour and salt into a medium bowl. • Use a pastry blender to cut in the butter until the mixture resembles coarse crumbs. • Add enough milk to form a stiff dough. • Press the dough into a disk, wrap in plastic wrap, and refrigerate for 30 minutes. • Preheat the oven to 375°F/190°C/gas 5. • Set out two 12-cup mini-muffin pans. • Roll out the dough on a lightly floured surface to a thickness of ⅛ inch (3 mm). • Use a 2-inch (5-cm) fluted cookie cutter to cut out rounds. • Gather the dough scraps, re-roll, and continue cutting out rounds until all the dough is used. Press the dough rounds into the prepared cups. • Syrup Filling: Drop teaspoons of the maple syrup into each pastry base. • Sift the flour and baking powder into a medium bowl. • Beat the butter and brown sugar in a medium bowl with an electric mixer at high speed until creamy. • Add the egg and vanilla, beating until just blended. • Mix in the dry ingredients and milk. • Spoon the mixture evenly into the prepared cups. • Bake for 15–20 minutes, or until golden brown. • Transfer to racks to cool.

COCONUT AND ALMOND TARTS

Pastry: Sift the flour and salt into a large bowl. • Use a pastry blender to cut in the butter and lard until the mixture resembles fine crumbs. • Mix in the ice water to form a smooth dough. • Shape into a ball, wrap in plastic wrap, and refrigerate for at least 30 minutes. • Preheat the oven to 350°F/180°C/gas 4. • Butter twelve 2 x $^3/_4$-inch (5 x 2-cm) tartlet pans. • Roll out the pastry on a lightly floured surface to a thickness of $^1/_4$ inch (5 mm). Use a pastry cutter to stamp out twelve rounds to slightly larger than the tartlet pans. Press the pastry rounds into the prepared pans. • Filling: Heat the raspberry jelly in a small saucepan until liquid. Brush $^1/_4$ teaspoon jelly over each pastry base. • Beat the egg white in a medium bowl with an electric mixer at high speed until stiff peaks form. Use a rubber spatula to fold in the superfine sugar, coconut, and almonds. • Spoon the coconut mixture evenly into the pastry bases. • Bake for 20–25 minutes, or until golden brown. • Cool the tarts completely in the pans.

Makes: 12 tarts

Preparation: 40' + 30' to chill

Cooking: 20–25'

Level of difficulty: 2

PASTRY
- 1¼ cups/180 g all-purpose/plain flour
- ⅛ tsp salt
- 4 tbsp butter, cut up
- 4 tbsp lard, cut up, or vegetable shortening
- 1–2 tbsp ice water

FILLING
- 2–3 tbsp raspberry jelly
- 1 large egg white
- ⅓ cup/70 g superfine/caster sugar
- 2 tbsp shredded/desiccated coconut
- 2 tbsp finely ground almonds

PLUM CAKES

Preheat the oven to 350°F/180°C/gas 4. •
Butter a 12-cup mini muffin pan. • Cut each
half-plum into three. • Sift the flour, nutmeg,
cinnamon, and salt into a medium bowl. Stir in the
almonds. • Beat the butter and confectioners'
sugar in a large bowl with an electric mixer at high
speed until creamy. • Mix in the dry ingredients and
egg whites. • Pour the batter evenly into the
prepared cups and place a piece of plum on top of
each. • Bake for 25–30 minutes, or until a
toothpick inserted into the centers comes out
clean. • Transfer to racks to cool.

Makes: 24 cookies

Preparation: 25'

Cooking: 25–30'

Level of difficulty: 1

- 8 oz/250 g firm-ripe plums, halved and pitted
- ½ cup/75 g all-purpose/plain flour
- 1½ tsp finely grated nutmeg
- ¼ tsp ground cinnamon
- ⅛ tsp salt
- 1¼ cups/180 g finely ground almonds
- ¾ cup/180 g butter, softened
- 1⅔ cups/250 g confectioners'/icing sugar
- 6 large egg whites

STRAWBERRY ALMOND CAKELETS

Makes: 24 cookies
Preparation: 25'
Cooking: 25–30'
Level of difficulty: 1

- ½ cup/75 g all-purpose/plain flour
- ⅛ tsp salt
- 1¼ cups/180 g finely ground almonds
- ¾ cup/180 g butter, softened
- 1⅔ cups/250 g confectioners'/icing sugar
- 6 large egg whites
- 12 strawberries, cut in half

Preheat the oven to 350°F/180°C/gas 4. • Butter a 12-cup mini muffin pan. • Sift the flour and salt into a medium bowl. Stir in the almonds. • Beat the butter and confectioners' sugar in a large bowl with an electric mixer at high speed until creamy. • Mix in the dry ingredients and egg whites. • Pour the batter evenly into the prepared cups and place a slice of strawberry on top of each. • Bake for 25–30 minutes, or until a toothpick inserted into one comes out clean. • Transfer to racks to cool.

GLAZED COFFEE MADELEINES

Makes: 20–24
cookies

Preparation: 25'

Cooking: 10–12'

Level of difficulty: 1

- ½ cup/75 g all-purpose/plain flour
- 2 tbsp unsweetened cocoa powder
- ⅛ tsp baking soda
- ⅛ tsp salt
- 2 large eggs
- 1 tsp freeze-dried coffee granules
- ½ tsp vanilla extract/essence
- 1 cup/150 g confectioners'/icing sugar
- ½ cup/125 g butter, melted
- 2 cups/500 ml Chocolate Frosting (see page 952)

Preheat the oven to 375°F/190°C/gas 5. • Butter two madeleine pans (for 20–24 madeleines). • Sift the flour, cocoa, baking soda, and salt into a medium bowl. • Beat the eggs, coffee granules, and vanilla in a large bowl with an electric mixer at high speed until blended. • Beat in the confectioners' sugar and continue beating until thick. • Mix in the dry ingredients and butter. • Spoon the batter into the prepared cups, filling each three-quarters full. • Bake for 10–12 minutes, or until springy to the touch. • Cool the madeleines in the pans for 15 minutes. • Transfer to racks and let cool completely. Spread with the frosting.

RASPBERRY ALMOND FRIANDS

Preheat the oven to 350°F/180°C/gas 4. •
Butter a 12-cup mini muffin pan. • Sift the flour
and salt into a large bowl. Stir in the almonds. •
Beat the butter and confectioners' sugar in a large
bowl with an electric mixer at high speed until
creamy. • Mix in the dry ingredients and egg
whites. • Pour the batter evenly into the prepared
cups and place a raspberry on top of each. • Bake
for 25–30 minutes, or until a toothpick inserted
into the centers comes out clean. • Transfer to
racks to cool.

Makes: 24 cookies

Preparation: 25'

Cooking: 25–30'

Level of difficulty: 1

- ½ cup/75 g all-purpose/plain flour
- ⅛ tsp salt
- 1¼ cups/180 g finely ground almonds
- ¾ cup/180 g butter, softened
- 1⅔ cups/250 g confectioners'/icing sugar
- 6 large egg whites
- ½ cup/125 g raspberries

BLUEBERRY ALMOND FRIANDS

Makes: 24 cookies

Preparation: 25'

Cooking: 25–30'

Level of difficulty: 1

- ½ cup/75 g all-purpose/plain flour
- ⅛ tsp salt
- 1¼ cups/180 g finely ground almonds
- ¾ cup/180 g butter, softened
- 1⅔ cups/250 g confectioners'/icing sugar
- 6 large egg whites
- ½ cup/125 g blueberries

Preheat the oven to 350°F/180°C/gas 4. • Butter a 12-cup mini muffin pan. • Sift the flour and salt into a medium bowl. Stir in the almonds. • Beat the butter and confectioners' sugar in a large bowl with an electric mixer at high speed until creamy. • Mix in the dry ingredients and egg whites. • Pour the batter evenly into the prepared cups and place some blueberries on top of each. • Bake for 25–30 minutes, or until a toothpick inserted into one comes out clean. • Transfer to racks to cool.

PETIT-FOUR FANCIES

Preheat the oven to 375°F/190°C/gas 5. • Line two 13 x 9-inch (33 x 23-cm) baking pans with parchment paper. • Sift the flour, cornstarch, baking powder, and salt into a large bowl. • Beat the egg yolks and granulated and vanilla sugars in a large bowl with an electric mixer at high speed until pale and thick. • Mix in the dry ingredients. • With mixer at high speed, beat the egg whites in a large bowl until stiff peaks form. • Use a large rubber spatula to fold the beaten whites into the batter. • Spoon half the mixture into a separate bowl. Mix in the cocoa powder and rum. • Mix the orange and lemon zest into the remaining mixture. • Spoon one mixture evenly into each of the prepared pans. • Bake for 12–15 minutes, or until golden brown and springy to the touch. • Cool in the pans for 15 minutes. • Turn out onto a sheet of waxed paper dusted with confectioners' sugar. • Use 1-inch (2.5-cm) cookie cutters to cut out pairs of shapes from each cake. • Stick the cake shapes together in pairs with the preserves. • Mix the confectioners' sugar and lemon juice in a small bowl to make a spreadable icing. • Spoon the icing over the shapes, letting it run down the sides. • Decorate with a combination of the nuts, candies, and marzipan fruits.

Serve as an after-dinner treat with sweet dessert wine.

Makes: 35–40 cookies

Preparation: 50'

Cooking: 12–15'

Level of difficulty: 2

- 1 cup/150 g all-purpose/plain flour
- 1 cup/150 g cornstarch/cornflour
- 1 tsp baking powder
- 1/8 tsp salt
- 6 large eggs, separated
- 3/4 cup/150 g granulated sugar
- 2 tbsp vanilla sugar
- 2 tbsp unsweetened cocoa powder
- 1–2 tbsp dark rum
- 2 tsp finely grated orange zest
- 2 tsp finely grated lemon zest
- 2/3–3/4 cup/220–240 g apricot preserves or jam
- 3 1/3 cups/500 g confectioners'/icing sugar
- 3–4 tbsp fresh lemon juice
- Chopped nuts, sweets, sugar flowers and petals, chocolate flakes, candied fruits and peel, colored sugar crystals, silver balls

NUTTY TARTS

Makes: 24 cookies

Preparation: 45'

Cooking: 10–15'

Level of difficulty: 2

PASTRY
- 1¼ cups/180 g all-purpose/plain flour
- ⅛ tsp salt
- ¼ cup/50 g granulated sugar
- Grated zest of 1 orange
- 4 tbsp butter, cut up
- 1 large egg yolk, lightly beaten

PINE NUT PECAN FILLING
- ¼ cup/50 g granulated sugar
- 1 tbsp water
- ¾ cup/75 g finely chopped pecans
- ¼ cup/30 g pine nuts
- 2 tbsp honey
- 1 tbsp light/single cream

Pastry: Sift the flour and salt into a medium bowl. Stir in the sugar and orange zest. • Use a pastry blender to cut in the butter until the mixture resembles coarse crumbs. • Mix in the egg yolk to form a smooth dough. • Press the dough into a disk, wrap in plastic wrap, and refrigerate for 30 minutes. • Preheat the oven to 350°F/180°C/gas 4. • Butter twenty-four mini-muffin cups. • Roll out the dough on a lightly floured surface to a thickness of ⅛ inch (3 mm). • Use a fluted 2-inch (5-cm) cookie cutter to cut out twenty-four dough rounds. • Press the dough rounds into the prepared cups and prick all over with a fork.
• Bake for 10–15 minutes, or until the pastry is just golden. • Transfer to racks to cool. • Pine Nut Pecan Filling: Mix the sugar with the water in a small saucepan. Wash down the sides of the pan with a pastry brush dipped in cold water to prevent sugar crystals from forming. Cook over low heat until the syrup is golden, about 10 minutes. • Mix in the pecans, pine nuts, honey, and cream until well blended. • Spoon the filling into the cups and let cool completely.

ALMOND TARTLETS

Makes: 12 cookies

Preparation: 30'

Cooking 25–30'

Level of difficulty: 1

Preheat the oven to 350°F/180°C/gas 4. • Set out a 12-cup mini muffin pan. • Roll out the pastry to a thickness of ¹/₄ inch (5 mm). Use a 2-inch (5-cm) cookie cutter to stamp out twelve rounds. • Line the cups with the pastry rounds. • Brush with 1 teaspoon of cherry jelly. • Mix the cake crumbs, almonds, and flour in a medium bowl. • Melt the butter in a small saucepan. • Stir in the sugar and remove from the heat. • Add the egg. • Fold in the dry ingredients and vanilla. • Spoon the mixture into the prepared cups. • Bake for 25–30 minutes, or until golden brown and a toothpick inserted into a center comes out clean. • Turn out of the cups and let cool. • Brush with the apricot jam. • Mix the confectioners' sugar with the water. • Spread with the frosting.

- 4 oz/125 g store-bought flaky pie pastry
- ¹/₄ cup/90 g cherry jelly or cherry jam
- ¹/₄ cup/30 g plain cake crumbs
- ¹/₂ cup/75 g finely ground almonds
- 1 tsp all-purpose/ plain flour
- ¹/₂ cup/125 g butter
- ¹/₂ cup/100 g granulated sugar
- 1 large egg, lightly beaten
- ¹/₂ tsp vanilla extract/essence
- 3 tbsp apricot preserves or jam
- ³/₄ cup/125 g confectioners'/ icing sugar
- 1 tsp warm water or more as needed

Makes: 36 cookies

Preparation: 30' + 30' to chill

Cooking: 12–15' per batch

Level of difficulty: 2

MINI MINCEMEAT TARTLETS

P astry: Sift the flour and salt into a large bowl. • Cut in the butter until the mixture resembles coarse crumbs. • Stir in the almonds and sugar. • Mix in the milk and almond extract to form a soft dough. • Form the dough into two 9-inch (23-cm) logs and refrigerate for 30 minutes. • Mincemeat Topping: Melt the butter with the corn syrup and molasses in a small saucepan. • Mix in the raisins, cake crumbs, candied peel, currants, and allspice. • Add the egg. • Preheat the oven to 375°F/ 190°C/gas 5. • Butter and flour three 12-cup mini muffin pans. • Slice $1/2$ inch (1 cm) thick and press into the cups. • Spoon the topping into the cups. • Bake for 12–15 minutes, or until the pastry is golden. • Cool for 5 minutes. • Mix the confectioners' sugar with enough lemon juice in a small bowl. • Drizzle over the tops of the cookies.

PASTRY

- $1^{1}/_{3}$ cups/200 g all-purpose/plain flour
- $^{1}/_{8}$ tsp salt
- 6 tbsp butter
- 2 tbsp ground almonds
- $^{1}/_{4}$ cup/50 g sugar
- 4 tbsp milk
- $^{1}/_{4}$ tsp almond extract/essence

MINCEMEAT TOPPING

- 2 tbsp butter
- $^{2}/_{3}$ cup/150 ml light corn syrup/ golden syrup
- 2 tbsp light molasses
- $^{1}/_{3}$ cup/40 g golden raisins
- $^{1}/_{4}$ cup/50 g cake crumbs
- 2 tbsp chopped candied peel
- 1 tbsp currants
- $^{1}/_{2}$ tsp allspice
- 1 large egg
- 5 tbsp confectioners'/ icing sugar
- 2 tbsp lemon juice + more as needed

BUCKWHEAT COOKIE CAKES

Makes: 24–30 cookies

Preparation: 25' + 30' to set

Cooking: 20–25'

Level of difficulty: 2

- ²⁄₃ cup/100 g all-purpose/plain flour
- ²⁄₃ cup/100 g buckwheat flour
- 1 tbsp unsweetened cocoa powder
- 1 tsp baking powder
- ¹⁄₈ tsp salt
- 1 tbsp ground almonds
- 6 tbsp butter, softened
- ¹⁄₂ cup/100 g firmly packed soft brown sugar
- 3 large eggs
- 2 tbsp milk
- ¹⁄₂ tsp vanilla or rum extract/essence
- 2 oz/60 g semisweet/dark chocolate, finely grated
- 2 oz/60 g white chocolate, coarsely chopped

Preheat the oven to 350°F/180°C/gas 4. • Butter two 12-cup mini muffin pans. • Sift the all-purpose and buckwheat flours, cocoa, baking powder, and salt into a medium bowl. Stir in the almonds. • Beat the butter and brown sugar in a large bowl with an electric mixer at high speed until creamy. • Add the eggs, milk, and vanilla, beating until just blended. • Mix in the dry ingredients and semisweet chocolate. • Fit a pastry bag with a plain ¹⁄₂-inch (1-cm) tip. Fill the pastry bag, twist the opening tightly closed, and squeeze out small rounds into each prepared cup. • Bake for 20–25 minutes, or until lightly browned and a toothpick inserted in the centers comes out clean. • Cool in the pans for 3 minutes. Transfer to racks and let cool completely. • Melt the white chocolate in a double boiler over barely simmering water. Spoon the chocolate into a small freezer bag and cut off a tiny corner. Pipe chocolate lines over the tops in a decorative manner. Let set for 30 minutes. Transfer to racks to finish cooling.

COFFEE ÉCLAIRS

Makes: 10 éclairs

Preparation: 45' + 15'
to chill

Cooking: 30'

Level of difficulty: 3

Preheat the oven to 425°F/220°C/gas 7. • Line a baking sheet with parchment paper. • Place the pastry in a pastry bag fitted with a $3/4$-inch (2-cm) tip and pipe ten 4-inch (10-cm) strips of pastry onto the sheet. •Brush the egg over the pastry. • Bake for 15 minutes. Reduce the oven temperature to 400°F/200°C/gas 6 and bake for 15 minutes more. • Transfer to racks to cool. • Using a sharp knife, carefully cut each éclair in half lengthwise. • Coffee Cream Filling: Beat the cream, sugar, and coffee granules in a large bowl until stiff. • Coffee Frosting: Mix the confectioners' sugar and coffee in a small bowl. • Place the filling in a pastry bag with a $1/4$-inch (5-mm) tip and cover the bottom half of each éclair with 3 tablespoons of filling. Cover with the top half of the éclair. • Spread the top of each éclair with the frosting. Refrigerate for 15 minutes. Decorate with the coffee beans.

- 1 recipe Choux Pastry (see page 952)
- 1 large egg mixed with 1 tsp water

COFFEE CREAM FILLING
- 2½ cups/625 ml heavy/double cream
- ⅓ cup/70 g granulated sugar
- 1 tbsp freeze-dried coffee granules

COFFEE FROSTING
- 1½ cups/225 g confectioners'/ icing sugar
- 1 tbsp freeze-dried coffee granules, dissolved in 1 tbsp boiling water
- Chocolate-covered coffee beans, to decorate

APRICOT MUFFINS

Makes: about 12 muffins

Preparation: 10'

Cooking: 15–20'

Level of difficulty: 1

- 2 cups/300 g all-purpose/plain flour
- 1 tbsp baking powder
- 1/4 tsp salt
- 2/3 cup/70 g chopped dried apricots
- 3/4 cup/180 ml cold water
- 1/2 cup/125 g butter, cut up
- 3/4 cup/150 g firmly packed brown sugar
- 1/2 cup/125 ml milk
- 1 large egg, lightly beaten
- 2 tsp vanilla extract/essence

Preheat the oven to 350°F/180°C/gas 4. • Butter and flour a 12-cup muffin pan, or line with foil or paper baking cups. • Sift the flour, baking powder, and salt into a large bowl. • Bring the apricots and water in a saucepan over medium heat to a boil. Reduce the heat and simmer for 5 minutes. Remove from the heat and beat in the butter and sugar until the sugar has dissolved. Stir in the milk, eggs, and vanilla. Stir the apricot mixture into the dry ingredients. • Spoon the batter into the prepared cups, filling each 2/3 full. • Bake for 15–20 minutes, or until a toothpick inserted into the center comes out clean. • Cool the muffins on racks.

ORANGE TARTLETS WITH MERINGUE

Pastry: Sift the flour, confectioners' sugar, and salt into a medium bowl. • Cut in the butter until the mixture resembles coarse crumbs. • Add the egg and enough water to form a dough. • Divide the dough in half. Wrap in plastic wrap, and refrigerate for 30 minutes. • Preheat the oven to 400°F/200°C/gas 6. • Set out four 12-cup mini-muffin pans. • Roll out the dough on a lightly floured surface to a thickness of $1/8$ inch (3 mm). • Use a 2-inch (5-cm) round cookie cutter to cut out rounds. • Gather the dough scraps, re-roll, and continue cutting out rounds until there are at least 48 rounds. • Press the rounds into the prepared cups and prick all over with a fork. • Bake for 8–10 minutes, or until the pastry is pale gold. • Cool completely in the pans. • Drop $1/2$ teaspoon of the orange curd into each pastry base. • Meringue Topping: Stir the egg whites, water, cream of tartar, and salt in a double boiler until blended. Cook over low heat, beating constantly with a hand-held electric mixer at low speed until the mixture registers 160°F (71°C) on an instant-read thermometer. Transfer to a bowl and beat at high speed, gradually adding the superfine sugar until stiff peaks form. • Fit a pastry bag with a $1/2$-inch (1-cm) star tip. Fill the pastry bag with the meringue and squeeze over the tarts in a decorative manner. • Bake for 6–8 minutes, or until lightly browned. • Cool completely in the pans. • Decorate with the orange curls and dust with confectioners' sugar.

Makes: 48 cookies

Preparation: 40' + 30' to chill

Cooking: 14–18'

Level of difficulty: 3

- 1$2/3$ cups/250 g all-purpose/plain flour
- 2 tbsp confectioners'/icing sugar
- $1/8$ tsp salt
- $2/3$ cup/150 g butter, cut up
- 1 large egg
- 1–2 tbsp water
- $1/2$ cup/125 ml orange curd

MERINGUE TOPPING

- 2 large egg whites
- 2 tsp water
- $1/8$ tsp cream of tartar
- $1/8$ tsp salt
- $1/2$ cup/100 g superfine/caster sugar
- 1 tsp finely grated orange zest
- curls of orange zest, to decorate
- 1 tbsp confectioners'/icing sugar, to dust

CHOCOLATE MADELEINES

Sift the flour, baking powder, and salt into a medium bowl. • Beat the eggs in a large bowl with an electric mixer at high speed for 3 minutes. • Gradually add the granulated and vanilla sugars, beating until the batter falls off the beaters in ribbons. • Fold in the dry ingredients. • Melt the chocolate with the butter in a double boiler over barely simmering water. • Gently fold in the chocolate mixture. • Refrigerate for 30 minutes. • Let rest at room temperature for 15 minutes. • Preheat the oven to 375°F/190°C/gas 5. • Butter two madeleine pans (for 20–24 madeleines). • Spoon the batter into the prepared pans. • Bake, one pan at a time, for 10–12 minutes, or until brown and springy to the touch. • Cool the madeleines in the pans for 15 minutes. • Transfer to racks to cool. • Dust with confectioners' sugar.

Makes: 20–24 cookies

Preparation: 30' + 45' to chill and rest

Cooking: 10–12' per batch

Level of difficulty: 2

- ³⁄₄ cup/125 g all-purpose/plain flour
- ½ tsp baking powder
- ⅛ tsp salt
- 3 large eggs
- ½ cup/100 g granulated sugar
- 2 tbsp vanilla sugar
- 4 oz/125 g bittersweet/plain chocolate, coarsely chopped
- ½ cup/125 g butter, cut up
- ⅓ cup/50 g confectioners'/icing sugar

BUSY MADELEINES

Makes: 20–24
  cookies

Preparation: 20'

Cooking: 12–15'

Level of difficulty: 1

- ½ cup/75 g all-purpose/plain flour
- 1⅔ cups/250 g confectioners'/icing sugar
- ⅛ tsp salt
- ½ cup/75 g finely ground hazelnuts
- 4 large egg whites
- ¾ cup/180 g butter, melted
- 1 container (8 oz/250 ml) chocolate hazelnut spread (Nutella), softened

Preheat the oven to 375°F/190°C/gas 5. • Butter two madeleine pans (for 20–24 madeleines). • Sift the flour, confectioners' sugar, and salt into a large bowl. • Stir in the hazelnuts. • Beat the egg whites in a large bowl with an electric mixer at high speed until stiff peaks form. • Fold in the dry ingredients, followed by the butter and chocolate hazelnut spread. • Spoon the batter evenly into the prepared pan. • Bake for 12–15 minutes, or until a toothpick inserted into one comes out clean. • Cool the madeleines in the pans for 15 minutes. Transfer to racks and let cool completely.

MINI LEMON PIES

Pastry: Sift the flour, confectioners' sugar, and salt into a medium bowl. • Use a pastry blender to cut in the butter until the mixture resembles coarse crumbs. • Add the egg and enough water to form a stiff dough. • Divide the dough in half. Press the dough into disks, wrap each in plastic wrap, and refrigerate for 30 minutes. • Preheat the oven to 325°F/170°C/gas 3. • Spread the hazelnuts on a large baking sheet. Toast for 7 minutes, or until lightly golden. • Transfer to a large cotton kitchen towel. Fold the towel over the nuts and rub them through the towel to remove the thin inner skins. Pick out the nuts and coarsely chop. • Increase the oven temperature to 375°F/190°C/gas 5. • Set out four 12-cup mini-muffin pans. • Roll out the dough on a lightly floured surface to a thickness of $1/8$ inch (3 mm). • Use a 2-inch (5-cm) round cookie cutter to cut out rounds. • Gather the dough scraps, re-roll, and continue cutting out rounds until there are at least 48 rounds. • Press the rounds into the muffin cups and prick all over with a fork. • Bake, one batch at a time, for 8–10 minutes, or until the pastry is pale gold. • Cool completely in the pans. • Lemon Filling: Mix the lemon curd and cream in a small bowl. Spoon the filling into the pastry bases. • Decorate with the chopped hazelnuts and lemon zest.

Makes: 48 cookies

Preparation: 40' + 30' to chill

Cooking: 8–10'

Level of difficulty: 2

PASTRY
- 1$2/3$ cups/250 g all-purpose/plain flour
- 2 tbsp confectioners'/icing sugar
- $1/8$ tsp salt
- $2/3$ cup/150 g butter, cut up
- 1 large egg
- 1–2 tbsp water

LEMON FILLING
- $1/2$ cup/125 ml lemon curd
- 4 tbsp heavy/double cream
- 1$1/2$ cups/225 g hazelnuts
- Curls of lemon zest, to decorate

868

DUNEDIN MADELEINES

Preheat the oven to 375°F/190°C/gas 5. •
Butter two madeleine pans (for 24 madeleines).
• Sift the flour, baking powder, baking soda, and
salt into a medium bowl. • Beat the eggs and
sugar in a large bowl with an electric mixer at
medium speed until blended. • Mix in the dry
ingredients, followed by the butter, lemon zest and
juice, and vanilla. • Stir in the almonds. • Spoon
the batter into the prepared pans, filling each one
about three-quarters full. • Bake for 10–12
minutes, or until springy to the touch. • Cool the
madeleines in the pans for 15 minutes. • Transfer
to racks and let cool completely.

Makes: 24 cookies

Preparation: 25'

Cooking: 10–12'

Level of difficulty: 1

- ½ cup/75 g all-purpose/plain flour
- ½ tsp baking powder
- ⅛ tsp baking soda
- ⅛ tsp salt
- 2 large eggs
- ½ cup/100 g granulated sugar
- ½ cup/125 g butter, melted
- ½ tsp finely grated lemon zest
- 1 tbsp fresh lemon juice
- ½ tsp vanilla extract/essence
- ¼ cup/30 g finely chopped almonds

CAROLINE BAY MADELEINES

Makes: 20–24
   cookies

Preparation: 20'

Cooking: 12–15'

Level of difficulty: 1

- ⅔ cup/100 g all-purpose/plain flour
- 1⅔ cups/250 g confectioners'/icing sugar
- ⅛ tsp salt
- ½ cup/75 g finely ground pistachios
- 4 large egg whites
- ¾ cup/180 g butter, melted
- 1 tbsp honey
- 1 tsp almond extract/essence

Preheat the oven to 375°F/190°C/gas 5. • Butter two madeleine pans (for 20–24 madeleines). • Sift the flour, confectioners' sugar, and salt into a medium bowl. • Stir in the pistachios. • Beat the egg whites in a large bowl with an electric mixer at high speed until stiff peaks form. • Use a large rubber spatula to fold in the dry ingredients, followed by the butter, honey, and almond extract. • Spoon the batter evenly into the prepared pans. • Bake for 12–15 minutes, or until a toothpick inserted into one comes out clean.
• Cool the madeleines in the pans for 15 minutes.
• Transfer to a rack and let cool completely.

THREE KINGS PALMIERS

Makes: 12 cookies

Preparation: 30'

Cooking: 20–27'

Level of difficulty: 2

- ⅓ cup/70 g superfine/caster sugar
- ½ tsp ground cardamom
- 1 sheet frozen puff pastry (about 8 oz/ 250 g), thawed

Preheat the oven to 350°F/180°C/gas 4. • Butter a cookie sheet. • Stir together the sugar and cardamom in a small bowl. Lightly sprinkle a surface with 1 tablespoon of the sugar mixture. • Unfold or unroll the pastry to an 10-inch (25-cm) square. • Sprinkle with 1 tablespoon of the sugar mixture. •

Mouthwateringly good with a slight Eastern flavor.

Fold the long sides of the pastry over to meet in the center. Sprinkle with 1 tablespoon sugar mixture and fold in half lengthways. • Slice the pastry into 12 portions. • Place the cookies cut-side down 2 inches apart on the prepared cookie sheets. • Sprinkle with the remaining sugar mixture. • Bake for 10–12 minutes, or until just golden. • Transfer to racks to cool.

SNACKING MADELEINES

Makes: 12 cookies

Preparation: 40' + 45' to rest and chill

Cooking: 10–12'

Level of difficulty: 1

Sift the flour, baking powder, and salt into a medium bowl. • Beat the eggs, honey, and granulated sugar in a large bowl with an electric mixer at high speed until pale and thick. • Use a large rubber spatula to fold in the dry ingredients, lemon zest and juice, and vanilla, followed by the butter. • Refrigerate for 30 minutes. • Let rest at room temperature for 15 minutes. • Preheat the oven to 375°F/190°C/gas 5. • Butter a madeleine pan (for 12 madeleines). • Spoon the batter into the prepared pan. • Bake for 10–12 minutes, or until golden brown and springy to the touch. • Cool the madeleines in the pan for 15 minutes. • Transfer to racks and let cool completely. • Dust with confectioners' sugar just before serving

- 1 cup/150 g all-purpose/plain flour
- 1 tsp baking powder
- 1/8 tsp salt
- 2 large eggs
- 1/2 cup/125 ml honey
- 1/4 cup/50 g granulated sugar
- Grated zest of 1 lemon
- 1 tbsp fresh lemon juice
- 1/2 tsp vanilla extract/essence
- 6 tbsp butter, melted
- 1/3 cup/50 g confectioners'/icing sugar

Makes: 24 cookies

Preparation: 30' + 45'
to chill

Cooking: 10–12'

Level of difficulty: 2

- 1 cup/150 g all-purpose/plain flour
- 1 tsp ground cinnamon
- ½ tsp baking powder
- ¼ tsp ground nutmeg
- ⅛ tsp salt
- 3 large eggs
- 1 tsp vanilla extract/essence
- ⅔ cup/170 g granulated sugar
- ½ cup/125 g butter, melted
- ⅓ cup/50 g confectioners'/icing sugar

NUTMEG MADELEINES

S ift the flour, cinnamon, baking powder, nutmeg, and salt into a medium bowl. • Beat the eggs and vanilla in a large bowl with an electric mixer at high speed for 3 minutes. • Gradually add the granulated sugar, beating until the batter falls off the beater in ribbons. • Fold in the dry ingredients and butter. • Refrigerate for 30 minutes. • Let rest at room temperature for 15 minutes. • Preheat the oven to 375°F/190°C/gas 5. • Butter two madeleine pans (for 20–24 madeleines). • Spoon the batter into the prepared pans. • Bake for 10–12 minutes, or until brown and springy to the touch. • Cool the madeleines in the pans for 15 minutes. • Transfer to racks and let cool. • Dust with the confectioners' sugar.

WHITE CHOCOLATE TARTLETS

S ift the flour and salt into a medium bowl. • Beat the butter and sugar in a large bowl with an electric mixer at high speed until creamy. • Add the egg yolk, beating until just blended. • Mix in the dry ingredients. • Cover with plastic wrap and refrigerate for 30 minutes. • Preheat the oven to 350°F/180°C/gas 4. • Set out three 12-cup mini muffin pans. • Form the dough into balls the size of walnuts and press into the cups. • Prick all over with a fork. • Bake, one pan at a time, for 12–15 minutes, or until just golden. • Transfer to racks to cool. • Melt the white chocolate in a double boiler over barely simmering water. Fill each tartlet with the melted chocolate and serve.

Makes: 36 cookies

Preparation: 30' + 30' to chill

Cooking: 12–15' per batch

Level of difficulty: 1

- 1 ³/₄ cups/275 g all-purpose/plain flour
- ¹/₈ tsp salt
- ¹/₂ cup/125 g butter, softened
- ¹/₂ cup/100 g granulated sugar
- 1 large egg yolk
- 3 oz/90 g white chocolate, coarsely chopped

RASPBERRY TARTS

Makes: 12 tartlets

Preparation: 50' + 1 h
to chill

Level of difficulty: 1

S et out the tartlet shells. • Process 1 cup (250 g) raspberries in a food processor until pureed. • Transfer the raspberries to a large bowl and stir in the confectioners' sugar, liqueur, lemon zest and juice, ricotta, and yogurt. • Sprinkle the gelatin over the water in a saucepan. Let stand 1 minute. Stir over low heat until the gelatin has completely dissolved. • Stir the gelatin into the raspberry mixture and refrigerate until thickened. • Beat the cream in a medium bowl with an electric mixer at medium speed until stiff. Fold the cream into the raspberry mixture. • Spoon the raspberry mixture into a pastry bag with a $^1/_4$-inch (5-mm) plain tip. Pipe into the tartlets. Decorate with the raspberries. • Refrigerate for 1 hour before serving.

- 12 store-bought tartlet shells
- 1 cup/250 g raspberries + about 24 extra
- $^2/_3$ cup/100 g confectioners'/ icing sugar
- $^1/_2$ cup/125 ml raspberry (or other berry fruit) liqueur
- Grated zest and juice of 1 lemon
- $^2/_3$ cup/150 g ricotta cheese
- 1 cup/250 ml plain yogurt
- $1^1/_2$ tbsp unflavored gelatin
- 4 tbsp cold water
- $1^1/_2$ cups/375 ml heavy/double cream

PISTACHIO MUFFINS

Makes: 10–12 small cakes

Preparation: 45'

Cooking: 20–25'

Level of difficulty: 1

- 1¼ cups/180 g pistachio nuts, blanched and finely ground
- 1 cup/200 g granulated sugar
- 4 large eggs, separated
- 2 tbsp grated orange zest
- ½ cup/75 g cornstarch/cornflour

Preheat the oven to 325°F/170°C/gas 3. • Butter and flour 10–12 little cake molds (or a muffin tray). • Stir together the ground pistachios and sugar in a large bowl. • Beat the egg whites in a large bowl with an electric mixer at high speed until stiff peaks form. • Stir the egg yolks and orange zest into the pistachio mixture. • Use a large rubber spatula to gradually fold the pistachio mixture into the beaten whites, alternating with the cornstarch. • Spoon the batter into the prepared molds, filling each ¾ full. • Bake for 20–25 minutes, or until a toothpick inserted into the center comes out clean. • Cool the cakes on racks.

MINI REDCURRANT PIES

Pastry: Sift the flour, confectioners' sugar, and salt into a medium bowl. • Use a pastry blender to cut in the butter until the mixture resembles coarse crumbs. • Add the egg and enough water to form a stiff dough. • Divide the dough in half. Press the dough into disks, wrap each in plastic wrap, and refrigerate for 30 minutes. • Preheat the oven to 375°F/190°C/gas 5. • Set out four 12-cup mini-muffin pans. • Roll out the dough on a lightly floured surface to a thickness of $1/8$ inch (3 mm). • Use a 2-inch (5-cm) round cookie cutter to cut out rounds. Gather the dough scraps, re-roll, and continue cutting out until there are at least 48 rounds. • Press the rounds into the prepared cups and prick all over with a fork. • Bake, one pan at a time, for 8–10 minutes, or until the pastry is pale gold. • Cool completely in the pans. • Redcurrant Filling: Bring the redcurrants, sugar, and water to a boil in a medium saucepan over medium heat. • Simmer for 5–7 minutes, or until tender. • Transfer to a food processor or blender and process until pureed. • Mix the custard powder with enough water to form a smooth paste and stir into the puree. • Return the mixture to the saucepan and bring to a boil over medium heat, stirring constantly. • Spoon the filling into the pastry bases and refrigerate for 1 hour

Makes: 48 cookies

Preparation: 45' + 90' to chill

Cooking: 8–10' per batch

Level of difficulty: 2

PASTRY
- 1⅔ cups/250 g all-purpose/plain flour
- 2 tbsp confectioners'/icing sugar
- ⅛ tsp salt
- ⅔ cup/150 g butter, cut up
- 1 large egg
- 1–2 tbsp water

REDCURRANT FILLING
- 2 cups/500 g redcurrants
- 1½ cups/300 g granulated sugar
- 1⅓ cups/330 ml water
- ⅔ cup/100 g custard powder
- 2–4 tbsp water

BUTTERFLY CAKES

Makes: 20–24 fairy cakes

Preparation: 15'

Cooking: 10–15'

Level of difficulty: 1

Preheat the oven to 350°F/180°C/gas 4. • Arrange 20–24 foil baking cups on baking sheets. • Sift the flour, baking powder, and salt into a medium bowl. • Beat the butter, sugar, and vanilla in a large bowl with an electric mixer at medium speed until creamy. • Add the eggs, one at a time, until just blended after each addition. • With mixer at low speed, gradually beat in the dry ingredients, alternating with the milk and lemon juice. • Spoon the batter into the baking cups, filling them half full. • Bake for 10–15 minutes, or until golden brown. • Cool the cakes on racks. • With mixer at high speed, beat the cream in a medium bowl until stiff. • Cut a small circle about $^1/_2$-inch (1-cm) deep from the top of each cake. Fill with $^1/_2$ teaspoon of jam and 1 teaspoon of whipped cream. Cut the tops in half and arrange like butterfly wings.

- 2 cups/300 g all-purpose/plain flour
- 2 tsp baking powder
- $^1/_4$ tsp salt
- $^2/_3$ cup/150 g butter, softened
- $^3/_4$ cup/150 g granulated sugar
- 1 tsp vanilla extract/essence
- 2 large eggs, at room temperature
- $^1/_2$ cup/125 ml milk
- 1 tbsp fresh lemon juice
- $^1/_2$ cup/160 g strawberry jam
- 1 cup/250 ml heavy/double cream

LEMON RAISIN ROCK CAKES

Makes: about 12–15 cakes

Preparation: 10'

Cooking: 15–20'

Level of difficulty: 1

- 1½ cups/225 ml all-purpose/plain flour
- 6 tbsp butter, melted
- 1 tbsp grated lemon zest
- 2 tsp baking powder
- 1 large egg, lightly beaten
- ⅓ cup/70 g granulated sugar
- 2 tbsp fresh lemon juice
- ⅔ cup/120 g raisins
- 2 tbsp raw or coarse sugar

Preheat the oven to 375°F/190°C/gas 5. • Butter a baking sheet. • Beat the flour, butter, lemon zest, and baking powder in a large bowl with an electric mixer at medium speed until well blended. • Add the egg, sugar, lemon juice, and raisins. • Drop heaping tablespoons of the batter onto the prepared sheet, spacing them 2 inches (5 cm) apart. Sprinkle with the sugar. • Bake for 15–20 minutes, or until golden brown. • Cool the cakes on racks.

Makes: 24 cookies

Preparation: 1 h + 30'
to chill

Cooking: 15–20'

Level of difficulty: 2

- 1⅓ cups/200 g all-
  purpose/plain flour
- ⅛ tsp salt
- 6 tbsp butter, cut
  up
- ⅓ cup/50 g finely
  ground hazelnuts
- ⅓ cup/70 g
  granulated sugar
- 1 tbsp vanilla sugar
- 2–3 tbsp water

Almond Rum Filling

- 3 tbsp butter,
  softened
- ¼ cup/50 g firmly
  packed light brown
  sugar
- 1 large egg + 1 egg
  yolk
- ¼ tsp almond
  extract/essence
- ⅓ cup/50 g all-
  purpose/plain flour
- ⅔ cup/100 g finely
  ground almonds
- 3 tbsp milk
- 1 tbsp rum
- ¼ cup/90 g apricot
  preserves or jam

ALMOND RUM TARTS

Sift the flour and salt into a medium bowl. • Use
a pastry blender to cut in the butter until the
mixture resembles coarse crumbs. • Mix in the
hazelnuts and granulated and vanilla sugars. • Mix
in enough water to form a soft, but not sticky,
dough. • Press the dough into a disk, wrap in
plastic wrap, and refrigerate for 30 minutes. •
Preheat the oven to 375°F/190°C/gas 5. • Set out
two 12-cup mini-muffin pans. • Almond Rum Filling:
Beat the butter and brown sugar in a large bowl
with an electric mixer at high speed until creamy. •
Add the whole egg and almond extract, beating
until just blended. • Mix in the flour, almonds,
2 tablespoons milk, and rum. • Roll out the dough
on a lightly floured surface to a thickness of
⅛ inch (3 mm). • Use a 2½-inch (6-cm) fluted
cookie cutter to cut out twenty-four rounds. Press
the dough circles into the prepared cups. • Gather
the dough scraps and re-roll. Use a 1-inch (2.5-cm)
star-shaped cookie cutter to cut out twenty-four
small stars. • Drop ½ teaspoon of the apricot
preserves into each pastry base and spoon in the
filling. • Place the pastry stars lightly on top of the
filling. • Beat the remaining egg yolk with the
remaining milk and brush over the stars. • Bake for
15–20 minutes, or until the pastry is pale golden
and the filling has set. • Cool completely before
removing from the pans.

ANISEED DREAMS

Preheat the oven to 325°F/170°C/gas 3. • Spread the nuts on a large baking sheet. • Toast for 7 minutes, or until lightly golden. • Increase the oven temperature to 375°F/190°C/gas 5. • Line a cookie sheet with rice paper. • Transfer the almonds to a food processor, add the sugar, and process until finely ground. • Mix the almond mixture and flour in a medium bowl. • Beat the egg whites and salt in a large bowl until stiff peaks form. • Fold in the dry ingredients and almond extract. • Fit a pastry bag with a 1-inch (2.5-cm) plain tip. Fill the pastry bag, twist the opening tightly closed, and squeeze out 1-inch (2.5-cm) stars spacing 1 inch (2.5 cm) apart on the prepared cookie sheet. Sprinkle with the aniseeds. • Bake for 12–15 minutes, or until pale gold. • Let cool completely.

Makes: 20–25 cookies

Preparation: 30'

Cooking: 12–15'

Level of difficulty: 1

- ¾ cup/125 g blanched almonds
- 1 cup/200 g granulated sugar
- 2 tbsp all-purpose/plain flour
- 2 large egg whites
- ⅛ tsp salt
- ¼ tsp almond extract/essence
- 1 tbsp ground aniseeds

COFFEE RAISIN COOKIES

Makes: 24 cookies

Preparation: 10'

Cooking: 12–15'

Level of difficulty: 1

- 2/3 cup/100 g all-purpose/plain flour
- 1 tsp baking powder
- 1/4 cup/45 g golden raisins/sultanas
- 1/2 cup/125 g butter, softened
- 1/2 cup/100 g granulated sugar
- 1 tbsp coffee extract/essence
- 2 large eggs
- 1/2 cup/75 g confectioners'/icing sugar
- 2–3 tbsp boiling water

Preheat the oven to 400°F/200°C/gas 6. • Set out about twenty-four mini-cupcake paper cups on a baking sheet. • Stir together the flour and baking powder in a medium bowl. Stir in the raisins. • Beat the butter, sugar, and 2 teaspoons of the coffee extract in a large bowl with an electric mixer at medium speed until creamy. • Add the eggs, one at a time, until just blended after each addition. • With mixer at low speed, gradually add the dry ingredients. • Drop heaping teaspoons of the mixture into the baking cups. • Bake for 12–15 minutes, or until a toothpick inserted into the centers comes out clean. • Cool the cookies completely on a rack. • Sift the confectioners' sugar into a medium bowl and add the remaining coffee extract and enough water to make a soft frosting. Frost the top of each cookie.

PARTY
COOKIES

HONEY BEE COOKIES

Makes: 28 cookies

Preparation: 25'

Cooking: 15–20'

Level of difficulty: 2

- 1¼ cups/180 g whole-wheat flour
- ½ tsp baking powder
- ⅛ tsp salt
- 2 tbsp honey
- 6 tbsp extra-virgin olive oil
- ½ tsp vanilla extract/essence
- 1 large egg
- 1–2 tbsp milk (optional)
- ⅓ cup/50 g confectioners'/icing sugar

Preheat the oven to 350°F/180°C/gas 4. • Butter two cookie sheets. • Sift the flour, baking powder, and salt into a medium bowl. • Mix the honey and olive oil in a large bowl until well blended. • Add the vanilla and egg, beating until just blended. • Mix in the dry ingredients to form a soft dough. • If the dough is stiff, add the milk. • Fit a pastry bag with ½-inch (1-cm) star tip. Fill the pastry bag, twist the opening tightly closed, and squeeze out small heaps, spacing 2 inches (5 cm) apart on the prepared cookie sheet. • Bake for 15–20 minutes, or until lightly browned. • Transfer to racks to cool. • Dust with the confectioners' sugar.

CHRISTMAS BAUBLES

Makes: 35–40 cookies

Preparation: 50'

Cooking: 30–40'

Level of difficulty: 2

Preheat the oven to 300°F/150°C/gas 3. • Line three cookie sheets with parchment paper. • Beat the egg whites in a large bowl until frothy. • Gradually add in the confectioners' sugar until stiff, glossy peaks form. Set aside two heaped tablespoons of the meringue in a small bowl. • Fold in the almonds, flour, cinnamon, almond extract, and salt into the remaining meringue mixture. • Form the dough into small balls and place 1 inch (2.5 cm) apart on the prepared cookie sheet. • Coat each cookie top with the reserved meringue. • Bake for 30–40 minutes, or until just golden. • Cool on the sheets until the cookies firm slightly. Transfer to racks and let cool completely. • Frosting: Mix the confectioners' sugar and water in two separate bowl. Add drops of each food coloring to each bowl. Drizzle over the tops of the cookies.

- 3 large egg whites
- 1⅔ cups/250 g confectioners'/icing sugar
- 1½ cups/225 g finely ground almonds
- 2 tbsp all-purpose/plain flour
- 2 tsp ground cinnamon
- ¼ tsp almond extract/essence
- ⅛ tsp salt

Frosting
- ½ cup/75 g confectioners'/icing sugar
- 4 tbsp hot water
- 2–3 drops red and green food coloring

| Makes: 16–25 bars |
| Preparation: 20' |
| Cooking: 30–35' |
| Level of difficulty: 1 |

CHRISTMAS PECAN BARS

- 1 cup/150 g all-purpose/plain flour
- ½ tsp ground cinnamon
- ⅛ tsp salt
- 4 tbsp butter, melted
- ¾ cup/150 g granulated sugar
- 1 large egg, lightly beaten
- ⅔ cup/70 g finely chopped pecans
- ½ cup/125 g fresh or frozen cranberries
- 2 tbsp confectioners'/icing sugar, to dust

Preheat the oven to 350°F/180°C/gas 4. • Butter a 9-inch (23-cm) square baking pan. • Sift the flour, cinnamon, and salt into a medium bowl. • Mix the butter and sugar in a medium bowl. • Add the egg, beating until just blended. • Mix in the dry ingredients, pecans, and cranberries until well blended. • Spread the mixture in the prepared pan. • Bake for 30–35 minutes, or until just golden and a toothpick inserted into the center comes out clean. • Cool completely in the pan. • Dust with the confectioners' sugar and cut into squares.

PRETTY PINK TWISTS

Makes:	20–25 cookies
Preparation:	30'
Cooking:	10–12' per batch
Level of difficulty:	1

Preheat the oven to 350°F/180°C/gas 4. • Set out two cookie sheets. • Sift the flour and salt into a large bowl. • Beat the confectioners' sugar and butter in a large bowl with an electric mixer at high speed until creamy. • Add the egg and peppermint and vanilla extracts, beating until just blended. • Mix in the dry ingredients. • Divide the dough between two bowls. • Mix the crushed candy into one bowl and the food coloring into the other bowl until well blended. • Form tablespoons of the candy dough into 4-inch (10-cm) ropes. Repeat with the colored dough. • Twist one candy dough rope and one colored dough rope together to form a striped rope. • Shape one end of the rope into a curve to resemble a candy cane and place 2 inches (5 cm) apart on the prepared cookie sheets. • Bake for 10–12 minutes, or until firm to the touch. • Transfer to racks to cool.

- 1½ cups/225 g all-purpose/plain flour
- ¼ tsp salt
- ⅔ cup/100 g confectioners'/icing sugar
- ⅔ cup/150 g butter, softened
- 1 large egg
- 1 tsp peppermint extract/essence
- ½ tsp vanilla extract/essence
- ¼ cup/50 g crushed red-and-white candy canes
- Few drops red food coloring

PINWHEEL COOKIES

Makes: 24–28 cookies

Preparation: 40' + 30' to chill

Cooking: 10–12'

Level of difficulty: 1

- 2½ cups/425 g all-purpose/plain flour
- ½ tsp baking soda
- 1 tsp ground cinnamon
- ⅛ tsp salt
- 1 cup/250 g butter, softened
- 6 tbsp granulated sugar
- ⅔ cup/100 g finely ground almonds
- ½ cup/90 g dried currants
- 2 tsp caraway seeds (optional)
- 1 large egg, lightly beaten
- 2 tsp water

Sift the flour, baking soda, cinnamon, and salt into a large bowl. • Cut in the butter until the mixture resembles fine crumbs. • Stir in the ½ cup (100 g) sugar, almonds, currants, caraway seeds, if using. • Add the egg and mix until firm. • Refrigerate for 30 minutes. • Preheat the oven to 400°F/200°C/gas 6. • Butter two cookie sheets. • Roll out the dough to an 8 x 6-inch (20 x 15-cm) rectangle. • Brush lightly with water. Sprinkle with the remaining sugar. • Cut the dough into ½ x 6-inch (1 x 15-cm) long strips and shape into rounded ropes. Form each rope into a tight circular coil in a circular manner. Transfer the cookies to the prepared cookie sheets, flattening them slightly. • Bake for 10–12 minutes, or until golden brown. • Transfer to racks to cool.

VALENTINE CARD COOKIES

Makes: 6–8 cookies

Preparation: 45' + 30' to chill

Cooking: 10–15'

Level of difficulty: 1

- 2 1/3 cups/350 g all-purpose flour
- 2 tsp ground cinnamon
- 1 tsp baking soda
- 1/2 tsp ground cloves
- 1/8 tsp salt
- 1/2 cup/125 g butter, cut up
- 2/3 cup/140 g granulated sugar
- 4 tbsp light molasses/treacle
- 1 tbsp finely grated lemon zest
- 1 large egg, lightly beaten
- Colored candy writers, to decorate

Sift the flour, cinnamon, baking soda, cloves, and salt into a medium bowl. • Use a pastry blender to cut in the butter until the mixture resembles fine crumbs. • Stir in the sugar, molasses, lemon zest, and egg to form a stiff dough. • Press the dough into a disk, wrap in plastic wrap, and refrigerate for 30 minutes. • Preheat the oven to 375°F/190°C/gas 5. • Butter a cookie sheet. • Roll out the dough on a lightly floured surface to a thickness of 1/4 inch (5 mm). • Use a 4-inch (10-cm) heart-shaped cookie cutter to cut out the cookies. Gather the dough scraps, re-roll, and continue cutting out cookies until all the dough is used. • Use a spatula to transfer the cookies to the prepared cookie sheet, placing them 1 inch (2.5 cm) apart. • Bake for 10–15 minutes, or until lightly browned. • Transfer to racks to cool. • Use various colored candy writers to pipe a message onto each cookie.

JAM STARS

Makes: 24–36
  cookies

Preparation: 50' + 30'
  to chill

Cooking: 8–10'

Level of difficulty: 2

Sift the flour and salt into a large bowl. • Stir in the granulated and vanilla sugars. • Cut in the butter until the mixture resembles coarse crumbs. • Mix in the egg and egg yolks and vanilla. • Divide the dough in half. • Wrap in plastic wrap and refrigerate for 30 minutes. • Preheat the oven to 350°F/180°C/gas 4. • Roll out the dough to a thickness of $1/8$ inch (3 mm). • Use differently sized (1-, $1^1/2$-, and 2-inch (2.5–5-cm) star cutters to cut out the cookies. Continue cutting out cookies until all the dough is used. • Transfer the cookies to cookie sheets, placing them 1 inch (2.5 cm) apart. • Refrigerate for 10 minutes. • Bake for 8–12 minutes, or until just golden. • Transfer to racks and let cool completely. • Stick the differently sized cookies together with the preserves—the largest at the bottom, the smallest on top. • Dust with the confectioners' sugar.

- 3 cups/450 g all-purpose/plain flour
- $1/8$ tsp salt
- 1 cup/200 g granulated sugar
- $1/4$ cup/50 g vanilla sugar
- $1/2$ cup/125 g butter, cut up
- 1 large egg + 3 large egg yolks
- 1 tsp vanilla extract/essence
- 3 tbsp damson plum or raspberry preserves
- $1/2$ cup/75 g confectioners'/icing sugar

Makes: 36 cookies
Preparation: 35' + 30' to chill
Cooking: 12–15' per batch
Level of difficulty: 1

- 1 cup/250 g butter, softened
- 1³⁄₄ cups/275 g confectioners'/icing sugar
- 2¹⁄₂ cups/425 g all-purpose/plain flour
- 1 tsp vanilla extract/essence
- 1 tsp almond extract/essence
- 1 cup/100 g finely chopped pecans

SOFT PECAN WEDDING CAKES

Beat the butter and ³⁄₄ cup (125 g) confectioners' sugar in a large bowl with an electric mixer at high speed until creamy. • Mix in the flour, vanilla and almond extracts, and pecans. • Refrigerate for 30 minutes. • Preheat the oven to 350°F/180°C/gas 4. • Butter three cookie sheets. • Form the dough into balls the size of walnuts and place 2 inches (5 cm) apart on the prepared cookie sheets. • Use the bottom of a glass to flatten them slightly. • Bake, one sheet at a time, for 12–15 minutes, or until lightly browned. • Transfer to racks and let cool completely. • Roll in the remaining confectioners' sugar until well coated.

DECORATED COOKIES

Sift the flour, baking soda, and salt into a medium bowl. • Use a pastry blender to cut in the butter until the mixture resembles fine crumbs. • Stir in the brown sugar. • Add the honey and enough egg to form a stiff dough. • Press the dough into a disk, wrap in plastic wrap, and refrigerate for 30 minutes. • Preheat the oven to 375°F/190°C/gas 5. • Butter two cookie sheets. • Roll out the dough on a lightly floured surface to a thickness of $^1/4$ inch (5 mm). • Use various shaped cookie cutters to cut out the cookies. • Gather the dough scraps, re-roll, and continue cutting out cookies until all the dough is used. • Use a spatula to transfer the cookies to the prepared cookie sheets, placing them 1 inch (2.5 cm) apart. • Bake for 7–10 minutes, or until pale gold. • Transfer to racks to cool. • Spread the tops of the cookies with the preserves. • Roll out the fondant on a surface lightly dusted with confectioners' sugar to a thickness of $^1/4$ inch (5 mm). • Cut out the same shapes to top the cookies with the fondant. Place the matching shape of icing on top of each cookie. • Use a paint brush to decorate the tops of the cookies with the food colorings.

An ideal way to spend a rainy afternoon with your children.

900

Makes: 25–30 cookies

Preparation: 50' + 30' to chill

Cooking: 7–10'

Level of difficulty: 2

- $^1/2$ cup/75 g all-purpose/plain flour
- $^1/4$ tsp baking soda
- $^1/8$ tsp salt
- 2 tbsp butter, softened
- $^1/4$ cup/50 g firmly packed light brown sugar
- 1 tbsp honey
- 1 large egg, lightly beaten
- $^1/4$ cup/90 g apricot preserves or jam
- 7 oz/200 g ready-to-roll fondant icing
- few drops various food colorings

TRICK OR TREATERS

Makes: 12–16 cookies

Preparation: 25' + 30' to chill

Cooking: 10–15'

Level of difficulty: 2

- 1½ cups/225 g all-purpose/plain flour
- ¼ tsp baking soda
- ¼ tsp salt
- ½ cup/125 g butter, softened
- ½ cup/100 g firmly packed light brown sugar
- 1 large egg
- 2 oz/60 g semisweet/dark chocolate, coarsely chopped
- 7 oz/200 g store-bought ready-to-roll white fondant
- 2 drops orange food coloring (or red and yellow)

Sift the flour, baking soda, and salt into a medium bowl. • Beat the butter and brown sugar in a large bowl until creamy. • Add the egg, beating until just blended. • Melt the chocolate in a double boiler over barely simmering water. • Stir the melted chocolate into the butter mixture. • Mix in the dry ingredients to form a stiff dough. • Press the dough into a disk, wrap in plastic wrap, and refrigerate for 30 minutes. • Preheat the oven to 350°F/180°C/gas 4. • Butter two cookie sheets. • Roll out the dough on a lightly floured surface to a thickness of ¼ inch (5 mm). • Use a 3-inch (8-cm) cookie cutter to cut out the cookies. Continue cutting out cookies until all the dough is used. • Transfer the cookies to the prepared cookie sheets, placing them 1 inch (2.5 cm) apart. • Bake for 10–15 minutes, or until just golden. • Transfer to racks and let cool completely. • Knead the white fondant frosting until malleable. • Divide the fondant into two portions. • Place one portion in a bowl and mix in the orange food coloring until no white streaks remain. • Roll out the plain fondant on a surface lightly dusted with confectioners' sugar to a thickness of ⅛ inch (3 mm). • Use the cookie cutter to cut out enough fondant rounds to cover half the cookies. • Brush the fondant rounds with water. • Place wet-side down on top of half the cookies. • Repeat with the orange fondant and place on top of the remaining cookies. • Use an edible black candy writer to draw spooky designs.

PINEAPPLE COOKIES

Preheat the oven to 350°F/180°C/gas 4. • Set out a 9 x 5-inch (23 x 12-cm) loaf pan. • Beat the egg and sugar in a large bowl with an electric mixer at high speed until creamy. • Mix in the pecans, pineapple, coconut, and vanilla until well blended. • Turn the mixture into the pan, smoothing the top. • Bake for 15–20 minutes, or until lightly browned. • Use a wooden spoon to mix the mixture after removing it from the oven. • Cool completely in the pan. • Form the mixture into balls the size of walnuts and roll in the confectioners' sugar.

Makes: 18–20 cookies

Preparation: 25'

Cooking: 25–30'

Level of difficulty: 1

- **1 large egg, lightly beaten**
- **½ cup/100 g granulated sugar**
- **½ cup/50 g coarsely chopped pecans**
- **½ cup/50 g coarsely chopped crystallized pineapple**
- **½ cup/60 g shredded coconut, toasted**
- **½ tsp vanilla extract/essence**
- **⅓ cup/50 g confectioners'/ icing sugar, to dust**

Makes: 25–30
cookies

Preparation: 1 h + 1 h
to chill

Cooking: 10–15'

Level of difficulty: 1

- 4 tbsp butter
- 1 tbsp honey
- 1/3 cup/70 g light brown sugar
- 1 1/2 cups/225 g all-purpose/plain flour
- 2 tsp ground cinnamon
- 1 tsp ground ginger
- 1/2 tsp baking soda
- 1/8 tsp salt
- 3 tbsp milk
- 1 large egg, separated
- 2 tbsp very finely chopped candied red and green cherries

CHRISTMAS COOKIES

Melt the butter with the honey and brown sugar in a small saucepan. Let cool slightly. • Sift the flour, cinnamon, ginger, baking soda, and salt into a medium bowl. Mix in the butter mixture, milk, and egg yolk until stiff. Refrigerate for 1 hour. • Preheat the oven to 350°F/180°C/gas 4. • Butter two cookie sheets. • Roll out the dough to a thickness of 1/4 inch (5 mm). • Use a 2-inch (5-cm) star-shaped cookie cutter to cut out the cookies. • Place 1 inch (2.5 cm) apart on the sheets. • Lightly beat the egg white and brush over the tops of the cookies. Sprinkle with the cherries. • Make a hole in one point of each cookie. • Bake for 10–15 minutes, or until golden. • Let cool completely. • Thread ribbons through the holes and hang on the Christmas tree.

FLY TRAP COOKIES

Prepare the cookies and let cool completely. • Fondant: Bring the sugar, water, and cream of tartar to a boil in a medium saucepan. Wash down the sides of the pan with a pastry brush dipped in cold water to prevent sugar crystals from forming. Cook, without stirring, until the mixture reaches 238°F (114°C), or the soft-ball stage. • Sprinkle a lightly oiled baking sheet with cold water. Pour the fondant syrup onto the sheet and let cool until warm, 10–15 minutes. When ready, the fondant should hold an indentation made with a fingertip. • Work the fondant, lifting from the edges toward the center, folding it until it begins to thicken, lose its gloss, and turn pure white. • Dust your hands with confectioners' sugar and knead the fondant until smooth. Place in a bowl and cover with a clean cloth. Let stand overnight. • Knead the fondant until malleable. Roll out on a surface lightly dusted with confectioners' sugar to a thickness of $1/4$ inch (5 mm). • Drape the fondant over the cookies and cut out the fondant to fit the tops of the cookies. • Warm the preserves in a small saucepan over low heat until liquid. • Spread the preserves over the cookies and place the fondant layers on top. • Melt the chocolate in a double boiler over barely simmering water. • Spoon the chocolate into a freezer bag and cut off a tiny corner. • Pipe over the cookies in concentric circles. • Let stand for 5 minutes until set. • Draw through the lines from the center outward to create a spider's web effect.

Makes 30 cookies

Preparation: 1 h

Cooking: 8–10'

Level of difficulty: 3

- **30 Best Sugar Cookies (see page 495)**

FONDANT

- **2 cups/400 g granulated sugar**
- **$3/4$ cup/180 ml cold water**
- **$1/4$ tsp cream of tartar**
- **2 tbsp confectioners'/ icing sugar, to dust**
- **$1/2$ cup/160 g apricot preserves**
- **4 oz/125 g bittersweet/plain chocolate, coarsely chopped**

HAMANTASCHEN

Beat the shortening and $^1/_2$ cup (100 g) sugar in a large bowl with an electric mixer at high speed until creamy. • Add 2 eggs, beating until just blended. • Stir in the honey, 1 tablespoon lemon juice, water, and vanilla. • Mix in the flour to form a smooth dough. Press into a disk, cover with plastic wrap, and refrigerate for 30 minutes. • Preheat the oven to 375°F/190°C/gas 5. • Butter three cookie sheets. • Chop the prunes coarsely. • Mix the prunes, walnuts, remaining 1 tablespoon lemon juice, 1 teaspoon cinnamon, and 1 tablespoon sugar in a small bowl. • Roll out the dough on a lightly floured surface to a thickness of $^1/_4$ inch (5 mm). • Use a 3-inch (8-cm) cookie cutter to cut out the cookies. Gather the dough scraps, re-roll, and continue cutting out cookies until all the dough is used. • Drop teaspoons of the prune mixture into the center of the cookies. • Lift up three sides of each circle to form a triangular shape, pinching the edges of the dough together to seal. • Beat the remaining egg and brush over the cookies. Mix the remaining sugar and 1 teaspoon cinnamon and sprinkle over the cookies. • Use a spatula to transfer the cookies to the cookie sheets, placing them 2 inches (5 cm) apart. • Bake, one sheet at a time, for 12–15 minutes, or until just golden at the edges. • Transfer to racks and let cool completely.

Makes: 40–45 cookies

Preparation: 25' + 30' to chill

Cooking: 12–15' per batch

Level of difficulty: 2

- 1½ cups/375 g vegetable shortening
- 1 cup/200 g granulated sugar
- 3 large eggs
- 3 tbsp honey
- 2 tbsp lemon juice
- 6 tbsp cold water
- ½ tsp vanilla extract/essence
- 4 cups/600 g all-purpose/plain flour
- 1 lb/500 g dried pitted prunes, soaked overnight and drained
- 1¼ cups/125 g coarsely chopped walnuts
- 2 tsp ground cinnamon

FESTIVE WALNUT CRANBERRY BARS

Preheat the oven to 350°F/180°C/gas 4. •
Butter a 9-inch (23-cm) baking pan. • Sift the
flour and salt into a medium bowl. • Mix the butter
and sugar in a medium bowl. • Add the egg,
beating until just blended. • Mix in the dry
ingredients, walnuts, and cranberries. • Spread the
mixture in the prepared pan. • Bake for 30–35
minutes, or until golden and a toothpick inserted
into the center comes out clean. • Cool completely
in the pan. • Cut into squares. • Mix the
confectioners' sugar and water in a small bowl.
Add the food coloring until well blended. Drizzle the
glaze over the tops of the cookies.

Makes: 16–25 bars

Preparation: 20'

Cooking: 30–35'

Level of difficulty: 1

- 1¼ cups/180 g all-purpose/plain flour
- ⅛ tsp salt
- ½ cup/125 g butter, melted
- ¾ cup/150 g granulated sugar
- 1 large egg, lightly beaten
- ⅔ cup/70 g finely chopped walnuts
- ½ cup/125 g fresh or frozen cranberries
- 1 cup/150 g confectioners'/icing sugar
- 2–3 tbsp hot water
- 2–3 drops red food coloring

PASSOVER COOKIES

Makes: 36–45 bars

Preparation: 25'

Cooking: 30–35'

Level of difficulty: 1

Preheat the oven to 325°F/170°C/gas 3. • Oil a 13 x 9-inch (33 x 23-cm) baking pan. • Beat the eggs and sugar in a large bowl with an electric mixer at high speed until pale and thick. • Beat in the oil until well blended. • Mix in the matzo meal and cocoa. • Pour the batter into the prepared pan and sprinkle with the pecans. • Bake for 30–35 minutes, or until dry on top and almost firm to the touch. Do not overbake. • Cool completely before cutting into bars.

- **5 large eggs**
- **2½ cups/500 g granulated sugar**
- **1¼ cups/310 ml vegetable oil**
- **1¼ cups/180 g matzo meal**
- **1½ cups/225 g unsweetened cocoa powder**
- **1¼ cups/125 g finely chopped pecans**

Makes: 24 cookies

Preparation: 40'

Cooking: 10–12'

Level of difficulty: 1

- 1⅓ cups/200 g all-purpose/plain flour
- ⅛ tsp salt
- ½ cup/125 g butter, softened
- 6 tbsp granulated sugar
- 1 large egg, separated
- 1 tsp finely grated orange zest
- 3 green candied cherries and 3 red candied cherries, finely chopped, to decorate

CHRISTMAS RINGS

Preheat the oven to 400°F/200°C/gas 6. • Butter two cookie sheets. • Sift the flour and salt into a medium bowl. • Beat the butter and ¼ cup (50 g) sugar in a large bowl with an electric mixer at high speed until creamy. • Add the egg yolk, beating until just blended. • Mix in the dry ingredients and orange zest. • Form tablespoons of the dough into 6-inch (15-cm) ropes. • Shape into circles with slightly overlapping ends and place 1 inch (2.5 cm) apart on the sheets. • Brush with the egg white and sprinkle with the remaining sugar. • Decorate with the cherries. • Bake for 10–12 minutes, or until lightly browned. • Cool on the sheets until the cookies firm slightly. Transfer to racks and let cool.

CHRISTMAS BUTTER COOKIES

Preheat the oven to 325°F/170°C/gas 3. • Set out two cookie sheets. • Sift the flour, cinnamon, and salt into a large bowl. • Use a pastry blender to cut in the butter until the mixture resembles coarse crumbs. • Stir in $^2/_3$ cup (140 g) sugar and the coffee. • Press the dough into a disk and knead it lightly. • Place the hazelnuts on a large plate. • Form the dough into balls the size of walnuts and roll in the hazelnuts until well coated. • Place the cookies 1 inch (2.5 cm) apart on the cookie sheets, flattening them slightly. Sprinkle with the remaining sugar. • Bake for 20–25 minutes, or until faintly tinged with brown on top and slightly darker at the edges. • Cool on the sheets until the cookies firm slightly. • Transfer to racks to finish cooling.

Makes: 30–34 cookies

Preparation: 25'

Cooking: 20–25'

Level of difficulty: 1

- 1½ cups/225 g all-purpose/plain flour
- ½ tsp ground cinnamon
- ⅛ tsp salt
- ⅔ cup/140 g + 2 tbsp granulated sugar
- 2 tsp freeze-dried coffee granules, dissolved in 1 tbsp hot water
- 1 cup/250 g butter, cut up
- 2 cups/200 g coarsely chopped toasted hazelnuts

BOWTIE COOKIE

Makes: 1 large cookie

Preparation: 30'

Cooking: 8–10'

Level of difficulty: 2

- 6 tbsp butter, softened
- ¾ cup/125 g confectioners'/icing sugar
- 4 large egg whites, lightly beaten
- ½ cup/75 g all-purpose/plain flour
- ⅛ tsp salt
- 1 tbsp unsweetened cocoa powder

Preheat the oven to 400°F/200°C/gas 6. • Butter a cookie sheet. • Use a pencil and ruler to draw a 12 x 8-inch (30 x 20-cm) rectangle on a sheet of parchment paper. Draw triangles, points facing inward, at each end of the rectangle to resemble a double-edged bowtie. Cut out the template. • Place the template on the prepared cookie sheet. • Beat the butter and confectioners' sugar in a large bowl with an electric mixer at high speed until creamy. • Stir in the egg whites, followed by the flour and salt. • If the mixture separates, place over barely simmering water and mix. • Set aside 2 tablespoons of the mixture. Stir the cocoa into the remaining batter. • Use a thin metal spatula to spread a small amount of plain cookie batter around the inside edge of the template to form a border. • Spread the remaining plain batter in the center of the template. • Spoon the cocoa batter into a small plastic freezer bag. Cut off the corner and pipe over the edges. • Bake for 8–10 minutes, or until just golden. • Use a spatula to loosen the edges and transfer to a rack to cool completely.

Make this giant cookie on Father's Day or for a special guy's birthday.

917

GERMAN SPICED COOKIES

Preheat the oven to 375°F/190°C/gas 5. •
Butter two cookie sheets. • Sift the flour,
cinnamon, cloves, mace, and salt into a large bowl.
• Stir in the lemon zest, aniseeds, and black
pepper. • Mix the honey, molasses, and granulated
sugar in a medium saucepan over low heat. •
Cook, stirring constantly, until the sugar has
dissolved completely. • Add the butter and remove
from the heat. • Add the egg, beating until just
blended. • Mix in the dry ingredients to form a stiff
dough. • Drop teaspoons of the dough 2 inches
(5 cm) apart onto the prepared sheets. • Bake for
12–15 minutes, or until firm and golden brown.
• Cool on the sheets until the cookies firm slightly.
• Transfer to racks and let cool completely.

Makes: 30–35
   cookies

Preparation: 40'

Cooking: 12–15'

Level of difficulty: 1

- ¾ cup/125 g all-purpose/plain flour
- 1 tsp ground cinnamon
- ½ tsp ground cloves
- ½ tsp ground mace
- ⅛ tsp salt
- ½ tsp grated lemon zest
- ⅛ tsp ground aniseeds
- ⅛ tsp ground black pepper
- 6 tbsp honey
- 6 tbsp light molasses/treacle
- ¼ cup/50 g granulated sugar
- 2 tbsp butter
- 1 large egg, lightly beaten

ALL SAINTS COOKIES

Makes: 12–16 cookies

Preparation: 40' + 30' to chill

Cooking: 10–15'

Level of difficulty: 1

- ¾ cup/125 g all-purpose/plain flour
- ½ tsp ground cinnamon
- ¼ tsp ground cloves
- ⅛ tsp salt
- 6 tbsp butter, softened
- ⅓ cup/70 g granulated sugar
- 1 large egg yolk
- 2 tbsp milk + more as needed

Sift the flour, cinnamon, cloves, and salt into a medium bowl. • Beat the butter and sugar in a large bowl until creamy. • Add the egg yolk, beating until just blended. • Mix in the dry ingredients and enough milk to form a soft dough. • Press the dough into a disk, wrap in plastic wrap, and refrigerate for 30 minutes. • Preheat the oven to 350°F/180°C/gas 4. • Butter a cookie sheet. • Roll out the dough on a lightly floured surface to thickness of ½ inch (1-cm). • Use a 2-inch (5-cm) cookie cutter to cut out the cookies. Gather the dough scraps, re-roll, and continue cutting out cookies until all the dough is used. • Use a sharp knife to mark a cross on top of each cookie. • Use a spatula to transfer the cookies to the prepared cookie sheet. • Bake for 10–15 minutes, or until deep golden. • Transfer to racks to cool.

CHURCH WINDOW COOKIES

S tir together the confectioners' sugar, flour, salt, butter, cream, and vanilla in a large bowl to form a smooth dough. • Press into a disk, cover with plastic wrap and refrigerate for 30 minutes. • Preheat the oven to 400°F/200°C/gas 6. • Line two cookie sheets with parchment paper. • Roll out the dough on a lightly floured surface to a thickness of $^1/_8$ inch (3 mm). • Use Christmas-shaped cookie cutters, such as holly, stars, and snowmen, to cut out the cookies. Continue cutting out cookies until all the dough is used. Use a spatula to transfer the cookies to the prepared cookie sheets, placing them 1 inch (2.5 cm) apart. • Use a sharp knife to cut a small hole in each cookie. Place a candy piece in each hole. • Bake for 5–7 minutes, or until the cookies are lightly browned and the candies have melted. • Let cool completely.

Makes: 25 cookies

Preparation: 40' + 30' to chill

Cooking: 5–7'

Level of difficulty: 2

- 1$^1/_4$ cups/180 g all-purpose/plain flour
- $^1/_3$ cup/50 g confectioners'/icing sugar
- $^1/_8$ tsp salt
- $^1/_2$ cup/125 g butter, softened
- 1 tbsp heavy/double cream
- $^1/_2$ tsp vanilla extract/essence
- 25 lightly crushed hard candies, mixed colors

SPICED CRISPS

Makes: 28–32 cookies

Preparation: 40' + 1 h to chill

Level of difficulty: 1

Cooking: 8–10'

- 2 cups/300 g all-purpose/plain flour
- 2 tbsp ground cinnamon
- 2 tsp ground cloves
- 1½ tsp ground ginger
- 1 tsp baking powder
- ¼ tsp salt
- ⅔ cup/150 g butter, cut up
- ⅔ cup/140 g granulated sugar
- ½ cup/125 ml light corn syrup/golden syrup
- ⅓ cup/30 g coarsely chopped almonds
- 1 tbsp finely grated lemon zest
- 1 tbsp finely chopped mixed candied peel
- 1 tbsp flaked almonds

Sift the flour, cinnamon, cloves, ginger, and baking powder into a large bowl. • Melt the butter with the sugar and corn syrup in a medium saucepan. • Let cool for 10 minutes. • Stir in the almonds, lemon zest, and candied peel. • Mix in the dry ingredients. • Refrigerate for 1 hour, or until firm. • Preheat the oven to 375°F/190°C/gas 5. • Butter two cookie sheets. • Roll out the dough to a thickness of ¼ inch (5 mm). • Use a 2-inch (5-cm) cookie cutter to cut out the cookies. Continue cutting out cookies until all the dough is used. • Transfer the cookies to the prepared cookie sheets, placing them 1 inch (2.5 cm) apart. • Place a flaked almond piece on top of each cookie. • Bake for 8–10 minutes, or until just golden. • Transfer to racks to cool.

CHRISTMAS CHERRY COOKIES

Makes: 35 cookies

Preparation: 20'

Cooking: 8–10'

Level of difficulty: 1

- 1½ cups/225 g all-purpose/plain flour
- ½ tsp baking soda
- ⅛ tsp salt
- ½ cup/125 g butter, softened
- ¾ cup/150 g firmly packed light brown sugar
- 2 large eggs
- 1½ cups/150 g coarsely chopped pitted dates
- 1½ cups/150 g coarsely chopped walnuts
- ½ cup/90 g golden raisins/ sultanas
- 4 tbsp whiskey
- 18 maraschino cherries, drained and cut in half

Preheat the oven to 350°F/180°C/gas 4. • Butter two cookie sheets. • Sift the flour, baking soda, and salt into a large bowl. • Beat the butter and brown sugar in a large bowl with an electric mixer until creamy. • Add the eggs, beating until just blended. • Mix in the dry ingredients. • Stir in the dates, walnuts, raisins, and whiskey to form a stiff dough. • Drop teaspoons of the dough 2 inches (5 cm) apart onto the prepared cookie sheets. Top each cookie with a half cherry. • Bake for 8–10 minutes, or until lightly browned. • Transfer the cookies to racks to cool.

BUTTER DIAMONDS

Preheat the oven to 350°F/180°C/gas 4. • Butter a 10½ x 15½-inch (26 x 36-cm) jelly-roll pan. • Sift the flour, cinnamon, ginger, and salt into a medium bowl. • Beat the butter and sugar in a large bowl with an electric mixer at high speed until creamy. • Add the almond extract and egg yolk, beating until just blended. • Mix in the dry ingredients to form a smooth dough. • Firmly press the dough into the prepared pan to form a smooth, even layer. • Beat the egg white and water in a small bowl and brush it over the dough. Sprinkle with walnuts. • Score the dough into 1-inch (2.5-cm) diamonds. • Bake for 15–20 minutes, or until lightly browned. • Cool completely in the pan. • Cut along the lines and divide into diamonds.

Makes: 18 cookies

Preparation: 20'

Cooking: 15–20'

Level of difficulty: 1

- **2 cups/500 g all-purpose/plain flour**
- **1 tsp ground cinnamon**
- **1 tsp ground ginger**
- **⅛ tsp salt**
- **1 cup/250 ml butter, softened**
- **1 cup/200 g granulated sugar**
- **1 tsp almond extract/essence**
- **1 large egg, separated**
- **1 tbsp cold water**
- **1 cup/100 g finely chopped walnuts**

PEPPERMINT LOLLIPOPS

Makes: 24 cookies

Preparation: 30' + 30' to chill

Cooking: 6–8' per batch

Level of difficulty: 2

- 2 cups/300 g all-purpose/plain flour
- 1½ tsp baking powder
- ¼ tsp salt
- 6 tbsp butter, softened
- 6 tbsp vegetable shortening
- ¾ cup/150 g granulated sugar
- 1 large egg, lightly beaten
- 1 tbsp milk
- ½ tsp vanilla extract/essence
- ½ cup/50 g crushed peppermint candies

Sift the flour, baking powder, and salt into a medium bowl. • Beat the butter, shortening, and sugar in a large bowl with an electric mixer at high speed until creamy. • Add the egg, milk, and vanilla, beating until just blended. • Mix in the dry ingredients to form a smooth dough. • Divide the dough in half. Press into two disks, wrap in plastic wrap, and refrigerate for 30 minutes. • Preheat the oven to 350°F/180°C/gas 4. • Set out four cookie sheets. • Roll out the dough on a lightly floured surface into a 12 x 9-inch (30 x 23-cm) rectangle. • Use a fluted pastry wheel to cut into twelve 3-inch (8-cm) squares. • Repeat with the remaining dough. • Use a spatula to transfer the cookies to the cookie sheets. Do not place more than six cookies on each sheet as there must be space for the craft sticks. • Sprinkle with the crushed candies, pressing them lightly into the dough. • Cut 1-inch (2.5-cm) slits in each corner toward the center of the square. Fold every other corner into the center to make a windmill shape. • Press craft sticks into the base of the squares, pressing the dough around them so that they are firmly held. • Bake, one sheet at a time, for 6–8 minutes, or until just golden at the edges. • Cool on the sheets until the cookies firm slightly. • Transfer to racks to cool.

Bake these attractive cookies for children's birthday parties.

CAT FACE COOKIES

Beat the butter and sugar in a large bowl with an electric mixer at high speed until creamy. • Beat in the honey, flour, cocoa, and egg white. Add the rum and lemon extracts. • Refrigerate for 1–2 hours. • Draw the outline of a cat's face and ears (about 3¼ x 3 inches/8.5 x 8 cm) on a acetate square or plastic lid. Cut along the outline to make a stencil. • Preheat the oven to 325°F/170°C/gas 3. • Line three cookie sheets with parchment paper. • Place the stencil on the parchment at the top corner of the cookie sheet. • Hold the stencil in position and spread a thin layer of the mixture across it with a rubber spatula, making sure the ears are filled in! • Carefully lift the stencil and place on the parchment next to the cat face you just made, spacing 2 inches (5 cm) apart. • Do not place more than eight cookies on one sheet. • Bake, one sheet at a time, for 6–8 minutes, or until the edges are firm. • Cool on the sheets until the cookies firm slightly. • Transfer to racks to cool. • Decorate with the chocolate chips to resemble eyes and noses.

Makes: 20–24 cookies

Preparation: 30' + 2 h to chill

Cooking: 6–8' per batch

Level of difficulty: 2

- 2 tbsp butter, softened
- ¼ cup/50 g granulated sugar
- 1 tbsp honey
- 3 tbsp all-purpose/plain flour
- 1 tbsp unsweetened cocoa powder
- 1 large egg white
- ¼ tsp rum extract/essence
- ¼ tsp lemon or vanilla extract/essence
- ¼ cup/45 g semisweet/dark chocolate chips

SWISS CHRISTMAS SHAPES

Beat the egg whites and superfine and vanilla sugars in a large bowl with an electric mixer at medium speed until thick and glossy. • Mix in the rum, butter, cocoa, cinnamon, and cloves. • Mix in the ground almonds and baking powder to form a stiff dough. • Press the dough into a disk, wrap in plastic wrap, and refrigerate for 30 minutes. • Preheat the oven to 350°F/180°C/gas 4. • Line four cookie sheets with parchment paper. • Discard the plastic wrap. Roll out the dough between sheets of waxed paper to a thickness of $1/4$ inch (5 mm). • Use a $1^1/_2$-inch (4-cm) heart-shaped cookie cutter to cut out the cookies. Gather the dough scraps, re-roll, and continue cutting out cookies until all the dough is used. • Bake, one sheet at a time, for 8–10 minutes, or until pale gold and firm at the edges. • Transfer to racks to cool. • Icing: Mix the confectioners' sugar with enough water to make a thick, spreadable icing. Spread over the tops of the cookies.

Makes: 45–50 cookies

Preparation: 45' + 30' to chill

Cooking: 8–10'

Level of difficulty: 1

- **2 large egg whites**
- **1$1/4$ cups/250 g superfine/caster sugar**
- **1 tbsp vanilla sugar**
- **1$1/2$ tbsp dark rum**
- **1 tbsp butter, melted**
- **2 tsp unsweetened cocoa powder**
- **1$1/2$ tsp ground cinnamon**
- **$1/2$ tsp ground cloves**
- **2$1/2$ cups/375 g finely ground almonds + more as needed for rolling**
- **$1/2$ tsp baking powder**

ICING

- **1$1/3$ cups/200 g confectioners'/icing sugar**
- **2 tbsp hot water + more as needed**

EASTER CURRANT COOKIES

Makes: 16 cookies

Preparation: 40'

Cooking: 10–15'

Level of difficulty: 1

- 1¼ cups/180 g all-purpose/plain flour
- 1 tsp baking powder
- ⅛ tsp salt
- 6 tbsp butter, softened
- 1 cup/200 g granulated sugar
- 1 large egg, lightly beaten
- 1 tbsp dried currants

Preheat the oven to 325°F/170°C/gas 3. • Butter a cookie sheet. • Sift the flour, baking powder, and salt into a medium bowl. • Beat the butter and sugar in a large bowl with an electric mixer at high speed until creamy. • Add the egg, beating until just blended. • Mix in the flour to form a smooth dough. • Knead in the currants. • Transfer the dough to a lightly floured surface and roll out to a thickness of ¼ inch (5 mm). • Use a 3-inch (8-cm) cookie cutter to cut out the cookies. • Gather the dough scraps, re-roll, and continue cutting out the cookies until all the dough is used. • Arrange on the prepared cookie sheets, placing them 1 inch (2.5 cm) apart. • Bake for 10–15 minutes, or until lightly browned. • Transfer to racks to cool.

ZESTY COOKIES

Preheat the oven to 375°F/190°C/gas 5. •
Butter two cookie sheets. • Sift the all-purpose
and rice flours, baking powder, and salt into a
medium bowl. • Beat the butter and sugar in a
large bowl with an electric mixer until creamy.
• Add the egg and lemon zest, beating until just
blended. • Mix in the dry ingredients. • Drop
tablespoons of the dough 1 inch (2.5 cm) apart
onto the prepared cookie sheets. • Bake for 8–10
minutes, or until pale golden. • Transfer to racks
to cool.

Makes: 20–24 cookies

Preparation: 25'

Cooking: 8–10'

Level of difficulty: 1

- 1¾ cups/275 g all-purpose/plain flour
- ⅓ cup/50 g rice flour
- 1¼ tsp baking powder
- ⅛ tsp salt
- 4 tbsp butter, softened
- ¾ cup/150 g granulated sugar
- 1 large egg
- 1 tbsp finely grated lemon zest

ALMOND GARLANDS

Preheat the oven to 350°F/180°C/gas 4. • Set out three cookie sheets. • Sift the flour, baking powder, and salt into a medium bowl. • Beat the butter and sugar in a large bowl with an electric mixer at high speed until creamy. • Add the egg yolk and almond extract, beating until just blended. • Mix in the dry ingredients and almonds until well blended. • Fit a pastry bag with a ½-inch (1-cm) star tip. Fill the pastry bag, twist the opening tightly closed, and squeeze out 2-inch rings onto the cookie sheets, spacing them 1 inch (2.5 cm) apart. • Bake, one sheet at a time, for 8–10 minutes, or until golden brown. • Cool on the sheets until the cookies firm slightly. Transfer to racks and let cool completely.

Makes: 40–45 cookies

Preparation: 25'

Cooking: 8–10' per batch

Level of difficulty: 1

- 1½ cups/225 g all-purpose/plain flour
- ½ tsp baking powder
- ⅛ tsp salt
- 1 cup/250 g butter, softened
- ½ cup/100 g granulated sugar
- 1 large egg yolk
- ½ tsp almond extract/essence
- ⅓ cup/50 g finely ground almonds

Preparation: 45' + 30'
to chill

Cooking: 8–10' per
batch

Level of difficulty: 1

- **2 cups/300 g all-purpose/plain flour**
- **¼ tsp salt**
- **1 cup/250 g butter, softened**
- **6 tbsp milk**
- **¾ cup/150 g granulated sugar**

FILLING

- **½ cup/125 g butter, softened**
- **½ tsp vanilla extract/essence**
- **2 cups/300 g confectioners'/icing sugar**
- **1½ tbsp milk**
- **Few drops green food coloring**

CHRISTMAS TREES

Sift the flour and salt into a medium bowl. • Beat the butter in a large bowl until creamy. • Mix in the dry ingredients and milk to form a smooth dough. • Refrigerate for 30 minutes. • Preheat the oven to 375°F/190°C/gas 5. • Set out three cookie sheets. • Roll out the dough to a thickness of ¼ inch (5 mm). • Use a 2-inch (5-cm) tree-shaped cookie cutter to cut out the cookies. Continue cutting out cookies until all the dough is used. • Dip the cookies in the sugar and place 1 inch (2.5 cm) apart on the cookie sheets. • Bake for 8–10 minutes, or until just golden at the edges. • Let cool completely. • Filling: Beat the butter and vanilla in a medium bowl until creamy. • Beat in the confectioners' sugar and milk. • Add the green food coloring. • Stick the cookies together in pairs with the filling.

MINT SPRITZERS

Preheat the oven to 400°F/200°C/gas 6. •
Butter two cookie sheets. • Sift the flour and
salt into a medium bowl. • Beat the butter, sugar,
egg, and vanilla and mint extracts in a large bowl
with an electric mixer at high speed. • Mix in the
dry ingredients, followed by the food coloring. •
Refrigerate for 30 minutes. • Insert a star-shaped
design plate into a cookie press by sliding it into
the head and locking in place. Press out the
cookies, spacing about 1 inch (2.5 cm) apart on
the prepared cookie sheet. • Bake for 8–10
minutes, or until just golden at the edges.
• Working quickly, press a chocolate into the
center of each cookie. • Cool on the sheets until
the cookies firm slightly. • Transfer to racks and
let cool.

Makes: 30 cookies

*Preparation: 25' + 30'
to chill*

Cooking: 8–10'

Level of difficulty: 2

- 1 cup/150 g all-
  purpose/plain flour
- ⅛ tsp salt
- ½ cup/125 g
  butter, softened
- ⅓ cup/70 g
  granulated sugar
- ½ large egg, lightly
  beaten
- ½ tsp vanilla
  extract/essence
- ½ tsp mint
  extract/essence
- Few drops green
  food coloring
- 30 Hershey kisses

MARSHMALLOW PARTY COOKIES

P reheat the oven to 375°F/190°C/gas 5. •
Butter three cookie sheets. • Sift the flour,
cocoa, baking powder, and salt into a medium
bowl. • Use a pastry blender to cut in the butter
until the mixture resembles fine crumbs. Stir in the
sugar. • Mix in the egg yolk. Press the dough into a
disk, wrap in plastic wrap, and refrigerate for 30
minutes. • Roll out the dough out on a lightly
floured surface to a thickness of $1/4$ inch (5 mm). •
Use a 2-inch (5-cm) cookie cutter to cut out the
cookies. Cut out the centers from half of the
cookies with a 1-inch (2.5-cm) cookie cutter. Gather
the dough scraps, re-roll, and continue cutting out
cookies until all the dough is used. • Bake, one
sheet at a time, for 10–15 minutes, or until golden
brown. Transfer the cookies with holes to racks. •
Place a marshmallow on the top of each whole
cookie and bake for 3 minutes, or until the
marshmallow has melted. Immediately stick a ring
cookie on top of each marshmallow base. •
Transfer to racks to cool.

Makes: 20–24
cookies

Preparation: 40' + 30'
to chill

Cooking: 10–15' per
batch

Level of difficulty: 1

- **1½ cups/225 g all-purpose/plain flour**
- **2 tbsp unsweetened cocoa powder**
- **1 tsp baking powder**
- **⅛ tsp salt**
- **½ cup/125 g butter, cut up**
- **½ cup/100 g granulated sugar**
- **1 large egg yolk, lightly beaten**
- **20–24 white marshmallows**

PINK DRIZZLERS

Makes: 20 cookies

Preparation: 40' + 30' to chill

Cooking: 8–10'

Level of difficulty: 1

- 1 cup/150 g all-purpose/plain flour
- ¾ cup/125 g cornstarch/cornflour
- 2 tsp unsweetened cocoa powder
- 1 tsp ground cinnamon
- ½ tsp allspice
- ½ tsp baking soda
- ¼ tsp ground ginger
- ¼ tsp freshly grated nutmeg
- ¼ tsp salt
- ½ cup/125 g butter
- ¾ cup/140 g granulated sugar
- 1 tbsp light corn syrup/golden syrup
- 2 large eggs
- 2–3 tbsp raspberry preserves
- 3–4 tbsp confectioners'/icing sugar
- 3–4 tsp warm water
- 2 drops red food coloring

Sift the flour, cornstarch, cocoa, cinnamon, allspice, baking soda, ginger, nutmeg, and salt into a medium bowl. • Beat the butter, sugar, and corn syrup in a large bowl with an electric mixer at high speed until creamy. • Add the eggs, beating until just blended. • Mix in the dry ingredients to form a smooth dough. Press the dough into a disk, wrap in plastic wrap, and refrigerate for 30 minutes. • Preheat the oven to 350°F/180°C/gas 4. • Butter two cookie sheets. • Roll out the dough on a lightly floured surface to a thickness of ½ inch (1 cm). • Use a 2-inch (5-cm) cutter to cut into rounds. • Transfer the cookies to the prepared cookie sheets, placing them 1 inch (2.5 cm) apart. • Bake for 8–10 minutes, or until firm. • Cool completely on the cookie sheets. • Stick the cookies together in pairs with the preserves. • Mix the confectioners' sugar, water, and food coloring to make a soft frosting. Spread the frosting over the tops.

SPICY GINGER SANDWICHES

Sift the flour, cocoa, allspice, cinnamon, ginger, and salt into a medium bowl. • Beat the butter and sugar in a large bowl with an electric mixer at high speed until creamy. • Add the egg yolk and lemon zest and juice, beating until just blended. • Mix in the dry ingredients and almonds to form a stiff dough. • Press the dough into a disk, wrap in plastic wrap, and refrigerate for 30 minutes. • Preheat the oven to 350°F/180°C/gas 4. • Set out three cookie sheets. • Roll out the dough on a lightly floured surface to a thickness of ¼ inch (5 mm). • Use a 2-inch (5-cm) cookie cutter to cut out the cookies. Gather the dough scraps, re-roll, and continue cutting out cookies until all the dough is used. • Use a spatula to transfer the cookies to the cookie sheets, placing them 1 inch (2.5 cm) apart. • Bake, one sheet at a time, for 25–35 minutes, or until lightly browned and firm to the touch. • Transfer to racks to cool. • Stick the cookies together in pairs with the preserves.

Makes: 14–16 cookies

Preparation: 25' + 30' to chill

Cooking: 25–35'

Level of difficulty: 1

- ⅔ cup/100 g all-purpose/plain flour
- 2 tsp unsweetened cocoa powder
- ½ tsp ground allspice
- ½ tsp ground cinnamon
- ½ tsp ground ginger
- ⅛ tsp salt
- ¾ cup/180 g butter, softened
- ½ cup/100 g granulated sugar
- 1 large egg yolk
- 1 tbsp finely grated lemon zest
- 2 tbsp fresh lemon juice
- 2 cups/300 g finely ground almonds
- ⅓ cup/60 g raspberry preserves

BASIC
RECIPES

VANILLA SUGAR

*Makes: 2¹/₂ cups/
300 g*

*Preparation: 7–10
days*

Level of difficulty: 1

- **2¹/₂ cups
  granulated sugar**
- **2 vanilla pods, cut
  into 2 or 3 pieces**

Fill a glass jar with the sugar. • Add the vanilla pods, seal tightly, and set aside for 7–10 days. When you open the jar, the sugar will be flavored with vanilla. • As the pods have a long aromatic life, just add more sugar as needed.

CINNAMON SUGAR

*Makes: 2¹/₂ cups/
300 g*

*Preparation: 7–10
days*

Level of difficulty: 1

- **2¹/₂ cups
  granulated sugar**
- **3 cinnamon sticks,
  broken into halves**
- **4 cloves**

Fill a glass jar with sugar and place the cinnamon sticks and cloves in it. • Let stand for 1 week and use as needed. Add more sugar when necessary.

CHOCOLATE FROSTING

Stir together the confectioners' sugar and cocoa in a double boiler. Add the butter, vanilla, and enough of the water to make a firm paste. Stir over simmering water until the frosting has a spreadable consistency, about 3 minutes.

Makes: 1 cup/ 250 ml

Preparation: 5'

Level of difficulty: 1

- 2 cups/300 g confectioners'/ icing sugar
- ¼ cup/30 g unsweetened cocoa powder
- 2 tbsp butter, softened
- 1 tsp vanilla extract/essence
- about 2 tbsp boiling water

CHOUX PASTRY

Place the water, butter, sugar, and salt in a large pan over medium-low heat. When the mixture boils, remove from the heat and add the flour all at once. Use a wooden spoon to stir vigorously until a smooth paste forms. Return to medium heat and stir constantly until the mixture pulls away from the pan sides. Remove from the heat and let cool for 5 minutes. • Add the eggs, beating until just blended after each addition. • Use as required.

Makes 1 recipe

Preparation: 15'

Cooking: 10'

Level of difficulty: 3

- 2 cups/500 ml water
- ⅔ cup/150 g butter, cut up
- 1 tbsp sugar
- ¼ tsp salt
- 1⅔ cups/250 g all-purpose/plain flour

ITALIAN BUTTERCREAM

S tir the water and sugar in a saucepan over medium heat until the sugar has dissolved. • Cook, without stirring, until the mixture reaches 238°F (114°C), or the soft-ball stage. • Beat the egg yolks in a double boiler with an electric mixer at high speed until pale. • Gradually beat the syrup into the beaten yolks. • Place over barely simmering water, stirring constantly with a wooden spoon, until the mixture lightly coats a metal spoon. • Immediately plunge the pan into a bowl of ice water and stir until cooled. • Beat the butter in a large bowl until creamy. Beat into the egg mixture.

Makes: 2 cups/
  500 ml

Preparation: 25'

Level of difficulty: 1

- ½ cup/125 ml
  water
- ¾ cup/150 g
  granulated sugar
- 3 large egg yolks
- 1 cup/250 g butter,
  softened

COFFEE BUTTERCREAM

*Makes: 2 cups/
    500 ml*

Preparation: 25'

Level of difficulty: 1

- **2 tbsp very strong coffee, lukewarm**
- **¾ cup/150 g granulated sugar**
- **3 large egg yolks**
- **1 cup/250 g butter, softened**

Stir the coffee and sugar in a saucepan over medium heat. • Cook, without stirring, until the mixture reaches 238°F (114°C), or the soft-ball stage. • Beat the egg yolks in a double boiler with an electric mixer at high speed until pale. • Gradually beat the syrup into the beaten yolks. • Place over barely simmering water, stirring constantly with a wooden spoon, until the mixture lightly coats a metal spoon. • Immediately plunge the pan into a bowl of ice water and stir until cooled. • Beat the butter in a large bowl until creamy. Beat into the egg mixture.

INDEX

959

C

961

963

D

E

F

967

P

971

T

Tea Cakes

Treacle

Toffee

V

Vanilla

Walnuts

Whole-wheat

Wine

Yeast